THE FIFTH DAUGHTER in a patriarchal society, and an indigenous Bedouin in Israel, Amal came into this world fighting for her voice to be heard in a community that did not prize girls. At birth it was only her father who looked at her and said "I see hope in her face. I want to call her Amal [hope] in the hope that Allah will give us boys after her." Five brothers were indeed to follow.

Hope is a Woman's Name is a rare look at Bedouin life from the even rarer perspective of a Bedouin girl. Amal challenged authority from birth, slowly learning where her community's boundaries lay and how to navigate them.

As a shepherd at the age of 6, Amal led her flock of sheep across the green mountains of Laqiya, her village in the Negev in southern Israel. Given such responsibility, though rarely recognition, Amal came to understand her community and forge her skills as a leader.

Aged 13 and frustrated by the constraints put on her education as a girl, Amal set up literacy classes for the adult women in her village. She aimed to teach them not only how to read, but to value education itself: "I wanted them to taste an education so that they would never again deprive their daughters of one."

This was the beginning of a lifelong career initiating projects that would help create change for the Bedouin – a minority within Israel's Palestinian minority – and for their women in particular. She established economic empowerment programmes for marginalized women, helped found an Arab-Jewish school, and created organizations to promote shared society.

At every turn she had to face the challenges of tradition – as well as the prejudices of Israeli society – to create new possibilities that would allow women to empower themselves.

Amal has learnt to embrace every aspect of her complicated identity – Bedouin, Arab, woman, Palestinian and Israeli citizen – to help create social change, build bridges with other communities and inspire hope.

From an early age Amal had to fight for a good education. She proceeded to get a BA in social work from Ben Gurion University in Israel and a PhD in social work and community organizing from McGill University.

Amal became an activist very young and went on to found several NGOs, including the Arab-Jewish Centre for Equality, Economic Empowerment and Cooperation. She is the recipient of many international prizes, was nominated for the Nobel Peace Prize (2006), included in Genius 100 Visionaries of the Future (2017), and awarded the New Israel Fund's Human Rights Award (2013).

Hope is a Woman's Name

HOPE
IS A WOMAN'S NAME

Amal Elsana Alh'jooj

HALBAN
LONDON

First published in Great Britain by
Halban Publishers Ltd.
2022

www.halbanpublishers.com

ISBN 978 1 912600 11 3

Typeset by AB, Cambridgeshire

Printed in Great Britain by
CPI Group (UK) Ltd, Croydon CR0 4YY

To my grandmother, Jidatee, who taught me that a free woman
has nothing to fear

To my father, Abouee, who always believed in me

To my mother, Ummi, for whom I am full of admiration

To my brothers and sisters who share this story

To Anwar who has shown such independence throughout his life
and has proved the perfect partner

And to Moad and Adan, may you find hope and justice in your
own lives

Contents

University Years

Professional Activism:
Roads Through the Cracks of Citizenship

Navigating Minefields

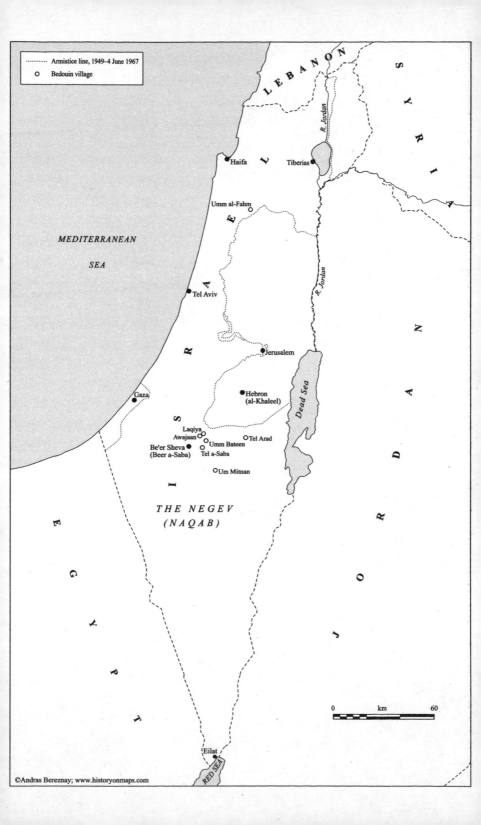

Armistice line, 1949–4 June 1967
○ Bedouin village

LEBANON

SYRIA

R. Jordan

Haifa

Tiberias

ISRAEL

Umm al-Fahm

MEDITERRANEAN
SEA

R. Jordan

Tel Aviv

Jerusalem

Hebron
(al-Khaleel)

Gaza

Dead Sea

Laqiya
Awajaan ○ Tel Arad
Umm Bateen
Be'er Sheva
(Beer a-Saba) Tel a-Saba

○ Um Mitnan

JORDAN

THE NEGEV
(NAQAB)

EGYPT

km
0   60

Eilat

RED SEA

©Andras Bereznay; www.historyonmaps.com

Acknowledgements

WRITING ABOUT ONESELF poses a particular challenge in societies where the self doesn't exist. In my community, one exists as a member, not as an individual. Without having to navigate the expectations of my parents, the family, the community, the government, or donors to my NGOs, the writing of this book allowed me to put myself in the centre of the story, to tell it the way I saw and felt it and, above all, to reflect freely.

For the most part, the writing came easily. There were countless stories to tell, so many moments where my personal identity – Arab, Bedouin, Palestinian, Israeli citizen, Woman – was at odds with what the world was asking of me and so many times when I had to confront political challenges on my doorstep. While I wrote, I laughed loudly, I cheered, I sobbed. I expressed every emotion that had been stolen from me. The process fulfilled my need to live my life the way I would have liked, without the constant fights that my every action seemed to provoke.

Reliving my memories through writing allowed me to see my life more clearly. There were still some choices I had made that I regretted and felt angry about, but writing about them helped me reflect on these choices and let me see all the pieces of the puzzle that make up my life. I saw how I had been punishing myself before others did and in writing I found self-compassion and a deeper love for my parents. I strengthened the relationship with my mother. Her memory became an integral part of my own and whatever residual anger I felt towards her dissipated into an ocean of love and understanding. I saw my father with even more admiration, gaining a newfound respect for his strength to stand up against tribal pressures, and as for Basma, my incredible older sister, I wasn't able to put myself in her shoes until I wrote her story. It was only then that I stopped being angry and was able to see her again as my hero.

The reality of male domination convinces us women that being professional requires keeping the personal tucked away. It took me many years to understand that the personal is political and that denying the personal is to give up on presenting ourselves as a whole. As a social and political activist, I came to understand how my daily experiences have shaped my awareness, how the past has affected my present, and how reconciling my multiple identities has been my only way to find my place in the world. When we know our story, we can root deeply into the ground and grow into a tree whose branches embrace the stars.

I decided to write my memoirs because I believe that, as a woman activist, it is important to document my experiences and my story for the generation to come. In the words of Walid Saif, when we criticise the government, we are called heroes but when we criticise our own community, we are called traitors and the whip and sword of the tribe are used to punish us. I believe that history belongs to the one who writes it and if we want to own our history, we have to write it. My story is a contribution to herstory.

On this journey, I have been very fortunate to meet many wonderful people who influenced this book and to whom I am deeply thankful. One woman who contributed significantly to this book is Marisa Samek. Marisa worked closely with me, squeezing my soul, in her gentle way, for its juice. She took my first drafts and through our discussions elevated them to the vibrant memories recounted in this book.

I would like to thank my publisher Martine Halban who never gave up on me. I met Martine in 2013 at a Human Rights Award event in London. After sharing a part of my story with her, she approached me to write this memoir. I told her that I was busy completing my PhD and would do it afterwards. Martine sent me emails throughout my PhD asking if I had finished. Thank you, Martine, for your persistence and the tremendous support of you and your team all along the way.

To my old friend, Dr Clinton Bailey, who made sure that all the Bedouin-Arabic phrases were translated and transliterated correctly. Clinton's love for my people and our culture inspired me when I met him in my youth and continue to inspire me to this day. I couldn't have found a better person to make sure my phrases meant what I wanted them to mean.

My special thanks also go to my friends, Emad Balkis, Nida Samaha, Asma Nassar, Rabbi Lisa Grushcow, Soryl Rosenberg, Paula Klein, and Aziza Alui with whom I had many interesting conversations that influenced my work. Their support encouraged me to continue.

I also want to thank my people – the Bedouin community – who have been tough but without whom my vision and my dreams wouldn't have had a chance to see the sun. I realize how challenging my ideas were for them but also realise how privileged I was to serve them.

My special thanks to Ummi, Abouee, Basma, and all my brothers and sisters who each shared their memories to bring my story to life. Ummi in particular would send me WhatsApp messages in the middle of the night to correct the name of an uncle or revise a date she had given me.

My final and deepest thanks are for my family: my husband Anwar Alhjooj, my son Moad, and my daughter Adan who have provided tremendous emotional encouragement and support all the way. Their confidence in me gave me strength during the hardest moments. Their love paved my road. I love you.

Note on Transliteration

I HAVE USED many Arabic terms and phrases in this memoir. As these may differ from uses in other Arabic dialects, they have been transliterated to reflect the a-Sana tribal pronunciation.

Depending on the context in which they are used, place names appear both as we refer to them in Arabic and as they are known in Hebrew. For example, the Arabic term "Naqab" – the region in which I grew up — is also rendered in the Hebrew, "Negev". This also applies to individual towns in the region: the Arabic "Beer a-Saba" is also referred to by its Hebrew name, "Be'er Sheva", and the Arabic "Tel a-Saba" also appears as "Tel Sheva".

The Motherland

Birthing Hope

WHEN I OPENED my eyes, I saw the video camera beside my bed that I had brought to film the birth of my twins, Moad and Adan. I rolled over to the other side, feeling the bandage on my stomach where they had performed the C-section, and my eyes fell into my mother's. She was sitting a few feet away from me and the look on her face was as foreign to me as my two newborns who had entered into this world only a few hours before. I knew these rooms well. I had worked at this hospital as a social work student and then later had partnered with them to provide services for Bedouin children. The management knew me by name and many of the doctors and nurses recognized my face. Everything there was familiar – everything except my mother's look of pure tenderness.

Whenever my mother looked at me, I only remember seeing her mouth in two shapes: a small, tight grimace or a wide-open shout. "Why can't you act more like a lady?" "What do you think you are doing protesting them?", "Don't even think about men." Every time I caused her trouble, she would look up to the sky and pray, "Allah, send down your *goofa* [basket] and take her." When I was a child, I would peer up at the clouds and wait for Allah's giant wicker basket to descend and whisk me away. Sometimes when my mother was really desperate, she would ask Allah to take all of us girls (me and, at that time, my four sisters). But the jab that was reserved just for

1

me was, "When you were born, I didn't want you. When you were born, I wished that you were dead."

Now, under the bright fluorescent lights, her mouth rested in a gentle smile. Tears streamed from her eyes and she looked like she wanted to reach out and take me back into her womb. As soon as she noticed that I was awake, she rushed towards me and covered my face with kisses.

"*Al-hamdulillah! Al-hamdulillah!* [May Allah be praised!]" She held my hand in hers.

"Ummi, why are you crying?" I asked.

For the next month, while she stayed with me in my home, my mother unravelled the answer to that question. During late nights of rocking the twins to sleep, sweeping the kitchen floor, or sitting with me while I fed the babies, my mother told me, as if for the first time, the story of how I was born. It was a story I thought I knew, but there are many ways to tell a story and there are many stories we don't tell.

In the past, when she told the story of how I was born, she told it to hurt me. This time, when my mother shared with me the details of the days surrounding my birth, she spoke not of her disappointment but of her fear. From her story, I saw that, while my mother seemed to oppose everything I fought for, she suffered from the same oppression that I had stood up against since I was a young child. Here is her story of my birth, woven together from her memory, my father's memory and the memory of my sisters and aunts.

A Face Like a Full Moon

UMMI'S EYES FLUTTER open. She is lying down and staring up at the ceiling. It is perfectly white, from corner to corner. Her gaze moves from the ceiling to the off-white walls and down to the white sheets she is lying on. *Everything here is so clean.* The sheets are starchy and crisp, the cushions are plush and full, and, from the door, she can see people with fresh faces and tidy clothes bustling down the hallway.

She looks down at her arms. Even her own body looks different under these lights. *Everything is shining. Everything except me.*

She closes her eyes and tries to understand where she is. She strains her ears for the familiar sounds – the dogs, the sheep, the children. Nothing. She listens again.

"Where are you? Get up! Why are you lying down?"

Ummi's body twitches and she opens her eyes. She is still alone in that shiny room. Her mother-in-law is nowhere to be seen but she hears her voice in her head shouting commands.

Why am I lying down? Within the confines of those crisp, white sheets, Ummi does not know who she is. She has spent her entire life in the tribe where she has always been defined by who she belongs to. As a woman, you are "daughter of", then "wife of", then "mother of". Now, as the wife of my father, she spends every hour throwing herself at her mother-in-law's feet. She had no right to rest. While her body sought refuge on that cot, her soul shook with fear. How frightening the unfamiliar can be when it undermines everything we know about the world and our place in it.

A young woman approaches holding a tray. Her head is uncovered and she is facing straight ahead, walking with confidence without looking around to see if anyone is watching her. *She walks like a gazelle. What does she want? Allah, she is coming here.*

She walks right up to Ummi's bed. "Hajar a-Sana*? Is that you?" she asks in broken Arabic before continuing in Hebrew.

Ummi's hands are shaking and her eyes, full of tears, are desperately searching for something familiar. Her eyes follow the young woman as she puts the tray on the table next to the bed.

"Please enjoy your breakfast." Ummi looks over at the tray. Among the unfamiliar items, she recognizes hard boiled eggs and a carton of milk. A small victory. *Is this for me? Why? Why is she serving me?*

---

* a-Sana reflects the pronunciation of the tribe's name in Bedouin Arabic, but I am known in the West as Amal Elsana, and also sometimes Amal el-Sana. Alh'jooj is my married name.

3

"After you finish, please take a shower and I will bring your baby to you to feed." The nurse mimes breastfeeding.

Ummi doesn't understand the words, but she understands the motion. The nurse disappears down the hall. My mother looks around furtively. She is very hungry but the voice in her head stops her from reaching towards the tray. *What if this food is not for me? I didn't pay for it. What will happen if I eat it and she comes back and finds out. I don't have money. She might kick me and my baby out.*

The word "baby" triggers a memory of last night's events and, suddenly, she remembers arriving with Abouee (my father) to deliver me. This was her first time in a hospital. All my sisters and my older brother were born in the tent.

She looks around the room again, taking it all in. A few feet from the bed, there is a curtain with a picture of a smiling baby's face inside a bright yellow sun. From behind the curtain she can hear a man and a woman speaking quietly. She cocks her head to one side to catch what they are saying. It's Arabic. *Al-hamdulillah.* Relieved to find something more familiar than a couple of eggs and a carton of milk, Ummi reaches towards the curtain. Her legs brush against one another and she feels a sticky wetness. She stops moving, pulls the bed sheet over her head and looks down at herself. She recoils. She isn't wearing any underwear. As she thinks about these strange people having seen her naked, her cheeks flush and shame grips her heart.

"Allah, cover me. Protect me," she whispers.

She runs her hands through her hair and her heart starts pounding in her chest as she realizes that her head is bare. Her eyes scan the room. She is wringing the bed sheet tightly between her fists as she tries to think what to do. *What if a man comes in? What if my father-in-law comes in?*

She reaches towards the curtain separating her bed from the one beside her and carefully pulls it open until she can just see the corner of the other bed. Slowly, she pulls the curtain back further until she sees a head wrapped in a red scarf. *Al-hamdulillah.* Ummi pulls it back completely.

"Ukhti [my sister], do you have an extra scarf? I've lost my scarf. I had it when I came here, but I've lost it."

The woman sits up and points to the cabinet next to Ummi's bed. "It's in there, Ukhti. They put all your things in there."

Ummi opens the cabinet and finds her embroidered Bedouin dress, her white scarf and the shoes she had to borrow from her cousin. She looks back at the woman.

"There is a bathroom at the entrance of the room. Go take a shower. In that cabinet there are pads to clean yourself. Be quick. They're bringing the babies for the morning feed."

The friendly woman looks at the tray of untouched food beside Ummi and asks, "Why didn't you eat your breakfast?"

"I was afraid to eat it," Ummi replies. "I thought it was not mine—"

"No, no, no. It's yours. Eat, eat!"

"I can't pay for it. My husband will come in the evening and he can pay—"

"It's free. Eat, eat."

Now Ummi allows herself to examine the food more closely. She sees the fork and spoon but doesn't know how to use them.

"Eat with your hands, Ukhti." Ummi relaxes into the first smile she has had since arriving.

"*Shoukran*, Ukhti. Thank you." She scoops up the eggs, drinks the milk, and pushes the red jelly aside.

After finishing her breakfast, Ummi turns to the cabinet beside her bed and takes out her dress. She places her arms in first and then pulls the dress over her head. She starts sliding the heavy fabric down her body and then remembers her blood-smeared legs. *I must be covered. It doesn't matter if it gets dirty.* She slides the dress down her legs, then takes her scarf and wraps it around her forehead, knotting it at the back where her head and neck meet. She pulls out her cousin's shoes and places them on the floor in front of her.

"Don't you have any slippers?" the woman chimes in. "Your shoes will get wet in the bathroom."

Ummi shakes her head. She removes her shoes and walks, barefoot, towards the two doors a few feet from the bed. Unsure where to go, she looks back for help. The woman points to the door on the left.

Ummi enters the bathroom like a child entering a library. Every object in that room reminds her of how little she knows about the world outside her tribe. She is lost amid all this porcelain, chrome and glass. She sees a blue, nylon curtain and pulls it back. She looks up at a metal pipe coming out from the wall with a metal plate with holes on the end of it. Next to the curtain is another porcelain object: a round basin of water. Her breath shortens as she tries to decode the things around her. Above one of the porcelain pieces is a mirror with a shelf below it and on the shelf are two small bottles. She decides that the basin of water must be for cleaning her face. She grabs one of the bottles of what smells like soap, kneels down on the floor beside the basin and splashes the cool water on her face. She dips her hands in again and is interrupted by a soft knock at the door. It's the woman from the other bed. "Ukhti, Ukhti, do you know how to use the shower? Let me in. I will show you."

Ummi opens the door and lets the woman enter. The woman flips a switch on the wall and the tubes on the ceiling light up. The woman walks over to the shower, turns the tap and water pours from the metal plate. The woman is speaking to her, but Ummi is somewhere else. *How can you just flip a switch and there is light? How can you just turn a tap and there is water?* Ummi's thoughts are interrupted when the woman points to the porcelain basin and explains that it is used for eliminating human waste. Ummi gulps silently. She nods her head to hide her shame. This day has been one humiliation after another. Her cheeks burning, she thanks the woman and closes the door behind her.

Ummi rubs her face between her hands disgusted. She pulls off her dress and steps into the shower. She fiddles with the tap, hot water pours onto her head and shoulders, and she jumps back. She steps out of the shower, turns off the water and tries the other tap.

The water is freezing. She closes it, opens the hot one again and steps beneath it. *It's better like this.* In the tent, she only ever uses cold water. For hot water, she needs to follow the cow and sheep tracks, collect their *jalle* (their droppings) that has been dried from lying out in the hot sun, start a fire with them and heat the water.

Now, while her body is turning red, her thoughts drift to her mother-in-law.

"Wake up! Go and get the water for tea!"

Her mother-in-law's harsh whisper rouses Ummi from her sleep. Although her body aches from yesterday's labour, she doesn't linger. She gets up from the floor, dusts off her dress, and checks on her three girls sleeping on the floor beside her. They are like angels snuggled together, their rosy cheeks billowing gently with their sleeping breath. She covers them with the heavy red rug she received as a wedding gift from her mother and moves silently to the other side of the tent to make herself a cup of tea.

As she reaches for the kettle, her mother-in-law snaps at her again. "We don't have enough water. Go and get water. You will have plenty of time to drink tea."

Her mother-in-law's tongue is a whip that bears down upon her soul. Her words have beaten Ummi so many times that she barely flinches anymore. The only sign of her submission is that her neck is slightly stooped, used to nodding, "Yes, Amee [my Mother-in-law]," when she would rather say no. She steps away from the warm glow of the fire and walks to the back of the tent where she gathers up two large metal containers and loads them onto either side of the donkey.

Under the hot stream of the shower, she feels the pangs of thirst and hunger that greet her every morning as she lumbers over to the well at the main entrance of the tribe. She moves her body closer to the stream, making sure the water reaches every pore. She unties her scarf, soaps it, and starts to scrub. Gently at first, then harder and harder. How hard does she need to scrub to wash away the pain of a lifetime? She drops her makeshift washcloth to the floor and tears cascade down her cheeks. In her anguish, she seeks refuge in another memory where she can be with herself.

Ummi opens her eyes and gasps for air. She rubs her eyes, but stops when she realizes that it isn't her eyes that are foggy. *What if I faint here and people find me naked? Allah, what will they say?* She turns off the tap and hears a knock and a voice through the steam. She covers herself with a towel and moves towards the door.

"Ukhti, Ukhti, are you all right? Please open the door."

"Yes, I'm OK."

"They've brought your baby to feed. Come! Ukhti, you have a baby girl. Her face is like a full moon."

Ummi feels her naked rear on the bathroom floor. She looks up and sees the woman from the other bed crouching beside her, rubbing her shoulders, and the nurse holding a glass of water.

"You spent too much time under the hot water," the woman warns her as she reaches for the glass and brings it to Ummi's lips.

The words "you have a baby girl" hover like a dark cloud. The woman helps Ummi into her clothes and walks her back to her bed. Ummi crawls in and as soon as her head lands on her pillow, she falls into a deep sleep. "I thought that I was dead," Ummi says whenever she tells this part of the story, "and when I woke up, I didn't know if it was day or night."

When Ummi wakes up, it is time for the evening feed and the nurse is moving from one bed to another, pushing two cribs alongside her. She peers at the small, plastic tag on one of the babies' wrists, then glances over at Ummi's bed. She does this a few times, squinting down at the tag, then studying Ummi's face. Every time she looks over, Ummi averts her eyes. "I was praying that she wouldn't bring you to me. I didn't want you. I wished and wished that while I slept you had died so that when your grandmother arrived with your father I could tell them that it was a boy but that he had died."

The nurse moves away from her bed and the knot in Ummi's stomach loosens a little. *Maybe Allah heard me.* Before she has a chance to let out a full breath, the nurse turns around and walks right over to her. Without a word, she takes Ummi's hand and examines the blue ID bracelet and checks it against the bracelet fastened snugly to the baby's fat wrist.

"Are you Hajar a-Sana?"

Ummi nods.

The nurse continues, "*Hada bint inti?* [Is this thing yours?]"

Ummi's eyes take me in. "Your face looked like a full moon. Your skin was light – not dark like mine. You also didn't have any hair."

The nurse points at me and asks, "Why is she light and you are dark?"

Tears are pooling in Ummi's eyes. Trying to hold them back, she sniffs and swallows before answering, "She is mine." She points at me and then back at herself. "Her father has light skin."

The nurse lifts me out of the crib and places me on Ummi's lap. She asks her to feed me, then leaves.

As soon as the nurse turns her back, Ummi returns me to the crib. "I was not going to feed you. I wanted you to starve and die."

"Allah, why? Why another girl? Why? Why?" she is asking through her tears. Her mother-in-law's voice bears down on her: "We have fed you for seven years and all we have got is one boy and five girls! My son deserves better than you. He's done with you. I'll find him another wife."

Ummi thinks of Abouee. *What will I tell him? How will I look at him? I've failed him. I've destroyed him.* She clutches her stomach and rocks herself back and forth.

Her whimpering grows into loud, uncontrollable sobs. The woman next to her opens the curtain. "What is it, Ukhti? *Allah yibaarik feekee* [God bless you]. What is it? What's wrong?"

Ummi continues to cry.

"Ukhti, do you have any boys?"

Ummi doubles over and lets out a low, desperate moan. "Only one. And now five girls."

The woman sits down beside her and gently squeezes her shoulder. "Listen."

9

Ummi is still bent double, crying.

"Listen, Ukhti." The woman squeezes harder and Ummi raises her head. "What's your name? What's the name of your son?"

"Salmaan," Ummi says between sobs, and she sits up and wipes the tears from her eyes.

"I am Um Khaalid [mother of Khaalid]. Listen Um Salmaan, this is your fate. We women can't do anything about it. If your man is a good man," she continues, "he will treat you well. He won't abandon you and your children." Um Khaalid pauses, then asks, "Is he coming to visit you?"

Ummi nods and notices a shift come over Um Khaalid. "Then you must show him that you are sad. You must show him that it is not in your hands. You have to cry. He should see how red your eyes are so that he feels compassion for you."

Um Khaalid looks over at me in the crib and picks me up.

"*Haraam!* You must feed her. This is Allah's creature." She places me in Ummi's lap. "She is an innocent baby. Allah will punish you if you starve her."

Ummi holds me close to her chest and feels my little body pressing against her tear-soaked dress. She brings her mouth to my forehead and kisses it gently while inhaling my sweet smell. She closes her eyes and her nipples tingle as if to invite me to drink. I have my first breastmilk and Ummi accepts Allah's will.

While feeding me, Ummi's mind wanders to the tragedy of two months ago. She is cleaning the *saj** when the sound of shrieking from the west side of the tribe interrupts this daily ritual. She runs towards her parents' tent, her mind racing. Who could the wailing be for? There is not one of her twenty brothers and sisters that she is willing to spare. When she approaches, she sees all of her older sisters crouched down together, contorted with grief, as they shriek and throw sand in their faces. A black woman named Nayfa, who lived with the family and whom Ummi referred to as "our slave", runs

---

* A big, domed metal dish on which bread is quickly cooked. Pieces of wood or coal are lit beneath it and in our case, the *saj* sits on stones.

towards her with open arms. Although Nayfa lived mostly with Ummi's family, she moved between the two sides of the tribe, healing the sick, delivering babies and sharing gossip.

"Allah protect you! Allah protect you, my *babaabi* [lord]. It is your father. It is your father."

Ummi runs towards her mother, who has collapsed next to the central rod of the tent, and embraces her. Nayfa examines the belly protruding from Ummi's dress and proclaims: "That is a girl. If this was a boy, he would die after running in this heat."

"Shut your mouth," my grandmother retorts. "Don't bring the devil around here."

When Ummi tells that story she always adds, "I should have known then. Only girls can endure such pain."

Around seven o'clock in the evening, Abouee came to visit Ummi in the hospital. My father was different from most Bedouin men. For many years, he had been exposed to a more urban lifestyle. He had left the tribe at the age of twelve to work as a farmer on an Iraqi Jewish family's moshav. He was twenty-eight when I was born and financially better off by that time than anyone else in the tribe. He owned his own delivery business, driving his red Volvo truck all across Israel to deliver fruit and vegetables. In other ways, my father was Bedouin through and through. Not least in his reverence that bordered on fear of his mother, Jidatee (my grandmother).

My father, dressed in a tank top and shorts, walked towards Ummi, followed by Jidatee and then his father, Jidee (my grandfather). Jidatee had donned her most luxurious clothes to celebrate the birth of her much-anticipated grandson: a traditional Bedouin dress ornately embroidered with blue, brown and yellow flowers, a crepe abaaya (a thick coat also worn by men) and a golden Bedouin niqaab, which consists of a hood and a gold chain that descends from the top of the hood, sits on Jidatee's nose and attaches to both ears. My mother's relief at seeing Abouee's smiling face faded as soon as she saw my grandmother. In a culture where a woman is supposed to walk behind her husband, Jidatee's impressive attire and her order in the party added to Ummi's terror. As soon as Abouee greeted her, Ummi started sobbing to win her mother-in-law's compassion. Jidatee didn't even look at her. She took one look at the little creature in Ummi's arms and spat: "It's a girl." Ummi sobbed harder. Jidee came closer but Jidatee kept her distance.

"Binti [my daughter]," Jidee said calmly, "it doesn't matter." He placed his hand on Ummi's head. "Allah will never desert you."

Abouee tried to lighten the mood by cracking a joke. "Don't worry. As long as she looks like me." Ummi lifted me up and turned my face towards him. "The moment I looked at your face," Abouee would tell me years later, "I felt a deep connection with you. You know when you see someone that you love and your whole body pulses with joy? When I saw you, I felt tears coming to my eyes, but I was afraid that my mother would notice."

Jidatee looked at Abouee and said, "*Ya waladi* [my son], another girl. How will you show your face to the tribe? This woman," her head gestured to Ummi, "has broken your back."

Ummi's eyes are begging for Jidatee to soften, knowing that her life is in her hands. Jidatee will be the one who will decide if her days will be bitter or sweet. Ummi watches the tattoo on Jidatee's chin – the tattoo of the tribe – shrink as she purses her lips tighter and tighter.

"What do you say, Haj?" she barks at Jidee.

"It's for Allah to say," he replies.

She clicks her tongue. "Tck. It's in human hands now. I won't let my oldest son lose his power because of this."

Ummi knows that Jidatee means that she will try to find another wife for Abouee.

"I accept my fate," Abouee says looking deeply into Ummi's eyes. "I believe in Allah. Allah won't forget me." Abouee looks at me and says, "I see hope in her face. I want to call her Amal [hope], in the hope that Allah will give us boys after her."

"Which Allah?" Jidatee turns to leave, ordering Jidee after her. "*Yalla, Haj.*"

Now, the three of us were alone. Abouee knew that he could only linger for a moment. He leaned in and whispered in Ummi's ear, "I promise you. For as long as I am alive, I will never marry another woman." He squeezed her hand then stood up to leave. As he was passing through the door, the nurse entered to retrieve me.

"*Mabrouk!* [Congratulations!]" she said to Abouee and then, in Hebrew, "You have a beautiful girl." She shook Abouee's hand. "She looks just like you." Ummi remembers the proud look on Abouee's face before he disappeared down the hall.

Ummi is sitting there in shock as she feels tears coming again. The nurse turns to her and with a big smile she says, "Now I get it. Your baby looks just like her Ashkenazi dad!"

His father hung back, waiting for him. "Poor you. Your mother is very angry."

Abouee didn't reply. He knew that his mother would do everything she could to marry him off to another woman and he was already trying to figure out how to prevent that. When they reached the red Volvo truck, he opened the passenger door for his mother, placed his hand beneath her foot, and hoisted her inside.

"You wait here. I am going to buy some candies for the good news," he announced.

"Jump in, jump in. We have no time." She murmured to herself, "Candies! What for? You're not bringing home any prize."

Abouee ignored her. He stopped at the first kiosk on the street and asked the Jewish shopkeeper, in Hebrew, for a bag of candies. The shopkeeper handed him a bag and Abouee asked for two more.

"That's a lot. What are they for?"

"My wife just gave birth to a new baby girl who's a warrior."

The shopkeeper smiled. "*Mabrouk*, Akhi [my brother]," he said, handing Abouee the candies.

Abouee jumped into the truck as if he was jumping onto a horse and dropped the bags on his mother's knees. She flung them onto her husband's lap. Abouee started the engine, rolled down the windows, and started the drive home. For the entire ride, the only sound above the revving of the engine was Jidatee's gold niqaab clinking in the wind.

My eldest sister, eleven-year-old Basma, is waiting with her friends for my father's truck to appear on the main street between Be'er Sheva and Arad. She has told me, "I was sure it was a boy. I was telling my friends, 'Wait, wait, Abouee is going to bring lots of candies because Ummi gave birth to a boy today.'" She is waiting outside the tent and it is getting dark. She places her ear on the dirt road to listen for the sound of our father's Volvo, but she doesn't hear it. Together with the other girls, they start singing a song that our grandmother taught her to make our father come home faster.

Oh rooster, rooster, singing in the pot,
Bring my father to this spot . . .

After the last verse, Basma places her ear to the ground and shoots up. "It's Abouee's truck! It's Abouee's truck!"

She darts down the road barefoot because she can't wait even ten minutes to hear the good news. She reaches the Volvo, jumps and grabs onto the large wing mirror on the driver's side.

"Abouee, Abouee, what's the name of my brother?" she yells.

"Amal. Her name is—"

"It's a girl. Where's the *amal* in that?" Jidatee cuts him off. Abouee tosses Basma a bag of candies. "Here! Give it to your friends."

Basma pitches the candies back at him. "No one wants your candies." She jumps down from the truck and runs back towards the tent.

On her way, Basma passes through our uncle's tent. One of our cousins steps out and asks with excitement, "What is it, Basma? What is it?"

Without stopping, Basma shouts, "Another sister."

After a few paces, Basma looks back at our cousin, who is kneeling on the ground, tearing at her hair and throwing fistfuls of sand in her face.

A Tent, a Saj and a Donkey

TWO MONTHS AFTER my birth, Ummi's breasts stopped producing milk and she put me on goat's milk. She watched her mother-in-law put on her black abaaya and ride out on her donkey, knowing that she was going to visit another family in the village to inspect a possible new wife for my father. For the entire day she worked in a waking nightmare, startled by every sound, fearing the *zagareet* announcing the match and sealing her fate.

Ummi remembers: "I worked very hard to serve the whole family, your uncles, aunts, grandparents. I used to walk for three kilometres to the *jiheer* [well] and carry the water back to where your grandmother had left a pile of clothes as tall as I am under the noonday sun for me to wash by hand. Standing up after three hours of kneeling there washing the clothes was one of the hardest things, let me tell you. I'd bake and cook for everybody. My children were served last. How stupid I was! I thought that if I proved my loyalty to my mother-in-law that she'd stop searching for a new wife for your father. I heard her discussing it right in front of me! I knew her plans, but I never had the courage to stand up to her. Every time they mentioned a new plan I'd ask if that woman was prettier than me. At that time, I felt like all the women on earth were prettier and more deserving of your father than I was."

This time was crucial for both my parents. Abouee needed to draw the line between his commitment to himself, his loyalty to his parents and his responsibility to the tribe. Despite the promise he made to my mother that he wouldn't remarry so long as she gave me the name Amal, the choice wasn't really up to him. It was a collective decision that he could influence but ultimately had to submit to. My father worked himself to the bone to demonstrate his authority as the main breadwinner. He was supporting not only his family, but also his father's new family – my grandfather had married a second wife a few years before my father got married – and his sibling who was studying abroad. Ummi could do nothing except wait and pray.

It was winter, the end of February. A time when even Tel Arad's harsh land is awash with green and the smell of rain fills your every breath. Tall grass perks up between the houses and the soil is soft. Ummi's youngest sister, Na'ama, was eight years old and the same age as one of her daughters, also named Na'ama. They were playing together, pressing their little hands into the mud and sculpting the wet soil. Na'ama and Na'ama heard my father's sisters, Hesen and Maryam, young teens, sharing the latest gossip about their brother's wedding and exchanging self-indulgent plans for what they were going to wear for the occasion. Na'ama, my mother's sister, ran over to defend Ummi. She accused the girls of lying, but Maryam wasn't going to be chastised by the little sister of the woman she saw as her servant. She screamed for help, Na'ama and Na'ama fled for safety to the tent of their grandmother (Ummi's mother), and when Abouee's father arrived to investigate, Maryam accused Na'ama of attacking her. He believed his daughter's crocodile tears and rode to Ummi's mother's tent, where he threw the canvas aside, made straight for my grandmother, *agaal** in hand, and walloped her until she cowered at his feet. When Ummi returned from the well, chaos greeted her. Hesen and Maryam called her terrible names and she ran to her mother's tent, only to find her trembling by the fire, the marks of the *agaal* visible in the marks on her arms and the fear in her eyes. That is when Ummi decided that enough was enough. She wasn't going back to my father's family.

Since her father had recently died, she needed to seek out her oldest male relative, her brother Salaame, and ask for his protection. Salaame was working in an orchard in the centre of Israel and timing was crucial. Still exhausted from the day's work, Ummi fastened her *shash*** firmly around her neck and placed me on her shoulders. She left my other siblings at home and her twelve-year-old brother Talab, who had travelled to the city many times, accompanied her to the bus

---

* A black cord made of goat's hair worn doubled on a man's head to keep his keffiyeh in place.
** A long white scarf worn loose under a black abaaya.

stop. Women weren't allowed to travel alone then, and even if it had been permitted, she wouldn't have known how to take the bus.

Basma remembers that when our father came back from work that day, before he could even enter the house, Maryam and Hesen ran over to him and started telling him the story about how Ummi slapped them. Jidatee egged them on. Basma waited until Abouee was alone. He was getting ready for bed when she shared what she knew: Jidee had struck Jidatee – Ummi's mother – and Hesen and Maryam were inventing a drama that never happened. Now Abouee understood the severity of the issue. It was no longer a private spat, but a tribal case.

A week later, Abouee went to my mother's side to negotiate. During that time, Basma didn't attend school and took care of our four siblings since Ummi was living with Salaame in his shack in the middle of a fruit orchard surrounded by orange trees, a paradise compared to Tel Arad's dusty plains. That's where Abouee met with Salaame, who was known inside and outside the tribe for his strength of character. Abouee admired him and they had always been close, but now that his sister's honour was at stake, the negotiations were tense. The two men spoke beneath the fruit trees. Salaame was very wise. He agreed to settle the issue on one condition. "If you want my sister back," Salaame told him, "you have to grant her a decent life. You have to build her a tent and bring her everything she needs to have her own, independent life."

When Ummi told me this story for the first time, I asked what independence meant to her.

"There are three things," she answered, "three things every woman needs: a tent, a *saj* and a donkey."

The next day, Abouee brought her those three things. He came to her with good-quality fabric to build a solid tent for her to live in, a *saj* so she could earn her keep by baking, and a healthy donkey so she could easily get around. By giving my mother these things, he freed her from her mother-in-law's cruelty and allowed her to start a life that was all her own.

Ummi said that the morning she woke up in her own tent, the sun had never seemed more radiant, the air had never smelled so fresh, and the animals' bleats had never sounded more beautiful. She felt like she owned the universe. When we own ourselves, we do. She tied her donkey next to her tent and hung her *saj* on the *al-waasit*, the central pole of her tent. The early morning light had just caressed Tel Arad's hills and the soil was still cool to the touch. Barefoot, she tiptoed out to face her tent. She smiled and let out an easy breath.

In her new tent, Ummi got pregnant again. She received the news with mixed feelings, but she had faith that life was opening itself up to her. The first time she had delivered a boy, my elder brother Salmaan, Ummi's closest brother, Daahish, had visited her in a dream and brought her a gift. This time Daahish gave Ummi a white dress embroidered with dainty yellow flowers, but when she stretched out her arms to pull the dress over her head, a searing pain shot from her wrists out to her fingers.

The night my mother felt that it was time to deliver, my father brought his Volvo truck to outside her tent and my mother clambered up the steps to sit next to him. Her waters broke on their way to Soroka Hospital and at the junction that links al-Khaleel (Hebron) to Beer a-Saba (Be'er Sheva), my brother's head descended into this world. My father called him Yousef, as this was the very spot where the prophet Yousef was left at the bottom of a well by his eleven brothers. Once it was known that she had delivered another baby boy, another future man capable of defending the tribe, Ummi's worth, in the eyes of the tribe, was restored and her relationship with her mother-in-law changed. Jidatee no longer perceived my mother as an object she could order about, but saw her, at last, as a woman deserving of her respect.

However, just as the dream foretold, thirty days after she delivered Yousef she became very ill and needed to be hospitalized. She feared that she would not live to enjoy her newborn son. When she was well enough to walk, she made her way to the hospital entrance and waited all day for my father to arrive with Yousef in his arms. She returned to her room in tears.

The woman in the bed next to her gave her a reassuring smile and offered to read her palm. "You will have many children," she told her, "a lot of human wealth. You should walk with your head embracing the sky."

The woman's name was Aliza and she was an older Moroccan Jewish woman who spoke Arabic. Ummi and Aliza became close friends. They would sit together discussing the two topics that they had in common: children and food. After the family updates, the conversation would turn to different dishes and Aliza, a superb cook, would share recipes with my mother and explain them in detail. Aliza's semolina milk cake was one of the first desserts Ummi learned how to make and it is still one of our favourites. Ummi was discharged from the hospital before Aliza but would ask my father to visit her every so often to take her Bedouin bread and cheese. Ummi always calls Aliza "my Jewish friend, Aliza" and emphasizes that Aliza is a good Jew, not like other Jews; that she is an Arab Jew.

Worthy of Meat

I MAY HAVE been only four years old when Ummi caught me pulling back the *ma'anad*, the fabric that separates the women's section in the tent from the men's. I wanted to watch the trial that Jidee, my father's father, was presiding over. Jidee was the judge in our tribe and his wisdom was respected across the Naqab (Negev). His *diwaan*, the tent reserved for men, which comes from the Arabic word "to discuss", was always bustling with some kind of business, be it matters of the heart, such as consulting on a marriage, matters of money, such as the sale of horses or cattle, or matters of politics and public well-being – on which his counsel was highly regarded. Regardless of who entered, the most powerful sheikh or the most wretched beggar, Jidee met each plea with a patient ear and a careful tongue. He listened for truth and spoke with justice.

When the dogs barked, you knew that someone was approaching the tent. My youngest uncle, whose job it was to care for any horses that our guests rode in on, could tell whether the bark signalled a familiar face or a strange one. If a stranger arrived, Jidee greeted him outside the entrance of the tent, saying: "*Ahalaan wasahalaan ya hayalah ba-thayf. Beetkou umatraahkou* [You are most welcome, my guest. This is your house and your place]." The stranger, tired from the day's ride, would dismount from his horse and shake Jidee's hand before being gently ushered inside.

It was one of those days when the *diwaan* was full of men. They argued and shouted. If I had been inside, I imagine that I would have seen their hands moving just as passionately as their mouths. Everyone wanted to have his say. On the women's side, things were very different. We spoke in muted tones, whispering so that no one would hear us. The commotion on the other side rose in a crescendo until Jidee's voice pierced the roar and silenced the other men. I always wanted to know what was going on in there. Why were the men shouting? Why could Jidee tell them what to do? Why would they listen? Were they afraid of him? With me, he was always soft and gentle, like a lion basking in the midday sun.

When I could no longer contain my curiosity, I edged towards the *ma'anad*, and slowly pulled it back until I could see the right side of Abouee's face. His light eyes were shadowed by a furrowed brow and his head was turned towards Jidee, who sat at the head of the tent, facing the entrance. On either side sat a scattering of men, some of whom I knew and others whom I had never seen before. The strangers, like this land, were dusty and dry, their skin dark and wrinkled from exposure to the sun. I so badly wanted Abouee to look at me. I pulled the *ma'anad* back further until I had Jidee's full face in view, my eyes staring intently at Abouee, burning with a child's desire to be seen. Finally, our eyes met and his gaze enveloped my little body, warming me like a sheepskin coat. My body relaxed, but a needle – Ummi's sharp nails – stabbed me in my arm. Before I could scream, Ummi's other hand gripped my face as she dragged me away from the *ma'anad*, my arm's soft flesh still caught between her claws. I jerked and kicked, but I couldn't escape.

She spoke in a furious yell-whisper. "Why are you doing this? Are you out of your mind? Do you want to kill me?"

It was strictly forbidden for the girls to peer into the *diwaan*. It was even more forbidden for a girl to stare at a man she didn't know. Jidatee, with her air of authority, came over from the other side of the tent where she was supervising the preparation of the evening meal and bluntly pushed Ummi aside. "Leave her," she commanded. "She's just a kid." Ummi released her grip and walked away in silence. Ummi knew her place.

Jidatee bent down and wrapped her arms around me, her cheek resting near mine just for a moment. She looked into my eyes and firmly wiped away my tears. "Don't listen to her," she said, her head motioning towards Ummi. "Your mother is stupid and ignorant." Together, we walked back to where Jidatee had been supervising the preparation of the goat that would later be served in the *diwaan*. She added another piece of wood to the fire and took a seat next to the pot of boiling water and goat meat. I sat down on the dirt floor beside her. My eyes on the fire, I whispered, "She is stupid and ignorant," repeating it to myself like a lullaby. Jidatee hated people she thought were weak, and Ummi was one of her main targets. Every time Ummi beat me, Jidatee would take my side, saying, "She doesn't understand you. You are strong. She is weak." I didn't understand the hypocrisy then, but later I would recognize how women in the tribe internalized their own oppression and abused each other accordingly. As I grew up, I would come to understand why the same woman who saved me from Ummi's abuse treated Ummi worse than the mud beneath her feet.

This must have taken place in the fall, because I remember that we were using the winter tent. That tent is made of a mix of camel and goat hair; it is heavy and thick, black with white and brown

21

stripes. The fabric is so heavy that it requires the strength of twenty men to carry it. The tent is divided into three sections: the *diwaan*, the women and children's section, and the kitchen. A few feet away from where I was sitting with Jidatee, Ummi was baking the bread. The bread we eat is as large as a serving platter and slightly thicker than a crepe. It takes about twenty seconds to bake. Lay it on one side, flip it on the other, and it's done. Every couple of minutes, Ummi pushed five or six coals from the fire under the *saj* to ensure that the bread would bake evenly. She knew how many coals to add by looking at the bubbles in the dough. A rug covered the floor where she rolled the dough and tossed it in the air, deftly spinning it around until it grew large enough to cover the *saj*'s entire surface. Baking the bread was torture, but with Jidatee watching, Ummi didn't dare stop to rest, even as the smoke blinded her and the fire burned her shins and calves, which were red from sitting so close.

As the women worked, the aroma of baking bread and braised goat wafted through the tent and mingled with the coffee that had been brewing in the *diwaan* all afternoon. Two of my sisters were seated in another corner of the tent, washing a seemingly endless stack of large metal serving platters. Whenever there are guests, women are put to work. Amid the hushed bustle, Abouee quietly entered and pointed towards the pot, enquiring politely if the meal was ready.

Jidatee left her post, moved closer to Abouee and asked: "Did they solve it?" Her dark eyes gleamed.

"Yes, yes."

"*Al-hamdulillah!*" She clapped her hands together. In our tradition, we only serve the meal once the issue has been resolved. The two parties will share bread as a sign of peace and a commitment to cease fighting. If the problem is not resolved, the men will only drink coffee.

Jidatee barked at Ummi: "Prepare the food for serving. It's time!"

Ummi leaped up from the fire, grabbed the metal plates, and lined them up on the floor of the tent. I counted them with my eyes.

There were seven. Like in a well-rehearsed play, everyone took their places. Ummi and Abouee lifted the pot of stewed goat and placed it on the floor. Now came the time for everyone to play their part in a coordinated dance of speed and precision. Ummi and my sisters were on first. They tore the bread into small pieces and covered the platter with them. Then, Jidatee swooped in, delivering a careful splash of hot soup, a mixture of broth and yogurt, which was followed by Ummi firmly planting a full flatbread to soak up the soup. For the grand finale, a male solo in this female production, Abouee added the last but most important flourish: healthy morsels of savoury goat meat that had been stewing since the early afternoon. They loaded up the platters one by one until all the food was laid out in seven magnificent and mouth-watering arrangements. Jidatee and Abouee sent each other a silent signal that it was time to place the feast before our guests. For the second act, Abouee lifted one platter in each hand and disappeared swiftly into the other side of the tent. Ummi and my sisters stood in a straight line just behind the curtain that separated us from the *diwaan*, each holding a platter, and Abouee moved back and forth, gracefully taking the plates from their hands and placing them before the guests. When every last platter had been brought out, Jidee's voice proudly declared: "*Medo eidayko ala ali qasma allah ya hala wahayaala* [Dip your fingers into the food that Allah has given to you]."

After all that work, everyone on the women's side, including my brothers, had to endure act four, the waiting game. We had been enveloped in that sumptuous aroma all afternoon and the tease of seeing that tasty feast was almost too much for our empty stomachs to bear. All the children sat impatiently around the fire, counting the minutes till the guests would finish eating so that we could devour their leftovers. Some of us kept perfectly still, forcing an inner calm, while those of us who were less disciplined fidgeted and wriggled, desperately distracting ourselves from our desire for food. After what felt like an eternity, we heard a shift. The voices of satisfied stomachs stepping out of the *diwaan* to wash their hands rippled into a tsunami of excitement on our side of the tent.

"The food is coming! The food is coming!" my brother squealed.

My mind conjured up a particularly plump piece of meat I recalled Abouee ladling on top of the fresh bread and yogurt soup. I ran my tongue along the inside of my mouth and licked my lips in anticipation. My uncle appeared from behind the curtain, approaching us with two half-full platters in his hands. He saw our enthusiasm, but didn't smile. His dour expression told us to keep it down since the guests were still there. We ran towards him, our arms reaching out towards the plates, but Ummi snatched them from him first.

"Sit!" she growled.

We crowded around her, craning our faces as close as we could. With one hand, she stacked the dishes and with the other she swatted us away like the persistent flies on a horse's back. She placed the platters on the ground, her hands moving quickly as she reorganized them, putting all the meat onto one platter and the yogurt soup and bread onto another. She kept the platter with the meat tucked behind her, and pushed the other one towards us. Like a pack of dogs, we rushed towards it. Sitting around the platter in a circle, we thrust our grubby hands into the warm mush, rolled the bread and yogurt together into a gooey ball, and devoured one ball after another.

Jidatee was sitting away from us, arranging other platters and handing them to my cousins to bring to their families for dinner. Everyone in the tribe waited eagerly for this meal because goat was a luxury we ate only on very special occasions. Even if they only received a small portion of meat atop a large serving of bread mixed with yogurt soup, just a morsel of that sumptuous flesh was enough for everyone to feel like they had been fed. Ummi was sitting with us without eating, watching in silence. Each one of us was trying to get as much bread onto our side of the platter as we could. When she could see the metal of the plate through the pieces of bread, she would cut more and toss it into the dish, only breaking her silence to warn us to move our hands away as she poured more soup over the plate.

With the edge taken off our hunger, the pace of our hands moving towards our mouths slowed. But it was only the calm before the storm. For this pack of dogs, the fight for food was nearing its deadliest stage, the part that I hated the most. Ummi turned to the platter of meat behind her and started to pull it apart, dividing it between the seven of us. It wasn't really a contest. We all knew where we stood and we all knew why the girls got the scraps. Ummi started by handing the meat to my brothers: big, juicy chunks dripping with hot soup. I eyed them with envy. Now, it was our turn. To Basma, she tossed a scraggly bone with only a pinkie nail's worth of goat flesh. Basma didn't seem to care. Without even inspecting her meagre share, she popped it in her mouth.

I looked at the piece that had landed in my hand. It was pathetic: a splintered bone covered almost entirely in fat. My stomach sank. I don't know if it was the fat or the injustice that repulsed me, but I couldn't take it. I tossed the bone back into the dish and waited for Ummi's reaction.

"*Inshaala ma takli* [So you won't eat]," she said without even looking at me.

My other sister rushed to grab my sad, discarded bone and suck out the marrow. Fuelled by my rage, I leaped up and began yelling at her, my finger condemning her for this betrayal. The commotion drew my uncle from the *diwaan*. The light was fading, but we could see his eyes, blazing with anger. They could hear me shouting from the other side.

"Beat her!" Ummi demanded in a harsh whisper. "She threw her piece of meat back and today she was trying to get into the men's side."

My uncle grabbed my arm and dragged me deeper inside the tent. The more I fought, the harder his fingers twisted around my arm. "I have told you a million times! You can't be around men and you can't be in there. It's only for men." With those words, he released my arm and pushed me to the ground. I landed face first and tasted the dirt.

Jidatee came to my rescue again. "Leave her! She didn't do anything wrong. Her mother is exaggerating." My uncle stalked off and Jidatee waited till I picked myself up before going back to whatever she had been doing before the commotion started. Dusting myself off, I looked over at Ummi, who was busy washing the platters as if nothing had happened. I was furious at her indifference. That was when I noticed my brother standing next to Jidatee, a fat piece of meat still dangling in his right hand. My eye on the prize, I ran towards him at full speed. With rage and determination on my side, I yanked the meat from his hand and bolted from the tent. His whimpering for Ummi followed me out into the darkness. I heard Ummi yelling after me, threatening to kill me if I didn't come back that instant.

Jidatee, my biggest ally, turned to my brother and said, "Run. Go and get your meat. If you catch her, it is yours. If not, you don't deserve it."

My brother and my sisters all sprinted after me. My little legs moved swiftly beneath me, carrying me faster and faster away from the voices shouting at me in anger or cheering my brother on. I ran and ran and ran until the only sound I could hear was the rhythm of my feet hitting the sand. I made it to the very top of the hill that overlooked my parents' tent. Finally, I stopped. I caught my breath and with a quick prayer to Allah turned around. No one was behind me.

A wave of relief coursed through my body. I sat down and opened my hand to see that decadent chunk of meat nestled safely in my palm. The soup had dribbled between my fingers and down my arm, coating it in a sticky mess of yogurt and dust, but I didn't care.

Raising the meat to my nose, I inhaled its delicious smell. Then I brought the meat to my lips, kissing it before opening my mouth and biting off the tiniest piece. Closing my eyes, I savoured the taste of triumph. I swallowed and felt the meat nourish my entire being.

"Yes," I said with a smirk. "You earned it."

The Land of Olives and Thyme

THE ISRAELI GOVERNMENT wants you to believe the official story: that we are not indigenous to the land. The official story is that we wandered in from Saudi Arabia and Egypt during the time of the Ottomans. While we don't have written documents to counter this claim, our oral history relayed from generation to generation tells a different story. According to our traditions, our herds have grazed on the Naqab's grass since the Bronze Age and her lands continued to give us life even as she changed hands from the Nabateans, to the Byzantines, to the Romans. Our traditions are a product of our semi-nomadic lifestyle of moving with the seasons, settling our tents away from the wind and riding towards the sun in order to sustain our herds. As you can imagine, semi-nomadic people don't fit neatly into a delineated territory, nor do they abide by the laws laid down by the prevailing power. During those times, we answered only to the stern law of nature and to our own tribal codes, which ruled every element of life in the tribe: the roles of men and women, the customs of birth, marriage and death, and how crime was punished and justice exacted.

According to Abouee, the sedentarization of the Bedouin began with the Ottomans, who introduced the Land Law in 1858, declaring all land in the region to be uncultivated and state-owned. As a result, we were incentivized to register our land in order to prove ownership. By that time, we were organized into seven major tribal confederations, each consisting of several tribes. The largest was made up of thirty tribes, the smallest of five or six. My tribe belonged to the second largest, the Al-Tiyaaha, and we were known for being noble and educated. According to my grandmother, we were originally Iraqi and belonged to that majestic civilization before we made our way from Iraq, through the treacherous mountains of Jordan, which wasn't of course called Jordan at the time, to the vast desert of the Naqab in historic Palestine.

Abd al-Kareem, my paternal great-grandfather, was a fierce leader of the tribe who fought alongside the Ottomans. Abouee was named after him. When the Ottomans finally ceded to the British in 1917, the British administrators appointed a sheikh from a different tribe in order to temper the a-Sana power in the region. Abd al-Kareem went to the chief British administrator and threatened him at gunpoint. Then the British understood that our tribe had many allies in the region, and they appointed Abd al-Kareem's brother, Ibraheem, my maternal great-grandfather, as sheikh instead.

Whoever ruled over our territory tried to garner our favour through promises and bribes. The promises were always the same: "If you leave this land, you can have that one, where there are many more Bedouin, and you will have an official title, which means they will report to you." Some Bedouin from other tribes fell for these schemes and were willing to give up their territory in exchange for more favourable political ties and a greater number of people to rule over. But not Sheikh Ibraheem. Ibraheem was more diplomatic than his brother and was deeply principled. Throughout the Naqab, the other Bedouin tribes referred to him as "The Righteous". He conducted meetings with the British tactfully and respectfully, but always with an eye for what was best for his people.

The British continued the process of sedentarization by building villages and establishing laws. By 1946, it was estimated that 14 per cent of the Bedouin lived in permanent structures. We chose to remain in the desert, but we owned several permanent buildings in Beer a-Saba, where Sheikh Ibraheem held meetings and other formal gatherings. When proponents of the Zionist project started buying land in the region, Sheikh Ibraheem gathered the heads of the Bedouin tribes and asked them to place their swords on the Quran and swear that they would not sell a single dunam to the Jews. Later, in 1936 when the Palestinians revolted against the British over growing Jewish immigration, Palestinian leader Amin Al-Husseini and the King of Jordan, Abdullah I, selected Sheikh Ibraheem to represent the Bedouin tribes at the subsequent negotiations. The role he played during this event is crucial to understanding Israel's future dealings with my tribe and our dedication to political activism. He worked tirelessly to oppose the settlers and advocate for the tribes in the region. People from across the Naqab sought his counsel and he negotiated with the Zionist leaders on their behalf – never betraying his principles and never accepting a higher seat in exchange for his people's autonomy.

When my grandmother spoke about her father, Sheikh Ibraheem, she spoke with pride beyond pride. Even if she was reclining from the day's work, when her father was mentioned, she would sit up, pull her shoulders back and wait for complete silence before opening her mouth. In the way that I could always predict my father's arrival by the revving of his truck engine, my grandmother could always tell when her father was approaching by the cloud of dust his horse kicked up as he rode into the tribe. She never hid inside the tent, even if a group of ten or twenty men arrived with her father. He would hand her his horse in front of the whole caravan, and charge her with its care. My grandmother was the eldest daughter and she knew where her father went, the cases he was dealing with, and the parties involved. Ibraheem didn't refrain from discussing political affairs with her because she was a woman. At this time, prior to the urbanization of our community and the subsequent shift to a more conservative Islam, women were part of the whole and helped the tribe survive. My grandmother fondly recalled participating in the resistance against Israeli soldiers, a stockpile of ammunition hidden beneath the rug where she sat breastfeeding when the soldiers stormed the tent. Although she never received a formal education, she understood the political landscape: the intricate affiliations between tribes, the names of the Zionist movement's leaders and their respective platforms, and which plots of land the tribe now owned and who had sold it to them. And, while it may take an entire university course to explain the difference between colonialism and settler-colonialism, my grandmother distinguished these two concepts by the simple fact that when the British came, they came alone, and when the Jews came, they came with their wives and children.

My grandmother also perceived the sad truth that "*Alyahood wid-*

hum blaad bedoon l'baad" – the Jews want land without people. Before the Nakba* in 1948, there were roughly ninety thousand Bedouin in the Naqab. Three years later, there were eleven thousand. During the war, some tribes fought, some fled and others were expelled. Each tribe's experience depended on their allegiances and their numbers, which affected their decision to resist or not. Those who left headed to Jordan, Gaza, Sinai, the Hebron mountains and the West Bank. At that time, Bedouin tribes were fractured: there were members of our tribe who fled to Gaza and Jordan while others, around eight hundred, stayed behind to defend the homeland we had spent years cultivating. We also cooperated with the Egyptians to protect Beer a-Saba, but we did not have the strength to defend these lands. The Israeli forces had guns that outmatched our British rifles and we were forced to relocate to an area north-east of Beer a-Saba. Jidatee remembers that after the Israeli forces claimed Beer a-Saba, her father went to an outdoor faucet near a house he owned there. He asked to drink at it, but the Jewish settler who had taken up residence refused. "You foreigner," Sheikh Ibraheem said. "I installed this pipe with my own hands, and I have the documents to prove that these houses belong to us." The Jewish settler moved aside and let him drink.

For many Palestinians, the process of expulsion ended when the state was established in 1948. For my people, our dispossession didn't end there. Even after Israel established itself as a country, the government continued its attempts to empty the land of its indigenous people. Between 1949 and 1953 it was possible for the Bedouin to move freely to visit their relatives who had fled to the surrounding regions. Some tribes stayed in order to avoid having their land taken over by Jewish settlers. Others left, in the hope of reuniting with the rest of the tribe and returning at a later date. The government took advantage of these movements and claimed the territory the Bedouin tribes left behind by enacting the 1950

---

* During the Nakba, which means catastrophe in Arabic, approximately 700,00 Palestinians were expelled, or fled, from their homes, turning them into refugees. This is also known as the Israeli War of Independence.

Absentee Property Law, which authorized the state to nationalize nearly all the land in the Naqab. The government justified these actions on the basis that we were nomadic people who had no official records of our land holdings, and, therefore, no rights to this soil. Moreover, some of the territory we had previously inhabited was designated as a military zone, which denied us access to those lands. Without official documentation, neither the trees we planted nor the fields we cultivated were sufficient proof to back up our claim.

Jidatee told me that our tribe was expelleed twice; the first time was from Laqiya in 1950 at gunpoint. We fled to the mountains and were allowed to return a couple of weeks later. For the next three years, we lived in Laqiya, but under highly restrictive conditions. Finally, in 1953, although Sheikh Ibraheem had been granted a provisional judgement against the Israeli military governor and the company developing our land, Israeli forces arrived in tanks and armoured cars, circled the village and swiftly moved in. Chaos descended. Guns at the ready, they fired them in the air to scare everyone and shot anyone who resisted. "*Yalla! Yalla!*" was their only intelligible demand, but what they wanted was clear. The women were begging and pleading, men fighting and throwing stones, and people running in all directions. Clutching their children, families tried to fight back, but they were beaten until they had no choice but to comply. Eventually everyone was loaded onto trucks, squeezed between their cows, camels, goats and sheep.

They were going to relocate my tribe to Tel Arad, but my great-grandfather Ibraheem wanted to go to Jordan, fearing that Tel Arad was a death sentence. Although this contravened the armistice with Jordan, the Israeli military governor didn't try to stop him. The land they wanted would be emptied of one more Bedouin tribe; he didn't care where the tribe went. He considered us weeds in a garden, to be managed and removed, rather than trees in the desert, important features of the land which had a place, and whose place had a purpose.

With heavy hearts, my tribe walked with whatever we could carry towards the Jordanian border, which, at the time, was near Hebron.

When we arrived, we did not receive the warm welcome that my great-grandfather was expecting. Instead, we were held there for fifty days. Fifty days that destroyed my great-grandfather's life. Ibraheem would have preferred to go to Jordan and collect his energy until he could plan his next steps, but the Jordanian authorities refused to let my tribe in. My great-grandfather spent many hours fiercely negotiating with the military governor and consulting with the rest of the tribe in the *diwaan*. Finally, the United Nations Truce Officers intervened. Ibraheem hosted a meeting with the Jordanian officials, the Israeli military governor and the United Nations officers. The Jordanian officials did not want to allow the Israelis to reduce their Palestinian population by sending Palestinians over the border; they claimed that it would create a precedent and that Jordan's lands were becoming overcrowded with refugees. One afternoon the military governor drove by the *diwaan* in his jeep and ordered Sheikh Ibraheem to go to Tel Arad, a barren swathe of land west of the Dead Sea. This news crushed him, but he was not going to fight to enter another land where the government would not welcome his people. An account from one of the United Nations Truce Officers, an English military observer named E.H. Hutchison[*] describes my great-grandfather's tremendous character, strength and diplomacy and the tragic shift from pride in leading a carefree people to a sense of defeat, shame and humiliation at not being able to protect them. We were sent to Tel Arad to die, and forty days after we arrived, my great-grandfather was found wrapped in a blanket, lifeless and cold. He left behind a legacy of principled action, of advocacy on behalf of the Naqab Bedouin, and a diplomacy that demonstrated the sophistication of our tribe and of our people.

On my mother's side, Ummi's father was concerned that upon arriving at Tel Arad, the authorities would arrest his brother due to his actions in the resistance. After consulting with the tribe, it was

---

[*] *A Violent Truce: A Military Observer Looks at the Arab–Israeli Conflict 1951–1955*, E.H. Hutchison (1958).

decided that Ummi's family would sneak into Jordan and seek shelter there. Ummi remembers the journey well. She remembers the unforgiving desert sun, the sand that scorched her feet, the dust that covered her face and clothes, and the feeling of being so parched that even her skin was thirsty. Ummi's mother and father rode at the front of the caravan, her mother on a camel and her father on a horse. They were followed by their modest herd of animals – a few donkeys, some goats, sheep, and cows – shepherded by my mother and the brother closest to her in age. Her two older brothers brought up the rear of the train. My mother walked along the middle, near one of the donkeys where her two baby brothers lay nestled in a pair of saddlebags. She would run back and forth, running ahead to keep the animals in line and then sprinting back to swat the flies from her sleeping brothers' faces. Her bare feet scurried across the sand, carelessly stepping on pebbles and plants so that by the end of the day her feet were caked in blood and dirt. After walking to a safe distance from the border, near Hebron, her parents stood in front of the caravan to discuss where to put the tent. The twenty of them were covered in grime and exhausted from the day's trek, from the fear of being caught, and from moving onwards without knowing where they would end up. Ahead, they could see the stone houses of a town – Ummi's first glimpse of such structures – but decided it would be safer to set up camp outside the town. They later joined the rest of the tribe in Tel Arad.

For more than twenty years, we lived in a camp with tents and makeshift shacks scattered across Tel Arad's dusty mound. We lived like prisoners in a country where we once roamed free. Unable to grow anything on Tel Arad's salty and dry expanse, we risked our lives to find menial work in the nearby Jewish towns, sneaking out under the cloak of night to tend to their fields or develop their land. In 1976, when I was four years old, we were finally granted the right to return to Laqiya, our beloved home. I was so young, but the day that we returned is burned in my memory. We drove from Tel Arad towards our promised land in large trucks loaded with dismantled shacks and tents. My siblings, aunts, uncles and cousins sat together in the back of Abouee's truck, squashed between our belongings, singing, laughing, dancing, lifting ourselves up onto the sides of the truck, craning our necks to see the land ahead as the desert wind carried our songs away.

Although we had lived there for twenty-three years, Tel Arad was always only temporary. While I had never stepped foot on Laqiya's soil, I had visited her a thousand times in my mind, seeing her rolling green mountains and wells streaming with sparkling water. Her name means "the meeting point between Gaza and Hebron", and I was sure she was heaven. As we drew nearer, my sisters and aunts raised their voices, singing "*Bilaadi, bilaadi, bilaadi laaki hobbi wa fouwaadi* [my land, my land, you deserve my love]," as we younger children repeated the words after them with elation and glee. We were all in a giddy state of relief and disbelief. As the first truck in our caravan entered the village, it raised the Palestinian flag, a beacon of victory and an act of defiance. We had finally returned to the place where we had always belonged.

I peered over the side of the truck and watched the members of my tribe embrace in celebration. Each *fahad* (section of the tribe) was scoping the land and discussing how to divide the territory for their families and the families of their married sons. The *zagareet* resounded across the plain as more and more women added their voices to the jubilant chorus. We didn't do much work that day. We unpacked our things and concocted plans for our new lives. Once the sun had descended behind Laqiya's blessed mountains, we crawled into the back of Abouee's truck and slept packed together like a flock of sheep, content to have returned to our pasture and eager for the morning graze.

The second day, everyone was in motion. Men carried large planks of wood for building cabins, the women unloaded the trucks and prepared the *saj* pita, and even the children scurried around helping wherever they could. My job was to stand close to Abouee as he erected our shack and hand him the right-sized nail. I listened with rapt attention and dutifully obeyed his commands of "A long one!" and "A short one!", absorbed in my role of helping him to fashion these barren planks of wood into our family home.

Laqiya is seventeen kilometres north-east of Beer a-Saba, in the Ijbaal al-Laqiya mountains that connect Beer a-Saba to al-Khaleel. We built our homes on the lap of the mountainside, not too close to the peaks, in order to be shielded from the wind, and not too near the valley, to avoid being flooded in the winter. This area is known for its many wells and freshwater springs, as well as its caves that were used as dwelling places in the previous century. We later used them to store our crops or to provide our shepherds with refuge from the sun. From the place where we would build our house, facing west or south, I saw the mountain. Looking north or to the east, I saw the fields stretching far beyond me before ascending upwards, becoming once again part of those proud yet silent peaks.

By the time our shack was complete, it comprised two rooms as large as a school classroom that opened onto a cement patio – the *hosh* – which was enclosed by a wall made of concrete blocks. The rooms had large glass windows and the doors were fitted with a lock and key, none of which I had ever seen before. We loved our new home, in no small part due to the fact that Abouee had allowed us to carve our names in the soft cement in our room and in the *hosh*. Next to our room, Abouee and Ummi constructed an arbour for our grapes that shaded the area between the shack where we lived and another shack that we used as a kitchen. The kitchen shack was constructed from sheets of corrugated metal, and on one side of the kitchen, Ummi had set up our tent where she would prepare the food. In the winter, the kitchen was my favourite place to be. The metal did little to protect against the cold so we would sit huddled together on the dirt floor by the fire. I sometimes think that those nights are the reason that everyone in my family has a loud voice. As we sat together in that tin shed, we would have to yell at the top of our lungs to be heard over the rain pounding against the roof.

The village wasn't equipped with modern plumbing or electricity.

Our only sources of water were three wells, a large one located in the centre of the village, and two smaller ones in the mountains. We used to bathe in a corner of the kitchen that Ummi had designated for us. We heated the water in a pot on the fire and would sit in a large metal dish while one sibling poured the water over your body and the other scrubbed you raw. Ummi hated it when the water spilled outside the bathing area and onto the kitchen floor, threatening to turn her neatly packed dirt floor into a puddle of mud. I was happy that this unpleasant activity only took place once a week. For our other needs, we ventured into the valley, and we girls had to wait for the cover of night before we were allowed to relieve ourselves.

During those first months in the village, we were on a mission to root ourselves for good. We built homes, planted orchards, raised sheep and did everything we could to ensure that, this time, no one could deny that these lands were ours. Planting olives, figs and grapes, with a fence around them of prickly pear cacti, was not only for sustenance but to prove that we had been here all along. We lived by the words of the Palestinian poet Mahmoud Darwish: "We will stay in the land as long as the thyme and olives are rooted." Our orchards told the Israeli government that our roots in this land ran just as deep.

We divided the valley into farms and orchards, built dams to water our crops, and dug roads between the shacks and tents. Next to Jidee's shack was the *diwaan*, where the men gathered to drink coffee and discuss tribal affairs. The *taboon*, a communal oven made from mud and hay, was set up in the middle of the village, where the women would take turns preparing the bread for the entire tribe. I remember the morning baking with special fondness. The women would arrive very early and place their babies in cloth hammocks tied to the shelter covering the *taboon*. They would fire up the oven and by late morning the entire village would be bathed in the scent of freshly baked bread. The scene at the *taboon* was a kind of paradise for me. The hens strolled about while the women worked, sitting together on the floor, rolling out the dough, purposeful but also carefree, laughing, gossiping and enjoying the experience of hard labour in the company of good friends. They worked all morning, resting only for a quick breakfast of fresh bread dipped in small bowls of olive oil and zaatar.

The first years after returning to our village were marked by breathing life back into the land. When we weren't caring for our crops and animals, we children would roam the wheat fields playing tag or hide-and-seek. Nothing compares to times when the old and young work together under the open sky. I still remember my grandparents' harvest songs and the contentment and peace that come from living with the land. Although it may have been different for the adults in the village, as a child I don't remember anything from the outside world interrupting our lives. But one day, in the fall of 1978, I came to understand that things were not so simple.

I was six years old and in first grade. We were sitting at our desks, listening to the day's lesson, when our teacher stopped mid-sentence and walked towards the window. We ran to look. The windows faced the village's main dirt road, where an unfamiliar procession was making its way towards the school. There were two white police jeeps at the head followed by two bulldozers and an endless line of white cars behind them. I sensed my teacher's fear. I had no idea what was happening, but another teacher entered the class and the two of them whispered to each other frantically. As the line of bulldozers and white cars drove closer and closer to us, teachers streamed into the schoolyard and formed a human barricade against the oncoming threat. The jeep neared the schoolyard and the principal cried out: "This is a school! What do you want? There are children here. You are scaring the children!" He stretched his arms out in front of him and commanded the other teachers to do the same. Not everyone wanted to fight. Some teachers stayed behind, refusing to leave the classroom and join the resistance. Most of the teachers who joined the principal were teachers from the Arab communities in the north, government employees who had been sent to support the disadvantaged schools in our area. The jeeps ploughed onwards.

Silence descended over the yard. Once they were through the gate, the jeeps halted. After that, nothing happened. No one rolled down a window and no one got out. Whether the people in the vehicles wore uniforms was hard to see, because the windows were tinted, which only exacerbated our sense of facing a non-human enemy. Then, just as swiftly as they had rolled in, the procession backed out of the driveway and headed straight for the field of prickly pear cactus adjacent to the school.

The bulldozers led the charge in digging up these beautiful green giants. Impressive plants more than two metres tall, they had been planted over a hundred years ago by the Abu Garin Bedouin who lived nearby, but these yellow monsters paid no heed to that. With no hesitation, their shovels plunged deep into the soil and uprooted a hundred years' worth of history.

I had run out of my classroom and was frantically searching the schoolyard to find my sisters. The principal's voice rang out. "Protect our trees! We must fight and protect our trees!" Across the field, I saw soldiers with shovels and shears making their way towards a newly planted olive orchard. Like everyone else, I ran. I didn't know what I was supposed to do, but everyone was running so I ran with them. Some ran towards the bulldozers, others towards the orchard.

I saw my uncle* being pinned down by two policemen, struggling in their grip. My aunt, who was in ninth grade, was enlisting my sister Basma and their friends to stop the bulldozers. "They don't harm women," she assured them. "Let's go!" The group of six girls sprinted towards the bulldozers, gathered stones and hurled them.

We younger children were trapped in the centre of the chaos. We tried to run back inside the school, but we couldn't swim against the current of teachers running towards the fields. I saw my aunt, the one who had been confident that women were safe from civic brutality, fighting a policeman. He pushed her aside and two policewomen beat her to the ground. I couldn't see her head, but I saw her legs flailing

---

* The children of my grandfather's second marriage were at school with me.

in the air and then fall down motionless. They dragged her to the jeep. The police hit anyone who stood in their way, striking them with a wooden bat. Another group of students ran for higher ground, and from the top of the hill they slung sizeable boulders onto the police in the field below, but their success was short-lived. Outnumbered many times over, once the police started to chase them, the students fled for the village.

Amid the confusion, Ummi found me. Her face pale with fear, she grabbed my wrist and asked me where my siblings were. Without waiting for my answer, she ran. Fast. So fast that my feet barely grazed the ground by her side. "Hit them!" she screamed, telling me to fling rocks at the police officers around us. Suddenly we noticed a police officer coming towards us. Ummi stopped in her tracks and said in broken Hebrew, "I just want to take my children. They are small. Please, please let me go." He let her pass. I don't remember if and how she found my siblings, but by the time we crossed the mountain, our village was crawling with police officers who were searching for anyone who had retaliated. We arrived at our shack to find my uncle and cousin hiding in my parents' room. My sister ran inside to alert us that the police were coming to search our house. When a woman gets married, she receives a large wooden chest, an *edde*, which is roughly two metres long and has three or four drawers where she can keep her things. Traditionally, mattresses and blankets are piled high on top of the *edde*, reaching up to the ceiling. Ummi quickly folded my uncle and cousin in two large separate quilts at the summit of the mattresses.

"Don't move!" she whispered. With a wave of her hand, she gestured the rest of us to the kitchen, where we sat pretending to eat dinner.

The police arrived and Ummi greeted them with a calm that my child self couldn't comprehend. When the officers asked if she was hiding anyone, my mother pointed to us and said in a mix of Arabic and simple Hebrew: "*Ma fi . . . kloom. Yeladim ketanim* [No one is here. Only small children]." They walked past her to search the shack and she no longer seemed so serene. Although her face was expressionless, I could tell that she was holding her breath as she kept her gaze fixed on the floor. A couple of minutes later, the voice of one of the police officers allowed us to breathe again: "*Ayn kloom* [There is nothing]," and they left. We wanted to stand up and cheer, but my mother's hand warned us to stay seated and silent. Then we heard a commotion at Nayfa's house. She welcomed the officers with her typical greeting – "*Habaabi, habaabi* [My lord, my lord]" – and then walloped one of them across the head with a rock.

We later learned that Nayfa had hidden one of our teachers in her shack. It wasn't just any teacher, it was one of the government-hired teachers from the north, from Akka (Acre). Being in the Negev cut us off from the rest of the Arab community within Israel. These teachers exposed us to the world outside. They exposed us to the discourses of nationalism, communism and the possibility of political activism. This is one of the reasons why they were the first to join our fight: they didn't see the invasion as a crime only against the Bedouin, but as an act of nationalist terror against all Palestinian citizens of Israel. As a government employee, the teacher would most certainly lose his job, and yet he defended our fields as if he was protecting his own land and fighting for his own rights. And Nayfa! We couldn't believe it. She had risked her life to save a stranger to the tribe. From that day on, we regarded her as a hero.

Abouee's Story

JIDATEE OFTEN TOLD me that, when I was a few months old, she peered closely at my forehead to examine the angle at which my hair grew, and after a few minutes of intense concentration, she knew that boys would be born after me. Ummi, however, wasn't convinced, and with another girl in tow, the fear that Abouee would take a second wife hovered around her like a dark cloud. The women in the village came to comfort her.

"*Illi min Allah zayn* [What comes from God is good]," they

would say, but then follow up their reassurance with a knowing look in their eyes and the inevitable "A man can't stay with a woman who delivers girls. You know that. You're not the first and you won't be the last. God help you." A woman who could not produce boys could expect her husband to remarry and she couldn't fault him for it. The tribal doctrine against girls ran so deep that these visits always ended with the common saying: "*humm al-banaat lal-mamaat* [The burden of girls lasts until your death]," – a saying which Ummi used against my sisters and me often and with complete sincerity. While the rumours that Abouee was going to marry again made their way around the tribe, Ummi remained silent on the matter. If she didn't ask Abouee about it directly, she wouldn't have to face the pain.

Abouee was twenty-eight years old when I was born. He was young and handsome, full of adventure, and eager to experience the world outside the tribe. Later, when I was older, I asked him if it was his love for my mother that discouraged him from taking a second wife.

"It wasn't something that I wanted to do," he replied, his white turban framing his face that had aged well and always maintained its dignity no matter the time or the circumstance. "I never thought of myself as someone who follows the rules of the tribe. It wasn't really because I loved your mother. I didn't know her. The first time I saw her was on our wedding night when I entered the tent and she was sitting on our wedding bed."

Abouee's lips curled into a half-smile. A smile that seemed to convey the mixed emotions that come with a complex memory: longing, sadness, but also love and warmth. He laughed.

I leaned in closer. "What's so funny?"

"My brother was so creative. He loved me so much that he spent the whole day preparing a special mattress for my wedding night that would be as comfortable as the bed we had seen at our Jewish boss's house."

Abouee's brother passed away just shy of his fiftieth birthday. Abouee rarely spoke about him, but they had been very close. The

41

two of them supported the family because Jidee had vowed never to work for anyone other than himself. He had tended to his own fields, but lost them when his land was confiscated under the military regime. This theft marked him deeply and he could not bear to work for any Jewish authority when *"Al-ard ard abuuna wal-gourb yetroduuna* [the land is our father's and the stronger are kicking us out of her]," so the burden of supporting the family was placed on Abouee and my uncle, who suffered from a weak heart.

"He dug out and flattened the floor of the tent and filled it with hay. On top of the hay he placed a thick, camel-hair carpet and on top of the carpet he placed a soft mattress filled with wool. As good as an Aminach!" We both chuckled. I didn't doubt that this handmade bed would be just as good as Israel's top-grade mattress brand. Even better, I would say, because it was made with a brother's love and care.

"On our wedding night, your mother was wearing a black gown decorated with red embroidery. Over her head she wore a black abaaya and her face was covered in gold jewellery that hung from her forehead. It was dark, but a very faint flame flickered in the oil lamp. I remember it moving with the wind. The singing and the *zagareet* filled the desert around us. I approached her and sat down in front of her. I wanted to see her face, but she looked away and tried to hide her eyes. I placed my hand on her shoulder and she started and turned herself completely away from me. I knew she was afraid and I wanted to ease the situation. To comfort her, I said, 'Welcome to your new home.' She didn't say anything in return."

Ummi's memory of this moment is very different from Abouee's. While he remembers the details, she only remembers her fear. Her body, mind and soul drowning in it. She trembled at being alone with a man for the first time and she trembled at the thoughts that poured through her: *Why would a man like this marry me? He is so handsome and strong. He knows the world outside the tiny village. A man like that would never want me. Why would he want to marry a stupid, skinny, dark-skinned illiterate woman like me?*

Greater than all of these fears combined was Ummi's fear of what was expected of her that night. As a Bedouin woman, you are told all your life to protect your honour, that your honour determines your value, and that any dealings with men who are outside your immediate family – from looking at them to speaking to them – will destroy your reputation and ruin your life. How then, on your wedding night, are you supposed to let all of this melt away? How are you supposed to be the perfect bride: firm yet surrendered, bold yet gentle, an immaculate virgin, yet a poised woman yearning to be taken?

Abouee continued, "I waited and then her voice came, 'Do you really want me?' Her voice trembled. I didn't know what to tell her. I wanted to say yes, but I didn't really want to lie beside her. I didn't know her except for her name and her family. I laughed softly and she looked at me. Then I said, 'It depends. If you behave, I will love you forever.'

"You know that it wasn't that my mother chose her for me, which is the case in most marriages. My mother wanted me to marry another woman, a light-skinned one like her. I rejected her choice, but I didn't directly challenge her authority. My mother was a strong woman, as you know, and I didn't want to be her enemy. So, when she shared her plan to marry me off, I said nothing. The next day, I asked my father if my uncle Aamir had a girl of marrying age. I admired my uncle. I loved his charisma and I wanted my children to be like him.

"That evening, my father went to my uncle and asked him for your mother's hand in marriage. When we came back, my mother came to my father to take his horse back to the stable. My father leaped off the horse, passed her the reins and said, 'Let us hear your *zagareet* and a *mabrouk* to your son who is getting married.' She followed him, incredulous, and asked, 'Whose daughter is the worthy girl?'

"My father replied, 'His uncle Aamir. His daughter Hajar.' 'What!' She stopped in her tracks. 'The dark-skinned one? Why not the other one? She is much prettier. Hajar is very skinny. She can't do housework. She can't serve.' My father ignored her, pretending he couldn't hear her. My mother looked back at me and I smiled, gently, with confidence, that smile that I knew she couldn't resist. Then her frown turned into a smile. She held my gaze and turned her head towards the west, cupped her hand around her mouth, and let out a triumphant *zagareet*. Women and men nearby rushed to our tent to shower us with their *mabrouks*.

"I've always respected your mother. She is a good woman who brought comfort and joy to my life. I didn't want to hurt her, and my dreams extended beyond getting a second wife, and even beyond having boys. I was busy building my reputation and my financial future. I was busy learning new things about other communities, not only about my tribe. I used to sneak off to Yaffa [Jaffa] to watch movies – to discover the world outside Laqiya. Only when I returned to the village did I hear the rumours about my getting remarried. I needed to make sure no one had the chance to discuss it with me. I felt sorry for your mother because she was there. She was in the middle of this fire and she had no dreams beyond raising you and keeping the family together."

Although Abouee was not concerned with the petty affairs of the tribe, ever since the day that I was born, Ummi had felt like her survival depended on delivering boys after me. And, to be fair, despite what Abouee thought, maintaining his social position within the tribe was also contingent on his having sons – whether he cared about that or not. As a child, I carried this responsibility close to my heart. I always knew that my name was given to me to express my family's hope for sons. While most girls in my tribe might have felt diminished knowing that they were a prayer for someone and something else, this fact emboldened me. Something about it inspired me to refuse to take my life for granted. Instead, I sought to prove that I belonged. I sought to prove that I was much more than just a means for bringing a boy into this world.

Fridays: Victories and Defeats

I BOTH HATED Fridays and anticipated their arrival with uncontainable excitement. Since it was the eve of the Jewish sabbath and the Moslem holy day, I didn't have school. Everything – buses, shops and public institutions, Jewish or not – closed early in preparation for the day. Abouee would return home well before sundown. Usually, his red truck could be seen driving down the dusty road towards our shack by early afternoon.

Friday evening was also when we had access to the rest of the Arab world. From 5.30 to 7.30 p.m., the main channel on Israeli television would show the Friday movie, an Egyptian blockbuster in Arabic with Hebrew subtitles. The phrase *"Urshaleem al-Qouds**" will forever be burned in my memory as a sign for everyone to gather around the tiny black and white television that Abouee had installed in our room.

Friday was also the day that Ummi would prepare an elaborate meal of chicken or fish, two foods that we only had on that special day. Not one Friday night dinner went by without my being confronted with the inequality I faced as a girl. Each week I found myself in the same bind: I could either keep my mouth shut, accept the sad scrap that I was offered and be allowed to watch the Friday movie with my family. Or, I could take a stand and defend my right to equal treatment. In this scenario, I might come out victorious during the meal, but I would most certainly miss the movie for talking back to Ummi. It was one of the hardest lessons in picking your battles that a six-year-old could learn.

The day that Abouee bought our first television felt like a historical event. As usual, we all stood outside our shack waiting for him to arrive. Most evenings, we would follow the truck in the distance, cheering, *"Abouee jaa! Abouee jaa!"* [My father's back! My father's back!] until he stepped into the *hosh*. The day Abouee

---

* Officially the Israeli way of saying Jerusalem in Arabic, using the Christan (Urshaleem) and the Muslim (al-Qouds) names.

brought home our television, we could make out the glint of a toothy smile through the windshield as his truck pulled into our driveway. Abouee leaped into the *hosh* and beckoned the eldest boy, Salmaan, towards the truck. He climbed inside and reappeared with the novel contraption.

"It's a TV! It's a TV!" we cried. Our skipping around the *hosh* turned into a rampage as we charged towards Abouee to express our love. He waded through our arms and legs, trying to make it to the house, when Jidee's voice ordered us to desist. "*Allah yaateek al-aafya ya waladi* [Let your father rest. He must be tired]." His reprimand didn't dampen our spirits. We left Abouee and gathered around to inspect the TV that Salmaan carried proudly. Together with my eldest sister, Basma, he carried the TV into the house while Jidee supervised.

We kept the small television in the children's room. It rested on a crate that had once contained one of the few exports that Israel was known for at the time: Jaffa oranges. A long cord ran from the TV and out of the window, all the way to the battery in Abouee's truck, which powered it. On Friday evenings, we gathered around the TV in a semicircle, the shorter children in the front and the taller ones seated behind. There were nine of us by then and the minute we saw the lady with blonde hair appear inside this mysterious, magical machine, all hell would break loose. We would jump up from the mattress we were sitting on, wave our little fists in the air, and mosh each other around the room. Once the initial excitement had subsided, we changed games, now pretending to be our favourite stars. Great lovers, like Hussein Fahmy and Naglaa Fathi, or the action heroes who played opposite Adel Adham, who was often the villain. Our frenzy ended in us wrestling each other to the ground until my parents couldn't take it anymore. "Quiet! Be quiet!" It was one of the rare times Abouee shouted. Ummi punctuated her shouts by hurling her slippers at us, then ordering us to return them to her, and throwing them again. On the evenings our excitement drove us too wild, Abouee would rise from his spot at the left side of the mattress, silently make his way over to the TV and turn it off. We would immediately stop yelling, scramble back to our spots on the floor, and pray that we hadn't lost the privilege of watching the film together.

We ate our special Friday meal before the movie. We didn't have a fridge so Ummi cooked daily and on weekdays we always ate the same things: lentil soup, potatoes, rice, tomatoes and cheese, with a daily meal of fatt. Just as the Italians have their staple of pasta with its infinite varieties of sauce, we have fatt. It is a *saj* pita broken into small pieces and soaked in different types of soup. Sometimes tomato and onion, other times lentil. During the winter, we ate hobeza – a leafy green similar to spinach – with onion and lemon, a soup that is also known as "poor people's meat", one of my favourites. We ate one large meal in the early evening and either you made it in time and you ate or you were late and ate only *saj* pita without anything to dip it in – if you were a girl, that is. With the boys, Ummi was more lenient. We sat together around one dish. Sometimes we sat so tightly packed together that only one hand feasted. You were squashed between your siblings, facing away from the food, while your scooped hand reached in and desperately carried the hot mush to your mouth as fast as possible before someone else's hand intercepted your path. Mealtime was also silent. If you mouthed off, everyone was expected to ignore you and not leave you anything to eat. The fact that I fought during mealtimes suggests that my will to be treated equally was greater than my will to live. In retrospect, perhaps one reason that Ummi found my outbursts so threatening was because I was willing to fight this fundamental structure of the tribe in order to defend my individual rights.

On Fridays, at the beginning of the day, Ummi undertook a serious investigation to find out what the rest of the family would be cooking. She would sidle up to my aunts and casually enquire about their culinary plans for the evening. This was essential because if you prepared a different dish from the rest of the tribe, you risked being obliged to share a portion of the food with whoever might show up at your door that evening. If Ummi cooked the same meal as everyone else, we could usually expect the evening to pass without any hungry visitors calling from the *hosh*.

Those evenings, when you walked the dirt paths between the shacks, you could see everyone engaged in the same end-of-week rituals. The afternoon was the time to slaughter the animals for the evening meal. The chickens squawked their desperate yelps, their nervous feet hopping in a dead man's dance until they collapsed. The sand would be spattered with chicken blood or, if we were having fish, littered with dirt-encrusted skins, and the air would have the unmistakable scent of exposed flesh. If the weather was wet, the chickens would be covered in a thick sludge. In the summer, they were covered in fine desert dust. It was my sisters' job to clean the chickens and prepare them for Ummi to cook. For the eleven of us, there would be two chickens with *saj* pita and broth, plus rice. My sisters would wait until the chickens stopped running and then would ask us younger siblings to retrieve the bird. They dropped the chickens into a pot of boiling water, plucked their feathers, then cleaned them with flour, lemon and salt. Ummi always inspected the chickens before cooking them. She dipped her nose towards the raw, pink flesh and sniffed. If there was a smell she didn't like, she would order my sisters to clean them again with more salt and lemon.

Fridays brought out a complex mix of emotions in me: anger, love, hate, hope and anticipation. Every time we sat down for the meal, I promised myself that I would keep quiet. I promised myself that I would ignore the gnawing pain in my gut that told me that this wasn't fair. I promised myself that I would act appropriately, that I would not challenge Ummi. This was a hard commitment for a six-year-old to make, but I knew that if I lost my composure, then I would also lose the food and film, which meant missing out on my favourite part of the day: arguing over the best character with my brothers and sisters during the movie.

Abouee didn't always watch the film with us. Sometimes, he would go to the *diwaan* after dinner, especially if there was some important matter to discuss or if the head of the tribe was entertaining a guest. My father would have preferred to stay home, but Friday evenings and Saturdays around noon were reserved for discussing tribal affairs. Unlike other fathers who spent all their free time at the *diwaan*, gossiping and drinking coffee, Abouee gave us the limited free time that he had. I think that's how he maintained his identity and independence. He kept himself and the tribe's criticism of him at arm's length. "I wanted to be my own master," he told me years later. He wanted to think and act in the ways that he thought were right, rather than feel compelled to act according to the tribe's rules. Traditionally we had a short-term outlook, living according to the cycles of nature and moving with the sun. Now that we had been forced into a more sedentary way of life, it was hard for people to adapt, but Abouee did. He was an adept planner and savvy businessman who thought deeply about how to secure a stable financial future. Abouee used to wear shorts and have casual conversations with the Jewish women he met at work. He needed to minimize his engagement with the austere tribal morality that would have quashed his ability to be himself. While he usually stayed home on week nights to spend time with his parents, children and siblings, on some Fridays, he would, without too much resentment, join the tribal discourse, as a way of showing respect and preserving his status within the community.

One particular Friday, I promised myself, as I had done every week before then, that I would obey all the rules for the meal. Before we sat down to eat, I told myself, not exactly in these words, that if I were to adjust my expectations, everything would be all right. We were sitting together in the *hosh* and the usual excitement that I loved about Fridays was there: Abouee's comforting presence, the sense of relief from the week's end, the anticipation of the after-dinner entertainment. I was wrapped up in all of it until Ummi handed me a chicken wing. Nine pairs of eyes glanced from my hand to my face and back again. I could feel them waiting to see what I was going to do, but this time I stayed calm. Ignoring them as best I could, I fixed my gaze on the wing in my hand and brought it closer to my mouth. Allah himself must have been testing me because my brother interrupted my new-found serenity and waved a fat chicken leg right in front of my face. "You got the wing!" he taunted. "Girl! Girl! Girl!" He kept waving that sumptuous morsel in front of my nose and I could feel the blood surging to my head.

Khalas with my peaceful plan, my good intentions, my realistic expectations. My brother had gone too far and now he was going to pay. Abouee's forceful cries of "*Khalas [That's enough of that]* Stop! Eat!" and "Ignore him!" did nothing to dissuade me from attacking my tormentor. I rushed towards my brother like a raging bull, shattering the teapot and cups as I ploughed through them to lunge at him. In one swift leap, I yanked the meat from his hand and pitched it over the *hosh* wall.

"Bring her to me now." Abouee's voice cut short my victory. "Come here. I'll kill you."

"This girl needs to be corrected," Ummi weighed in. "She is not well raised. Beat her! I'm tired of her."

My sisters pinned me down and, even if I had been able to escape, I didn't want to. Running away would have been an explicit act of rebellion against Abouee. I was willing to ignore my mother's orders, but I didn't want to defy my father. He was my champion. My guiding star in this bewildering desert. I waited, propped up by my siblings, my heart pounding in my chest. I averted my gaze to avoid seeing Abouee's angry eyes. I knew what they looked like when he was angry: two red coals burning in his head. Tears pooled in my eyes and dripped onto the dirt floor. Waiting for Abouee to strike me was more agonizing than the blow I was expecting to receive. He raised his hand in the air and Ummi egged him on.

I waited for the slap, but he was buying time, hoping that someone would save him from the task. Before his hand landed on my cheek, Basma, who knew Abouee didn't want to hit me, intervened: "Please, *Abouee*, don't hit her. Leave it to me." Ummi had reached the limit of her patience. She stepped in and slapped me hard across my shoulder blades and again on the back of my head. Basma tried to stand between the two of us when Jidee's usual Friday greeting of "Where are you, Arabs?" interrupted the chaos. This greeting is a vestige from our life in tents. Without a door to knock on, calling out from afar is a polite way to signal your arrival so that the host has time to prepare to receive you. His words couldn't have come at a better time.

Abouee answered quickly: "Here. Here. *Ya*, Haj, come in."

As soon as Jidee entered the *hosh,* he sensed he had entered a wrestling ring.

"What's going on here?"

"Your granddaughter is causing trouble," Abouee replied. "She is not well behaved. I warned her that I would tell her Jidee."

Jidee looked at my defiant face streaked with tears. Without breaking eye contact with me, he passed his firm but fair judgement: "She has too much free time." He continued: "This is not good. From now on she must herd the sheep. This will keep her busy and give you some rest from her mischief."

The Lunch Box

UMMI USED TO wake me before sunrise and I would follow her to the barn, my bare feet quietly slapping the cool, misted dirt. Before sending the sheep out to graze, Ummi milked their swollen udders, collecting milk for us and leaving enough milk for the lambs. I helped by holding the sheep steady. With my little arms wrapped around their necks, I tackled them to the ground. Ummi stood behind me, pinned down one of their legs and massaged the udder to draw out the fresh, warm milk. We worked in near-silence, except for Ummi telling me to release this lamb and bring her another, while the baby lambs' bleats filled the shed with an impatient morning prayer. After we finished the milking, I would walk over to the lambs' enclosure – we kept them separate from their mothers so that they wouldn't drink all their mothers' milk – and release them, quickly moving out of their way as they clambered towards their breakfast.

Ummi would then return home to prepare our breakfast, while I tried to separate the mothers from their lambs – another difficult task. I needed to get the lambs out of the barn to the grazing area on the hill next to our shack. By now, the sun would have risen, daylight would be descending upon the tribe and you would see smoke emanating from the shacks and tents nestled into the mountainside. You would hear the familiar music of another morning in Laqiya: the crying of babies eager for their morning meal, mothers yelling at their children to get ready for school, and the desperate yelps of siblings taking turns washing their hair under the cold stream of the *ibreek* (the pitcher we used to shower with).

Every morning, Jidee led his impressive black horse to graze in the valley where my lambs were. And every morning, when he arrived at the place where I was, he would tell me to graze further up the hill and leave the long grass for his horse, a pure-bred Arabian beauty whose silky black coat shimmered in the morning sun. I hated that his horse received preferential treatment. I wanted that tasty-looking grass for my lambs. I would obey him, but, when he left, I would bring my lambs back down to enjoy the grass that I knew they found most delicious. I remember feeling so satisfied watching them mow the field with their stubby front teeth. I imagined how pleasing it must be to be a lamb enjoying a meal of fresh, long grass. In fact, it was many years, more than ten, before I could look at a field of long grass without thinking how happy my lambs would be if they were there.

When I saw the first group of children pass me on their way to school, it meant that it was time for me to head back. After corralling the lambs back into the barn, I would skip over to the kitchen and hope that one of my siblings had left me something to eat. I usually arrived to find an empty platter with a smear of eggs, tomatoes and cheese and console myself with bread dipped in sweet, milky tea.

In my memory, Ummi was able to prepare and serve us breakfast in under half an hour because she had twelve arms. Her wrists and fingers dashed from one place to the other, serving tea, tearing bread and clearing empty dishes from where we ate on the floor. She saw nine hungry mouths and we saw her relentless hands, moving from one place to the next. While she worked, against the backdrop of dishes clanging and mouths chewing was my brothers' whining: "My tea is too cold", "Well, my tea is too hot", or "There's hay in my tea!" Ummi responded to these requests with as much immediacy as she could muster. In answer to the first complaint, Ummi would add more tea to my brother's glass. To the second, she would add more milk. If she didn't do it just right, my brothers were known to scream and threaten not to finish their food. The girls never acted this way. We were expected to serve ourselves and each other modestly, grateful for what we received, and if we weren't, we usually accepted our share in silence. Although I wished to be treated like a boy, my brothers' constant griping sickened me. As boys, they had been socialized to believe that their sex granted them the right to treat our mother as their personal slave. They often acted spoiled and entitled. I didn't want that. I just wanted things to be fair.

Each of us had only one set of school clothes: one pair of trousers, one shirt and one pair of shoes. If any of those items were dirty, we didn't attend school that day. When we returned home from school, Ummi made us take off our school clothes and put them in the closet. For whatever reason, I never had a spot in the closet, but I had my own wooden chest I had claimed with a fat red marker where I placed my carefully folded clothes instead.

It wasn't until my teens that I actually embraced having thick, unruly curls which sprung out in every direction. When I was a kid, Basma's daily domination of my mane by means of assertive braiding led me to hate my wild locks. In order to make sense of them, she braided them in one or two tresses that were so tightly woven they gave me headaches. After this torture was over, Basma manoeuvred me into my school jeans, blue shirt and sandals, while she braided her long blonde hair and got dressed in her school clothes. Once we were both dressed, I would grab the plastic bag containing my lunch and off we'd go: she striding several paces in front of me, purposeful and impatient, me running behind, trying to keep up.

Basma tied my hair so tight that I couldn't lower my head to draw or write. Once, the pain was so unbearable that I left my classroom in search of her to loosen my braids. Our school was divided between elementary and middle school and we weren't allowed to cross between the two sections without permission. To enforce this rule, teachers roamed the yard, sticks by their hips, ready to reprimand any student who crossed their path. When I couldn't find Basma, I sat down in the middle of the schoolyard and began to cry. Suddenly, a male teacher with thick, blond curls walked towards me. I panicked and thought of running away, but he seemed kind, so I stayed put. He squatted down in front of me and asked why a little girl with such beautiful hair was crying.

"I don't want to tie my hair," I wept. "It hurts. I can't write. I can't draw." I tilted my head forwards to show him the spot on the back of my head where the braid was tugging painfully at my neck and scalp.

He leaned forwards and asked, "How would you like me to tie your hair?"

His head was very close to mine so I could observe his unrestrained curls.

"Why can't I have hair like yours? Abouee said that I can be just like the boys."

He laughed, lifted me in the air and spun me around, the momentum easing the sharp tension I'd been feeling in my head all day.

"Amal, what are you doing here?" Basma's voice broke into the moment. "Go back to your class."

The teacher looked at Basma. "Is she your sister?"

Basma grabbed my hand.

"Can you tell Basma not to tie back my hair anymore?" I asked him.

His eyes lit up and he put on an authoritative voice. "You are not allowed to tie back her hair anymore. See?" and he pointed to the places I had shown him.

Basma smiled, and while she walked me back to my class, she carefully untied my hair, tussled it gently, and allowed it to flow free.

My first day at kindergarten, a girl entered the classroom carrying a dazzling, colourful lunch box. A blue, red and pink rectangular case with shiny silver zips. I looked at the plastic bag I carried my lunch in and I felt sorry for myself. I convinced my cousin, a boy who was in the same class as me, to steal her box and throw it in the well. We couldn't just steal it because we knew that if we brought it home our mothers would notice and punish us for taking it. I had already found a way to justify the crime: if I didn't have a fancy lunch box, no one should. The plan went smoothly. I remember cornering the girl during the break, snatching the box from her hands and running away while she cowered and cried. At the sight of her tears, I felt sorry and ashamed so I tossed it to my cousin, but he didn't want to carry the shame either. It was too late to turn back. Our guilt followed us all the way to the well in the centre of the village. We watched the box disappear into the dark and heard the single muffled splash. As we walked to our respective shacks, I made my cousin swear that he wouldn't tell a soul – meaning our parents and our grandfather.

"We are in this together," I said.

"I won't tell, but those other children saw us and they will tell the teachers and they will beat us tomorrow."

The next day, our kindergarten teacher, a heavy-set blonde woman who always reminded me of a tyrannosaurus rex, called us both to the front of the class and without a single word, without even asking us what we had done or why we had done it, she pushed us between the open door and the inside of the classroom wall and slammed the door into us. The door handle hit my chest again and again and again. I didn't have room to turn around and put my back to the door so I placed my hands over my heart. We screamed and cried and when she finally let us out she demanded that we never

55

steal again. I could hardly get out the words to agree because my front teeth were bleeding so badly. We returned to our desks and she forbade us to cry, sternly saying that she didn't want to hear our bad thief voices. I looked over at the girl whose box we had stolen and she looked back at me. Her eyes looked sad, but I didn't know if she felt sorry for me or for her lunch box.

In the evening, we faced another trial, this time from our uncle who had heard about the incident from his fiancé, the teacher's assistant. He lined us up against the wall and started a fierce interrogation: "Why did you steal her lunch box? Where is it?"

We exhaled sharply.

"Answer me! Why did you do it?"

My cousin looked at me, which told my uncle that the whole thing was my idea. He looked me dead in the eye. "Why did you steal it and where did you put it?"

My voice quivered. "Why should she have a pretty lunch box and I get a plastic bag? That isn't fair."

He brought his face inches from mine. "What's unfair? Did she take yours?"

I said nothing.

"Answer me. Is it yours?"

I shook my head.

"Then it's not a question of fairness. You did something wrong. You took something that didn't belong to you and for that you should be punished." Then, he turned to my cousin. "And what about you? Don't tell me it's not fair."

My cousin explained that it wasn't his idea and that he did it because I had asked him to. That made my uncle even angrier. "Are you a man?" he roared. "Answer me! Are you a man?"

My cousin nodded.

"If you are a man, why would you follow a woman? Are you out of your mind? I wanted to spare you, but now I'm really ashamed of you. Show me your palms."

My cousin slowly opened his hands. My uncle looked at them

and hit him twice on each hand with a wooden stick. He did the same to me.

Then he walked away, mumbling to himself with incredulity, "She told me to do so . . . *Wallah*, this is nice. This is exactly what we need here . . . What kind of a man is this?"

From that day on, I figured that being a shepherd was safer than going to school. In the field, I was free to do as I pleased and no one would punish me. My parents allowed me to skip kindergarten and tend to the flock instead.

The Lost Lamb

ROAMING THE MOUNTAINS with my flock unleashed my imagination. It was as if the vastness of the desert created an equally vast landscape within me, an expanse where my dreams could finally be free. Unlike at home where I was subject to Ummi's strict codes, with the sand, sky, trees and dirt as my companions a new code emerged, one that was determined by my ability.

I yearned so fiercely for the freedom that boys enjoyed that there were nights when I'd pray that I would wake up and find myself transformed into one. In many ways, I already felt like one. Abouee used to bring me round to the *diwaan*, where I would sit with the men, which is very unusual and shows my father's openness. This introduced me to the world of men. Most of my time was spent playing with my brothers and cousins in the fields, and I could never, for the life of me, be a good girl and sit still like Ummi wanted me to. Being a shepherd allowed me to escape the attempts to tame me and freed me from the social position that had been defined for me. Every time they tried to push me back into that role, their suppression fed my desire to resist. I became a force of fifty hands and legs, pushing and kicking with all my might to stay out of their container. And although each time I defended this freedom, I was slammed to the ground, the feeling of determination was so strong that it lifted me back onto my feet.

Having time to myself, time that I could delineate and order instead of following Ummi's rhythm, paved the road for my budding sense of self and independence. Away from the tribe's concerns, I consorted with nature and all her relatives: the proud mountains and receptive valleys, the bold rocks and timid stones, the relentless midday sun and the cool full moon, and the reverent night sky that shimmered with a million dazzling stars. This family coexisted in complete harmony. Here no sibling was better than the rest. That world became mine. It was there, amid my sheep and the tall grass, that I found acceptance without conditions or prejudice.

Every morning I would wait for the sun to rise so I could take my sheep and cow to the mountains to graze. Caring for the sheep and our single cow became my main responsibility and I wanted to do it as best I could. I trained the sheep to walk at my pace and to recognize my whistle so that I didn't need to run around to herd them. At a whistle from me and a wave to where I wanted them to go, they would lift their heads from the pasture, turn around and start grazing in that direction. One job of the shepherd is to keep the disobedient ones from disrupting the rest. My flock had one bad sheep, so I gave her the responsibility of leading the rest. I tied a bell around her neck and when it was time to head home, I would lead her first, and the sound of the bell would signal to the rest of the flock to follow.

One day, one sheep was lagging behind the rest. Every time I tried to make her join the others, she would scurry back to where we had been grazing before. After a while, I realized she was looking for something: her newborn, the youngest of the flock, was missing.

I led my flock to search the valley and asked a couple of women who lived in that area if they had seen the baby lamb. They hadn't, so I continued back up the hill, keeping my eye on the sun that was sinking towards the west. Panic set in. I wouldn't be able to search much longer. Night fell on Laqiya's mountains, but I continued to search for the lamb, leading my sheep from one place to the next, retracing the day's graze. I spotted the shepherd star – the sign that it was time to return home. I needed to think fast and decide what to do. Ummi was waiting to milk the sheep and the lambs were waiting to return home so that they could feed. I came up with a plan: the sheep would head home on their own and I would stay behind with the mother to look for her baby. I gave the lead sheep the sign to return home, and when she lifted her head from the grass and started walking towards our shack, the other sheep followed suit.

Without the rest of the flock, the mother sheep and I were able to move much more quickly. I returned to all the places I remembered and stopped to search behind large rocks and any bushes in our path, keeping the worried mother by my side. I didn't want to disappoint her, but I too was worried and scared. Worried about what my punishment might be if the lamb was lost and scared of walking alone in the dark. The land that was so inviting by day terrified me by night. Illuminated though it was by the stars and the moon, the sand looked like it might swallow me whole and there was no telling what creatures lurked across the plain. Running from one place to the next, I met Abouee's aunt, a woman in her sixties, which we consider to be very old.

"What's happened," she asked. "Why are you all alone?"

Between large sobs I told her that I had lost my lamb and asked her if she had seen it.

She looked at me with her sun-worn face full of comfort, reached for the pitcher on the floor by her shack and offered me a drink of water.

"Listen, *ya bintee*. It's true that you are the shepherd and that you are the one who leads the flock. But, but . . ." – she paused – "the true leader knows when to rely on his people to lead and be willing to trust them. Let your sheep lead you. Don't push against her. She knows where her newborn is."

She squeezed my shoulder and motioned with her head that it was time to go.

I released my sheep and off she went, sprinting into the dark. I scurried after her. She ran in a large circle, scanning the area, stopped for a moment and then started running towards the valley to the east of where we were, bleating loudly, calling to her baby. We reached a large bush and I heard a faint cry. I ran towards the sound and found the lamb, his leg tangled in a thorny root. I freed him and he leaped towards his mother, nuzzling her with his small pink nose until he found her teat and started to suck. He was very hungry. I waited till he finished, then picked him up in my arms and the three of us walked back home.

The shack was enveloped in darkness and the noise of the evening tasks – milking the sheep and the cow, feeding the animals, preparing dinner for the family – had all subsided. I first went to the barn to check that my entire flock had made it home. I counted them: fifty-seven. I took a deep breath, then entered the kitchen, still carrying the lamb in my arms. My family was sitting around the fireplace eating dinner, their faces lit by the fire's red glow.

As soon as Abouee saw me, he clapped his hands and commanded everyone to clap for me.

"I told you!" he declared proudly. "I said you didn't have to worry, that she would bring the lamb and his mother back." He looked at me, his face gleaming.

"Come, come, *bint abouha* [daughter of her father]! Sit next to me." He dusted off the spot on the mattress beside him and ordered Ummi and my sisters to serve me dinner. At that moment, I was treated like a boy and I felt like I had been promoted from daughter to son. My true measure of success was the fact that Abouee, a man who had all the qualities I valued, made it clear to my brothers that tonight I was the hero, I was the esteemed guest. This was a turning point. My sense of success came not from feeling like a boy, however, but from feeling that I had beaten the boys at their own game. I received special treatment because I was worthy of it, because I had challenged myself, worked hard and come out on top.

Two Lines

WHEN I WAS a shepherd, I refused everything Ummi asked of me. When we fought, I would say, "God! Come take that woman, the one in the black dress with red embroidery."

"Are you talking about me?" she would shout from the *hosh*.

"No. I didn't say your name!" I'd yell back.

Every evening when I returned from the field or the mountain, Ummi reminded me to lower my voice. She forbade me from laughing too loud, talking too much, or playing with the boys. Our fights always followed the same script: she commanded me to be small, I resisted, and she beat me.

It was Jidatee who saved me from Ummi's hand. She taught me how to be calm, how to let my mother's words fly off my back instead of stabbing me in my chest. She'd say that I was strong and Ummi was weak and that is why she would never understand me. "You are like me. Strong and determined. You are not afraid to fight." Jidatee was always undermining Ummi. If Ummi was trying to punish me, then Jidatee would protect and praise me. I don't know if their animosity towards each other was because of their mother-in-law, daughter-in-law relationship or if they really had conflicting views on how girls should behave. It often seemed that my behaviour gave them an outlet to express their resentment of each other.

When my youngest aunt got married, she was the first bride in our village to wear one of those extravagant white chiffon wedding dresses that we associated with brides from the West. We had only ever seen such things in newspapers or in the Egyptian films on Friday nights. My aunt had recently turned seventeen. She was sweet and timid and stunning. Her straight brown hair rested just below her shoulders and she had honey-brown eyes enclosed in long, thick lashes.

When my sisters and female cousins saw her dress, we gasped with wonder: the bodice embroidered with rhinestones, the crinoline skirt large enough to shelter four or five of us beneath it, and the puffy, white sleeves, layered in chiffon, were like figments from a dream. Even the smell was new and intoxicating. We jumped at the chance to carry the dress in our arms, to caress the nylon lace between our fingers, and slyly press our noses into whichever part we could to catch a hint of this faraway scent. When she donned the magic garment on her wedding day, all the children ran over to touch her, but the elders swatted us away, ensuring that this fairy had room to breathe.

The wedding party took place in Jidatee's room, where women of all ages gathered to fawn over the new bride. They eyed my aunt with delight and envy, imagining themselves in that dress, either harkening back to their own wedding day or dreaming of the day they prayed for. That small wooden room absorbed the sounds of the *zagareet*, the babies crying, the old women admonishing us little ones for playing hide-and-seek behind the guests, and the rest of the women standing in two lines facing each other, singing and clapping in celebration.

Although the room was full, the sound was muted, resting like the fog that sits on the sand during the winter months. In this fairy tale, the white dress's real magic was to hide my aunt's sorrow. She was being forced to marry her cousin, according to a tradition that has been codified in our saying: "*Al-bint lolaad amha* [the girl is for her cousin]." Back then, as even still today, there wasn't much of a choice. Her marriage had been arranged even before she knew the secret pains of womanhood. She loved someone else, but had to keep her desires hidden away, not only to protect her own reputation, but to avoid bringing serious harm to everyone involved.

They thought that the white dress would lighten her dark soul. After five days of living in her shack with her new husband, she appeared at our shack one morning, very early on a Saturday. Abouee sat in the tent next to the kitchen eating his breakfast with Jidatee. When my aunt arrived, my eyes traced the tears streaming down her pale cheeks. Jidatee jumped as if she had been bitten by a ferocious desert snake and rushed over, not only out of concern for her, but to ensure that their conversation did not take place in front of Abouee. My aunt told her that the green patrol* had stamped her shack, meaning that it was going to be demolished later in the week. Jidatee let out a sigh of relief. Ummi called out, "*Khayr khayr ya saatir?* [God protect us, what's happened?]"

"Nothing," Jidatee called back. "The government is destroying her shack."

All urgency vanished. "*Al-hamdullilah*," Ummi said as she reached Jidatee. "I thought she had left her husband."

"Me too," Jidatee replied.

Witnessing this exchange raised two questions for me: Why would Jidatee be relieved that my aunt hadn't left the husband she hated and why would the government destroy my beautiful aunt's shack? These are the questions I have been trying to answer since that day.

Wrestling with the dual identity of being a woman in a patriarchal society and an indigenous minority in a nationalist state, why do my rights as a woman seem to be at odds with my rights as a Palestinian Bedouin? How is it that my own community oppresses my aunts and sisters, forbidding them to marry whom they please, policing who they talk to and the kind of work they do, but, when it comes to fighting against the state, we are encouraged to see every Israeli as a common enemy? It was from my conversations with Jidatee that I gathered the seeds of knowledge to begin asking these questions. Jidatee was patient and encouraged me to question. She also brought to the process an unrelenting faith, teaching me to keep a cool head and channel my anger into intelligent action. Jidatee belonged to the generation when the Bedouin were treated with more respect. During her time, the Bedouin sat around the table with the Ottomans and the British, and were highly educated and politically aware. From hearing her story, I understood why my mother wasn't like her.

---

* Israeli government unit that deals with the environment and destruction of "illegal" buildings, among other issues.

Ummi's generation suffered from the Nakba, and the Six-Day War and its consequences, when fear and control ruled their lives. Forcing us into an urban lifestyle stripped women of their importance in the tribe. My mother's entire reality centred on domestic affairs, whereas my grandmother was a player in public life.

Jidatee had her own room in my youngest uncle's shack and we took turns sleeping with her in her bed so that she wouldn't sleep alone. This room was an enchanted alcove that smelled of cloves and olive oil soap. It was warm and safe and I felt liberated every time I walked through that door and crossed the threshold into her world. We all loved sleeping there and sometimes we could convince Jidatee to let all the girls – my sisters and cousins – sleep there together. She would agree to our request, but only on the condition that we kept very quiet since the *diwaan* was only a shack away and my uncle, who slept in the adjacent room, wouldn't hesitate to send us back to our parents' shacks if our chatting reached his slumbering ears.

One day, Basma and I went to sleep with Jidatee. I was so happy to be there with my favourite older sister. She was my hero and I loved copying her actions and pretending to be her because she was strong, smart, beautiful and very popular in the village. When my siblings and I slept together on our single mattress, I always crawled next to Basma to snuggle beside her under the same quilt. Basma was, and still is, a voracious reader. She would wait patiently until everyone fell asleep, place the oil lamp next to her pillow, roll onto her stomach and pull out the book she had been waiting to devour all day. Her satisfaction while she read was contagious. She smiled, she sighed, and from time to time she would retrieve a notebook and pencil she kept tucked away beneath her pillow and write something down in a slow, careful hand. Sometimes I would catch her crying while she read. Whatever was in that universe of hers I could hardly wait to discover. By the time I was five years old, Basma had already started to teach me how to read and write. By the third grade, I had my own books and notebooks that I too kept tucked away beneath my pillow. Finally, I discovered what was worth waiting a whole day to enjoy. I discovered a universe because of her, a universe that shaped me. I adored books and could be seen walking around the village with one in my hand. The best place to read was sitting on a slab of cool stone while I waited for my flock in the mountains, or, if it was summer, in the shade of an olive tree.

Basma was reading *Jafat a Domoua Aldomua* (*Dried Tears*) by the famous Egyptian novelist Yousef Alsebaai. We placed an extra mattress next to Jidatee's bed and once Jidatee had fallen asleep, Basma asked me to bring the oil lamp closer to our side of the room. She pulled out her novel and gave me a piece of paper to occupy myself. Then, Jidatee rolled over. The half-moons of her eyes landed on the book in Basma's hands. She reached her arm out and Basma's wrists shook as she handed her the book. Jidatee flipped the book over to inspect the cover: it was an illustration in pastel colours of a man and a woman locked in an embrace, their cheeks resting tenderly against each other. Basma and I looked at one another. I could tell she was afraid of what might happen next.

"This is what you are wasting your time on?" Jidatee said accusingly. "I thought you were reading something useful. Where did you get this?" Her voice grew louder with each question. "Who gave it to you?"

"It's my uncle's book, Jidatee," Basma answered quickly. "I took it from his library."

Like most men in my tribe, my uncle had attended high school in the north where the education system was better. If you wanted to have a future, you went to the north, either to Haifa or to the Israeli-Arab villages in the Triangle area*, adjacent to the Green Line.** When my uncle finished high school, he brought home many books that either became part of his private library or that he donated to the library in our village.

"Did you ask him before you took it? Did he see you?"

"Yes."

---

* A concentration of Israeli Arab towns and villages in central and northern Israel.
** The demarcation line of the 1949 Armistice Agreements between armies of Israel, Egypt, Jordan, Lebanon and Syria after the 1948 Arab-Israeli War, known as the Nakba to the Palestinians and the War of Independence to Jewish Israelis.

"Did he see this?" she asked, pointing to the man and woman on the cover, as if this image was enough to assure her of the depravity of the book.

"Yes, Jidatee. He's read it."

"You can't read this. It will ruin your brain, you hear me?"

Basma looked at me and raised her eyebrow to let me know not to believe what Jidatee was saying.

"Yes, but my uncle read it."

"Your uncle can read whatever he pleases. He's a man."

"Please, Jidatee. Give it back. I just want to finish this one. I promise I won't read these kinds of books anymore."

Jidatee ignored her and rolled over towards the wall. Basma and I kept looking at each other, then Basma pulled the quilt over her body. I didn't understand why she gave up so quickly. "Now what?" I whispered. She held up her five fingers, telling me to wait.

"Should I move the lamp away?" I asked. She vetoed my request by drawing a sharp line with her hand. Jidatee noticed that the lamp was still on and she rolled towards us, this time asking me to hand over my paper and pencil. She turned the paper to the clean side and drew a long straight line.

"Do you see this?"

Basma nodded.

"This is the border of our tradition."

She then drew a second line, parallel to the first one and very close to it. "Do you see this one?"

"Yes, Jidatee."

"This is God's border. Make sure you never cross either of these lines. You must walk in between them. Cross and you are finished."

Basma took the paper and stared at it. Jidatee turned over onto her back without waiting for Basma to respond.

"But, Jidatee, it is very narrow. How am I supposed to walk in between these lines without crossing them?"

Jidatee said nothing. She was already sleeping or pretending to.

Basma gave the paper and pencil back to me. I looked closely at the two lines and thought to myself, "It is really very hard to walk there." I drew two new lines, this time much wider apart, and handed the paper back to Basma.

"There. I made you new lines. Now you can walk between them easily."

Basma looked over at the lines that I had drawn. She leaned over and hugged me tightly.

"I wish it was that easy," she whispered, "but we can't draw our own lines."

"Why not?" I asked. "Who draws them?"

She squeezed me tighter. "Go to sleep, sister. They will make sure to answer you when your time comes."

Taking Revenge While Keeping Your Hands Clean

A BOUEE USED TO bring me to the *diwaan* and let me sit on his lap. At first the other men didn't like it, but they came to accept it. Maybe because they felt sorry for him for having mostly girls or maybe because they didn't want to face his temper. Whatever the reason, no one ever confronted him about it.

The *diwaan* always fascinated me. I wanted to know why women weren't allowed to be there. What were the men hiding from us? I was particularly curious because every time Abouee returned home from the *diwaan*, Ummi begged him to share the day's news with her. These conversations were always the same. She would ask him what he had heard and he would say, "Oh, nothing really," while Ummi helped him to remove his jacket. She would say, "*Taieb*, OK," not really believing him. Abouee never felt right about sharing other people's stories, but Ummi's curiosity was insatiable. She would gently ask again, this time applying a little more leverage. "Oh, but I saw *flaan's* [so and so's] car parked out in front of the *diwaan*," and then with feigned concern, "I hope everything is alright with him."

My father saw past all her pretence. He had no patience with idle gossip so he would say something harsh to end the conversation and Ummi would drop it.

The day after one of these conversations, when my aunts and my mother's friends gathered at the *taboon*, each one of them had a piece of the puzzle and if they were missing something, they made it up. They feared having Jidatee around because she, like my father, had no time for gossipy tales. If she heard them weaving stories, she would shake her head and say: "*Khafan Allah ya banat!* ["Fear God! Shame on you, girls!] Finish baking and go home." They would fall silent, but shoot each other sideways glances in solidarity, irritated that Jidatee had ruined the best part of the communal baking.

My mother also hated having me around because when I heard Ummi and her sisters gossiping, I threatened to report her to Jidatee. One time, I heard them gossiping about the woman who had just left the *taboon*. "I'm going to tell Jidatee!" I threatened them. Ummi whipped her plastic slipper in my direction. "How dare you sit among the adults. This is not your place." I dodged the slipper and ran to find my grandmother who returned to have the final word: "*Ga'daat a-kharab albuit* [You are ruining households]. I will tell Abd al-Kareem." Abd al-Kareem is my father's name and Jidatee used it to scare my mother. Ummi's eyes narrowed and she gestured towards me, placing her index finger over her thumb and waving it menacingly, telling me that she would kill me later. Allowing me to be a shepherd meant that there was no one around to stop her from inventing a story from scratch and ruining the entire village by late afternoon.

My flock grazed in different areas depending on the seasons. In the winter and spring, we grazed in the mountains, in the fall and summer, in the fields. During the summer months, the fields were sown with seasonal crops, mainly wheat and barley, and, every second year, Jidee would add lentils and chickpeas. There were places in the fields that lay fallow every second year, but the wheat and barley were a full-time affair because they were essential to our survival.

One of the skills you acquire herding sheep is to make sure that your flock does not enter other people's fields. Allowing your sheep to graze in someone else's pasture can be considered theft and you risk being chased by dogs or beaten by the field's owner. It was summertime, I was ten years old, and I was leading my sheep and cow very carefully on a narrow footpath between two fields. The sun's piercing rays beat against my neck and the sweat rolled down my back. I walked slowly, my gaze fixed on the path in front of me, my thoughts set on finding shelter. The insects didn't seem as bothered by the baking heat, and a desert fly landed on my cow and bit her on the neck. Her whole body jerked and she leaped in the air. I tried to hold her steady, but she escaped my grip and ploughed through the field to the left of the path. I chased her, but before I could catch her, a white car drove towards me at full speed. I ran in the other direction and the car raced towards me. I knew that cars couldn't accelerate in the dirt, so, terrified, I made circles in the dust, my circles growing smaller and smaller as the car drew closer and closer. Finally, I was close enough to the car that I grabbed his wing mirror and begged him to stop, promising over the sound of the engine that this would be the last time that I trespassed on his field. The man in the car pushed me off his mirror, got out of the car and slapped me across the face. He dragged me by my curly hair and threw me to the ground, warning me never to use this path again. He got back in his car and drove away. I lay there in the dust until I saw his car returning to the village.

When I told Ummi, she cursed the day he was born and swore that she would show him the noon stars. She fed me and let me lie down, a luxury we are only afforded when we are sick. Jidatee heard Ummi and came right away. She looked at me and knelt down, checking my legs, face and head, and tying my hair back. She didn't swear or raise her voice. Instead, she calmly asked me who had done this to me. I told her that I didn't know his name, but that he had a white van. She muttered his name and said, "Your father will deal with him when he is back." Anger flashed in her eyes. She ordered Ummi to cover me with a blanket, and said: "He has no respect for us to beat our girl . . . He doesn't understand the rules of respect. I will make Abd al-Kareem teach him a lesson on how to respect other people's daughters." When Ummi heard that Jidatee was going to tell Abouee, she became very worried.

"No need," she said. "I will go and talk to him. Don't make this a big issue. We are one tribe and he is our cousin."

Jidatee looked at her down her nose. "It is none of your business. This is our girl. We know how to make people respect our daughters." In Jidatee's words, I heard that I belonged to my father and to his lineage. In her eyes, my mother's role was just to bring boys into the world.

In the early evening, I heard Abouee's truck arriving home from work and started to cry. I needed his support. Ummi came running to her room, where I was lying down on the mattress, and whispered in my ear: "Don't say he chased you with his car. Say only that he pushed you. You don't want to cause a big fight in the tribe. You don't want to get Aboukee into trouble. Be careful. I trust you." This was one of her more tender moments reserved for the times she wanted me to save her skin. She delicately patted my head and wiped my tears.

Abouee's voice entering the shack felt like a soothing balm for my wounded heart. I couldn't see what was happening, but I heard the usual rituals taking place: my sisters rinsing Abouee's hands and face, placing the prayer rug towards Mecca, and Abouee praying while my sisters and mother prepared the evening meal. Everyone then went to the kitchen to eat the evening meal. Dinner was over when I heard Jidatee telling Abouee the story as I had told it to her. I heard my mother attempting to speak over her, trying to minimize what had happened.

"Where is Amal? Come here," Abouee called.

Ummi came rushing into the room where I was lying. "Your father wants to see you." Her eyes and mouth flashed a reminder of our agreement.

I struggled to stand up. I fixed my shirt and hair and stepped out onto the *hosh*. The minute I saw Abouee, I hugged him and tears pooled in my eyes. My despair ignited a fury within him. Ummi tried to suppress it with her refrain of "We are all one tribe," but Jidatee put it more clearly: "Teach him a lesson, but be smart. Don't get yourself or the tribe in trouble. It's not worth it."

Abouee gently moved my face from his shoulder and told me to go with him. We climbed into his truck and he reversed out of our driveway. We spotted Jidee walking towards our house. Over the noise of the truck, Jidee asked him where he was going. Sensing something wasn't right, he said, "I hope nothing bad has happened."

"*Khayr khayr* [Blessing, blessing]," Abouee replied, which means that, even if the situation is bad, some good will come out of it.

We didn't talk during the drive. I didn't even look at my father's face. I just stared at the dirt road ahead. When we arrived at the *diwaan*, Abouee parked the truck, told me to stay put, and got out. His cousins saw him and came out to greet him, surprised to see him since they knew his feelings about idle gossip and endless cups of coffee. Without returning their greeting, he called for the man who had hurt me. All eyes followed the man as he rose from his seat inside the *diwaan* and walked to meet Abouee in the *hosh*. By now other men had gathered around the entrance of the *diwaan* to watch. The men formed a ring around Abouee and the other man. Everyone was waiting for a fight to erupt when Abouee called me to step out of the truck. The tension eased. Everyone knew that there wouldn't be a fight if a man had his daughter with him.

Abouee looked at the guy who had chased me. Pointing to me, he asked him: "Do you know whose daughter she is?"

The man nodded and said quietly, "Yes." He leaned towards his left leg, trying to keep it from trembling, but his voice betrayed him.

"So you know she's my daughter?"

The man nodded, but he wasn't looking at my dad. Abouee grabbed him by the arm and asked again: "Look me in the eye and tell me that you know who her father is."

The man hesitated, but Abouee didn't relent. "Look me in the eye. I'm talking to you."

71

Abouee came closer to him, and stooped down, staring straight into the man's eyes before continuing: "Did you chase her with your car and then beat her?"

Now the man was shaking so much that he could hardly hold himself upright. He bowed his head and blubbered an apology. "I am really sorry. Please forgive me. I just wanted to teach her to be more responsible and careful with other people's fields. I know we are cousins."

"What?" Abouee shouted. "What did you say? Teach her? Is she your daughter? You have no right to touch my daughters! Look at me," Abouee pressed even harder into the man's arm. "I am the only one on earth who is responsible for my daughters. Is it clear or should I make it clearer?"

The man nodded, wincing from the pain. "It's clear."

"I don't hear you."

"It's clear," he said again, this time loud enough to appease my father. "It's clear. Please forgive me."

Then Abouee turned to me and said: "And now you must apologize to her."

Everything up until this point had been difficult, but that seemed like a bridge too far. The man hadn't expected this and was shifting from side to side, reeling from the humiliation of having to apologize, in front of the entire *diwaan*, to a little girl.

"Apologize to her! Now!"

The man muttered it under his breath, spitting out the words like sunflower seed husks. "Forgive me." He didn't look at me and I could hardly hear him.

"Did you hear him?" Abouee asked me.

"No," I said, taking my revenge and feeling the weight of the day's events lift.

Abouee looked at him and commanded: "Look at her and say it loud and clear."

The man paused and then cleared his throat. "I am sorry. Forgive me." Even though I doubted his sincerity, I felt relieved. He looked so weak standing there in front of me that I swore I could see him shrinking. Or maybe I grew taller.

Abouce dismissed him with a wave of his hand and then told me to get back into the truck. His uncle came running, inviting him to stay for coffee, but Abouee dismissed him too.

I looked at Abouee and felt a stream of power surge into my body. I felt so strong. I asked Abouee why he hadn't beaten the guy up.

"I didn't want to get my hands dirty," he replied.

Later I learned that it was Jidatee's idea that Abouee take me with him. A clever woman, well versed in matters of justice, she knew that having me there succeeded in righting the wrong that I had suffered, protected us from future abuse, and prevented the need for revenge from escalating into a war within the tribe.

My Champion

WHEN BASMA GRADUATED from high school, Abouee agreed to send her to teachers' college in Beer a-Saba with several other girls from the village. Basma and the other girls travelled every day by bus to this bustling, mainly Jewish city, half an hour south-west of Laqiya. Although the tribe initially approved of these Bedouin girls receiving a good-quality education, their support was short-lived. Every day the women faced the reality that Beer a-Saba might only be half an hour away, but it was a far cry from the world of the village, and by the end of the first term, Basma was the only Bedouin student who remained in the programme. That was when people's attitudes shifted and they demanded that she withdraw from the college, on the basis that it wasn't safe for a Bedouin woman to travel alone to a Jewish city.

When Abouee refused to comply, the tribe attempted to leverage Jidee's authority, but Abouee convinced his father of his point of view. Unlike my father, Jidee had received a formal education. He attended school before the state of Israel was established and he regretted not having been able to provide his son with an education. Abouee was only eight years old when the founding of the country short-changed the Palestinian education system by installing a military regime that forbade those who were on the losing side of history from travelling to the cities in the centre and the north where the good schools were located. Despite having never received a formal education, Abouee was brilliant. Within one year, by his uncle's side in the *kouttab* (the school attached to the mosque), Abouee learned to read and write in Arabic. Later, he taught himself enough Hebrew to be able to find a job in a nearby moshav. By fifteen, he could read and write the language fluently and he would stroll around with that day's copy of the Hebrew daily, *Yediot Ahronoth*, tucked under his arm.

To reverse Abouee's decision about sending Basma to the college, the tribe resorted to its most powerful tactic: rumours. They spread lies about her in the *diwaan:* "She's walking around with men," they said. "We've seen her. Letting them stare at her, letting them carry her books, letting them gently graze their arm against hers." If that wasn't enough, a group of men from the village waited for Basma on her way to the bus stop, on her way to the school gate, or even on her way home and shouted at her: "Whore!", "Shame on you!", "No one will marry you," and "You deserve to die."

Ummi desperately wanted Basma to surrender. She hated being in the crosshairs of the tribe's scrutiny. One Friday, when Abouee was in the market in Beer a-Saba, he returned to his truck, turned the key in the engine, and a deafening bang threw him back into his seat. Someone had filled his tank with sugar, leaving him without the means to continue his work delivering produce across the desert.

After that, with all of us to support, including my uncle who was studying medicine in Italy, Abouee was flat broke. It took him six months to start all over again, but during those six months, we herded sheep together. He would go to the fields in the morning and return again at noon. By half past two, I'd be back from school, my mother would hand me my lunch and I would join him in the fields. It was as if my father and I had a secret life. We rambled over Laqiya's pristine hills, reading Arabic literature, and having spirited debates about the characters and themes, and what these stories told us about life's greater questions. We were two wanderers united by our love of nature, adventure, beauty and truth. He asked me to read poetry aloud and fondly corrected my pronunciation. We read stories and if we didn't like how they ended, we created our own conclusions. We read, we talked, we laughed. But, above all, we argued. We argued passionately, especially about the role of women in society. When he didn't agree, he would gesture to me to get up, and command me: "Stand over there. Imagine you are talking to a group of people. And, all these people," he would gesture to an invisible crowd, "don't agree with you. Show me how you would convince them." I'd think and take a deep breath and then begin, holding my head high and chest out, speaking as boldly as I could. During my speeches, he would stop me every so often to give me feedback. On more than one occasion he told me that I was too angry. "Relax," he would say. "When you're angry, you lose your power. Anger diminishes power."

Abouee became very interested in the books that I was reading in my elementary class and asked my sisters if these authors had books for adults. My sisters started lending him books from my uncle's library. Of all the tomes that sat on those shelves, what he loved most was classic Arabic literature from the time before Islam. He particularly loved Mu'allaqat Imru al-Qais and Tarafa Ibn al-Abd, two seminal writers who wrote extensively about identity and finding one's place in society – for al-Qais was an orphan and al-Abd was black. He learned about their lives and their struggle for justice within their own tribal systems, which helped him to understand why his own people resisted and fought against his ideas. He learned many of their poems by heart.

While we herded the sheep, nothing burdened Abouee. He felt free. But in the evenings, he was a different person, especially when Jidee and my uncles discussed the incident with his truck. When this discussion came around, he was forceful and stubborn. The voices for and against Basma's education resounded through the shack. My uncles pleaded with him, "You don't have any money, so give up on this, at least." Abouee's brother Abdallah and Jidee were the only ones who supported my father. They saw that his ferocity left no room to negotiate. Thanks to his stubbornness, his brothers and one of Ummi's brothers helped him to rent a gas station in Beer a-Saba, so his work routine switched from long-distance travelling and sometimes staying away from his family for days at a time to a job where he would be home every day by early evening. Once he had enough savings, he bought a small car to get him to and from work every day and to drive Basma to college and pick her up in the evening, allowing her to continue her studies in peace.

Within three years, Basma had finished her college degree and by the time she graduated, she had already done a year's teaching in the village because of the dire need for teachers. The day she completed her second year of teaching, two cars drove past the *diwaan* towards our house. Coffee cups froze mid-air. Cigarettes burned. The eyes sitting in front of the *diwaan* followed Abouee's small, white Honda and the other, unfamiliar vehicle: a shiny, yellow Toyota with Basma's profile in the driver's seat. When the two of them pulled into our *hosh*, Ummi showered the car with rice and said a prayer that this car would serve my sister in the best way possible. My sister was the first woman in our village to complete a college degree and the first to drive her own car. Until then, people in my tribe didn't understand the significance of sending Basma to college. They didn't understand that her education paved the way for material gain.

A Woman After All

FOLLOWING OUR RESISTANCE to the destruction of our trees in 1978, the government put our tribe under close supervision. By the eighties, the government was engaging in openly repressive

1   My great-grandfather Sheikh Ibraheem a-Sana

2   My paternal grandfather Haj Salmaan, Jidee

3   My paternal grandmother Rokaya, Jidatee

4   With my parents and my sister Na'ama (*right*), in our first independent tent

5   In our *hosh*, with my parents, my younger brother Nasouh and sister Narjis
    on the wall behind us, 1980

6   My father Abd al-Kareem, Abouee, on horseback

7   My father skinning a lamb for Eid al-Adha

8   My father with Na'ama on his lap, Basma standing to the left and my father's
      half-brother kneeling

9   Me (*third from right*) with my sisters, brothers and cousins outside my uncle's
      stone house in Tel Arad

10   My grandfather with my mother, Ummi, celebrating the birth of my youngest
      brother Muntasir

11 My brothers, sisters and cousins on my father's truck

12 With my family: Basma (*top left*), my aunt Na'ama (*top second from left*), my Aunt Maryam (*top third from left*), my brother Salmaan (*bottom right*) and me being held (*third from right*)

13 Uncle Abd al-Rahman, his sisters and sisters-in-law outside the *hosh* in the camp in Tel Arad

14 Me with blonde hair on a school trip to the Tel Aviv Zoo, in third grade

15 Sixth grade: with friends outside our school, Mourad my cousin (*on the right*) and me (*second from right*)

16 My first demonstration against house demolition and land confiscation, Laqiya 1982

17 A view of Laqiya

18 In seventh grade: With my friends and our teacher from the North, Ziad Majadla

19 On horseback with Aunt Safiya

20 With my family: my Italian Aunt Valeria (*second from left*),
   Na'ama (*third from left*), me (*second from right*), Narjis (*far right*)
21 Skinning a lamb with my father for Eid al-Adha

22 With my Uncle Abd al-Rahman and Narjis (*right*) in the factory
23 Me, aged 14, (*top row, centre*) with the Debka troupe
24 With Narjis (*right*) in 1988
25 With my tenth-grade teacher in the Bedouin Museum
26 On a trip to Tiberias in tenth grade

27　My grandmother, Jidatee, my uncle Abd al-Rahman and my cousins celebrating Eid al-Adha

28　My mother bathing two of her grandchildren

29 With my uncle Abd al-Rahman
30 My parents overlooking Jerusalem celebrating my Solomon Bublick Prize.

tactics, arresting anyone who opposed it, demolishing shacks and uprooting healthy olive orchards. My uncle and my father's two cousins were arrested for supporting the Palestine Liberation Organization. In response to the government's actions, the men in the village established an NGO called the Sons of Laqiya Association which nurtured political and social activism. Following Israel's invasion of southern Lebanon in 1982 and the subsequent Sabra and Shatila massacre, where Palestinian camps were ravaged by Lebanese Christian Maronites under the watch of Israeli forces, the association organized a demonstration.

The organizers, who comprised university students from my tribe, Arab students from the north and Jewish peace activists, chose me to recite a poem on stage. I remember not having suitable clothes, and when Basma and my aunt rehearsed the poem with me a few days before, they fashioned a pair of Abouee's old jeans into a skirt for me to wear. On the day of the protest, they helped me to get dressed and braided my long hair into one simple plait that ran down my back.

We dressed in black. Young men carried planks of wood and their brothers lay on top of them, as if dead, while the women marched alongside. This was the first demonstration that included women in the history of the Bedouin in the Naqab. We marched through the village until we reached the main well at the centre of the village, where we constructed a memorial for the victims of the massacre. It was erected next to a memorial for the activist Emil Grunzweig, a Jewish teacher who had been killed the week before at a peace rally in Jerusalem when a hand grenade was thrown into the crowd. When it was my turn to speak, I walked to the centre of the platform – we were using someone's truck as a stage – and looked out over the four thousand or so people gathered there. I wasn't afraid. Those days up in the mountains with Abouee had prepared me for this moment. The megaphone was so large that someone had to hold it up for me. I opened my mouth and my voice rang out, in a bold, unwavering cry:

Lan taddhab hadra demauke ya Sabra!
Gummi wantafidee ya Sabra!
Gummi wantafidee ya Sabra!
Ayna a-salaam, ayna a-salaam, ya jeel al kyiyaam?

[Your blood won't be shed for nothing, stand and rise!
Stand up and rise, Sabra!
Stand up and rise, Sabra!
Where is the peace for the generation in the camps?]

Later we would find out that the police arrested the students who had organized the protest and expelled them from the university. From that day forwards, the government clamped down even harder on political activism in the village. Their first step was to shut down our middle school and arrange for buses to transport the students to a school in one of the newly established Bedouin towns called Tel a-Saba (Tel Sheva). The idea behind this was to send the children of "trouble-making age" – teenagers – out of the village so that they wouldn't be there when the government was uprooting trees and demolishing homes. Tel a-Saba also had the advantage of being a much more disadvantaged town than Laqiya, where the people were not politically active or politically aware. The authorities thought that if they sent us to a place where the people did not have such a fervent and unified voice, our spirits could be broken and our attempts at dissent would dissolve in the sand.

Around that time, I was 11 and moving into sixth grade, but the leaders of the tribe enforced a strike at the local school to protest the shutting down of the middle school. Not everyone in the village supported the strike, but none of the young people from the a-Sana tribe attended school that year. After the breakdown of another round of negotiations with the government about reopening the school, there was a heated discussion about whether the girls should be allowed to travel outside the tribe to attend the school in Tel a-Saba. The other question was whether the girls should travel in the same buses as the boys, even though the classes were co-ed. The head of the tribe held a meeting in the *diwaan* to discuss whether to send the girls or not. Men shouted without catching their breath. Their hands gestured violently. The voices for and against were split down the middle. Amid the tumult, Abouee rose, picked up his shoes from the entrance and stepped out. Before leaving, he turned around and said: "My daughters' education is not a tribal affair. If there is no school here, I will send them to school in Tel a-Saba." His resoluteness encouraged other fathers and within a week all the girls from the a-Sana tribe were on a bus together travelling to their new school in Tel Sheva. For the boys, the fathers who wanted a good education for their sons sent them to the middle and high schools in the Triangle area, a concentration of Arab villages near Haifa, or to the Galilee.

Three years later, it was again time to decide where to send the children in my age group to school. I was certain that my father would send me to the north, especially because my grades were higher than those of anyone in my class, even the boys. In anticipation of my shiny new future, I started preparing for the entrance exams in English and mathematics and even helped my younger brother, Yousef, prepare as well. Yousef and I loved playing together. He was a generous and sweet boy whom all the other boys taunted for his soft heart. Ummi noticed my efforts, but remained silent. She was happy that I was helping my brother, and I thought that she was, like me, convinced that I would be attending school in the north. Once, while we were studying, my brother shyly told me that only boys were allowed to go to the north. I threw the books on the ground.

"What! If I'm not going, I'm not helping you."

He blinked. He was only trying to tell me what he knew to be true, but I kept yelling, "Who said I'm not going? Was it Ummi? She doesn't decide for me. I will talk with Abouee."

I ran to Ummi, insisting that I should go to Haifa and that she was not the one to decide for me, but she met my fire with her own.

"Are you out of your mind? Go with the boys? Sleep outside the house? You're mad. Aboukee has ruined your mind. I want him to hear your stupid ideas."

"They're not stupid." I held my ground. "Why not? I'm better than Yousef. You know that."

As I said this I sensed Yousef standing a few feet behind me.

"*Fashaarti* [In your dreams]," Ummi barked. "You will always be a girl. He will become better than you." She walked past me and put her arms around my brother. He freed himself from her and ran over to hug me.

"If you don't want me to go, I won't," he said, trying to comfort me.

After dinner, Ummi shared the day's events, her sharp tongue set on provoking Abouee's anger.

"Did you hear? She thinks that she's going to Haifa. She's crazy. Going to Haifa."

Ummi shook her head. "She wants to go to Haifa. She wants to drive me crazy. She wants to kill me." Her voice berated me like a police siren that I had no choice but to endure. I concentrated on chewing the bread in my mouth and waited for it to pass. She carried on: "I only just survived when Basma was at college. By the time she finished my eyes were in the back of my head. I'm not going to allow that to happen again. Why can't she continue studying in Tel a-Saba like her sisters? She's not better than them."

She collected the plates and placed them on a tray to carry them to the kitchen. She stacked them with the agility of someone who had done this a thousand times, then glanced upwards and uttered her famous prayer: "Send down your basket and take them back! Screw girls and the one who delivers them. The burden of girls lasts forever."

When dinner was over, my siblings dispersed, but I hung back so I could hear the rest of the conversation. I was hoping Abouee would call me to come and talk about what had happened. I waited and waited while he sat in silence. It killed me not to know what he was thinking. I trusted him, but there was a chance that Ummi had poisoned him against me and that I wouldn't be going to school in the north. I hid around the corner of the shack, just out of sight, and waited. *Why is he not telling me? Just tell me!* The voice in my head was persistent and frustrated; the silence felt like two hands gripping my heart and throat. Finally, in a loud voice, loud enough for me to hear, for I'm sure she knew I was lurking nearby, Ummi asked: "So what are you saying? She is thinking that she is going with her brother to Haifa. What should I tell her?"

Abouee shook his head and with his own loud voice he confirmed my worst fear: "Tell her no. She can't go. Girls are not allowed to sleep outside the house." His voice didn't contain any anger, but his words hit me harder than any beating ever had. The disappointment pained me, but the betrayal was worse. This man who I believed in. This man who always did what was right. This man was not going to fight for me? Why? Wasn't I worth it? I slid to the ground and buried my head in my knees, and my dreams dissolved into a million tears.

When my sisters found me, they gently tried to get me into bed, but I didn't let them console me. I didn't want to be the victim. I followed my sister Narjis, who is two years older than me, into our room. Narjis is the sensitive one, the one who bursts into tears whenever she sees anyone else crying. Everyone hated sitting next to her during the Friday movie because you couldn't hear anything over her sobs. I slid under the blanket between Basma and Narjis, but I knew I wouldn't sleep. My gaze was fixed on the ceiling, watching the lamplight flicker with the wind. I imagined myself at the school in Haifa, the big city's neon lights keeping me awake instead of the flame from my candle here in the shack. I had visited Haifa only once, a few years earlier, when my teacher took me to participate in a poetry competition. It was big and loud and full of cars and many different kinds of people. It was a city that stretched from the sky to the sea, Mount Carmel reaching towards Haifa bay. A city that embraced everyone and everything in between. That's where I wanted to be. I rolled over and looked at Basma sleeping beside me. *Never take things for granted. Doubt things. Ask questions and don't be afraid. Searching for answers is your life's path. Never give up on it.* This lesson from Jidatee came to my mind and then I remembered what Abouee had said: "Girls are not allowed to sleep outside the house." I couldn't believe he had said those words. Abouee, my father, the man who had trained me to stand up for what I believed in. That man couldn't be the same man who had said those words in the *hosh*.

That's when I decided to write Abouee a letter. I decided that I would talk to the Abouee inside that man in the *hosh*, the Abouee who had taught me that words are powerful.

I carefully pulled my legs out from under the blanket, making sure not to disturb my sisters. I scanned the bed. Everyone was sleeping. I took the oil lamp, held my breath and tiptoed out of the room. When I reached the kitchen I was alone. It was dark and scary. Sitting next to the fire pit, I took out my notebook and opened it in the middle where I would be able to remove a clean sheet without ripping it. I wrote:

Dear Abouee,

I know that the words I heard today are not yours. I know that you pushed your conscience away to be able to say them. These are not your words. These are the words that you fought against all your life. These are the words that you didn't want to include in your dictionary and, because of them, they blew up your truck. You paid the price to defeat these words.

You were able to harvest the fruit of your resistance by winning Basma's education. Why give up now? You know the way out. You did it. You are already the king of your own road. Why put yourself back in the dark?

Abouee, I know that you believe in me. You are the one who fuelled the revolution inside me. You are the one who made me believe in myself and reclaim the hope of my name to guide me through my journey.

You trusted me to do all the hard work. You trusted me to herd the sheep far from home and I was able to protect myself. I did all kinds of jobs that boys are not capable of doing. I showed you what girls can do and that, when we get the opportunity, we are better than boys. You saw that. Why is it that when I was doing everything to serve the family, you never said, "She is a girl and she can't be a shepherd. She can't farm. She can't carry heavy bags of wheat." I did all this as a girl, Abouee, not as a boy. Why now, when I want to do something for my future, all of a sudden I am a girl and I can't do it, I can't take care of myself?

You know that I can protect myself and make you proud of me. What happened to you, Abouee? You know me. I can't give up on the things I believe in and I believe that we women have the same right as men to be educated and to go to school. I will never give up on fighting for these rights. You know why I won't give up, Abouee? Because, "Ana bint Abouha". I am your daughter.

Please, Abouee, don't be the one who kills my dreams. You instilled them in me. Give them the opportunity to rise high. I'm talking to Abouee inside you and I want the answer from him. Not from the man I heard today.

I love you, Abouee, and I want you to know that you are the dearest to me in this world.

Bintak,
Amal

Big black drops fell onto the page as my tears mixed with the smoke from the lamp, leaving round black stains that looked like bruises. I walked back to my bed, but I didn't sleep. I stayed awake all night planning how to deliver the letter at just the right time and place so that Abouee could take it in.

The call for prayer from our small mosque broke the early morning silence and the day regained its life. Ummi and my three sisters were the first to rise. The daily routine began. Usually, it was me and my sister Narjis who would feed the animals, but I didn't want anyone to see me with my letter, so I went to the *taboon* and started the fire, then grabbed the metal bucket and walked down the road to milk our cow. Her quiet grace enveloped me in calm. I came closer and slowly petted her face. I hugged her large neck and, again, the tears came. Still sobbing, I released her neck, crouched down and washed her udder before starting to draw her milk. The steady stream of warm milk soothed me. When I finished, I did what Ummi had taught us to do: I scooped a bit of foam off the top and lathered it on my face. It was warm and smooth.

After I had handed the bucket of milk to Narjis, I walked over to Abouee's car, opened the door and placed my letter on the steering wheel, then went to prepare the feed for the sheep. I worked meticulously, concentrating on mixing the barley and bran and dividing the feed between the troughs. After a while, I heard Abouee's footsteps, but I focused on my task, pretending not to hear him. He entered the barn and sat on a bale of hay. He waited quietly until I finished pu and then he asked me to sit beside him.

"*Shuufee, ya bint*ee [Look my daughter]. You know how much I love you and I believe in you." He spoke softly. "You have unique abilities. I can't let you live away from me. I need you here next to me. You are my right hand. Who will take care of the sheep and who will water the olive trees? Who will help me here? Your sisters will marry soon and no one can replace you."

His expression became more sombre. "Amal, I might lose the support of my tribe. I can't raise you without the support of the tribe."

His words hit my heart in the same way the ocean's waves kiss and leave the sand. I was touched by how important I was to him, but I also had my own vision for my future. "Abouee," I said, "I will never become a lawyer if I study in Tel a-Saba. No one there does the *bagrut**. I don't want to be a teacher. I want to go to university."

He looked at me and took my hand between his. "You don't need good schools to teach you how to achieve your goals or to become what you want. The only thing you need is yourself. And that you have, even if you're studying in Tel a-Saba. Good schools are made for lazy people who need the teacher to teach them everything. You don't need that." Before I could reply, he stood up to leave. "I have to go. I'm late for work." He rose and then gently pressed my shoulder. "*Ana bint Abouha!*" He handed me my letter. "It's a good letter, keep it." I followed him with my eyes and smiled. Ummi saw him walking back from the barn. She noticed my smile and shouted: "I hope she didn't convince you."

"Leave her," he said and kept walking.

I looked at the letter in my hand and kissed it. This was my first feminist document and my first formal attempt to stand up for women's rights.

This conversation shattered the spell that I was equal to the boys. I drove the tractor, I carried the wheat, I did everything that the boys did. I felt like a chameleon: not a girl, but not a boy either, my own thing, a creature in between. This was the first time I realized that, as far as the tribe was concerned, I had always been a girl and now I was becoming a woman. No matter how far from being a woman I felt.

---

* Israel's matriculation exam.

Drawing My Own Lines

A Woman's Name

I HAD LET go of my dream of studying in Haifa and wanted to be close to home so that I could continue helping Abouee and my family. With the last of us at school, even though Basma and Maryam were working and my other sister, Na'ama, had married one of our cousins and left home, we still didn't have enough, because my father had sent our eldest brother to study pharmacy in Italy.

Abouee left his job at the gas station and decided to rent a grocery store in the centre of Beer a-Saba. He rented it from an elderly Iraqi Jew who wanted to retire and built an extension from which he sold animal feed. The feed was in high demand within the Bedouin community because we no longer had access to large areas of land where our livestock could graze. In the transition from being semi-nomadic with limitless grazing to living in permanent structures with cramped barns and small plots, we shifted from nomadic herding to intensive subsistence farming and could no longer rely on the bounty of the land to sustain our herds. This shift put the Bedouin community under significant financial strain. We were used to feeding our sheep for free and now had to choose between feeding our sheep or feeding our children. I couldn't abandon Abouee under those circumstances. Staying in Laqiya and attending school in the neighbouring village felt like the right decision. I felt I had been called on a mission.

It was a bright morning in mid-August and my younger brother, Yousef, was preparing to embark on his own mission. At thirteen years old, he was leaving for Haifa to receive the education that would allow him to build a better future for himself and for all of us. Yousef had been born on the same day as me but one year later; Ummi pampered him so completely that he never lifted a finger in our house. We prepared all of his meals and served him as though we were his personal servants, but he was so sweet that I never resented him for it. Yousef was not like the other boys in the village. He was, and still is, sensitive, quiet, thoughtful and kind.

Abouee's approach to raising my brothers was very different from Ummi's. He wanted my brothers to be strong men, independent and self-reliant, who understood what it meant to work hard. He used to send Yousef to fix cars with our male cousins, who were tough. When they bullied my brother, I defended him, but I also taught him how to throw a rock to hit a target perfectly, even if that target was a cousin's head. By helping to disguise my brother's sensitive side, I was playing into the patriarchal ideology that I hated, but I did it for my brother's sake. I wanted to protect him, to present him as having the kind of strength that our community associated with manliness so that he could survive a system that wasn't kind to boys who were sensitive rather than senseless.

That day that my brother left home was very difficult for me. Not because I wasn't allowed to go to Haifa like the boys, but because I wasn't able to go with my little brother who needed me more than anything. How would he manage in a strange city to learn everything himself? How would he stand up against the other boys who would taunt him, keep the best pieces of chicken for themselves, and even steal his schoolwork? There were thirteen of them and they had been given enough money to survive, but when you have limited resources, you need to fight. And my brother was no fighter. We saw my uncle's car approaching our shack and Ummi started crying. She pinched Yousef's cheeks.

"You are strong," Abouee told him. "You are a big man. I know that you will be OK. God bless you." He hugged him briefly, pushed him away and held his shoulders. "Be strong."

I saw the tears trapped in Abouee's eyes. Yousef was his favourite son and he couldn't bear to see him leave for Haifa, knowing that he would visit only once a month, if indeed there was enough money for him to come home. My younger brothers and sisters ran towards Yousef, saying their goodbyes through their gentle hugs and kisses. The older ones waited their turn, giving him a firm and loving squeeze that communicated just how much he would be missed. I hung back. I wanted to be last. Jidee appeared in our driveway. He hugged each of the boys who stood in a line and then proudly declared:

"You know why you are leaving your village? Because you will be coming back with diplomas that will guarantee your future." The boys nodded and I watched Jidee's hands as he spoke. "I want you to have one hand against any threat and I want you to be united." He made a fist. "Stick together. Share the bread. The one who has should give to the one who hasn't. Help each other with your schoolwork. God gave each of you different abilities. If you work together, you will all succeed." He waved his hands, gesturing towards all of them. He continued, this time more sternly: "I don't want to hear that the grandchildren of al-Haj Salmaan are fighting among themselves or are not doing well at school. Jidee," he said, referring to himself, "never had fights with other people. Be nice to other people. You are strangers in the city and only by good words and kind deeds will you be granted the people's love and respect. God bless you! *Yawlaadi!* [My sons] God protect you."

With these last words, all my cousins and my brother lined up to kiss Jidee. After they had embraced, Jidee held their shoulders and called them "wolf", "eagle", "horse", blessing them with the names of the powerful animals of the desert.

While he was talking Jidatee was praying silently and repeating what Jidee had said. Ummi and her sister Khaltee stood by, their eyes shining with tears. The head of our tribe also came to say goodbye. He was a man with a soft heart. He looked at these children with their bags that dwarfed their bodies and said: "*Walla dhe'ouf Haraam!* [You are sending the children away!] *Haraam!*"

Jidee and Abouee replied at the same time: "*Rijaal min solb rijaal* [They are the sons of strong men]."

I looked over at my cousin. The one who always fought against my ideas and who hated me for trying to prove that I could do better than the boys. We were the same age and would goad each other into arguments about women's rights. That day, as he was saying goodbye to everyone, he stared me straight in the eye and said: "You see. I told you. Girls are not equal to boys. I'm going to Haifa and you're staying here." I held my tongue, and didn't blink.

My uncle started rushing the boys into the car. I looked at Yousef. We hugged each other tightly and both started to cry.

"I'll miss you," he said.

"I love you," I whispered back. "Take care. You know how to be strong. Don't give up your things and don't let people take them away from you."

"To hell with this life!" I heard Ummi say to Abouee. "I wish she were a boy so that she could go with him. He needs her."

With my little brother gone and no one else needing me to look after them, I started listening more carefully to the voice that had been growing in my chest. I was still too young to understand the relationship between the power of the patriarchy and the power of the state, but I couldn't sit still. I knew that if I didn't channel these feelings towards fixing the broken things around me, rage and restlessness would consume me.

Traditionally, our parents were our first teachers, but the schooling put in place by the state had replaced this custom and, in doing so, created a mistrust of what we learned at school. Ummi didn't see my education as important; she thought it was important for me to help with the daily chores, to get married and to have a family. In elementary school, when I returned home from school, my mother handed me my lunch and sent me to the field with my cow and donkey. "But I have homework," I'd protest. "*Yalla!* There are more important things to do," she would reply, dismissing me with a wave of her hand. While she cared about my education, she didn't want my schooling to come at the expense of tribal values of community, solidarity and honour. I wanted to show my mother and the other women in the tribe that education is not separate from our culture. I came up with the idea of teaching the women in my tribe how to read and write. I wanted to create a bridge between the world of home and the world of school. Not only did I want the women to be able to help their children with their homework, but I wanted them to taste an education so that they would never again deprive their daughters of one.

Although the dynamics of the tribe were not as clear to me then as they are today, I knew that I needed to frame the class within a context that wouldn't be too controversial and that would make it easy for the women to join. I pitched the class as an opportunity for the women in the tribe to learn how to read the Quran. If I had presented it as a class about the importance of literacy for the promotion of women's rights, no one would have joined. I figured that by starting with something people were already open to, and that no one could oppose – because it is Allah's will – I would win everyone's support. But, of course, once these women knew how to read the Quran, they would be able to read other texts, their children would be able to ask them for help with their homework, and the women would naturally be more engaged with their children's education. I was not only subverting the norms of the tribe, but I was tackling how the state had Westernized our education system and created a rift between generations. I was, however, only thirteen years old. How would women in their forties and fifties allow me to teach them? How would they listen and accept my authority?

The Sons of Laqiya Association gave me a room at the local clinic. It was the very first session and I was nervous. I prepared my materials, placed the chairs in a semicircle and cleaned the blackboard. I heard Ummi and her cousin howling with laughter and calling out: "*Ya Mi'almah wayn intee?* [Where are you, teacher?]" They stood in the doorway, clutching their bags and leaning on each other, overcome with laughter, as if they were entering a comedy show. They kept laughing as they crept into their seats. They, like me, couldn't believe what was happening.

Once the rest of the women had finally entered the room, I stiffly told them where to sit because I wanted them to experience the cold discipline that we faced at school. I wanted them to be able to relate to their children's experience. The women jostled each other playfully. "I want to sit next to my cousin, miss!" one of them whined.

"Teacher, teacher," another called out. I turned and saw her sitting in my chair, laughing so hysterically that she fell over.

I calmly asked that everyone take her seat and be quiet. One of the women straddled the back of the chair, folded her hands on the top of it and said: "Like this, teacher?" The women erupted again. Another one opened her bag and pulled out her sandwich. "Teacher, teacher. I am hungry. Can I eat?"

The laughter raged on as they ignored my requests for quiet and started opening their bags and showing each other their school supplies. They had blue pens and notebooks of various different colours, pencils, erasers and sharpeners. They were comparing what each one had and laughing about how their husbands had bought them these supplies. I couldn't tell if they were laughing at me or at themselves. Maybe they were laughing because they felt like little children.

One of the women chimed in: "Finally, I know why my husband beats me! All these years, he wanted an educated woman. Now I understand. Today I will come back home and show him what I wrote!"

"Poor you!" they howled back. "He will chase you into the olive trees. You will sleep there tonight!"

They were in stitches, wiping the tears from their eyes and slapping their desks. I let them laugh until the laughter died down and the more serious students, mostly the grandmothers, started calling out for me to lead.

I asked the women to introduce themselves. They looked around at each other and the attention and focus that I had waited for so patiently vanished in an instant.

"What's your name?"

"What's your name?"

"What's your name?"

They poked each other and laughed as they put the question to one another. This game seemed endless. They really couldn't stop and I had reached my limit.

"I can't teach," I said. "I need to end the session."

The room fell silent.

The power of this moment was not lost on me. I felt something awaken in my chest. Outside the class, these women terrified me. Their voices berated me and their eyes scrutinized my every move. Their threats to denounce my misdemeanours to my mother held me in a vice that kept me from stepping out of line, but right now I was in charge. This shift in the dynamics astonished me. The silence in that room made it feel like my kingdom, but only for a moment. Beneath my sense of dominion, I noticed something else. It was a feeling even more overwhelming than the feeling of being in charge: it was the sense of responsibility that comes with it.

One by one, their names filled the silence: "Um Ahmad", "Um Khaleel" ["the mother of Ahmad", "the mother of Khaleel"]. These were their motherhood names, the names that they used within the tribe.

Interrupting them, I said: "I would like you to use your name. Your first, middle and last name."

They roared again with laughter.

"I've forgotten my name!" one woman called out. "The last time I heard it was on my wedding night."

"What happened that night?" another joked.

One of the grandmothers near the middle of the semicircle had been sitting quietly with her hands folded on her lap, but now she cut through the commotion. "Shame on you! Is this what you came for? And you," she looked at me, "either you teach us how to read the Quran or we leave now. What are these empty words? Our names? Who needs to know her name?"

"We will definitely learn how to read the Quran," I replied, "but," I took a deep breath, "I need your names to be written on your notebook so I know who is who when I am grading your work."

Another wave of laughter. "There are exams!"

"*La wallah!*"

"I am leaving!"

"What if I fail? My husband will divorce me."

"Don't show him, stupid! Burn it in the *taboon* or clean your ass with it!" The small room filled with cheers.

Finally, the laughter died down and the women introduced themselves. As each one said her name, I wrote it down on a card and placed it on her desk. Once all the cards had been handed out, something shifted. Each woman stared at her written name as if she were meeting herself for the first time. Some looked delighted, some surprised and others sad. Some wrinkled their noses and jeered at the mystery in front of them. Others held the card close to their faces, as if by squinting harder they would find some deeper meaning behind the strange strokes. In their faces I saw the challenges faced by all the women in our tribe: the challenges of divorce and abuse, of forced marriage, of exclusion from the public sphere, of self-denial and self-sacrifice, of fights between mothers and daughters, grandmothers and granddaughters, and mothers and mothers-in-law. But, above all, the story I saw was the story of missed opportunities. In that moment, it seemed that these women recognized that they each had a self, a self that was separate from the wants and needs of the tribe, a self that was allowed to have hopes and dreams of her own.

If I had been a formally trained Arabic teacher, it's hard to say whether or not things would have worked out. I would have come with what I knew, forcing them to learn my way. But because I arrived as a child with the simple goal of teaching them the tiny amount that I knew, we were able to learn together. I taught them with respect for their indigenous knowledge and we used examples and explanations that drew on their daily lives. One of the women learned how to write the letter "ta" by comparing it to a plate with two fried eggs on it. When she covered more than half of the blackboard with her clumsy rendition of the letter, I asked her, "Why is it so large? I still have more to give you to write!"

"Because I can't cook smaller portions!" she answered.

These women could only understand what I was teaching them through the lens of what they already understood and this observation shaped my teaching philosophy for years to come. If new knowledge is planted next to existing knowledge, we will always fall back on the stronger plant, on what we know. I needed to graft the new knowledge onto the existing one so they could grow together, as one sturdy plant.

A couple of weeks into the course, I told them that we would have a spelling test. That night, Ummi couldn't sleep. She paced back and forth in her room, reading the words again and again. As *Um al-Mou'ulima* (the mother of the teacher), she felt pressure to ace the test. Whenever my mother did her homework, she looked just like a little kid, lying flat on her stomach, propped up on her elbows, scribbling in her notebook. Seeing her like that would make us laugh. We couldn't understand why she wouldn't just sit on the ground and hold the book in her lap like our father did when he read a book or the newspaper. I did my best to offer these women an experience they had missed out on in their childhoods. The more conservative women in the group resisted, but slowly they came around and even enjoyed being students, which required them to take care of no one but themselves.

A few days before the test, some of the students came to our shack to ask what words they would be tested on. I refused to tell them, explaining that the teacher never gives the students a preview of the exam, but I promised that if they studied, they would do well. The class started each day after the noon call to prayer, when the women had finished preparing the day's meals and feeding their livestock. On the day of the test, the women waited for Ummi in the olive orchard near our shack. When they saw her coming down the path, they called out: "You have the words! She must have given them to you because you are her mother! Tell us! What are they?"

"*Haraam!*" she shouted back. "She didn't tell me anything!" They persisted, pleading with her to tell them what she knew. Ummi quickly lost her patience with them and stalked off towards the clinic.

I met up with the women in the orchard and we walked together to the class, passing the *diwaan*, where the head of the tribe stepped out to greet us. He knew all about our test since his wife was in my class. The gossip in the tribe was that some men were proud of their wives while others didn't really see the value in what we were doing.

"You have an exam today!" he called out to us. "I told my wife that if she fails I'll spank her!" Spanking was how our teachers would punish us at school. Everyone laughed and we continued on. As we neared the clinic, I saw three or four women from the class sitting under the shade of an olive tree with their notebooks in their hands. Their determination amazed me, and I felt proud.

Ummi was already standing outside the class when we entered and I announced that I would be changing the seating arrangement. They whined that they had got used to their chairs and that it wasn't fair of me to change their seats on the day of the test. "Don't worry!" I told them. "You've practised these words everywhere. Under the tree, in the kitchen, in your *hosh*. Now they are in your head. Not on the chair." They slowly moved to their new spots and I told them to put everything except a pencil into their bags and to place their bags on the floor beside their feet.

I looked around the class, checking that everything was ready for us to begin, and noticed my aunt sobbing at her desk. Her face was purple and she took large breaths in between her sobs. The other women in the class started to laugh at her. "Is this how you want other children to treat your child?" I asked sternly. "Put yourself in your child's shoes now and tell me how you would act!" They stopped laughing. I knelt down beside her and wiped away her tears. One woman brought her water. Another stood behind her and gently rubbed her back.

"Do you want to speak privately?" I asked.

"No," she said, shaking her head. She took a deep breath. "I know all the letters, but when you tell me the word, I write another word. If you ask me to write all the words you taught us, I will do so by myself. I don't know what to do. I don't want to fail. All my children are smart. I can't let them down."

At that time, we didn't know much in my tribe about learning disabilities, but I did know that my aunt was a very dedicated student. I understood from the intensity of her emotion that she was scared and frustrated.

"Right. Your children are smart," I said, trying to comfort her. "They are first in their class. Where do you think they get that from? You are also smart! I believe that you are just stressed. You need to relax and write the words by yourself. Don't follow me. Write the way you see and feel and you will be great. One of your children had the same problem and now he's a doctor. This is because you are very, very smart. You have a different way of thinking and seeing things."

She smiled at me shyly and I hugged her. "You can do it!"

The women in the class cheered until her face brightened.

I began dictating the words. They bent over their papers, gripping their pencils tightly between their fingers, each stroke clumsy yet deliberate. Most of them had never held a pencil before attending my class. I could hear one muttering, "Ah, yes, this is the letter that looks like a plate with two eggs on it."

The class lasted twenty-four weeks. As it drew to a close, I decided that I wanted to conclude it with another school experience: a graduation ceremony and a diploma. More than that, I wanted them to receive this diploma during a big formal ceremony, complete with speeches, entertainment, food and, most importantly, the right audience: their children and their husbands.

The Sons of Laqiya Association was very supportive of the graduation. The fact that we were using their facilities to host a graduation ceremony for a women's literacy class was a ground-breaking project that their donors would be happy to hear about.

The club had a spacious yard with a paved walkway lined with flowerbeds that led to an amphitheatre. We covered the stage of the amphitheatre in colourful rugs and built a wooden backdrop on which we painted CONGRATULATIONS TO THE GRADUATING CLASS in large, ornate letters. The diplomas I prepared were signed by me and by the head of the association.

The evening of the graduation felt like a holiday. The club sits at the foot of one of the hills at the north-western part of the tribe and I could see everyone making their way there. They were all dressed up and my grandmother stood at the entrance to the amphitheatre handing out flowers to people as they walked in. The whole village was there; all the men and all the children were eager to see the new phenomenon of literate mothers and grandmothers. Everyone took their seats and the voice of Fairuz, the famed Lebanese singer, drifted over them. People clapped and cheered, and their bodies swayed to the music. It was like the beginning of a fancy awards ceremony. No one could tell that the music was coming from an old cassette player, in front of which a little girl was holding a megaphone.

When the song ended, the head of the tribe, standing at the centre of the stage, secured his headscarf and began his speech.

"I am very proud of our women today. They didn't give up on getting an education. They had the courage to join in at this late stage in their lives. They are showing us that our old saying, 'Ta'aleem al-ikbar zai toubsh al-ijrar [Teaching the old folk is like breaking jars],' is not true. Today they are showing us that it is never too late for adults to learn. I am so proud of you all for knowing how to read and write, but I am most proud of my dear wife."

He looked at his wife, who looked at the ground, confused by this breach of etiquette. He noticed her modest reaction and caught himself. "We are also very proud of our daughter Amal, who has put in so much effort to educate these women and to make our tribe better."

He finished his speech and then the class representative spoke. After her speech, the head of the tribe read each woman's name –

her personal name, not her motherhood name – and handed her a diploma. I wondered how those women felt, standing in front of the entire tribe, being honoured for their intelligence and their perseverance. Their smiles told me that they felt proud, and I also felt proud of them for trusting me and for working so hard.

After the speeches, it was time for the play, which was put on by children in the tribe. The play opened with women sitting together in a circle, each doing her own work: one is chopping vegetables, another is working on her embroidery, a third is cleaning spinach. The girl enters the room and tells her mother that she has been accepted into high school and that she wants to enrol.

Without looking up from her task, her mother replies: "You know that even if men get to the moon, the place of women is in the kitchen. At the end of the day you will marry your cousin and you will be here in the kitchen."

After the mother joins an adult education programme, she takes on a whole different tone. In one scene, she is lying on her stomach doing her homework. Her children come back from school and ask her to prepare them something to eat.

"I'm busy!" she snaps. "Do you want Ahmad's mother to get a higher grade than me?"

In another scene, a woman who isn't part of the adult education programme walks into the *taboon*, where she is used to seeing her friends gossiping, drinking coffee and preparing food. Instead, she finds them quietly studying.

"They are saying the daughter of so-and-so is engaged to her cousin. Did you hear?"

They nod, but don't look up from their books. She tries harder, saying more outlandish things, but they don't lift their eyes from their notebooks. Finally, she gives up.

"What letter are you learning these days?"

At once they all start shouting, as if they were gossiping about the latest engagement, each one competing to be heard over the other about what they are learning. Other scenes from the play were taken directly from my classroom. I used the women's names and showed how they would draw the letters and relate them to the things they knew.

Everyone was laughing, shouting at moments of unfairness and clapping at moments of bravery. The first half of the play showed how women are treated in the tribe. In the second half, I showed what happens if we change that, if we allow women to follow their dreams. Giving women more freedom makes the tribe stronger, not weaker. People often resist change because they are afraid to see what is behind the wall that they know. I showed them that life beyond the wall was better and that their ignorance, fear, suspicion and prejudice were not just holding back women, but were holding back our entire community.

After the play, we called the women up onto the stage. The audience cheered and then the women went to join their families. Everyone stood up to greet them and their children started calling out for them. The younger ones ran towards their mothers and this time it was the fathers who ran after the children, grabbing them by the hand so they wouldn't interrupt their mother on her big day.

The Bicycle

GIRLS WEREN'T ALLOWED to ride a bicycle or even go near one. The first bicycle we had was bought for my brother, Yousef. That summer it was a trend. Almost all the boys in the tribe had one. Like many things in the tribe, such as buying a television or a car, it was a collective thing, not a formal collective decision, but the collective social pressure forced you to do what everyone else was doing even if you didn't have the means. If someone bought a horse, then by the end of the week there would be horses everywhere.

That summer, I was eight years old, which means Yousef must have been seven. It was a dry, dusty day and the sand was hot to the touch. Abouee's truck stopped in our driveway. He shouted at Yousef to come and help him unload the bike.

"My dad bought me a bike! My dad bought me a bike!" Yousef shouted. He hopped onto it, eager to show his cousins, and the bike started down the dirt road, without Yousef pedalling. He was picking up speed, rolling over pebbles and larger rocks, dipping in and out of the holes in the road. Children nearby ran after him, trying to keep up, giggling.

I blinked and the children were no longer chasing him, but piled on top of him. We girls ran towards him with Ummi shouting, "Go and get him!"

Basma arrived first. She pulled the other children off Yousef and found him lying on top of his bike. The bike was unscathed, but Yousef's forehead was covered in blood. Basma lifted him into her arms and told our other sister, Narjis, to pick up the bike. "Don't cry," she told Yousef. "Men don't cry. Especially men who ride bikes. If Ummi sees that you got hurt, she won't let you ride again."

My brother's sobbing stopped, and he stared at us silently from my sister's shoulder, drying his tears with his shirt sleeve and smearing blood down his nose and cheeks. Ummi met us in the middle of the road, barefoot, her head covered with her white *shash*.

"God! What's happened to you, my son? It's all my fault! I asked your father to buy you the bike. I did this to you." Basma put Yousef down, and when Ummi saw the blood she shrieked.

"Ummi, it's nothing," Yousef said. "See? I'm not crying."

Ummi told Basma to fetch dry coffee to fill the wound and stop the bleeding. Now that everybody was busy with my brother, I wheeled the bike behind the shack and called Narjis over.

"Are you crazy?" Narjis hissed. "You can't! Someone will see us."

But I was already sitting on it. I put my right foot on the pedal, trying to balance my weight, and placed my left foot on the other pedal. The bike teetered over and I fell to the ground.

"Let's go inside before anyone sees us!"

"No, wait. Just one more time."

"No. You're crazy, Amal, let's go before our uncle sees you."

"No one will see us. Don't worry. Just help me. Hold the bike from the back until I put my other foot on, then let go."

"No!"

"Please? Please?"

My sister seldom resisted my pleas. With her holding the handlebars in place, I was able to stick my feet under the straps attached to the pedals. She let go and stepped aside. I managed to pedal twice before falling again. By now she was very angry.

"If our uncle kills you, you deserve it." She left me on the ground and ran away.

I looked at the bike lying beside me. Its curvy frame was the colour of sand and it had a plush black seat and a big round lamp on the front. I saw myself racing down the dirt road near our house, my hair blowing in the warm desert wind, unrestrained and carefree. Abouee asked me to bring the bike back to my brother. I held the handlebars and walked it towards the *hosh*. I ran a little, gliding the back across the padded dirt, and it felt like I was riding it. When I reached my dad and brother, no one paid any attention to me. I wasn't there; the bike was.

"See?" Abouee said. "Your bike is OK, and you are also OK. Slowly, slowly you will gain control of it. It's always hard at the beginning. Bicycles are like horses. They need to feel safe so they can put confidence in you. If you give confidence to the bike, it will trust you and let you lead. Fear and hesitation are your enemies here. Be confident in yourself. Keeping your eyes on the road is your best tool."

My brother wasn't listening, he was fiddling with the bell, but I listened to my father's words and I listened carefully. *If it is like a horse or a donkey, then it's easy*, I thought.

The next day I woke up early to take the cow to graze in the field, and I asked my brother to join me, persuading him to come by telling him that he could practise riding the bike in a flat open space where he wouldn't hurt himself if he fell.

I rode the donkey and he wobbled along next to me, trying to ride but falling over every few feet, then dragging it until he mustered the will to try again. Once we were in the field, far from the tribe's eyes, my brother and I took turns. We'd get on, pedal and fall. Yousef held the back of the bike steady while I hoisted myself onto the seat and tried to balance. I noticed that if I focused on my feet, I would fall, but if I looked ahead, I'd be able to pedal a few times. By noon we both were able to cycle in a straight line, but we couldn't turn. We agreed that we'd come back the next day to practise. Before we went home, I made Yousef swear not to tell anyone that I had been riding the bike.

I couldn't sleep that night. I lay in bed, nestled between Basma and Narjis, imagining myself zigzagging across the golden wheat field. When the sun peeked her head through the cracks in the walls of the room, I scurried out, cursing the sun for taking so long. That day in the field, I felt like I had been practising all night. The bike no longer felt awkward. I mounted the seat with the same confidence I felt when I got on my donkey. I placed my feet on the pedals, looked ahead with my eyes fixed on my destination, and I was off. The freedom of racing through the wheat and cutting through the wind was no longer in my imagination. It was real and it felt amazing. I cycled in circles around the field, twisting and turning, pedalling with all my strength. I couldn't stop. My brother stood by our cow watching me for a while until he got bored and threatened to tell my uncle if I didn't give him the bicycle back.

My taste for cycling and its freedom outweighed my fear of being scolded or punished. I started cycling around our house and sometimes I'd steal the bike and ride around the nearby olive orchard. I slowly expanded my territory until I would ride all the way from our house to my grandmother's. When my uncle saw me, he would scream, but I ignored him and my grandmother protected me. "Leave her!" she would yell back. "She's just a child."

I was fourteen years old when my uncle Talab, who would go on to be a Knesset* member, got married. My mother bought a piece of

---

* Israeli Parliament.

fabric from the packman who used to travel from al-Khaleel to every village in the Naqab selling textiles, kitchenware, candies and other goods. He would stop at our house, where my aunts and my mother's friends would come to peruse his wares. In preparation for her brother's wedding, Ummi bought a piece of pink and white crepe that she wanted to send to Faatima, a seamstress she knew who lived in Khirbit a-Rass, a village just across from Laqiya.

When I returned from school that day, Ummi asked me to deliver the fabric to Faatima's house. In the past, whenever I was asked to go there, I would ride my donkey. Her village was just across the highway that connects Tel Aviv to the Dead Sea. But this time I told her that I would only go if she allowed me to take the bicycle.

"Absolutely not," she said with a scowl. "What do you want people to say? You are not a child anymore. You can't ride the bike across to another tribe. Your uncle will kill you."

"You want the dress to be ready on time? You send me now and with the bike, I'll be back before sunset."

I knew I had her. She looked at me, moved her eyes to the bike and back to me, then to the bike again and slowly back to me.

"Listen. You take the bike but take the shortcut." My mother had her rules, but she also wanted to have something special to wear for the wedding. "Go through the wheat farm. Don't go down the main road of the village and when you cross the highway, be careful."

I wanted to leap up and cheer, but I didn't dare gloat over this victory. She handed me a plastic bag with the fabric in it and gave me the instructions for the seamstress. I bolted towards the bike, worried that Ummi might reconsider, and hopped onto the seat in one motion, swinging my left foot over to the other side, as if I was getting onto a horse. I cycled towards Laqiya's main dirt road, taking the same route as my walk to school. I heard my mother's voice telling me not to forget that her brother's wedding was the following week and she needed that dress as soon as possible. "Tell her that your mom is in a hurry and I will pay her whatever she wants. Tell her—" She kept talking until her voice disappeared behind me in the late afternoon clouds.

This is Ummi. There is always something that needs to be said to ensure everything is under control. Every time she visited her mother who lived in the village on the other side of the mountain, she would gather us in the *hosh*. We would stand around her in a semicircle, like a soccer team taking advice from our coach. She would look at us, one at a time, and tell us what we were to do while she was away, and although she was only going for a day, she would give us enough work for at least a week. After delegating the tasks, she would launch into the list of rules that we had heard a million times. It always felt like she was going forever.

"Take care of your brothers," she would say. "Don't leave the house. Get the laundry inside before the sunset. I've baked the pita and filled the pot with cooked vegetables. Don't give away your food or bread if someone comes to ask. Say nothing is left. Milk the cow halfway. Let her baby enjoy the milk. I don't know when I'll be back. It will be evening and I don't have time to make the cheese."

She would ask us to bring her abaaya and she'd start walking, wearing her shoes for long journeys that were normally stowed away in a separate cabinet. Only a few paces from the house, she would turn around and give more orders. "If your father asks, tell him that I left shortly before he arrived."

She would resume walking towards the mountain. Then she would stop again and yell something else, her voice growing louder with each step. "Don't fight and don't forget to feed the hens and the sheep." She would turn around and continue, then stop, turn back and yell: "If your aunt asks, tell her that I will see her at your grandma's house."

We would wait for all of her commands until she was beyond the ridge of the mountain where we could no longer see her. The moment she disappeared, a wave of relief would course through my entire body and I'd grab whoever's hands were nearest mine and skip around shouting to celebrate the freedom of not having Ummi around. I wasn't celebrating the freedom from my chores – we often did more than she asked, just to please her. No. It was the freedom of not having her yelling new orders every five seconds. Just as we'd finish one task, she'd be on at us about starting the next one. With her around, there wasn't a single still moment, not an instant where you could rest your hands and catch your breath.

I was on the west side of the highway, waiting for a break in the cars. I watched them fly past me down the never-ending road. The last time I had left the village was four years earlier when I was too sick to be treated by the tribe healer and needed to see a doctor in Beer a-Saba. The city had seemed covered in a thick yellow dust and everything moved so fast. Ummi took me to an open-air Bedouin market where vendors sold goats, jewellery, intricately woven rugs and falafel. The falafel was so delicious that I would wish I could get sick again so that we could go back for more.

One car slowed and moved into the centre lane to turn into the village. As it veered in my direction, I saw that it was my history teacher. My heart sank, but, to my surprise, he waved and gave me a thumbs up. I was afraid that he would punish me for riding a bike. At that time, teachers were given free rein both in and out of school to discipline their students and do what they thought was right for your proper development.

I crossed the highway onto the dirt road that passed through the neighbouring village. Unlike Laqiya with her tidy shacks and lush orchards, this landscape was dotted with decrepit shanties whose corrugated metal roofs had completely rusted through in places. Some homes were attached to small plots of land where an emaciated goat or sheep grazed on a sunburnt patch of grass.

The first pair of eyes that caught me in their line of sight gave a silent sign to the others. Within minutes, all the children in the village stood on either side of the road pointing at me and laughing. "*Walad walad!* [She's riding the bike like a boy]!"

I didn't look at them because I didn't want to embarrass myself by falling over. If I wanted to enjoy the same freedom as boys, then I had to be better than them, and that meant a perfect track record in just about everything. Falling flat on my face in front of these strangers from another tribe would have been a huge blow to my ego now and in the future. The tribes have ears and Ummi would hear about it one way or another. "See," they would say, "that's why girls can't ride bicycles." I was not about to let that happen.

Faatima, the seamstress, walked towards me and interrupted my anxious thoughts. I gracefully slowed my bike and made an elegant dismount. "You came on your automatic donkey!" she called, laughing, showing a row of perfect white teeth. "Come in, *ya bintee*, show me what you've got this time."

I leaned my bike next to her broken wooden door and followed her inside.

Faatima was very poor and lived alone in her shack. I didn't know if she had ever been married; perhaps she had had a husband who died before giving her any children. I only remember that she was always lively whenever I saw her and that she was very beautiful. She didn't judge me for riding a bike. She smiled and her eyes conveyed a secret that I would come to recognize in other women throughout my life: a silent admiration of the freedom I had cultivated for myself. It was as if they were saying: "I was not able to do this and for that I am sad, but Allah, I am happy to see a woman who can."

The minute I entered, the same children who had been laughing at me rushed over and dragged my bike away. I bolted after them, yelling: "Give it back or I'll break your hands! Give it back!"

It is disrespectful to chase someone in their tribal territory. According to our traditions, I was supposed to tell Faatima – someone from the tribe – and she would take care of it. While I chased after those children, an old man came out from his tent and shouted, "What is going on? One of the children said they took her bike. Who is she?" Faatima was behind me and told him that I was *bint* a-Sana (daughter of a-Sana) and that the children had stolen my bike.

She grabbed my hand. "Don't worry. They'll bring your bike back." I stood immobile, but my heart pounded in my ears. I gasped for air, near tears. The old man commanded the boy to call the others and to bring back the bike, threatening to beat them. A minute later, a young man was walking towards us, my sand-coloured bike in one hand, the hand of the boy who had taken it in the other. Without saying a word, he handed both the bike and the boy to the old man.

The old man stood with the bike next to him and looked at the boy, who couldn't have been more than seven years old.

"Did you take her bicycle?" I noticed that no one questioned the fact that it belonged to me. The boy started crying and looked at the young man. "Dad, please! They told me to take it." The old man told the boy to look at him and not at his father. His leathery palm came down hard on the little boy's face.

"Tell me that this will be the last time you do that."

"*Wallah! Wallah!* I will never do it again! Please, please forgive me."

"Go to your father," the old man gestured with his chin. The boy ran towards his father and hid his face in his legs.

The old man looked at me. "We are sorry, *ya bintee*. These are ignorant children. Here. Take your bike."

I took it. My heart relaxed as soon as my hands touched the handlebars, and the seamstress and I started to walk back towards her shack. She shouted at the old man, "I hope the story ends here and that her family won't make a big deal out of this."

"Who is her mother?" he called back.

"Hajar *bint* Nasra."

"Ah, it is solved then. Nothing to worry about." He knew that my grandmother on my mother's side was from his tribe.

Once we were back at her shack, I gave Faatima the instructions that Ummi had drummed into me. She nodded, holding the fabric between her delicate fingers, her eyes already stitching the shapeless drape into its final form. Then I gave her the deadline.

"Your mother is dreaming. It won't be finished before the wedding, but I'll do my best."

She gave me some water and an apple and told me to take to the road before it got dark. I thanked her. We chatted a bit while I ate the snack. She asked me for news from our tribe so she could tell her clients who in Laqiya was getting married and who had delivered a baby. Then I mounted my automatic donkey.

The ride back was faster, because I now knew the route. It felt as if I was racing against the sun, which also wanted to get to its destination on time.

When I got home, I leaned the bicycle outside our shack and took off my shoes before entering. Ummi grabbed my wrist. "Your uncle was here and he knows that you went to Khirbit a-Raas. He wants you to go and see him."

"How did he know?"

"He said that people saw you."

People saw you. I hated those words. "Which people?" I said, not really expecting her to answer. Whenever anyone wanted to stop women from doing something, they used this phrase. You couldn't prove your innocence and you didn't know who had seen you, so you couldn't confront them. "People saw you" stunted our impulses, restrained our curiosity and diminished our freedom.

"Tell him you were doing it for work, not for play!" I heard her shout as I left the shack.

I couldn't hide. If I waited, things would get worse. I walked over to his shack and saw him standing in his *hosh*, waiting for me.

"Who do you think you are?" he shouted. "Where did you go? What did you do there?"

"I didn't go anywhere," I said. "I was cycling in the tribe."

"You are lying. Your teacher saw you. Is your teacher lying? Tell me. Would your teacher lie?"

"No. He wouldn't lie. He saw me. But I wasn't there playing. I was working. I was taking my mother's fabric to the dressmaker."

"Why didn't you ride the donkey?"

"What's the difference? The bike is faster, and I wanted to get home before sunset."

The corners of his mouth stretched out and down in disapproval. He came closer to me. "Look at yourself," he said. "You will soon be a woman." I hunched my shoulders. Although I still hadn't accepted it, my baggy T-shirts couldn't hide my emerging breasts.

My uncle took another step towards me and said, in a different tone: "Listen, niece. You know I care about you." The sweetness in his voice caught me off guard. "You are becoming a woman and the most important thing for a woman in this life is to protect her virginity. Riding the bike can tear the hymen and if that happens you won't be a virgin anymore."

There are two things that Bedouin fight for: *al-aard* (the tribal land) and *al-ard* (family honour). The first refers to our geographical territory, the second to our reputation. Sadly, all responsibility for the second falls on the women. Men can do whatever they please, but as soon as a woman's actions – or, God forbid, her virginity – are thrown into question, she brings shame to the entire family. Protecting your virginity is as important as protecting your land from invading forces, and is viewed in a similar way. The sexual education we receive is that protecting one's virginity is about keeping your hymen intact. We grow up believing that even getting close to a man can rupture this sacred flesh.

I tried to maintain my composure, but my left leg started to tremble. *What was he talking about?* I didn't know what to believe. The thought of having lost my virginity to a bicycle was one of the most terrifying things imaginable. The fear made my mind whirr and I furrowed my eyebrows, trying to make sense of his words.

"But we are riding donkeys. It's the same!" I finally said.

The sweetness vanished from his face. He grabbed my arm, enraged by another answer he found insufficiently respectful, and shot back: "There is a big difference, you understand?" His grip tightened. "Look. If I see you riding a bike one more time, I will break your legs. Go home now."

How many things are women denied under the guise of men protecting us, when, in truth, we are being manipulated and denied simple freedoms? I was so confused and angry and sad. What was the difference between riding a donkey and riding a bike? What did this have to do with my virginity? And why would my teacher tell my uncle? He had smiled at me when he saw me. He had given me a thumbs up. He had encouraged me!

I walked home with these thoughts running through my mind and went straight to Basma. She would have answers. I asked her if I had lost my virginity. Her eyes flashed.

"What happened? Why are you asking?"

I told her the story. She couldn't believe that I had said the thing about the donkey. Her concerned expression relaxed into laughter.

"Especially our hungry, skinny-backed donkey!" She slapped her knees and I started laughing too.

The following week I placed a thick towel on the bicycle seat and secured it with two strands of rope before riding over to collect my mother's dress for the wedding. Although I didn't really believe my uncle, I didn't want to risk it. This way, my mother would get her dress on time and my virginity would surely be safe.

Tel a-Saba

THE TOWN OF Tel a-Saba was very different from my village. It had government-built houses, power lines, bus stops and running water. The Bedouin here lived in concrete houses and apartment buildings, just like the Jews in Beer a-Saba. Tel a-Saba was established in 1967. It was among the first planned towns which the government established in order to resettle the Bedouin and "solve" the problem of semi-nomadic people inhabiting large areas which they wanted for Jewish citizens. The entire strategy was part of a crueller plan of forced urbanization and cultural denigration. Relocating the Bedouin served two purposes: the first was to free up their territory so that it could be developed for Jewish neighbourhoods or government projects. The second was to strip the Bedouin of their own traditions and acculturate us into Israelis in order to "civilize" us. The government systematically denied our culture, particularly through the education system. Our curriculum was state-mandated, and our principals and teachers were hired by the education minister under the direction of the security services, the Shabak*. So when our land was confiscated from us, not only did we lose our traditional livelihood, but we were forced to imbibe an ideology that was not our own.

The high school at Tel a-Saba had two thousand students. It consisted of three austere concrete rectangles with little personality, making it look more like a prison than a school. Two of the buildings housed vocational training programmes: one for the boys to learn woodwork, plumbing and welding, and another for the girls to learn sewing and housekeeping. I attended classes in the third building, which was for regular classes. Bedouin from almost every tribe in the south of the Naqab went to school here. It was rare that we had the opportunity to meet Bedouin from other tribes. This was the only legitimate space for us to be together. Most of the teachers were Palestinian Israelis from the villages and towns in the north and only two of the teachers were Jewish Israelis.

Despite the paved streets and urban architecture, Tel a-Saba preserved its tribal social structure. The town was divided into tribal sections with clear, albeit invisible, borders. Even the public spaces were designated according to the different tribes that lived in the township. The high school was the exception. It was a unique environment where we were all mixed together. This mixing, however, heightened the fear in every Bedouin parent of their daughter marrying a Bedouin boy from a different tribe. Very few girls from Tel a-Saba attended high school, and, if they did, most of them dropped out before tenth grade. And while we were granted the freedom of an education, it came with binding ropes of rules to protect our modesty.

The first day at our new school, our bus parked on the street in front of the iron gate that had been freshly painted. A line of students

---

* Hebrew acronym for *Sherut haBitahon haKlali* (General Security Service) – also known as Shin Bet – which deals with Israel's internal security.

formed to watch us step off the bus and their dark eyes peered at us through the gate as we hopped down the steep steps of the bus towards our unknown future. I couldn't understand what was so different about us until the school custodian came over and reprimanded us for what we were wearing. It was still a modest society by Western standards, but we were wearing knee-length shorts and fitted T-shirts. There wasn't a school uniform, but it was school policy that girls were not permitted to wear shorts or T-shirts and that if trousers were worn, they had to be paired with a large, loose-fitting, long-sleeved shirt that hung down to the thigh.

Our clothes weren't the only things that set us apart. Even before we showed up at the school, the other Bedouin knew about us. It was known that our village wasn't a planned town the state had created to manage the "Bedouin issue". Laqiya was part of our original land holdings, and the other Bedouin knew that our sheikhs had been prominent leaders throughout history and that our people were educated. If anyone from the Negev wanted to get involved in social campaigns or political activities, Laqiya was the prime address. University students from Ben Gurion University in Beer a-Saba and even students from the north would come to our village to learn about social justice advocacy and community development. In class, we were always the most active students. Once, in our history class, the teacher brought the students from Laqiya to the front of the class.

"I want you to be like them," he said to the entire class. "They are smart and they take their schooling very seriously. Remember. They don't have running water or electricity like you. They have generators that give them light for only three hours after the sun goes down. And you," he pointed to the rest of the class, "you have everything and yet you are stupid."

At that time, Laqiya was the most educated village in the Negev. We were one of the first villages in the south that allowed women to attend high school, already a couple of decades ahead of the other tribes, and we treated our teachers like prophets. We were quiet when we were asked to be quiet, participated when we were asked a question, and, if we saw a teacher in the village after school hours, we always greeted them. In Tel a-Saba, I'd see gangs of older boys chase teachers out into the schoolyard, pin them down and beat them up.

These same boys preyed on me and the other girls from Laqiya while we waited for the bus home that would sometimes arrive as much as an hour late. The days when the clock showed 2.45 p.m. and the spot in front of the school was empty, my stomach tightened with dread. It wasn't that I minded waiting, it was that we were vulnerable when we were sitting there alone. The boys closed in on us like a pack of dogs and endlessly howled, "*Ya banaat al-Laqiya, Ya sabab koul illa* [Laqiya's girls are the cause of all this world's troubles]," while pelting us with sharp, grey rocks.

Listening to teachers repeat themselves over and over again in a desperate attempt to get their students' attention was as agonizing as the noonday sun bearing down on your naked back. I couldn't stand it, so I started to cause trouble. In seventh grade, I ran for the school council against two male students, one in eighth grade, the other in eleventh grade. With the support of one of the teachers from the north, I campaigned in every class, my platform the equal treatment of girls at the school and the role of the Bedouin in advocating for the Palestinian cause. When I spoke, even the students at the back of the class lighting small paper fires looked to the front of the room and I ended up winning the election. The student in eleventh grade who ran against me became my deputy, but after a few weeks, he quit, ashamed to be bested by a much younger student, and not willing to take orders from a girl.

As student president, my first order of business was to campaign for girls to be allowed to attend the boys' soccer games. Not only were we not allowed to play, but we weren't even allowed to sit in the stands and cheer. When the boys in my homeroom were playing in a soccer tournament, I rounded up all the girls from Laqiya and we snuck onto the field carrying hand-painted signs supporting our team.

"Go, Aamir!"

"You can do it, Haj!"

"Go—"

Our cheering was cut short by an angry pack of boys who shouted at us to leave. We held our ground, but a minute later the game was suspended. Our team stomped over and the boys' red faces told us that we had dishonoured them by showing up. We lowered our signs and left the field in a dignified march. The next day, everyone was talking about those crazy girls from Laqiya who had made a scene at the soccer game. Several teachers hounded the gym teacher to punish us, but at the next game he joined us in the stands. He was also from Laqiya. That time our team won and we all marched singing, girls and boys together, to our classroom, starting a new tradition. This event catapulted me into popularity. When I walked down the hall, I was no longer a strange creature from Laqiya but a force in my own right. A force some people loved and others hated.

In December 1987, the intifada* erupted. I was in eighth grade and I was very angry. There were not many places where I encountered Jews. There was the time that I was sick and visited a Jewish doctor in Beer a-Saba. That happened only once. Another was when the Jewish Israeli police showed up with demolition machinery and tore down the homes in our village. That happened often. My other encounter with Jews was when I was herding my sheep. The military used the area around our village for navigation training. They would drop the new recruits, boys of eighteen with fresh crew cuts and pimples, next to our school and send them up the mountain to locate bits of paper that their commander had hidden somewhere on the terrain. I would surreptitiously watch the commander, snatch the papers before the soldiers could find them, and watch with giddy excitement as the soldiers walked around in circles, getting more and more frustrated. When I got bored of

---

* Palestinian protests and violence erupted against the Israeli occupation of the West Bank and Gaza, which resulted from the Six-Day War in 1967.

watching them, I would pop out of my hiding spot and taunt them with the bits of paper, only handing it over in exchange for a prize, usually a can of Loof, the Israeli army's equivalent of Spam.

I grew up seeing Jews as my oppressors: the people who stole our land and expelled our relatives to Jordan, to Gaza and to the West Bank. The people who stole our lands and left us to die with nothing. The people who stole our land and didn't give a damn about preserving our traditions or culture. This is the narrative I subscribed to which led me to reject learning Hebrew, motivated me to throw stones at the Israeli police, and, on Land Day, which commemorates the state-sanctioned expropriation of our territory, to set fire to car tyres and push them down the hill towards Israeli police jeeps. During the intifada, I wrote pages and pages of patriotic poetry championing our struggle and the Palestinian cause. The small library of books that I carried around with me at all times marked the shift from the innocence of my childhood to the tumult of my teenage years. I exchanged the gorgeous novels of Ihsaan Abd al-Qoudis, Naguib Mahfouz and Khalil Gibran for the complex works of Ghassan Kanafani, Samih Al-Qazim and Mahmoud Darwish. Before bed, on my way to school, or as I completed my daily chores, I recited their words under my breath, whispering with precision and passion my plea for a righting of this great injustice.

The protest music of Marcel Khalife, Ahmad Kaabour and Samih Choukcir rang in my ears. "I'm walking, standing tall / in my heart I have an olive branch and on my shoulder I have a coffin." I sang these lyrics while I waited for the morning bus. Leila Khaled and Dalal Mughrabi, bold women who fought alongside the PLO, a keffiyeh around their heads and a military rifle slung over their shoulder, became my heroes. Photographs of their dark eyes shining with possibility fuelled my dream of being a freedom fighter. I wore Yasser Arafat's scarf on my head and a necklace with a Hanzalah charm, the token cartoon of a small child looking out on his godforsaken homeland, dangled over my throat. The Palestinian flag decorated my school bag and I had marked every notebook in big, block letters with "PLO. ISRAEL NO. Free Palestine." This cause became greater than anything I had ever cared about. I wanted to fight for my people, and I was willing to die for them.

Now that my activism had shifted from liberating women to liberating the Palestinian nation, it was the only thing I talked about. I accosted anyone in the hall, students and teachers, and would launch into the injustice we suffered at the hands of the Israelis and that we needed to join this just and noble revolution. In April 1988, when Abu Jihad, the co-founder of the Palestine Liberation Organization, was assassinated in Tunisia, thousands of protesters from Gaza, the West Bank and even within Israel took to the streets. When I got to school the next day, I arrived at our homeroom before the teacher and jammed a wood chip in the keyhole. Once the rest of the students had gathered, I led them down the halls, calling on all the students to join us.

"Free Palestine!" I shouted. "Your brothers and sisters need you to stand up and fight. PLO! Israel no! PLO! Israel no!"

Boys and girls streamed into the hallway, probably more inspired by the opportunity to leave class rather than any belief in the protest, but with every new student who joined our ranks, their apathy transformed into action. The power of leading this sea of energy propelled me onwards and I felt unstoppable. We marched past the school entrance and into the schoolyard and I stiffened. While a handful of teachers had been quietly encouraging us from the sidelines, the rest of them now appeared before me as a wall of fed-up and angry authority figures. They shouted at us to return to class, shoving us back towards the school and some even dragging students inside.

The principal pointed to me and three other students. "My office now or I call the police."

We looked at each other and silently agreed that we were not going to see what would happen if we disobeyed him. We followed him to his office.

"Who do you think you are?" he said to me. "You really believe you can liberate Palestine? Wake up." He looked at my necklace and tore it from my throat. "You are not allowed to wear this at school." He was really shouting now. "If you want to wear it, stay at home with your mother."

I looked at my little Hanzalah on the carpet and my face grew hot with rage. I snatched up my charm and shouted, "Do you think I was expecting you to support our protest? I know you are all traitors. You work for Israel and you don't have the courage to raise your head in front of the government."

He pushed me. "You are expelled. I don't want to see you anymore unless your father comes to resolve this."

No girl had ever before caused enough trouble to be expelled. I stormed out, making sure to impress on the teachers standing outside that I was angry, and that I felt justified in my anger. Some teachers eyed me with disdain; others, I could tell by the way they held my gaze, were proud, but they didn't dare say anything.

The thing about standing up to power is that you don't think about what will happen next. It was still morning, I had just been expelled, and the bus to Laqiya wasn't due until 2.45. Now what? I decided that I would walk the twenty kilometres back home. With the morning's events playing in my head, I walked and walked, each step chipping away at my indignation. I passed through Abu Kaf-Umm Bateen, an unrecognized village, where I followed the wide paths that are for general use and only used the narrow ones, the paths that provide passage between family shacks, when I felt thirsty. On these paths I ran into women in long black embroidered dresses, some leading obedient goats and others carrying caramel-coloured babies swaddled in cotton sheets, hanging clothes on lines and fences, or sitting around, young and old women together, taking refuge in a patch of shade. At that time of day, I only encountered women. They offered me water, but their hospitality came with a concerned interrogation: "Who are you? Why are you walking alone?" In these parts, a woman on her own was always accompanied by one of her male relatives, even if that relative was her five-year-old brother. In my tribe, women had more freedom. After giving me water or directions, the women would ask me which tribe I was from and I'd tell them a-Sana and they'd say, "Ah, nice people. Their daughters are strong and well behaved. Take care and next time try not to walk by yourself. Don't bring trouble to your family." I'd nod and keep walking. After more than three hours, our village appeared on the horizon, nestling quietly in the lap of the mountain, stretching down over the fields. I took a deep breath and the comfort of being home put out the last embers of my anger. I passed our wheat field and felt proud of the sturdy green stalks carrying such heavy golden ears. The words of Mahmoud Darwish fell from my lips:

O you with bloodshot eyes and bloody hands,
Night is short-lived,
The detention room lasts not for ever,
Nor yet the links of chains.
Nero died, Rome did not:
With her very eyes she fights.
And seeds from a withered ear
With wheat shall fill the valley.

I arrived shortly after noon. When I entered our house, my little sister, Wafaa, who was three years old at the time, ran towards me, excited by my surprise visit. I threw my bag on the floor and scooped her up in my arms. When Ummi saw me, she cupped a worried hand over her face.

"What happened? Why are you back? How did you get here?"

I didn't know how to start. What to tell her? That I had been expelled?

"They let us out early today and I didn't want to wait for the bus—"

"Who drove you?"

"No one," I said. "I walked."

"Walked? Are you crazy? You are lucky that you weren't eaten by dogs. Are you out of your mind? What was the rush? Why didn't you wait and come with your sisters?"

I didn't answer.

With a wave of her hand she told me to go and feed the sheep and the cow and to give them water.

I left, grateful to be alone again. I tended to the animals, then sat down on a bale of hay. Their satisfied bleats provided no real comfort. Holding my head between my hands, I rubbed my temples and pondered what I would tell Abouee. What a story to tell him. His anger I'd have to face one way or another, but I hoped I would be spared his disappointment.

One Rotten Tomato

I WAS ALLOWED to return to school on one condition: I had to promise to stay away from politics and focus on my classes. I made that promise to the principal, but I told myself something else. I had to be true to myself, the self that I would carry around with me for the rest of my life. The principal would be out of my life three years from now.

I was still incensed by the killing of Abu Jihad and used the momentum from that to continue organizing political activities at school. My patriotism was as strong as ever and I convinced the girls from Laqiya and those taking the sewing class in the home economics programme to make small Palestinian flags that we would wave from our bus windows to show that the Palestinian spirit lived on. We worked in secret, smuggling in fabric and using the machines in between classes, to make sure that the principal wouldn't catch on. He kept a close eye on me now, but we outsmarted him. We created ten flags about half the size of a notebook, and hid them in our school bags, knowing full well that the other students would rat on us if they saw them. Our enthusiasm was contagious. We took our plan seriously, making sure each girl had her flag ready and that we all knew what we were going to do, and when it came to the agreed afternoon, we watched the bus pull into its usual spot. My body was pulsing with energy and my excitement eclipsed the slightest thought of the consequences.

We boarded the bus with purpose, took our seats, looked at one another, and started singing. Our voices filled the cabin with words condemning the occupation and verses yearning for a day when our land would be ours and we would be free. The driver was Jewish, but he didn't say anything. As soon as we turned onto the highway, we pulled out our flags and waved them from the bus windows. The green, white, black and red fluttered feverishly and we sang louder and louder to be heard over the roar of the highway. Five whole minutes of glorious freedom. Then, the bus stopped.

It was a Wednesday. I remember very well because I loved Wednesdays and I was in my second term of ninth grade. I always sat in the front seat to the right of the bus driver so I had a clear view of the road – I liked seeing where we were going – and if that seat was taken, I would sit on one of the elevated seats in the middle of the bus. That day we all sat in the back. All of a sudden, we heard police sirens and two police cars stopped in front of the bus. The girls at the front of the bus looked at us. We stashed our flags in our school bags and sat quietly with our hands folded in our laps. Three officers boarded the bus, two women and one man, and started searching between the seats for the flags. I looked down to avoid making eye contact, but I felt that they were coming for me. Fear gripped my stomach as I tried to remember what else I had in my bag in case they asked me to open it. There was my flag and my geography notebook full of maps of historic Palestine, but there was something else, something that really made me panic: my brother Salmaan's notebook filled with his poetry denouncing the occupation. He had given it to me right before he left for Italy to pursue his pharmacy degree. My hands started to sweat and tremble. My great-uncle had been detained for five years for actively promoting the Palestinian cause when he was studying medicine abroad and his nephew, my uncle

Abd al-Rahman, was detained for three months simply for being there at the same time. I couldn't put my brother's life at risk. Although the poems were written in Arabic, I worried that the police would wait for him at the airport and take him to jail as soon as he stepped off the plane. Abouee and Ummi's souls would turn to dust. And it would be all my fault.

The female police officer with pale skin and blonde hair looked over at us, her cold eyes scanning our ashen faces. The other female officer had a darker complexion, with black pools for eyes and matching long dark hair. The lighter one came towards me and said in broken Arabic: "*Ta'aalee ma'ei* [Come with me]."

Moving very slowly, I casually placed my bag in my friend's lap and stood up. She noticed and told me to bring my bag, pointing to it resting on my friend's knees. I could barely breathe. All my thoughts were on my brother's notebook. I was trying to picture where I had put it in my bag, which was a mess of papers, snack wrappers, books, pens and whatever else I had stashed in there. If I quickly reached in, would I be able to toss it away without being noticed?

The blonde police officer asked another girl to follow her. I passed my sister Narjis, but didn't look at her. I was afraid that they might take her as well. As the officers led us to their jeep parked across the street, the cars speeding along the highway slowed down and shouted: "These are young girls! What do you want from them? Let them go!"

Pressed against me in the back of the jeep, the other girl, Zahra, started sobbing.

"I didn't do anything!" Her tears ran down her cheeks and into the collar of her shirt.

"Cry louder," I whispered, "they'll feel sorry for you and get you back to your family." I didn't really know if that would work, but I wanted to distract the police so that I could retrieve my notebook. I decided that I would tear out the incriminating pages and eat them. While the officers tried to calm her down, I reached into my bag and fumbled around, keeping an eye on the police officers in the front seat, averting my gaze to the window whenever they looked over. Zahra was crying very loudly and the police still had their siren on. The car jostled from side to side as we took one sharp turn after another. I didn't know where we were going. My mind was focused on finding that notebook and protecting my brother's future.

My fingers brushed up against the rounded edge of the little book and my heart leaped. I grabbed it and waited for the right moment before pulling it from my bag and stuffing it between my underwear and my jeans. I exhaled silently. I could now focus on what was happening. I started thinking about my family's fate. What would happen to them? I'd heard that in some cases the government exacted a collective punishment on the entire family. I imagined the officers arresting my father or destroying our shack. My heart started pounding again. I banished this dark thought from my mind, reminding myself that I was a minor and that I hadn't done anything wrong. I had expressed an opinion. I had a right to fight for what I believed in. I thought about all my Palestinian heroes and their acts of resistance. I was one of them.

I was aware of the jeep braking frequently, which meant that we had entered a city. I was sure it was Be'er Sheva, but the travel time seemed to be twice as long as usual. The jeep finally stopped. The two policewomen asked us to get out. We stood beside the jeep and I looked around for clues of where we were, but I wasn't familiar with any places other than my village and Tel a-Saba.

My eyes landed on the sign on the building in front of us: MISHTERET ARAD (Arad police station). Arad. I had heard of it. I knew it was some distance away. Next to the Dead Sea. I remembered that my family used to buy provisions here when they lived in Tel Arad. A tall middle-aged man wearing a red hoodie stepped out of the building. He spoke to the policewomen in Hebrew. I caught enough of the conversation to understand that he would be taking us from here. Zahra started to cry again and begged him to let her go home to her family.

The police officers left and the tall man in the red sweatshirt told us to follow him into the building. While we walked, he scolded us in fluent Arabic. "Your families are very angry at you. You're causing trouble for them and for us."

At the word "families", my panicked thoughts started up again. We entered a large waiting room with fluorescent lights, white floors and wooden chairs. He offered us water, but it was the month of Ramadan, and I told him that we were fasting. He apologized for offering and I said that I needed to use the bathroom. He led me a little further down a corridor with the same bright, overhead lights. At the entrance to the bathroom, he told me to leave my bag outside. I said there were things I needed from it and he answered that everything I would need was in the bathroom, that I must leave the bag with him. I didn't really need anything from my bag but I didn't want him to suspect that I had the notebook on me.

I shrugged and walked into the bathroom. The lights were even brighter in here, showing just how clean it was. It smelled of nice soap, fruity and sweet, not like the soap we had at school or in our outdoor bathroom at home. I pulled the notebook out from my trousers, sat on the toilet, and first decided that I would only remove the pages that had the flag and the poems on them, but then thought about what would happen if they noticed the missing pages. I had no option but to tear out and eat every page. I ate the first one, then the second, and then I felt stupid. Why didn't I just throw them in the toilet? But what if they didn't flush away? I had to eat them. It was the only safe way. I swallowed one page after the other, but the paper kept getting caught in my throat. I changed my plan. I ripped out the remaining pages and rinsed them under the faucet in the sink, which made the ink disappear. I rolled the wet paper into a ball, threw the ball into the toilet and flushed, praying for it to disappear. It did. Now that my brother's name was safe, they could do what they wanted to me.

I walked out of the bathroom, straight past the tall man in the red sweatshirt, and sat next to my friend. She leaned towards me and asked if our fathers would come to pick us up. The man shouted at us to shut up. He disappeared and we waited. It felt like hours. I stared at the floor, then out of the window across from me, and then I searched the barren room for something else to stare at. I don't remember how long we waited, but I remember feeling hungry and thirsty and tired and scared. Finally, the tall man with the red sweatshirt returned with another man who took Zahra upstairs, while I followed the tall man to a room further down the hall.

When we entered, there was a younger man in a suit and a smart haircut sitting behind a neatly organized desk. Two photographs hung on the wall behind him – one of Yitzhak Shamir, the then prime minister, and another of Chaim Herzog, the president – and beside the photos hung an Israeli flag. A big one. It made my blood boil. The tall man in the red sweatshirt ordered me to sit. He sat across from me and the younger cop sat beside me. I finally learned their names. The tall man was Moshe, the handsome one Eran.

"Listen," Eran began, "I don't want to keep you here. It's Ramadan and your family must be worried about you, so if you tell me everything you'll be able to go home."

I didn't answer so he switched to nice easy questions. What grade was I in? Who was my homeroom teacher? Who was my favourite teacher? How many brothers and sisters did I have? What did my father do for work? He was gentle and I told him everything he asked.

Although I didn't know about it then, this encounter was laden with the social inequality between Mizrahi and Ashkenazi Jews. Moshe was a Mizrahi, a Jew from an Arab country, and Eran was an Ashkenazi, a Jew of Eastern European origin. And they were playing a "good cop, bad cop" routine where Moshe was the bad guy and Eran the good one. Eran was handsome and well dressed. Moshe was scruffy and dressed more like a gangster than a detective. Eran asked the easy questions and tried to win my favour, while Moshe just sat there, arms folded, scowling at me. I tried not to look at him but every so often he would cut me off and accuse me of lying.

Eran continued: "We know this is not the first time you've caused trouble. You were expelled from school last year. We know that your father is a good man who wants to live peacefully. We know that he works at a grocery store in Be'er Sheva in order to support your brother's studies in Italy."

When he mentioned my brother, my heart sank.

Moshe opened my bag and took out the flag. "Nice work. Who made it?"

"I did."

"Where?"

"At my school."

"Who helped you? Where did you get the material from?"

I decided to put everything on the school and keep my family out of this. "We have a sewing workshop and I made it during that workshop."

"It's not nice to lie. You are not in school for vocational training, so who made it for you?"

"I made it during recess. I went to the basement of the vocational training class—"

Moshe hit the table. "You are lying! Tell us who was with you. How did you learn about the flag? Do you have it at home?"

"No."

He hit the table again.

"Did you see it somewhere?"

"On TV," I replied.

"Which TV?"

"Israeli TV. Your TV."

Moshe slapped me across the face. "You are *chutzpanit*."

Eran brought his chair closer to me and said: "Listen. You are a smart girl. Your sister is a great teacher and your actions could destroy your future and her future."

By now, my cheeks were glistening with tears, but they did little to cool the heat on my face. It felt like a fire burning me up, consuming my eyes and my whole head. I couldn't think or speak.

At that moment, I wanted to be home, but home seemed very far away, like a dream I would never see again. Eran walked towards another desk and started writing something in a blue file while Moshe stood facing me and said: "If you don't tell us who asked you to do this, you will be put in jail and who knows what will happen to you there."

It was the height of the intifada. These policemen suspected that I had been recruited by one of the groups of organized Palestinian activists who were engaged in various levels of action against the state of Israel.

I said, "No one asked me to! I did this by myself!"

Moshe's beefy hands slammed the table a third time. "You are lying!" he shouted.

Then Eran uttered the chilling words: "You know that once you have an open file with the police, you won't be able to go to university." To Moshe he said, "Take her and bring the other girl. She will tell us who asked them to do this and I will send her home and won't open a file on her."

Moshe grabbed me by my braid and the pain at the back of my scalp was excruciating. I tried to shake off his hand, but he dragged me towards the stairs. I clung to the railing for an instant before yielding to his superior strength. He threw me on the couch and left. I looked around. It was an empty room with sofas and chairs. It didn't look like a jail. I thought he was taking me to jail. Now that I was alone, I broke down into loud, unrelenting sobs. I don't know if I was crying from the burning I felt on my scalp or from fear: fear of jail, fear of my school expelling me again, fear of my family's punishment.

It was already evening. I knew because I watched from the window the sun set over the hazy city of Arad. It was very quiet except for the sound of police cars driving in and out of the police station and, every so often, words of Hebrew being exchanged between officers. Nothing looked familiar. At this time at home, the sheep were waiting to be fed, hens were waddling towards the coop, mothers were calling their children to come home for dinner. Usually at this hour of the evening, I would feed my sheep. I missed them so much at that moment.

When I heard Moshe's voice, I recoiled. It was almost night, and I could feel my defences unravelling. That morning I had been Amal, a fearless Palestinian freedom fighter. Now I was a scared teenager who just wanted to be home in her bed, nestled between her two sisters. I kept my eyes glued to the window and tried not to look at Moshe. "*Ta'aalee warei* [Follow me]," he said in Arabic. At least he didn't pull my hair this time.

When I arrived in Eran's room, my friend was sitting there crying. "Your friend told us everything and she is leaving. Her father is already here. He has come to pick her up," Eran said.

I didn't know where to start. I didn't know whether to say that my friend had nothing to do with this and had played no part in it, or to ask if my father was coming to collect me. Why would he come? He must be angry and my grandfather would probably be even angrier.

"So, it was Amal who waved the flag on the highway?" Eran asked.

Before Zahra could answer, I jumped in: "Yes. It was m—"

"Why didn't you admit it from the beginning?" Eran said, cutting me off.

"You didn't ask me that. You asked me if someone told me to do it and no one told me to do it."

Moshe smacked me on the back and I almost fell over. Eran asked him to bring me some water and Moshe returned with a glass. "You won't make me break my fast," I said, narrowing my eyes. Inwardly I said, "You won't break my soul."

"It is already evening. You have to break your fast anyway," Moshe replied. I took the glass from his large, threatening hands, and he came closer, "You know you will need a lawyer and your father will need to pay a lot of money to get you out of here. Why do you do that to your father? He's a good man. He doesn't deserve this from you and I'm sure he doesn't like what you are doing."

I tried not to cry, but the tears came anyway. I couldn't bear the idea of my dad paying for my actions. I had never wanted that to happen. Why would he have to pay? They were my choices and my responsibility. As if he could read my mind, Moshe said, "You're only fourteen and your father will be responsible for what you've done."

"We respect your father," Eran cut in, "and we don't want to cause him any problems. Just give us the names of who told you what to do and I promise that you'll go home and no one will know that you told us."

"I have no names!" I said through my tears. "Nobody told me." I looked up at Eran. "I did it because I want to help my people."

Eran's forehead relaxed. He looked me in the eye, but for the first time he actually saw me. "Amal, you will be able to help your people by getting an education, by becoming a teacher and teaching them, or even by becoming a lawyer and defending them. In what way are you helping them with these stupid actions? You are putting yourself and your family at risk. Who benefits from that? No one." He leaned forward. "Listen to me: if there is someone who is pushing you to do this, just tell us. Don't be afraid. We will protect you. We are here to help you."

Eran stood up and asked Zahra and me to sign the papers on his desk. "I will send you home, but I will need to see you again with your father." I looked at the page of words in handwritten Hebrew. Although I knew how to read it, I couldn't understand any of it. I didn't want to ask. I just wanted to get home. I knew that the big fight wasn't with him, it was forty kilometres away with my parents.

After we had both signed, Moshe led us to the room where Zahra's dad was waiting. When he saw us, he stood up out of respect for the policeman and looked at his daughter with eyes that were full of rage and disappointment. He didn't greet her or ask how she was. Moshe asked him if he could drive me home too.

Zahra's father asked Moshe if my family had contacted the police. "No one has," Moshe replied. "I can take her if you can't."

"No, no, I will take her. I didn't want to take her if her father was on his way."

"No. Don't worry. No one is coming for her."

I felt abandoned. I was sad, but I knew that my father had his reasons and that I trusted them, whatever they were.

The whole way back to Laqiya, we drove in heavy silence. Nothing except the whirring of the engine, my friend's muffled sobs, and her father's face in the rear-view mirror, silent and focused on the road, acting as if we weren't there. He dropped his daughter off first. "Wait for me until I come back," he said. "My daughter is raised properly, but some girls aren't. And if there is one rotten tomato in the box, they will all turn bad." I knew he meant me, but I decided not to waste energy on a useless fight.

When we approached our shack, my mother was outside, eyes fixed on the road, waiting for me. The car stopped outside the *hosh* and my mother ran towards the car. I don't know if she knew that I was in it. I imagined she did that to every car that passed by the house. I got out of the car, and shakily closed the door behind me. I felt ashamed for bringing trouble to my mother and I was scared of what she might say. When my mother noticed that the man was a stranger, she wrapped her face with her scarf, showing only her eyes. She greeted him, the gratitude in her voice betraying her humiliation. She followed with an apologetic refrain of *"Hamm al-banaat lal-mamaat* [The burden of girls lasts till the grave]."

"You are right," the man replied. He spoke sincerely, his anger still apparent. "Girls need a very short leash. We can't let them do whatever they want, otherwise they will bring us trouble. Lots of trouble."

Ummi thanked him again before he got into his car and drove off into the darkness. She pushed me towards the *hosh* as if I was a stubborn cow. I lurched forwards, my head snapping back and forth. I thought I might fall to the ground. I had been fasting for the last twenty-six hours. We entered the *hosh* and my siblings ran over to greet me. The younger ones were worried about what had happened to me and the older ones were worried about what was going to happen. Now in the safety of our private space and away from disapproving eyes, my mother twisted my earlobe between her fingers and shouted in my face: "Are you stupid? How dare you do such a thing. Do you want to shame us? Do you want them to arrest your father? Can't you see what's going on? They don't think twice when it comes to protecting the state. They will make you disappear. No one will know where you are." She got more and more worked up with every word until she started hitting me on my back.

"Leave me!" I yelled back.

She ordered my siblings to bring her the broom handle. I prayed that she would leave my hair alone; my scalp was still tender. She grabbed my arm to keep me from running away and whacked me on my legs. "I will break them so you can't move again," she said in between cracking the broom against my shins.

My grandfather entered. "Where is she? Where is the one who wants to destroy the family? The one who causes trouble? I will make her see the stars during the day."

He removed his *agaal* from his head and flogged me on my back, the knot of the cord digging into the skin between my shoulder blades and forcing my head into submission.

"I am tired of her," Ummi wailed. "She causes us so much pain, so much trouble."

"The one who is not raised properly can be raised again and raised correctly," Jidee said before whipping me again.

Ummi wrestled her way between us. "I already beat her this much, Haj, and her father will come home and punish her. We will end up killing her."

At my father's name, my grandfather lost it. "Her father? Her father? He is the one that loosens the leash. I told him that he should shorten it, but he didn't listen. Let him defend himself."

My mother whispered to me to run inside while she distracted my grandfather. "Sit sit, *ya* Haj. It is Ramadan. *Yel'an al-banaat willi jabouhin* [Damn girls and the ones who bring them to life]."

I sat on the mattress, swallowing my suffering and thinking about what would come next. The meeting with Abouee would bring me the greatest pain, not in my body, but in my soul. Narjis quietly entered the room and handed me a small cup of sweet tea.

"Did they rape you in the jail?" she asked. I looked at her, but I didn't say anything. She continued: "I've read that they rape the girls so they can shame their fathers and make them cooperate with the security services."

"No one touched me. Don't worry." I heard my youngest uncle shouting, "Where is she? Where is she? That's what we need now! You want to free Palestine! Who do you think you are? Leila Khaled?"

He entered the room. "Stand up!" he shouted. He grabbed my hair and I almost fainted. I could feel every tiny hole in my head screaming. Instinctively, I took hold of his hand to soften his grip. "Put your hand down!" he shouted. My mother ran into the room. "Please, please. Leave her to her father." He pushed me onto the mattress. I thought I was going to vomit. I had no strength to cry or to fight or to talk back. I knew what was coming and I accepted it willingly.

I lay down on the mattress, nursing my head, my back and my legs, waiting for this nightmare to end. My sisters swarmed around me and tried to console me by distracting me with gossip. They said that the teachers were very angry because the principal was the one who had called the police. They told me that the bus probably wouldn't have been stopped if the principal hadn't called the cops. I was angry again, but I didn't have the energy to dwell on it.

About an hour later, Abouee arrived. My ears perked up when I heard him entering the *hosh*. This was the moment that I had been fearing the most. I had no idea what was going to happen. My father never acts in the way you expect him to. He's always a step ahead of you and he's always in control. He washed, prayed and sat for the iftaar*. My sisters brought in the different dishes and lined them up on the plastic sheet in the centre of the *hosh*. My mother summoned

---

*The meal taken at sundown to break the fast during Ramadan.

my younger siblings. She didn't call me. I was relieved, but a moment later I heard my name and my heart sank. I rolled off the mattress hoping to hear Ummi say, "Let her sleep. The morning has eyes," a wise phrase she uses when she knows it's better to postpone a discussion until the compassion of daylight.

I walked over and looked to see if there was a spot for me in the circle around the meal, but there wasn't. Abouee wouldn't speak about the issue over the iftaar and this was part of the punishment. I was forced to sit there, invisible and hurt, my mind racing with thoughts of the day's events and the shame I had brought to everyone. I was starving but I didn't dare reach for the food. Ummi asked my sister to pass me a date. I sneaked a sideways glance towards Abouee to read his face, but I was too scared to really look at him, terrified that I would encounter those two hot coals that signalled fury. I chewed the date, but hardly swallowed. I felt like everyone could hear me chew and was thinking: "How dare you hurt the family and still have an appetite."

Everyone started moving. The meal was over and it was time for tea. Still my father hadn't even looked at me. Ummi handed him a cup of tea. He reclined on the mattress and placed a pillow beneath his elbow, now ready to hold an audience with me.

"Come here." He pointed. "Sit in front of me." I walked towards him with my head down. I sat on my knees facing him, still not wanting to show him my face and not wanting to see his eyes.

"Head up and look at me," he ordered.

My family sat around, silently watching the drama unfold. It was a warm night, the sky was swimming in stars, the smell of the wheat wafted into our little *hosh* and a perfect crescent moon was visible just to the east of the mountain. But the fear in my heart blotted out all that beauty. The night was stifling: silent, tense, suffocating. Abouee was one of my closest friends. We always worked together, fixing the car or tending the farm. We never fought, not really. We disagreed, sure, but we always found a way to win each other over. With him, I always felt safe to be myself.

Ummi's voice broke the silence. "She got her portion today. Her uncle and her grandfather were here."

Abouee kept his eyes on me and said: "Do you understand what you did? Do you understand the consequences? I trusted you."

The tears came. I opened my mouth to apologize.

"Don't apologize. Tell me first why you did what you did. What was in your mind?"

"They killed Abu Jihad," I said quietly. "They stole our land. They destroyed our houses and even forbade us from carrying our flag." My words gave me confidence. "This is oppression and I want to stand against it."

"She saw others doing it and she did it. She doesn't understand," Ummi interjected, trying to soften my answer.

Abouee shook his head. "She does understand, but she doesn't understand that we all pay for this. *They* destroy our houses and *you* want to destroy your future and our family's future. What's left then? Nothing. You want them to take me to jail?"

"No, Abouee!" I sobbed.

"Look me in the eye."

Don't ask me to do that, I thought. Please.

I was trying to avoid them, but his eyes chased mine down.

"The family, and the future of the family, is what we have, and your role is to protect it not to destroy it. If you want to lift the oppression, there are many ways. Smart ways. Not stupid ones like this one. Do you understand me?"

He spoke with disappointment, not anger. Then his voice changed, perhaps to appease my mother, and he shouted: "Go to your room. This is the last time you do this. Next time I will stop sending you to school. You'll stay home and wash and clean. Get up. I don't want to see you."

Later I heard Jidee ask if the police had called Abouee. I heard Abouee say that the Shabak had come to his grocery store and warned him that he would pay a high price for my political activities if he didn't make me stop.

"You have to punish her hard," Jidee said. "We can't allow her to do whatever she wants. You must take her out of the school if necessary. We don't want trouble with the government."

"Don't worry, Father."

"I have to worry. You let the leash be too long. For girls, it must be short and tight."

"I'm not worried about the government. If the problems were just with the government, it would be easy. But if she gets in trouble with the community, it will finish us. I prefer dealing with the government to dealing with the community."

Here was another lesson that took me years to understand. The government was a stable system. There were laws and courts and trials and hearings. In the community, your fate could be determined by a single rumour. Abouee didn't know what would happen if I challenged the community. He knew that if I challenged the government, I might land in jail, but if I challenged the community, I might end up dead. He was a smart man who knew that trying to suppress my energy would make me rebel even more. Instead, he encouraged me to fight the state but to leave the tribe alone. This distinction reminded me of my grandmother's two inviolable lines. I realized then that she didn't have a line for the government. God's laws and the tribe's laws we had to respect, but we could fight against the government. That's where I had begun, but now I knew better. I knew now that if I wanted to fight, I needed to fight fair, so that no one except me would bear the burden of my actions.

When My Champion Abandoned the Race

WHEN I WAS a child, my eldest sister Basma was my hero. She walked around with regal grace, bright-eyed and emanating confidence. She was smart and hardworking. She was always there for me and she supported my activism. When I was expelled twice from school, she was the one who made sure they let me back in. She always told me, "Don't give up just because some people don't like your actions. Be yourself."

Being the eldest, Basma was obliged to *tiftakh tareeg la-khawaatha* (open the road for her sisters) and to marry as soon as possible so that her younger sisters could marry. A younger sister marrying before an older one could prompt dangerous rumours about the older sister's virginity or throw into question her ability to bear children. In our tradition, we have a saying that loosely translates to "the girl is for her cousin". Although this is no longer common practice, at the time, marrying one's cousin was desirable because it was the easiest way to perpetuate the bloodline.

One night, Basma, Na'ama, Narjis, Maryam and I were sitting on our mattress playing a game we called "matching grooms", in which, from the safety of our mattress, we would choose from among our cousins the one we each thought we would marry. I matched Basma with one of our cousins from our mother's side, and Basma screamed and slapped me across the face.

"If you dare to mention his name again, I will kill you," she warned.

She crawled onto Narjis, who was sleeping between us, and buried her face in her neck. I rubbed the spot on my cheek where Basma's palm had hit. I felt the weight of her burden. She wasn't only slapping me, she was slapping everything: the tradition, her destiny, and the fact that she was powerless to do anything about it. I was thirteen then and I wasn't aware that Ummi and our aunt, the mother of the despised groom, were cooking up a plan. I saw Basma's arguments with my mother. I saw my uncles walking with her in the field, taking her off for *makhlawiyya* (a private conversation) to try to convince her. I saw her trying to hold them off for as long as she could.

No one could conceive of a reason for Basma to refuse the groom. He was handsome enough, he had a job, he hadn't been previously engaged. It wasn't that the tribe didn't care about what Basma wanted; it was that we didn't live in a world where that concept mattered. In a tribe you are a member, not an individual. Happiness? A woman has a husband and now her sisters can get married and the tribe can live on. What else could possibly make Basma happy? From my mother's experience with her mother-in-law and her constant fear that her husband might, at any moment, marry another woman, I understood that our lives were not our own. What I wanted to know was who was making the choices for us? What was the role my mother played? My father? My grandparents? My uncles? My aunts? What was everyone doing to push Basma down a path where her soul was crushed between God's laws and the tribe's? Every day I saw her cry quietly on the mattress in our room, and I thought about those two lines and how Basma's spirit had no room to breathe. All that was left of her was a body, a parcel for a man to take and do with as he pleased, a pair of hands and feet for the tribe to make use of to produce another member.

"He's our cousin. It's good! What do you want?" Ummi shouted every day when Basma returned from the village school where she was teaching. Basma's refusal echoed through the shack. Her easy grace was gone and in its place was a desperation that turned her into a person I didn't recognize. Her red face would be a mess of tears, but our mother always had the last word, knowing how to twist the blade. "Forget about it! You want all your sisters to stay unmarried!"

"Leave me alone!" Basma would yell back and Ummi would walk away.

"Allah, take me," Basma would pray after retreating to our bedroom and burying her face in the quilt.

Basma swore that she would never marry him. She hated him. Ummi didn't entertain these notions of "love" and "hate". It was as if she didn't recognize those words. I don't know if this was Ummi's way of coping with the world around her or if she was treating Basma the way she had been treated: as an object whose role in the tribe was more important than what was in her heart. She never asked Basma how she felt. Not once did she console her, saying, "You think you hate him. Don't worry, dear Basma, love will come with time." Our mother had a mission to marry off her first daughter and there was nothing to discuss. It was tradition. At the time I thought her heartless, but I wonder now if her intransigence and disregard for Basma's pain were a product of her fear of challenging tribal rules. I know she found these conversations with Basma heartbreaking. Our mother was under tremendous pressure raising girls. One mistake from any of us would make her life very hard. This is the sad cycle that women find themselves in: oppressed women oppressing the next generation of women. And here is the other irony: for a system that has been upheld for hundreds, if not thousands, of years, we treat it as if it is incredibly fragile. The whole system is contingent on following the rules, the rules that have been laid down by our parents and by their parents before them and by their parents before them. It has always been this way and it always will. The tribe must be preserved and that means you must marry your cousin. Where is the room for *what if*s? What if that path between God's laws and the tribe's laws was not a tightrope, but a field? What if we women didn't have to fear going astray, but could dance between one path and the other, integrating the codes into a life that made sense to each of us, to find our own way to live in accordance with the tribe, with God and with ourselves? A major difference between Basma and me was that I knew that there were alternatives to the party line Ummi spouted and I was willing to stake anything to find them. My tenacity made my relationship with our mother very tough. I disobeyed her over and over again and drove her crazy.

One afternoon, I went and sat quietly next to Basma, whose blonde head was buried in her fine white arms.

"Why can't you object?" I asked her gently, afraid that I might receive a swift kick for my question. Her desperation sometimes made her react with anger. "Why can't you say loud and clear to Ummi that you don't want to marry him? She will be angry and she might hit you, but you will have done what you want."

She looked at me, with tears in her eyes. "This is not about some demonstration that I want to join. This is real life. I am the eldest and it is my responsibility to open the road for you. I know that they are forcing me to take a road that is not mine, but I have to take it for you so that you can move up the line."

"What road? What line? I'm not waiting in that line. I'm taking my own road. You have to stand up for yourself. How do you expect me to take my own road if you don't take yours?"

"You are stronger than me. They know that you are a rebel. You have already shown them. I have never stood up to them. Besides, your hesitation is not blocking your sisters' future."

Our sister Na'ama, the second eldest, was engaged to a man she loved, Aamer, another one of our cousins. There was a fear that if she had to wait until Basma married to accept his proposal, he might leave her for someone else. Basma gently pulled my braids and her fingers tucked in the strands that had worked their way loose. "Besides, your time will be different. You will be able to fight for your own road and open that road of power and resistance for other girls." She hugged me, her wet cheeks kissing mine, and said, "When it's your turn, I will support you. I will enjoy watching you widening those lines and taking the road you want."

A week later, our house was full of people. It was Basma's *henna*, her engagement party. Men sat around the *hosh* smoking and laughing and our living room was crowded with women in their finest party clothes. Ummi, my sisters and I were navigating the excitement, serving tea. All that motion and noise, the dresses swaying back and forth, the dancing, the clapping of the hands, the *zagareet*. Where someone else might have heard a celebration, I heard the devil's low laugh beneath it all. The noise masked the pain. A bizarre carnival where everyone's smiles took on a dark tone of delusion and despair. What were we celebrating? Basma's wedding or Basma's funeral? Basma wore a yellow dress. She looked like a wilted daisy sitting on the couch, just as dainty and just as dead. Her face was painted with bright make-up that made her forced smile look obscene. Couldn't everyone tell that she didn't want to marry him? Was everyone just pretending that everything was all right? And Basma – how could she go through with it? Why would she put her feelings aside and submit to a life without love?

Basma stood up to dance. Her smile widened as she took her place in the circle, raising her lovely arms, her hands graceful and poised. She joined the other women, the ones who'd been dancing for most of the afternoon. The beat of the *dorbaka* thumped through the shack. I watched her jump from one foot to another with feigned exuberance. She reminded me of a hen hopping around after its slaughter. Dance was a way for women to grieve without being seen. At weddings the ones who spent the longest time dancing were the women who bore the greatest burdens – the women who were beaten by their husbands, the women whose husbands dealt drugs, the women who'd been jilted for another woman, the women who had nowhere or no one who would hold them while they cried. These women danced until dawn, waving their arms, clapping their hands, shouting and smiling until the hostess gave them the sign that it was time for them to go home. These circles were their freedom, these dances their therapy. This was the only place where they could express the pain their bodies bore.

I was wearing a dark blue dress with long sleeves that had once belonged to Basma. In the past, when I'd worn it, I'd felt beautiful and proud. Now, watching this farce where everyone was playing the role they were forced to play, I felt angry. But I too played my part, pouring tea for the guests, thanking them for coming, and saying "yes, of course" when they said how happy I must be that Basma had found such a favourable match. I hated this game. I couldn't stand the dissonance between my heart and my mouth, and the whole time I was trying to suppress what felt like a volcano about to erupt in my chest. I observed Basma all evening from the corner of my eye. I judged her for giving up. Sitting down on a chair in the corner of the room, I held the teapot on my lap with one hand and caressed the folds of my blue dress with the other. I hated her weakness. *Why didn't she fight for herself? Why did she follow the road that others dictated for her?*

Basma's marriage snuffed out the light in my heart. Whatever embers had burned there before were now black and charred. Why would Allah give us the ability to love and hate and dream if we couldn't act on those feelings? Love and slavery can't coexist. And the salt in the wound was that, after years of repressing those feelings, of pretending they didn't exist, a woman was expected to be a wellspring of love, to nurture and care for her husband, her children and her new family. Where were we supposed to find this resolve? Like all things, love must be fed. It doesn't grow from responsibility and expectation, but from self-respect, from pleasure and from following the rhythm of one's own two feet.

The week following Basma's *henna* Abouee walked around with a sad smile. Ummi walked around like a soldier who had just come back from a war, smug and self-satisfied, but to me her pride seemed shallow, like the pride of a slave who had pleased his master. As always, my father and I spent Saturday doing whatever needed doing around the house or the barn. It was the end of the summer, nearing the harvest, and the weather was still very hot and dry. Mornings were only bearable until about ten o'clock and then we needed to work indoors till about four or five when the temperature was tolerable again. It was the time of year when the grapes were ripening on the vine. Fat, purple things, sweet as syrup, which we harvested to make *enbiyya*, a grape sauce that we mixed with tahini for my father's favourite winter breakfast or slow-cooked with chicken for a hearty evening meal. We would walk between the vines, cutting the grapes one by one, carefully selecting the good ones and discarding the rest.

Abouee pointed to a good grape, I picked it, dropped it into the container and followed his finger to the next one. Abouee loved working the land and tending to nature. It was a place where he felt at ease and our crops and animals responded to his touch. In that environment, his mind was clear and there was an open path to his heart. While we worked, he would talk about everything. One hour he'd be lecturing me on the varieties of grapes, their subtle differences, their flavours and their preferred growing conditions.

The next hour we'd be talking about politics or debating ancient literature or philosophy. When he grew tired of talking, a tune would roll off his tongue.

We sat under the almond tree to rest. As I cracked the nuts from their hard shells and ate them, I gathered my words and asked: "Abouee, do you think Basma is happy?" He remained focused on breaking open an almond, but I could tell my question had surprised him.

"It is in her hands," he said. "She will need to create it. She has the ingredients. Sometimes life chooses for us and we need to make the best of those choices. She is strong and she will be happy." He stood up and changed the subject. "Bring the container and follow me."

I dropped my handful of almonds and followed him. Abouee never talked at the expense of work. Work always came first. If you could keep up production while having a conversation, he would tolerate your questions. If I needed to ask him tough questions or was looking for answers, I always made sure we were working. I couldn't ask him these things at home when my mother was around, but out here in the field, in the open air, when our fingers were engaged and our lungs full of fresh air, I had the freedom to ask him things that daughters never asked their fathers.

Cutting the grape he was pointing to, I said, "If you choose our future grooms, why do we need to fall in love with anyone? I think we should give our hearts a break and only use our brains. I want to put my heart in a jar and throw it away. I don't think there's a need for a heart if love is not a valid feeling." I tossed the grape into the container and moved on to the next one.

"It is not like that." He cut a big grape and handed it to me. "It is just that you need to choose the right person."

"What right person?" I demanded, then said more calmly: "Who do you think is the right person?" I didn't want to close the door on these types of conversations.

Still looking at the vine, he continued, "You should be smart and try not to walk against the wind."

"What if I shield myself?" I asked, more as a statement than a question. "What if I am stronger than the wind?"

He turned to face me with deep care in his eyes. "Wind is OK, but try not to walk against a storm. With the wind, you know which direction it's coming from, but you can't protect yourself against a storm. A storm comes at you from every direction, even opposing ones. If you don't have the same strength as the storm you will be the object in its way, and you will be overturned."

I didn't want to be overturned by the storm and I decided that I would strategically navigate the wind, however strong. We walked home with four large containers brimming with sweet grapes. To be free, I decided to give up on marriage and seal my heart in a jar. I wanted to focus on building my strength and my power. I wanted to be a strong woman with no weaknesses, and I knew now that falling in love was a weakness.

Work is Liberating

ONE MORNING I awoke with a plan. I hadn't spent nights thinking about it; it was one of those moments when you wake up just knowing what you need to do. I'd seen enough of the fate that awaited me if I left my future to my mother and I wasn't about to let that happen. School ended for the day and, instead of boarding the bus that would take me home, I boarded a bus to Beer a-Saba. As soon as I paid the fare, my loose jeans and T-shirt weren't enough to shield me from the nauseating self-consciousness that paralysed me at the front of the bus. Every pair of eyes stared me down, all male eyes, and each heavy step forwards was a fight against the feeling that I was committing a terrible crime. I didn't feel comfortable going to the city without permission, but I knew I had to push against those lines.

When I stepped off the bus, my head spun as I took it all in. Shopkeepers calling out to passersby, girls my age holding hands with boys, some even hugging as they said goodbye, and crowds of people walking in every direction. I had been aware that a completely different world existed only seventeen kilometres from my village, but I had never wanted to explore it. I knew that these people had stolen our lands and exiled our relatives. They were our enemies. I felt afraid, but my determination was greater than my fear, and so was, to my surprise, my curiosity. Everything was different and I wanted to understand why.

I didn't know where to go so I consulted the map on the wall of the bus station. The city made little sense to me, but I knew that my father's store was located next to a historic site, Beer Ibraheem (Abraham's Well), one of the seven wells that gives Beer a-Saba its name. I started walking down the road towards the south of the city. Crossing the main street was my first obstacle. I had read about traffic lights, I had seen them on our small black and white TV, but this was my first time walking into the TV and seeing them with my own eyes. The cars flew past me and I took my lead from the other people crossing. That wasn't so bad. With every street, my unease lessened a little.

I passed a cemetery where a sign written in Arabic told me that it was a Muslim cemetery. I looked out across the cemetery, at the worn-down white gravestones shielded from the sun by the occasional tree. I looked around and noticed an old man standing close to the cemetery gate and asked him, in Arabic, how to get to Beer Ibraheem. He pointed. *That's good enough.* I walked in the direction he had indicated, and just as I decided I must be on the wrong path and was about to lose hope, I caught sight of the well and quickened my pace.

I stood next to the sand-coloured building, the modest dome that housed the well, and I looked north-west, as I had heard my father say to guests whenever they asked him where he worked. I saw a line of grocery stores and darted across the street to examine them more closely. I poked my head into the first, then the second, and, before I had even peered into the third, I saw through the window my father, sitting at the checkout counter reading the newspaper. My heart sank. I hadn't given any thought to what would happen if he found me here in the city by myself, but it seemed a good idea for me to make the first move. I took a deep breath and strolled in, casually saluting him as if he had been expecting me. My father is not an easy man to surprise, but my appearance made him drop his newspaper and blink several times. In that brief pause, I thought maybe he'd be happy to see me, but he wasn't.

"How did you get here?" he asked angrily. Not waiting for my answer, he walked around the counter, grabbed my arm and dragged me into the storeroom. "Are you crazy? What made you come here? This place is not fit for girls."

He left me, closing the sliding door to the storeroom behind him before returning shortly with a bottle of orange juice and a pastry filled with dates. "Stay here until I finish."

I felt bad that I had made my father angry, but how was I supposed to pave my own road if I wasn't willing to get a little sand in my eyes?

I sat down on a small stool to enjoy my cake and looked around the storeroom. The room was lined with shelves, some more organized than others, but things were mostly a mess, still in boxes and arranged in a way that made little sense to me. Everything looked like it had been unloaded quickly, had begun to be put away, but then the process had been interrupted. There were half-opened cardboard boxes with some of the items on the shelves, fresh produce lying next to cleaning products. I finished my cake and decided to get to work. I put all the canned food on one side: the peas, the corn, the tomato paste lined up together on a single shelf. On the other side of the storeroom, I made a space for the fresh legumes. In the back, I carved out some shelf space for the cleaning products and organized them by brand. Once I was happy with my system, I grabbed the broom next to the door and swept the floor, a task that looked like it hadn't been done in a very long time. I spent another twenty minutes dusting until I was satisfied. *This was worth it.* I admired my work for another moment and then pulled out my maths homework. I hated maths, but, somehow, at this moment, I had the patience for it. Perhaps because it was the one place where the answers were clear and straightforward, and I was looking for clear and straightforward answers to the big questions that were churning in my mind.

I was struggling with a problem when my father opened the door. He looked at the newly organized storeroom and his eyes widened with astonishment. His face opened into a smile. "God bless you! This is a great job, *ya bintee*."

I said nothing, but quickly packed up my things and felt a glow of pride. We got into Abouee's yellow van and he asked me what I thought we'd be eating for dinner. We took turns guessing, using this game to avoid a conversation about what had happened that day.

"I'm sure it's rice with tomato," I said.

He laughed. "God forbid!"

We both knew that this was the one thing my mother cooked that he hated.

"I hope it's lentils with chard, with Arabic salad, and baladi olives."

I was too excited about my success at the store to be hungry, but his way of describing the food was starting to make my mouth water. I asked him why some of the items had prices on them and others didn't. He explained that the older items were priced, but that he hadn't got around to pricing the newer stock. He had another worker, but this worker mostly spent his time in the section of the grocery store dedicated to animal feed.

"OK, next time I'll do the pricing." His face turned cold and the easy relations we'd established between us disappeared, but he didn't say anything. Umm Kulthoum came on the official Arabic radio channel. I turned up the volume and we pretended to be too absorbed by her to continue the conversation.

When we arrived home, Ummi came out to welcome Abouee. Her smile vanished when she saw me.

"Where have you been?" she demanded, but I knew this wasn't

a question that I was supposed to answer. If Ummi wanted to find out something, she had her ways of getting the information she needed. "I asked Narjis and she said you took the student bus to Beer a-Saba." There it was. I was so used to fighting with her these days that I didn't even brace myself for her reprimand. "How dare you go without my permission. Go inside and I will teach you a lesson." My father didn't say a word. He didn't even tell her that I had been with him.

I went to the girls' room where my sisters were huddled around the mattress, speaking excitedly. When they saw me, they clucked at me like a group of hens, curious but concerned.

"How did you go by yourself?" Maryam asked. "Were you scared?"

"I went to help Abouee," I said. "I didn't go to play."

My actions were so radical that they didn't know what to make of them. Narjis, who shared the chore of feeding the sheep, impatiently reminded me that it was my turn that day.

"Narjis! It's half past seven and you still haven't fed them?"

"It's your turn," she said bluntly.

We started arguing, me indignant that she had been such a stickler for the rules when what mattered most was that the sheep got fed and she angry that she had to pick up my slack when I decided to go off and do whatever I wanted. Ummi came in and added her own grievances: "Your father is very angry that you went to the store today. It is full of men and you went with your hair uncovered!"

I stopped yelling at Narjis and turned my attention to the bigger wolf. "He's not angry with me. You are."

"He is, but he doesn't know how to tell you."

"There were women who came to buy stuff too. It wasn't only men. If he wants me to cover my hair, I don't mind. Next time, I will."

She pushed me towards the door. "There won't be a next time."

I grabbed the sheep feed container from outside the shack. "There will be a next time," I shot back. I shook the container to make sure she was listening. "Next *times.*"

The next time I went to the store after school, I didn't even greet Abouee. I walked straight to the storeroom and started sticking the prices on the unpriced items. Abouee came in and said: "If you don't know the price just call me," and pointed to the telephone on the wall. I wondered if he said that for reasons of efficiency or to ensure that men wouldn't see me. Abouee's clients were mostly Bedouin from the south who didn't send their girls to school. If they saw a girl working in the city with her father, that would be an unusual sight for them, and it had the potential to cause trouble. I understood that my unorthodox way of doing things needed to fit within certain bounds if I was to carve out the freedom I wanted. I started covering my hair and did my best to avoid being seen so that Abouee would have no excuse to forbid me from working.

I loved the work, especially when my father would come into the storeroom at the end of the day and hand me all the cash to count and sort according to the value of the bills. I was full of ideas about how to improve his operation and earn him more money. During our car rides home, I'd question him about the business; he'd discuss it and then change the subject, still playing our little game. Once I asked him how he decided on the prices in the store. His answer didn't satisfy me so the next time I came by, I went to the other stores to see how they priced the same things. I shared this information with my father, asking him if he wanted to discount those items so that people would be more likely to buy from him.

One day, I was busy organizing the canned food on the shelves when a wiry, tanned man, with salt-and-pepper hair entered. I could tell he wasn't a Bedouin, but my father greeted him warmly.

"*Salaam*, my friend. Come. Meet my daughter. She is top of her class. She insisted that she wanted to help me. I allowed her because I believe girls can do much better than boys."

The man looked at the two of us, then he beamed at me. He said in perfect Arabic, "*Ahsan min meet zalama* [She is better than a hundred men]." They both laughed.

"This is my Jewish friend, Dr Bailey," Abouee said. "He is a professor at the Hebrew University and he works with the Bedouin in the south. He helps them."

I shook his hand. My father walked to the back of the store and we sat down near the front to chat. Since when did Abouee have Jewish friends? Since when could Jews be friendly? I didn't stand on ceremony, but asked him directly why a Jewish person would help the Bedouin community.

He switched to Hebrew. "I love Bedouin culture and life. This is my field of study. I don't know if I help them or not, but every time they ask for help, I do what I can."

He asked me about my school and what I wanted to be when I grew up. I said I wanted to be a lawyer to help my people.

"I am sure you will achieve whatever you plan to do. I can see the spark in your eyes."

He held my hand and saluted me, "*Forsa sa'eeda* [A pleasure to meet you]," and with a final smile he left.

Why was he so nice? Why would he help my people? I was very curious to know more about him and about the outside world through him. Over the next few months, Clinton Bailey also became my friend. He would come to the store on Thursdays, the day when all the Bedouin were in Beer a-Saba for the Bedouin market.

After I had been working at the store for some time, my father built a small factory next to our house so he could grind the animal feed himself and turn a higher profit. The factory consisted of two floors, one for grinding the feed and another for storing it. Our father transported the bags of coarse grain to the factory where Narjis and I unloaded the bags and poured them into the mill. Every aspect of the work was hard, especially cranking the generator to get the whole thing up and running. It took all the strength a thirteen- and fifteen-year-old had to turn the wheel, and, in the winter, when it was cold, we needed to turn it twice as much.

Every Saturday morning, Narjis and I woke up before everyone else, stepped into our work clothes, and wrapped a scarf around our heads so that only our eyes were visible before rushing over to the factory. After we'd ground the first few sacks of barley, the room would disappear in a cloud of white dust. We would fill each bag with fifty kilos of feed and then store the bags in the east section of the factory, layering them and betting who would be able to toss the bag onto the third layer. We never got it on our first try. We prepared the feed for the entire week, and each morning, before school, we loaded twenty bags onto Abouee's truck for him to take to the store.

I never felt like an employee. His leadership made us take ownership of our tasks and he never ordered us around. If we forgot to add a sack of grain to the truck or made a mistake weighing out the feed, he would debrief us at the end of the day, explain the problem, and together we would figure out what had happened and if we needed to put a different system in place to ensure it wouldn't happen again. While Narjis and I worked, Abouee wrote his instructions on the cement wall with a piece of chalk, sweetly drawing a large heart around them: *We need another 50 kilos*, he'd write, and next to it a version of his favourite slogan: *The joy of life is the work you put into it*. When Narjis and I went home for lunch, we'd shower and then Ummi would serve us lunch. Now, we got the nice pieces of chicken. Sitting with all my siblings, savouring a juicy chicken thigh, I felt how powerful it was to be a worker.

Other dealers in the region started buying feed directly from our factory in Laqiya rather than going to the city. I handed over the goods and collected the money. Our work clothes hid the fact that we were girls, which allowed us to be treated equally. One day, Abouee gave me money to give to one of our biggest accounts, a dealer from Gaza. I knew him well and was used to seeing him at the factory delivering wheat and oats. Whenever he saw me, I was in my uniform, covered from head-to-foot, but this time when he showed up, I wore jeans and a T-shirt and had my hair uncovered.

He approached me with tremendous respect. "Your father sent me to get the money," he said.

"Just a moment." I went inside and returned with a big brown envelope and paper and pen. I handed him the envelope, then asked him to sign the paper to confirm that he had received the money.

His eyes narrowed. "I've worked with your father for many years now and he's never asked me to sign."

"That's true. You used to get the money from him, not from me."

The man looked so confused that I could tell he was thinking about more than just the signature. His eyes searched for answers between me, the paper and the ground. "Sorry," he said finally. "You are the worker? It was your voice? Your voice is familiar."

I laughed because I knew that he was surprised to find out who he'd been dealing with all this time. "Yes. I am the worker and I am Amal, Abd al-Kareem's daughter."

He stepped back and examined me as if to make sure that the voice matched the face. He laughed too and asked me who the other worker was.

"My sister," I replied.

He looked up at the sky, smiling and shaking his head. "I can't believe this. All this time I thought you were a couple of men who worked for Abd al-Kareem!"

Still smiling, he looked down at the paper and signed. He pushed the paper towards me and started walking towards his car. "I have to tell you," he said, turning around, "you are a better businessman than your father." He waved goodbye. I ran inside feeling giddy and proud. When Abouee came back from work and finished his ritual of washing and praying, he sat down with all of us to eat.

"What did you ask that man to do? I saw him signing and he had a big smile on his face."

"Of course I made him sign. That's a lot of money. What if he denies that I gave it to him?"

"Our relations are not only about business. We are good friends."

"I understand, but business is business."

"Well, he's already told me that you are sharp and that I should give you more responsibility."

When he said that I knew he was letting me know that he

welcomed my ideas and was grateful for my role in our family business. Over time, I became more of a partner in the business and I expanded the grocery store by selling dairy products and holding a children's toy bazaar during the holidays. Abouee believed in me, but I knew he wouldn't tolerate failure.

Our village wasn't recognized by the state of Israel until the early nineties, which meant that we had no infrastructure, including electricity. The big dairy companies wouldn't supply our village with milk and cheese so I would meet the truck at the end of the paved road outside the village and carry the crates containing the goods back to the small grocery store Abouee had opened in the village. I kept a tight schedule: at five in the morning, I would meet the truck, carry at least fifty litres of milk and fifty containers of cheese back to the store, to open by six. Then I would run to the barn, feed the sheep, eat breakfast and catch the bus to school at quarter past seven.

I was a tough businesswoman. Most people who bought cheese from me paid me at the end of the month when they received their welfare cheques and I recorded every transaction in my notebook. I refused to sell to anyone who didn't pay up, which had repercussions for Ummi. "Business is business," I would explain, but she had to endure their dirty looks as she went about her business in the village.

The toy store came into being because I found out that I could make a large profit buying toys from Hebron and selling them in the village. I figured that people only bought toys around the two big holidays, Eid al-Adha and Eid al-Fitr, so I decided to open a toy bazaar in the run-up to them. On my first trip to meet with the toy sellers in Hebron, I took Narjis. We shared everything: our clothes, our bed, our blanket and even the shower. When we finished our work on Saturday afternoon, we scrubbed each other's backs until we were as red as two carrots. She was modest and I was wild. She used to make me promise that we'd keep our backs turned while we lathered our dusty bodies with soap. I'd promise, but a minute later I'd jump in front of her just to hear her scream.

Although Narjis is two years older than me, I was in charge. I rented a minivan with a driver, and Narjis and I travelled to Hebron. We went to Bab a-zaawiya, a historic market in the old city that has since been turned into apartments for Jewish settlers. In those days, it was the city's beating heart: a huge open-air market, nestled in biblical stones with sellers belting out the price of almonds and sweets, scarves and shoes, stall after stall, a patchwork of aroma and colour.

When we arrived, I asked about the wholesale toy dealers and we were ushered into a room full of men in suits.

"Let's go," Narjis whispered. "They won't sell anything to you."

A man in his twenties informed us that we were in the wholesale department and that they didn't sell to individuals. He pointed to another area of the market and told us to go there.

I stood my ground. "No, thank you. I am buying for my store."

"What store? What do you want?"

I pointed to the toys displayed in the hall. "I will choose from here and tell you how many units I need of each."

He accompanied us to the other side of the hall and I consulted Narjis about which toys to get.

"You're Bedouin," he said, hearing our accent.

I nodded.

After we had made our selection, one of his workers stacked the toys in the van.

"Next time come with your father," the dealer told me.

He was much taller than me, but I felt like I was looking down at him.

"Sure, man," I said, handing him the cash and pausing just long enough to see the look on his face. I liked showing men who was the boss.

We bought groceries at the vegetable market and couldn't resist picking up falafel for the whole family. In Beer a-Saba, it cost five times as much. I recorded the expenses in my notebook, then we hopped back into the minivan, Narjis taking the back seat and me sitting in the front next to the driver, as usual. The smell of the falafel filled the minivan, but I did my best to ignore it, knowing that I would enjoy it most sitting in the *hosh* with my brothers and sisters.

As we pulled into the village, my brothers ran over to greet us. They chased us to the store, where we unloaded the toys. Ummi waited until the driver left – she didn't know him – before coming out to inspect the toys. We had plastic trucks, cars and water guns for the boys and Barbies, stuffed animals and hair accessories for the girls. She squealed and congratulated us while my brothers and young cousins gathered behind her, whining for toys.

The bazaar would open in two days' time. I told the boys that they could pick a toy and I would save it for them. My brother Ibraheem, who was nine years old then, didn't like that idea. He wanted his water gun right away. I refused. Ummi grabbed the gun from the pile and gave it to him. Ummi always said she was lifeless before the boys were born. She never refused their requests, so their sisters had to make sure they were polite and responsible. I looked at the price list, charged her double as the dealer had suggested, and demanded she pay. Her jaw dropped. She shook her head, but I didn't budge. She stared at me to see if I was serious, and finally grabbed the bills from inside her dress and threw them at me.

In the days leading up to the holidays, I added community work to my already packed schedule. I trained children for a *debka* dance performance that we would give on the Eid at the community club. I cleared the piles of wheat and barley in the factory so we could practise. With each stomp, we kicked up large clouds of white dust that clung to our clothes. The mothers in the village complained, but they didn't stop their children from coming.

I remember when a girl of six left the group when her mother was beaten by her father, and the two of them, mother and daughter, moved to be with the mother's parents who lived in another village. A few weeks later, after seeking forgiveness from his wife and her parents, the father brought his wife and child back to the village.

They arrived the day before the performance. I ran into them on my way to Hebron to pick up some last-minute things for the celebration.

The girl's mother thrust a few bills into my hands. "Please, please buy the dancing uniform for my daughter and let her take part in the show tomorrow."

I tried to give the money back to her, telling her that I couldn't possibly train her daughter in time.

The woman pleaded with me, tears leaking from the corners of her eyes. I couldn't stand to watch her beg. "I'll be back by noon," I said. "Send her to the factory. I'll train her."

When I returned from Hebron, Ummi shouted at me to go and see what was happening in the factory. I heard music and when I walked in the dust almost choked me. My two brothers, Ibraheem and Ousaama, who were nine and ten, and our youngest sister, Wafaa, who was five, stood in a line, training the new girl. I hugged them and kissed their dusty little faces when, out of the corner of the factory, Jidatee appeared. Jidatee had seen the little girl sitting in the shade of the factory and asked my younger brothers if they knew the dance. They told her that Wafaa knew it, but that they needed music and weren't allowed to use the stereo without my permission. "You may need her permission. I don't," she had told them, before grabbing the stereo and leading the whole gang into the factory.

Between the ages of twelve and eighteen, I ran two adult literacy classes, a *debka* dance group, a theatre group and summer camps. I also organized village clean-ups. On the political front, I belonged to the Sons of Laqiya Association for which I organized Land Day protests each year and demonstrations against house demolitions. For the family, I took care of the sheep and the grocery store, ran the factory and organized the toy bazaar, and I still found time to do my homework.

My grandmother used to hold my arm, grab a piece of skin between her fingers, and say, "This piece of skin, the more you stretch it, the stronger it becomes. If you leave it, it will shrink. Train your body to serve you. Never fear physical work. With seven hours of sleep, everything will be as good as new."

University Years

Competing from Behind the Starting Line

A S A CHILD, I had always dreamed of becoming a lawyer. When Abouee joined me and the sheep to roam in the mountains after our day's work, he would pull out an empty crate of Jaffa oranges, turn it upside down and invite me to defend my case. The issues I defended were political and personal. Impassioned pleas for the Israelis to stop demolishing our houses, for girls to be allowed to play the same games as boys, and for the government to give us back our land. On top of that crate, I was on top of the world. I had something to say and someone to be. For political causes, I could usually win Abouee's favour. For feminist ones, Abouee would often respond with: "But, *ya bintee*, girls don't have the muscles to fight and protect themselves!" To which I would reply: "My muscles are here", pointing at my head.

But even though I had good grades, I was graduating from one of the most disadvantaged high schools in Israel and getting into law school was a long shot. We didn't receive a good enough education to compete with students from Jewish schools. Our matriculation exams were easier and when universities were looking at who to choose, we hadn't taken enough units in the necessary subjects to give us a fighting chance. The government provided education to marginalized communities, but not one that was substantial enough to give us an opportunity to change our circumstances and join Jewish society on an equal footing.

While preparing for my matriculation exams, I continued with all my other duties: working at the mill, running activities for children and teaching women how to read. My priorities were family, community and school, in that order. I would finish working at the factory, then fetch my book to study for my exams. One day after I'd spent a few hours organizing the sacks of ground barley, I admired my work for a moment, caressing my hands, which were rubbed raw from the burlap, then selected a couple of sacks in the corner of the factory as a perfect study spot. I brought my notes over to my makeshift desk and spread them out.

It was noon and Jidatee was passing through the factory on her way to the outhouse when she noticed me bent over my notes in deep concentration.

"It is very hot today, watch out for snakes," she said simply, the way people who live with the land do.

Almost as soon as she left, I saw something move behind the mill. At first, I thought it was a dog who had found his way into our factory, but when I went to take a closer look, the sight of a thick, black tail slithering wildly between the wall and the side of the mill sent me running out screaming for Abouee.

I barged into the *diwaan*, which was full of men eating lunch. That would have been bad enough, but to make matters worse Abouee was entertaining four guests, four strangers to the tribe. Abouee immediately ordered me to stop screaming. He apologized to the guests, blaming my hysterics on my overactive imagination, but one of the guests was more sympathetic. "Let's check," he said. "Just in case."

"No, no. Please finish your meal," Abouee said. The look he shot my way told me that I should be ashamed. The man who was inclined to believe me was resolute. He calmly got up from the rug, and walked with me back to the factory. Abouee and the other guests followed. Jidatee was waiting outside.

"It's hot," she said, "and she is tired from studying. Her brain has stopped working!" She jabbed her thumb at me.

The man picked up a stick from outside the factory and rapped it against the side of the mill. The sound made me jump and the black tail jolted in response. "It's here!" he shouted. "Get me a metal rod. A long one! Hurry. Move the children away."

At this point, the snake's presence in the factory was a huge relief. Interrupting guests during a meal was completely unacceptable and anything less than a real threat would have resulted in a severe punishment for me and, worse, humiliation for my father. All the men stood around the mill; my siblings and cousins who had heard me screaming through the village gathered at the entrance to the factory, craning their necks to see the action. The guest commanded Abouee to hit the opposite side of the mill. The tail slithered towards the guest and he whacked it as hard as he could, stunning it. Then he crouched down and jimmied the tool underneath the base of the mill, but most of the snake was still hiding under the grinder. The guest commanded the other men to push the mill to one side and we all gasped.

As a shepherd, I had seen many snakes. Most of them were the colour of sand with yellow dots, about the girth of three fingers and as long as my arm. One time, when I was trying to catch one of my goats who had escaped from its enclosure, I picked up a rock to throw so that it would run towards me, when a white snake slithered up my arm. But this snake was the biggest one I had ever seen. Three metres long with an oily black body as fat as my wrist and speckled with white and brown spots. Everyone was shouting. The men warned us all to stay back. The snake had wrapped its body around the rod and was wriggling violently. The guest was using all his strength to pin it down and Abouee struck the snake's head with a rock three or four times. With each strike the body twitched, until finally it stopped moving.

The story of the snake circulated around the village for months. It became an emblem of my determination. When I received my diploma – and only three of us studying at the school in Tel a-Saba did – people would congratulate me and tell whoever would listen that I was a hard worker who had studied as much as I could, even in a dusty factory with giant snakes. Anyone who ran into Jidatee would hear her say, "That's Amal. A book in one hand and a hoe in the other."

I wanted to pursue a law degree, but Ben Gurion University, the university closest to my village, didn't have a law school. There was no chance that I would be allowed to study in Haifa or Jerusalem and live away from my family. I decided not to fight that because I knew that I wouldn't get in anyway. From a day trip my high school had taken to BGU, I knew that the university had a social work programme, and I convinced my father that social work would be a better path since I was already engaged in community work. Abouee joked that a social worker was essentially a lawyer for the community. Filling out the application forms was confusing and difficult, but Basma sat with me until we'd completed them. After triple-checking that everything was right, we folded the forms into an envelope and Basma drove me to the mailbox at the entrance to Beer a-Saba. Dropping off that letter filled me with a vision of freedom. If I was accepted, I would be the first woman in my tribe to attend university. By that time, two of my brothers were studying away: Salmaan was doing his pharmacy degree in Italy and Yousef was in high school in Haifa. Basma and Na'ama were out of the house and both married. I was counting on Abouee to pay for my education, since all the money I made I gave to him.

Four weeks later, the head of the tribe who was responsible for the post sent his son to our shack with a letter from BGU. I held the letter in my hand. Up until that moment, I had felt the possibility of this new future. Now, with the official document between my fingers, I experienced a new sensation: fear. What if I *wasn't* accepted? I didn't have another plan. I opened the envelope and darkness filled my eyes. Just as when you spot a rogue horse in the desert, my gaze was drawn to the sentence: "Unfortunately, we must inform you that your application has been rejected." I sat down in the *hosh* and cried.

Narjis came over. "Don't be sad. You can try again."

Ummi walked over from the kitchen and contributed her two

cents: "Why don't you go to teachers' college? You can be a teacher like Basma. Being a teacher is good for women. You will have a job in the village."

"She doesn't want to become a teacher," Narjis shot back. "You know that she wants to go to university." She finished her sentence and looked at me to see if her answer satisfied me.

"But it is not in our hands," Ummi said. "We can't force them to take her."

I brushed them off and ran to the barn to be alone. I was angry that my many activities cut into my study time and I thought that maybe if I had studied more, I would have been accepted. When Abouee came home from work, Narjis told him about the rejection letter. He said nothing. He continued about his evening rituals, unfolding his prayer rug and touching his nose to the embroidered mat to recite his prayers. I imagine this time was used for reflection as well as devotion. He was never one to come up with a quick solution to a difficult situation. When he had finished, he sat on the mattress and my sister Maryam placed a tray of food in front of him: lentil and chard soup with Arabic salad chopped fine and dressed with olive oil from our orchard. And, of course, a pile of *saj* pita for dipping in everything.

I sat next to Abouee and ate in silence. I chewed but couldn't taste. My heart was heavy from falling so far from that place of promise and possibility. Abouee finished eating, tucked a pillow under his elbow, and sat back. Ummi drifted in and out, clearing the dishes more delicately than usual, then served him a cup of sweet tea. He took one sip and looked at me. "Have you fed the sheep?"

"Yes," I said. His question pulled me back into my surroundings. He continued as if on the same subject: "I don't want you to be sad. If they don't accept you this year, they will next year."

I didn't respond.

Basma entered the *hosh* with one hand on her belly, heavy with new life. She lived a short walk from us and would visit every day. I don't know if it was out of duty or the desire to get away from her husband. She used to say that being with us rekindled her humanity. She sat beside Abouee, and rested her elbow on his legs. I went inside to fetch the letter and handed it to her.

"Let your sister rest. Can't you see she needs to catch her breath?" Abouee said, patting Basma's back.

Basma unfolded the letter, but her smile faded as quickly as it had appeared when she saw me carrying it. "Don't be sad. It is not easy to get into university. You need very good grades."

"But I am one of only three people who passed the matriculation exams at my school! How come I—"

"At your school," Basma said with the irritatingly matter-of-fact tone of an older sister. "Do you know how many students apply from throughout the country? Do you think that you can compete with Jewish students who come from the best schools? You may be the best in your school, but you are not competing with your school's students."

I knew Basma was right, but I needed to hear something else. Something supportive.

Abouee sensed my hurt. "Don't worry, *Kul ta'akhayra feeha khayra* [every delay has its blessing]. Use this year to improve your grades and help me with my work. *Inshallah*, next year you will get in. I have a good feeling."

Maryam suggested that I take a teaching job, since many Bedouin schools hired high school graduates because they didn't have enough teachers. She had heard about a school in Um Mitnan, one of the unrecognized villages in the Naqab, that was looking for someone.

Taking Pride in Your Donkey

UM MITNAN IS a small village next to Dimona. The land between Laqiya and Um Mitnan is desolate and empty, like the face of the moon. It is a true desert, with hardly any vegetation and even fewer buildings. Most of the unrecognized villages are located in this area and the people there live without access to basic services, in harsh conditions. Since we didn't have a telephone, the only way to get in touch was to go to the school and speak to the principal in person. I travelled with a teacher from my village who taught at the elementary school there. I sat in the back seat because sitting beside him would have been considered improper. We drove in silence, listening to Fairuz coming out of the car speakers. Even her luscious tones couldn't breathe life into the barren silence between us, a silence that seemed to echo in the land around us. Or was it the other way around?

After forty minutes of driving, he broke the silence to tell me that the school was another fifteen minutes away on a dirt road. The car lurched and swerved until finally he pointed to a building I could just make out in the distance. "Do you see those shacks?" he asked.

As we pulled up to the school, I saw as many as thirty donkeys tied to the fence. I couldn't believe it. My uncles used to ride donkeys to school, but that was in the sixties. It was now the nineties. We parked the car in the small lot in front of the school and I followed him inside. The school consisted of four classrooms made from corrugated metal sheets forming a square. The classrooms opened onto a courtyard with a single tree at the centre. I could see the children running and laughing. As we walked past them, they stopped and stared at me. They knew the teacher and greeted him respectfully. They looked at me, curious but uncertain. Not only was I a stranger, I was also a woman where all the teachers were men.

The teacher took me to the principal's office, then went off to attend to his class. Waiting for the principal to return, I sat on one of the chairs in front of his desk and looked up at the two framed photographs that presided over the small room: one of Yitzhak Shamir, the prime minister, and another of Chaim Herzog, the president. Those pictures suffocated me. Why would Palestinian schools celebrate the very leaders who oppressed them?

When I was in fifth grade, our teachers had taught us the Israeli national anthem. They wanted us to sing it for Independence Day.

When the teacher left the class to fetch something, we tore down the flags, stuffed them in the bin, and lit a fire using a lighter one of the children had stolen from his father. The teacher returned and put out the fire, which posed more of a political danger than a physical one. He asked who was responsible and everyone pointed to me. When he asked me why I had done it, I replied, red-faced and furious: "They killed our brothers in Lebanon." He wasn't pleased, but my answer seemed to satisfy him. He told us that we didn't have to sing if we didn't want to.

I heard the principal's footsteps and left Herzog and Shamir to stare down at me from their tidy frames. The principal sat down and asked me if I had the *bagrut* certificate – the diploma awarded for passing high school matriculation exams – and I said that I did.

"Who is your father?" he asked. While this question might seem wildly inappropriate in most professional settings, prohibited even, I didn't think much of it. He was trying to assess if I was trustworthy, credible and accomplished, and asking about my family was a legitimate way to do that.

"Abd al-Kareem."

"Oh! The one who owns the grocery store next to Beer Ibraheem in Beer a-Saba," he said with a smile.

"Yes."

Then he looked at me more closely and said in a kind of astonished whisper: "Are you Basma's sister?" He knew Basma because they had attended teachers' college at the same time.

I nodded.

"I knew it! You look like her."

He pulled out a notebook from his desk drawer and started leafing through it.

"Look. We don't have a position right now, but we might have one next month. You can start now as a volunteer and if we get funding for the position then it's yours."

The offer caught me off guard. On the one hand, I wanted the opportunity to get to know life in a village that was different from my own, but, on the other hand, I wasn't prepared to work for free. I wanted to be paid and save up for university. On top of that, the situation was entirely unconventional. Why would a school funded by the education ministry have a teacher working for free? It made no sense. Not only would I be a female teacher in a school where all the teachers were men, but I was also an outsider, a Bedouin from a thriving village. Why would I volunteer my time and forgo an income to help a community other than my own when I could easily remain in Laqiya and continue earning money in Abouee's business?

I responded with a compromise: I would volunteer for two weeks and see if it worked for me, but in the meantime I would also look for a paid position at another school. He agreed, although I could tell my assertiveness surprised him. He stood up and asked me to follow him. One class was missing a teacher that morning and he needed me to replace him. I stopped mid-step. "But I'm not ready. I just came today to talk to you about the position."

He waved his hand. "You don't need to be ready. It's third grade and you know what to do. Ask them to copy the text. Just keep them quiet."

I didn't like the idea that schoolchildren were like animals who needed to be tamed, but drawing closer to the classroom I heard yelling, laughter and running feet. As soon as the children saw us, the sounds ceased as if someone had pushed the mute button on a remote control. Within seconds, they took their seats and stared straight ahead. Their stiff silence reminded me of how much control our teachers exerted on us as children. In the classroom, everything felt too tight, as if the looming threat of a beating made the room shrink.

The principal introduced me and made sure to say, loud and clear, that if anyone didn't behave they would be sent to his office. Then he looked at them. "Understood?"

All forty heads nodded in unison, with a speed rooted in fear.

Forty children sat squashed together at three long tables. There was hardly enough space for them to sit comfortably, let alone for their books, papers and pencils. Their clothes looked like hand-medowns, a wardrobe that rotated between siblings and cousins, allowing everyone to save face at school. I smiled at them, which told them "Don't take me too seriously," and the classroom reverted to a circus. I changed my face back into a scowl and they returned to their seats, backs straight, hands folded, looking more like rows of soldiers than children. Their obedience saddened me. It was born out of a fear so pervasive it had become commonplace. Fear narrows the mind and closes the heart. Rather than approaching authority with respect, we obeyed it out of fear. When we live in fear, we blindly accept the crumbs we are offered, saying, "*Todah, todah* [Thank you, thank you]," when we don't even have enough chairs for all the schoolchildren. When we live in fear, we thank the oppressor for simply allowing us to exist. The schools crushed our spirits from the start. That way we wouldn't question. That way we wouldn't rebel. In that context, fun could be a revolutionary act. I decided I would treat the class like a summer camp so the children could experience school without fear. We played a game to get to know each other. After a few minutes, I had breathed life back into the room.

I finished my first day exhausted but satisfied. On my way out, the children in my class stopped me in the schoolyard to wish me goodbye while the others whispered to their friends: "She's your teacher? Oh! You are lucky!"

When I got to the car, there was another teacher waiting for a lift. "Watch out," he warned. "If you continue like this, they'll ride on your back,"– meaning that they would take advantage of me.

"My back is strong and wide," I said. "Theirs are brittle and small. I prefer that they ride on mine rather than I ride on theirs."

He ignored me the entire journey home.

One day during my two-week trial, I stood in for the gym teacher with the sixth grade gym class, the highest grade in the school. The higher the grade, the fewer girls there were and the more who wore the scarf. To remove the walls between us, I started to wear the scarf. I wanted all the students, and especially the girls, to understand that, although we were from different tribes and different villages, our culture was the same. I wanted them to know that I too understood the struggle of coming from an unrecognized village.

The school didn't have physical barriers separating the girls from the boys, but at recess the divisions were clear. During class time, girls and boys sat together, but out in the schoolyard the boys played soccer and the younger girls played dodgeball while the older ones chatted. I used recess as a time to integrate myself with the children and to facilitate activities for them. We would play tag, run races and invent all sorts of games. As the only female teacher, I didn't feel comfortable sitting in the teachers' lounge. The principal and other teachers criticized me for playing with the boys, but I ignored them. I figured that as I wasn't being paid, I had the right to do what I wanted. I learned quickly that asking for permission sets a dangerous precedent, one that limits your freedom.

After three months, they hired me but only paid me a part-time wage even though I worked full time. As I gained their trust, the children opened up to me about their problems: difficulties they had at school and challenges they faced at home. I wanted to bridge the gap between the school and the tribe, to close the rift between those two very different worlds, so I began visiting families after school and encouraging homeroom teachers to join me. One time, a girl who wasn't in my class but whom I knew from our recess activities didn't show up for two weeks. When she returned, she hardly spoke and spent recess sitting alone. She told me that her father had left her mother and siblings for a second wife. He had kicked them out of the house and they were now living in a dilapidated shack with a dirt floor while her father and his new wife lived in the home where she had previously lived, an attractive wooden hut she passed every morning on her way to school. Her teacher and I visited the little girl's family that afternoon. We sat with her mother and drank tea. Although there was nothing we could do, our presence was enough to say: "We're here for you and we understand."

I stayed on at the school for almost an entire year. It was March and sports day was coming up. In my village, our school would organize a full day of activities for all the students with five or six different events and prizes at the end. I told the principal, Ali, that I wanted to organize the same thing at this school. I would need the teachers' participation and some equipment. Ali was used to my wild ideas by now. He let out a hollow laugh and pointed to the metal cabinet adjacent to his desk. I opened it and found nothing except a thick layer of dust and one deflated soccer ball sitting alone on the bottom shelf.

"We don't do sports day here. Why would we miss a day of school just for the children to play?" he asked.

"These children will learn more from playing sports than from sitting through a class!"

He didn't like the way I was talking, but I refused to give up. "You won't have to do anything. I will bring whatever we need from my village. The teachers can participate only if they want to and I will train the older children to facilitate the games."

That is another lesson I had learned: make it easy for people to say yes. If the principal didn't have to do anything, why would he object?

"Fine. But it won't be a full day. You can have the last two periods. This is a school, not a playground."

"Of course," I replied, although we both knew that I had won.

But how was I going to organize a sports day for five hundred students without any equipment? It was something I had said in the heat of the moment. I had convinced him with a savoury aroma when all I had in the pan was a little oil and an onion. I left his office and walked across the schoolyard, past the tree in the centre, and out of the gate where the donkeys stood tied to the fence. *A donkey race! Why not? If that's what we have, that's what we'll use.* At that moment, I saw the bigger picture. This wasn't just about using the resources we had, it was about transforming those resources into something meaningful, something to be proud of. For this sports day, we weren't going to play Western games like soccer or dodgeball; we were going to turn to the indigenous games that Bedouin had played on this land for as far back as the oldest among us could remember. I sat down next to one of the donkeys and made a list of the games that we used to play when we were young: donkey racing, long and short distance races, the potato sack race, jump rope and the wolf, the shepherd and the sheep. I classified them according to age groups and then I hurried back to Ali's office with the list in my hand.

He glanced up before returning to the document on his desk. "Is there something else? I see you are excited."

"Yes. This sports day will be *very* special."

I told him about the idea, waving my hands to convey my excitement and rouse his soul. I wanted him to feel it. When I finished, he stood up.

"Hasn't anyone told you that you are crazy?"

"Yes," I said, still smiling, still convinced that my idea was brilliant.

"Do you think that the students will ride their donkey in front of their classmates? They are ashamed of them. They arrive early so that even the teachers won't see them riding them."

"They will be proud of their donkeys after today," I said, seizing the air with my fingers, creating hope with my hands.

I left his office and went to sit on a small patch of green grass that was growing in one of the corners of the schoolyard. Anything that could grow in this tough climate was an inspiration, and inspiration was what I needed if I was going to get the children and the teachers on board. During recess, I gathered the fifth and sixth grade students and told them about sports day and the kinds of events we were going to organize. When they heard about the donkey race, the excitement that had been bubbling died down. They looked at each other and whoever owned a donkey stared at the dirt. There were almost thirty donkeys who showed up at the school each morning, and each donkey might bring with it as many as four children. Two or three rode on the donkey's back and one held the reins. I understood how they felt. I told them about my years as a shepherd herding sheep in Laqiya's green mountains. I told them

167

about riding a donkey from the field to my house and the fondness I had for him, even though he didn't always listen. They couldn't believe it. A teacher who was also a shepherd? Who rode a donkey? As I spoke, I could feel their shame turn to curiosity. They became less agitated, the ones who were looking down met my gaze, and finally one of the boys asked me what colour my donkey was.

"Brown," I said.

"Mine's black! And his name is Farhood."

Everyone laughed. It was a laugh of relief. The kind of laugh that is about accepting something that has been kept hidden away under the rug and realizing that there is nothing to be ashamed of.

"Every donkey participating in the race must have a name and his owner will decorate him in his finery and jewellery," I continued.

They all agreed and added that there must be prizes for the winners.

The week before the event, preparations were at their peak. Even the teachers who had at first held back took responsibility for different stations. This event was not only about bringing pride to indigenous identity, but also about dismantling the barrier between the school and the community. I insisted that the track for the donkey race not be restricted to the area around the school, but that it pass through the surrounding neighbourhood. When I sensed a positive reaction from the teachers and students, I decided to go one step further: I got the parents involved.

The teachers informed me that the fathers, who were mostly illiterate, rarely visited the school so as not to be shamed, and mothers never came by because they did not want to be seen by men they did not know. I suggested that we organize activities that would play to the parents' skills. We decided on a horse race for the fathers on the same track we had constructed for the donkey race. The students enlisted their parents: the boys went to the *diwaan* to find out who wanted to take part in the race and the girls went to the house of an elderly woman in the village to ask her advice on what kind of activity the women would enjoy. She suggested *seeja*, a strategy game similar to chequers, and they decided that the women would gather in a house near the school so they would have their own private space.

The night before sports day, I couldn't sleep. I imagined that all my students felt the same way. This was a significant day. A day for celebrating our culture, for not denying it in favour of a national curriculum.

As the car pulled up to the school, I saw that along the fence was a beautiful parade of donkeys, adorned in fabric of many colours and laden with fancy jewellery. Each donkey also had a card around its neck with its name written in big letters, so that everyone could pick one to cheer for.

When I got out of the car, one of the children rushed over and grabbed my hand to show me his donkey. "This is my donkey, Samhoud. I named him after yours." I laughed and congratulated Samhoud on his red and gold robe. The sun seemed to be smiling on us with gentle rays that brought love into the harsh lives these children had known. Today was an opportunity for us all to be proud of where we came from and proud of what we knew. With the children running with me and hugging me, I could hardly make my way to the teachers' lounge.

Ali the principal entered the lounge. He always dressed well, but today he looked extra sharp. Conversation died down and the teachers who had been reading the newspapers folded them and turned towards him.

"I expect everyone to cooperate with the students to make this day a success," he said. His enthusiasm and support meant a lot to me. Although he thought I was crazy – and regularly told me so – he understood how deeply I cared for the students. Each teacher received the equipment for their respective stations and left the lounge to set them up with their team.

The donkey race launched the festivities. Thirty donkeys stood in several rows. The morning sun shimmered on the creatures' glittering costumes and the riders sat atop intricately stitched saddles, the promise of victory in their eyes. It was perhaps the first time these boys had sat on their donkeys without shame on their faces. An ear-splitting whistle broke the anticipation. The donkeys and the riders sprinted off, weaving around the nearby village where men, women and children stood together on either side of the dirt path, clapping and shouting, singing the *zagareet* and cheering on their favourite riders as they stormed by. Next was the horse race. Seven fathers participated. The whole community had come together, and for a brief time there was a shared space in which men and women might celebrate together.

Sports day consisted of a series of events organized from different stations. Students of the same grade competed with one another and went together from station to station. At one point during the day, a female student and I walked over to the shack, a few metres from the school, where the women had gathered to play *seeja*. Women of all ages lounged on mattresses and embroidered cushions, dressed in their finest clothes. You would have thought you were at a wedding! Their earrings bounced when they laughed and the whole room felt like it was dancing. When the last round of *seeja* ended, I wrote down the name of the winner, congratulated her, and turned to leave. An old woman stopped me and said: "Please, *ya bintee*. Do not say the name of the winner in front of everyone. Say her son's name and give him the award."

I wanted to protest, but the words "the people of Mecca are the most knowledgeable about the valleys and the mountains" stopped me. When that saying entered my mind, I remembered that the people of a certain place are the most knowledgeable about the customs of that place. This was not my village so I should not impose my way of thinking on them.

"All right," I said. "But I'll say the name of her daughter, not her son."

The old woman laughed and looked to the others for their response before nodding her head in agreement.

At the end of the day, the students and teachers gathered in the schoolyard, where we had built a stage out of tables and heavy camel-hair rugs from which to hand out prizes. The mothers did not join us, but many of the fathers did.

In the weeks that followed, I received many invitations to visit families from different unrecognized villages near the school. After school, I'd leave with my students and together we would go to visit a mother here, an aunt there, and a grandmother someplace else. Sports day helped to break down the invisible yet palpable barriers between the school and the community.

I suggested to Ali that I organize literacy classes for women, similar to the ones I had taught in my village, and that we could host them at the school. His eyes widened while I spoke. Widened not in wonder, but in alarm. "We must be careful. You don't understand the traditions here. Yes, some people enjoyed sports day, but not everyone."

He continued, "One of the fathers asked that his daughter not participate in your classes. Some parents think that your presence at the school could corrupt the morals of the girls."

I had heard this answer before. He was using tradition to bury anything he wanted to get rid of. I looked him dead in the eye, just as Jidatee had taught me, and said: "These are also my traditions. I am from here. I am a Bedouin and I know how to respect our traditions." A week later I was teaching reading and writing to a group of seven women, and the mother of the girl whose father had complained was one of my students.

A Lesson in Politics

DURING THIS TIME, the Oslo process* between Israel and the Palestine Liberation Organization (PLO) was at its peak. I followed the talks closely, with mixed feelings. On the one hand, how

---

* A period of negotiations between Israel and the PLO that began in secret in Oslo in 1990 with the general aims of reaching a peace treaty and agreeing terms for Palestinian self-governance in Gaza and the West Bank.

could the PLO recognize Israel without a complete withdrawal from Gaza and the West Bank? On the other hand, I wanted so badly to find a solution that would allow me and my people to have our own state. The day Israel recognized the right of the Palestinians to a state meant everything to me.* Our flag, the emblem of our emancipation, had been my saving grace all these years. It had become a symbol of hope and freedom, something to rally us towards a common goal, but it was also a piece of my identity that I had to keep hidden. Now, I could let it fly. Now, a fourteen-year-old girl wouldn't be arrested for waving that flag on a school bus. Now that flag of mine was something I could share.

That day I entered the teachers' lounge and asked what people thought about the Oslo process. After an uncomfortably long silence, someone said: "We do not talk about politics in school and we do not interfere in matters outside the framework of education."

"You don't talk about everyday life?" I was itching for a fight. "Everything in our life is political."

Another teacher, Nayef, said: "We don't want to be fired or imprisoned, so if you want to talk about such things, please do so but not here and not with us. We have jobs that we want to keep."

He said it nervously, but it was clear that he was telling me to leave the room. His father was the sheikh of the local tribe, which meant that his words, no matter how timid or soft, were backed by authority. I felt sorry for these teachers. If they lived in a prison of fear, how would they be able to free our children?

I looked at Nayef and, at that moment, decided to respond regardless of his social position. I wanted the other teachers to see that we didn't have to fear someone because of their social class.

"I am entitled to speak about anything I want, and our students have the right to know what is going on." I came closer to him and continued: "If the Shabak ask, tell them that I was the one who spoke

---

* On 13 September 1993 Yitzhak Rabin, Prime Minister of Israel, and PLO leader, Yasser Arafat, shook hands on the White House lawn to mark the signing of a Declarations of Principles for peace between the Palestinians and the Israelis.

about Oslo." I finished my sentence and left the room leaving a well of disbelief behind me.

That morning I was teaching fifth grade Arabic literature. I asked the students to put away their books and take out a piece of paper. "Draw the Palestinian flag," I instructed them. Not one hand moved, and they shot nervous glances at one another: some didn't know how to draw the flag, others would never dare draw it at school. They fidgeted in their seats while I drew a map of Palestine with the 1967 borders.

"Who is watching the news?" I asked. "What's going on between the Palestinians and Israelis?"

One of the students raised his hand and answered, as children often do, with an example of how political conflict affects their daily lives. "I can go and visit my uncles in Gaza. There will be peace."

Most of the students more or less knew the shape of the map, but had no clue about the flag, her shape, her colours. The only ones who had an idea were those whose parents were originally from Gaza or the West Bank. I began discussing the current political situation and the importance of the Oslo process when Ali entered my class, wiped the board clean and ordered me to follow him to his office.

As soon as we were inside his office, Ali shut the door.

"You are crazy! What are you doing? Even if I agree with you, don't you see that there are eyes and ears that can report you to the Shabak?"

He turned his chair around and sat down, gripping the back of the seat with his hands. "I know that you don't care. I know that you are not afraid. You don't have children to feed, but me, I do." His voice grew louder. "I have children to feed and I will not let you ruin my reputation with the education minister." Then he fired me.

I didn't argue. I left the school and walked all the way to the highway with our conversation playing again and again in my mind. *What was wrong? Was he really scared? Or was he using his fear as an excuse not to talk about these issues?*

The next day I stayed home. Ummi asked why and I made up a

story about the school not needing any replacements that day. That evening Salaame, the teacher who used to drive me to Um Mitnan, came by our house. My brothers Ousaama and Ibraheem ran over to tell me that there was a man there to see me. Although this was unconventional, and even dangerous, my family was used to unfamiliar men coming to speak with me because I was so active in the community with the family business and my projects. My brothers followed me outside our *hosh* to where the visitor stood waiting, and walked over to his car to check that there wasn't another man inside.

The teacher greeted me and said that Ali, the principal, had sent him to ask me to return to the school.

"You have to come. If not for him, come for your students. This morning when I parked the car all the children were expecting to see you. They were very disappointed. They followed me, asking, "Where is *moalema* [teacher] Amal? You have to come back.""

I wanted to go back and Salaame had convinced me in a very smart way. He knew that if I returned it wouldn't be because Ali needed me, but because the children did. I returned the very next day, grateful to be there, but also aware that the teachers acted even more coldly than usual towards me. Nothing I did could win their favour. They would always see me as a threat. I stopped going to the teachers' lounge altogether and focused all my efforts on bringing more freedom into the classroom.

A couple of months after I'd been fired, Ali called us all into the teachers' lounge to announce an official visit from the head of the government department that oversaw the education of the Negev Bedouin. He wanted to orchestrate a typical piece of theatre: a group of girls waving the Israeli flag would greet the delegation at the gate; a group of boys would recite a poem in Hebrew; and, finally, the teachers would serve our guests Bedouin mansaf* in the lounge. The teachers nodded enthusiastically and suggested more ways to ingratiate themselves with these visitors. I shifted in my seat and the

---

* Lamb cooked in fermented yoghurt and served with rice.

teacher next to me could tell that I was going to say something that would make Ali angry. He nudged me. "Forget it. Let it go."

His intervention made me even more determined to speak up. "I think this is a great opportunity." Was she really saying something positive about all of this, their faces seemed to say.

"We can show him around and we can show him how three children sit together at one desk, how there are more than forty children per class, that we have no running water, and that our toilets are outhouses by the side of the fence."

By now I was used to the lengthy silence that followed after I opened my mouth. Ali adjusted his collar. "I don't want you to play any part in it!" he said. "If you want, you can stay at home. I don't need trouble."

I didn't push it, but there was no way I was staying home that day.

The day of the visit, everything was organized according to Ali's masterplan: an Israeli flag hung in every classroom and two flags adorned the gate that opened onto the schoolyard; what we called "the library" – two rickety shelves by the principal's office – was reorganized so the books were in alphabetical order; and the large metal water containers had been repainted a dark blue to hide the glaring orange rust that served as a reminder of the school's poverty. Ali rushed from one place to another, like the mother of the groom on her son's wedding day. I sat in the teachers' lounge watching everyone act like good little sheep trying to please the wolves in the hope that they wouldn't get eaten. A teacher rushed in. The convoy was approaching. That was the cue. I looked out into the schoolyard and saw Ali leading the teachers and the two groups of students, girls and boys, who had been carefully selected and repeatedly reminded that they should feel honoured. I could read his anxious and exaggerated gestures from the window: "Start waving," and, soon after, "Smile."

That was when I got my idea. While everyone was busy, I sneaked into Ali's office and spotted my prize: Herzog and Shamir. The presence of the two photographs conveyed more hypocrisy than this entire charade. I took them off the wall and stashed them under his desk. Turning to leave, I caught sight of him through the window walking back towards his office. I was trapped. As he entered, the door knocked against me. He saw me and glanced around, knowing that something was up. His eyes landed on the empty wall behind his desk.

"Please, please give me the photos," he begged. He glanced towards the window. "They're arriving. Please let me hang them back up. Please." He tugged at my wrist.

"You don't need them," I said, trying to remain strong although I could never bear seeing anyone beg.

"Please, Amal. Please."

We looked out of the window. The delegation was by the door. I pushed the photographs towards him and left the office, passing in front of the delegation without looking their way. *Why must he please his oppressor? Why must he pretend he enjoys these harsh conditions?* It was one thing not to complain about the challenges the school was facing, but quite another level of internalized oppression to brag about how satisfied you were.

The sun was very hot against my skin, as if it too was incensed by the injustice of this visit. I walked a short way beyond the schoolyard and plopped down on a brown rock. A few students came to sit with me and I explained to them that what was happening was not right.

"But these are our guests," one student protested.

"No," I said. "These are the people who are responsible for your education. They are the ones whose job it is to make sure you have everything you need: water, a paved road, transport to school that's not donkeys. You treat them as a guest if they come to your house. Then, they are *ahlan wasahlan* [welcome], but at school they should be held accountable by you. You should tell them the problems you have with the school."

They tried to look at me as they shielded their eyes from the sun. I could tell that they still didn't understand.

"Have you ever visited a Jewish school?" I asked.

176

"Yes," one student chimed in. "Last year they took us to a school at Kibbutz Hatzerim."

"And what did you see there?"

"Oh, they have buildings and a nice big playground like the ones we see on TV. Their washrooms are inside the building, not dry ones like ours. And not stinky so you can't do your thing. There it smells like spring flowers."

Another student jumped in: "It's their country. Not ours—"

"But this is our land!" another student said.

The voice of one of the teachers calling all the students to class interrupted our conversation. The play was over. Now I had to face Ali. I entered his office and before he had the chance to say anything, I said:

"I know that you are angry and I can't promise you not to do this again. Therefore, I prefer to end my service here and leave the school."

He shook his head. "Amal, what do you think? You think I work for the Shabak? That I agree with this situation? I don't. I really don't. But we can't do anything about it."

"That's the difference between you and me. I think we can and I want to teach the children that we can. But you, you are raising a defeated generation."

I took my bag and was about to leave when he offered to drive me to the city. I thanked him, but refused and told him that I would take the bus. When I arrived in Be'er Sheva, I decided to go to my father's store. I needed him. He was busy with a customer when I got there so I sat on his seat near the door to wait.

"I see that you finished early today," he said. My heart felt too heavy to answer.

"You know who was here half an hour ago?"

I cocked my head to one side.

"The principal of your school. He came to apologize that he had to fire you. He said you made his hair grey and you broke his tooth." Abouee grinned. "He said that you are a troublemaker and that I have to keep you on a tighter leash."

"That's what he said?" I asked.

"Yes." Abouee paused. I sensed there was something else. "But he also said that you should apply to university and that he would write you a letter of recommendation."

Who Decides My Maturity?

I APPLIED AGAIN. Three weeks later a letter from BGU arrived. My cousin handed it to me in front of Basma and Abouee. *What if they have rejected me again?* Basma read my mind.

"If they reject you this time, you have to contest it," she said.

Abouee gently squeezed my shoulder and waved his hand to say: "Whatever is there, just open it and read."

I tore open the letter and my eyes landed, again, on the word "rejection", but this time they had rejected me because I was too young. The regulations stipulated that I needed to be twenty-one. Basma and Abouee stood beside me, reading over my shoulder. "Well, this is not a rejection," Abouee said. "They are telling you to come back when you are twenty-one."

"I want to study now," I protested. "What am I supposed to do for the next three years?"

"You never waste your time. You are always busy with important things and . . ." His voice trailed off and his eyes looked out, as if he was consulting with someone or something very far away. "*Kul ta'akhayra feeha khayra* [Every delay has its blessing]," he finally said and continued to look towards the mountains behind our shack.

Fat tears rolled down my cheeks. I knew that things wouldn't come easily to my door so to trust in something beyond my control made me feel more powerless than ever.

Basma grabbed the letter from my hand. "This is discrimination," she said. For once, that word gave me hope. I knew that it meant there was something I could do about the situation.

"How's that?" Abouee asked.

"Jewish children enlist in the army for three years so that by the time they finish they're twenty-one. Why shouldn't Arabs be allowed to start earlier?"

I wiped my eyes with my sleeve.

"I don't think it's discrimination. This policy is for everybody. I don't think they'd allow a Jewish girl to start university at eighteen." Having grown up under the military regime, Abouee accepted what was given to him without questioning the assumptions that lay beneath. Like the teachers at Um Mitnan, Abouee regarded whatever the government provided as a favour and feared that if we contested it, we might lose it.

Later that evening, I brought the letter to Basma and we sat together outside her house, reading the whole thing aloud twice.

"What if you send a letter to the Minister for Education and explain your situation?" Basma suggested.

I loved the idea. It was the perfect antidote to my inability to sit still and hope for the best. I kissed her and ran back to the house, grabbed a few sheets of paper from the girls' room, sat down beneath our grapevine and began composing my first formal letter in Hebrew.

At school we learned classical Hebrew, the Hebrew of the Jewish bible, the Torah, which is not the same as modern written Hebrew and is even more distinct from modern spoken Hebrew. I introduced myself as a Bedouin girl who wanted to study social work because she believed in helping her people. I described the various projects I was doing in the village and used them to demonstrate that I was mature enough to attend university. I argued that selecting candidates based on their age might be appropriate for Jewish candidates but not for the Bedouin, who had to overcome very challenging conditions in order to study and receive good enough grades to enter university. I closed my letter by saying that experience, not age, demonstrated maturity and I did not need to be twenty-one to understand my people's suffering and to want to improve their lives.

My hand drew out each word with supreme confidence. I wrote knowing that the minister could not deny me. I felt the same conviction I had when I wrote to Abouee asking him to let me attend high school in Haifa, but this time I knew that I wouldn't be stopped. No one could say that I was not mature enough to study social work. I was already doing social work. I just didn't know that that was what it was called.

I finished the letter just as the moon appeared between the two mountains, encouraging me on my journey. I showed it to Basma, who hugged me when she had finished reading it and whispered: "This is also for me, Amal. This is for all of us."

We agreed that she would send the letter from Beer a-Saba in order to avoid our drawing attention to ourselves by sending it via the head of the tribe. Basma showed me the door between God's law and the tribe's laws, but of the two of us only I walked through it. We are different people, but, as with many things, it's all about timing. As the younger sister, I witnessed her struggles, which allowed me to devise strategies to protect myself. I learned how to carve a path between those two lines that governed our lives. I flew home that night, running under the canopy of stars shining down on our quiet village, and I prayed, certain that what would happen would be right.

Almost a month later Abouee's uncle, Nabhaan, came to our house looking for me. I was in the barn mixing the barley for the sheep when my brothers ran inside calling my name: "Amal, Amal! A Jewish woman is looking for you!"

My hair was a frizzy nest above my hot sticky forehead and my clothes were streaked with dirt. Ummi came in after my brothers, tutting at me to hurry and not keep the woman waiting. I didn't know what to do. I couldn't change or shower because the woman was sitting by the entrance to our shack. I wiped my hands on my pants and used the backs of my hands to dry my sweaty face. I hesitated before leaving the barn, but my brothers hurried me out.

Nabhaan sat on the long, crimson rug Ummi put out for special occasions and next to him was a middle-aged, fair-skinned Jewish woman with glasses and short, dark, curly hair. She wore simple clothes. Slacks and a button-down shirt.

Nabhaan introduced me. "This is Amal. She was feeding the sheep. She is our hero."

Nabhaan noticed my reluctance, then glanced at my hands. "Come, come. Don't worry about your hands. Naomi used to work in the barn on the kibbutz."

The woman introduced herself as Naomi Chazan, a recently elected Knesset member in the Meretz party, a party known for its left-leaning politics and championing of minority rights. She smiled without any pretence and patted the spot on the rug beside her. I tried to maintain a straight face. She sat semi-reclined, her elbow propped up against the pillow, just like Abouee. She couldn't have known that this posture was reserved for men, and for only the most important men at that. Sitting cross-legged with her back straight would have been much more appropriate. I sat down and she pulled an envelope from her handbag. The creased brown envelope didn't mean anything to me until she pulled out a sheet of white paper that I recognized as mine. The blood drained from my face. I inched away, afraid of what she might say.

Naomi broadened her smile and again patted the spot on the carpet beside her. "Come, come."

My siblings and cousins sat packed together, whispering to each other, and they tittered as Naomi shifted from one side to another, rearranging the pillow every few minutes. Their presence made me even more nervous. My worst fear was that she had come to reprimand me in front of everyone.

"You're the one who sent this letter to the Minister for Education, right?" I stared intently at the embroidery on the rug while trying to think of the safest answer. I took so long that Nabhaan stepped in and translated the question for me. I waved him off and finally said, "Yes. I did."

"*Kol hakavod!* [Congratulations!]" My entire body relaxed. She nodded her head approvingly. "You are a strong girl."

Ummi made a face that asked for a translation but instead Nabhaan said, in Arabic, "She is smart and strong like her father," which told Ummi that the conversation was going well. Naomi invited me to walk with her, Nabhaan told the others not to follow us, and Ummi handed Naomi and me small cups of sweet, black tea before we set off together in the direction of the olive orchard. We passed the kitchen tent and the barn and Naomi asked me about my work in the village. I spoke excitedly, waving my hands in the air as I described the literacy classes, the *debka* groups, the work I had done in Um Mitnan, and the women's organzation I had just started.

Naomi listened. She smiled and nodded along and didn't interrupt me. When I had finished speaking, she asked: "Why do you want to study social work?"

"Because I want to know how to help my people stand up against the housing demolitions carried out by the Israeli government and I want the women to be strong and able to speak up for themselves."

Naomi ignored the first part of my sentence and picked up on the second. "You know, a strong society is a society where women are involved and women have a say."

She placed her hand on my shoulder. "If you want to become a social worker, you will become a social worker. I'll take care of it."

One element of her party's platform was to empower women and she invited me to visit her at her office in Jerusalem. Jerusalem seemed very far away, but Naomi brought it closer in my mind. That encounter spurred a lifelong friendship. We were brought together by a rejection letter from the university, my sister's brilliant idea, my conviction that I deserved to study social work, and Naomi's commitment to bridging the worlds between women in this complicated little country. In the years to come, we would stand together many times in front of crowds, on panels, on boards. But that day we stood together under the same olive tree, two travellers walking the same road.

I later learned that the Minister for Education, Amnon Rubinstein, had sent my letter to Naomi, who decided to come and find me. She told me that she came to the village not knowing where to go, because the envelope had no address, only the name of the village and the tribe. When she drove into Laqiya, she asked about me and people pointed her in the direction of the a-Sana tribe and told her to ask for me once she got there.

A week later, I received an invitation to interview at Ben Gurion University's School of Social Work. Abouee and I practised together nightly in the *hosh*. Once, Jidatee sat with us, her eagle's gaze on me. She couldn't speak a word of Hebrew, but after I finished she put out her hand and said, "When you speak, look directly into the person's eyes, even if he is a man. *Bint ar-rjaal ma tistahi min ar-rjaal* [A woman raised by a strong man can face any man]."

We finished our day's practice and then Jidatee started her lecture. She was sitting on the rug next to Abouee, her back as straight as a cypress tree and her head raised slightly, like someone who knows their worth. "Remember who you are. Remember your purpose and don't get lost in the noise of the city. They [the Jews] are not like us. They have their religion and their culture and we have our own. Don't try to be like them. If you do, you'll lose your roots. You'll lose your ground. The only ground that you can stand on, firm and proud, is your own." Shivers ran down my arms. Her blue eyes stared into my soul and the tattoo* on her chin shook as a reminder of the weight of our bond. My feet felt firmly planted. My heart received every word she said.

Then, her tone changed.

"Don't think that by being away from the village you can do things that will ruin your name. The streets have tongues and the walls have ears. You have to watch your step and think of us, the ones who sent you and who believe in you. Do not disappoint us. You are *bint irjaal* [the daughter of a strong man]. Remember! The woman *is* her honour and once you lose it, you lose yourself and you destroy us. Don't bring shame to Aboukee. Let him be proud of you."

That night when I went to sleep next to Narjis I dozed off with the sweet taste of victory on my tongue. But when I awoke in the

---

* Known as a *washum*, it was customary for Bedouin women to be tattooed, to enhance their beauty. This custom is dying out.

morning, that sweetness had turned sour. I realized how heavy my burden was. With the same breath Jidatee had built me up and torn me down. By invoking my culture, she made me feel proud. By invoking my responsibilities as a woman, she made me feel degraded. Her words about protecting my honour felt like a cage and I their prisoner. From day one women are trained to imprison themselves so that others don't have to watch over them.

Seventeen Kilometres Away but Worlds Apart

IN THE DAYS leading up to the first day of university, I had many concerns. How would I feel in that world? What would it be like to sit next to a Jewish person? How would they look at me? Abouee sensed my concerns and did his best to alleviate them by telling me that not all Jews are racist. He reminded me that I had already met Jewish people who believed in our cause, people like Clinton Bailey and Naomi Chazan. He insisted that it was up to me to dictate how people treated me and that I should choose my battles wisely.

The first day of university I woke up early as usual. I fed the sheep and loaded the sacks of animal feed into Abouee's van and changed from my work clothes into my student clothes. I sat next to Abouee in the front seat. My hair was braided down my neck, I wore blue jeans and a black long-sleeved shirt. My uncle, Abd al-Rahman, had given me a brand new, dark-blue canvas backpack. I sat in the van and waited impatiently for Abouee to arrive. I wasn't impatient because I thought we were going to be late. I was impatient because I was nervous about my first day. When Abouee arrived, he winked at me and we drove out onto the highway leaving Laqiya asleep in the lap of the mountains that grew smaller and smaller in the rear-view mirror. We arrived at the entrance of the university campus sooner than I had expected. Abouee asked me if I had enough money, wished me good luck and said: "Remember. I trust you and I count on you. You will bring me pride and keep my head high."

I joined the students lining up for the mandatory security check by a guard who stood at the head of the line, rifling through each student's bag before allowing them to enter the campus. I observed the new things around me – a boy with red hair, a tie-dye kippah, very short denim shorts – and I felt like everyone was staring at me, my braids and fitted black shirt getting tighter and tighter under their imaginary scrutiny. When I arrived at the security desk, I did what I had seen the other students do: I opened my bag and placed it on the table. The security guard took a quick look inside and wished me a good day. When I looked up I could hardly believe that I had made it this far. A stone's throw from Laqiya, but a far cry from home. Immense concrete buildings lined with windows, a paved pathway that opened onto an immense grassy field where students sat in circles chatting and smoking, and a series of trellises where more students sat together enjoying the shade. The sheer number of people made me dizzy. And there were so many men. Everything captivated me, but I didn't have time to waste. The fear of letting my family down sat like a rock in my stomach, but also kept my head facing the horizon. I walked right past the field towards a flight of stairs that led up to the entrance of a building, sat down and pulled out the map that all the new students had received in the mail. I tried to make sense of the lines. Bedouin don't use maps; we use reference points. I fumbled with the map for a few moments before jetting off in the direction of my first class.

It was held in an impressive auditorium, with rows and rows of small wooden seats and a stage below. The room filled with students. I sat down in one of the middle seats; although I usually sat at the front of the class, I wasn't ready for that. The seats beside me filled up and all around me students chatted with one another as if they knew each other. I wondered how this was possible since it was the first year of the programme.

A bearded middle-aged man entered the class: Professor Jonathan Hanson, the head of the School of Social Work, one of the professors who had interviewed me. He placed his notes on the table and waited patiently behind the podium for the students to quieten down. How could the students be so disrespectful, I wondered. Here, teachers had to earn respect; back home, we gave it without question. Professor Hanson began the lecture and I stared at him, trying to hear him over the hum of chatter that persisted. This was an introduction to sociology. I couldn't make out a word of it, but all around me students were busy taking notes. My pen lay idle in my hand, my notebook blank. I recognized the shape of the words, but didn't understand any of them. The language I knew was that of the ancients, the language of the Torah. At some point, the professor noticed me and smiled. I smiled back. I prayed he wouldn't ask me a question.

When I left the class, the only thing I understood was that I didn't understand anything. On my way out, the professor greeted me and asked how everything was going. "OK," I lied. I didn't want to let on that I wasn't qualified to be there. He invited me to come to his office should I need anything. I thanked him and followed the other students to the next class, Foundations of Social Work. Our professor was an old lady who wore glasses and loose tailored pants. She had the desks arranged in a circle. We were about twenty students, all girls except for three boys. I took my seat among these mixed grains: a woman with light skin and blonde hair, another woman with skin the colour of milky coffee and dark, curly hair, and two students, a man and a woman, with fine features and ebony skin.

The professor asked us to introduce ourselves: where we were from, why we had chosen social work, and what relevant experiences we had had before coming to university. The knot in my stomach tightened further. I waited until everyone else had shared so I could gauge how far behind I was.

"I served in the army in the West Bank."

"I served in Gaza."

As we went around the circle, their faces changed in front of my eyes. It was one thing to see them as strangers, it was another to see them as enemies. I didn't want to, but I couldn't help it. Having served in the army united them and the introductions quickly turned into a game of "who knows who", identifying common friends and irritating commanders.

When it was my turn, my tongue stuck like dried cement to the roof of my mouth. That language stood between me and my ability to present my whole person. I reminded myself that none of them did what I did. Serving in the army did not make them social workers.

"I'm sorry if my Hebrew is not that good, but I will try my best," I began.

Their encouragement – "Go ahead. We understand some Arabic if you need to speak in Arabic," – didn't reassure me. I didn't want to be treated like a child.

"Thanks," I replied curtly. "I know Hebrew."

Whatever I lacked in grammar, I made up for in passion. I spoke about the women's organization that I had established, the literacy courses I had taught, and my experience as a teacher in the unrecognized village. Some students nodded along, visibly impressed, some ignored me with a lack of interest that I took personally, though in retrospect I doubt if it was personal, and then there were the ones who said exactly what I had wanted them to say. Things like: "Oh, are girls allowed to do that in the Bedouin community?" These patronizing remarks made me feel more at ease than any statement of approval. They gave me something to fight against.

"You are a social worker by nature!" the teacher said. I thanked her and immediately looked down at my notebook in order to avoid the gaze of the others.

When the class finished, the students left together to eat and I sat alone in the hallway waiting for my next class, which was due to start an hour later. People raced by me, taking confident strides, chatting loudly, not bothering to look around them, jostling each other, laughing and moving through space as if they had never been afraid to be seen. When my evening class finished at eight in the evening, I sat on the bench outside the campus and waited for Abouee to arrive. This was my first time alone in the city at night and although there were students all around me, the fact that there were people is what made me scared. I didn't want to get into trouble. I saw students hugging, holding hands, kissing, and talking to one another with their faces so close together that they might as well have been kissing. I sat with my hands folded in my lap and stared at the ground until I heard the familiar rumbling of Abouee's van. I climbed in and he asked me how things had gone.

"I thought I knew Hebrew but I hardly understood the professors and when the students talk with each other they use words that I've never heard before."

"Don't worry," he said. "It's like spoken Arabic. You will pick it up fast. I learned Hebrew from zero in two months."

The following week, I was walking towards the main dirt road in the village on my way to classes. I wore my unofficial uniform: a pair of faded blue jeans, an old sweater of Basma's, and my canvas backpack. My hair was tied in a side ponytail, a few loose curls bouncing on my forehead. As I passed Jidee's house I saw he was sitting under the olive tree fixing a saddle.

"Where are you going?" he asked.

"University." I joined him under the tree.

"God bless you, *ya bintee*."

He squinted at me and said: "You know that you are carrying the name of the tribe. I ask you to cover your hair. It would be bad for a stranger to see your beautiful hair. Women are like diamonds. We have to keep them protected."

I bowed, kissed him and left, but my thoughts answered for me: *Do I really want to be a diamond hidden in that fancy box?*

I waited on the road for an hour, but no minibus showed up. At that time, there was no public transport in the area. Instead, we shared taxis, six-person minibuses that drove along the highway and picked up people as they went. The waiting was made even more unbearable by the fact that, the longer I stood there, the more people from the tribe came by and asked me where I was going. Everyone had something to tell me about my family name and how to behave.

The First Bedouin Feminist

M Y SECOND MONTH at university, performing my daily ritual of checking the noticeboard in the social work building, I saw a note instructing me to go to the dean's office. He greeted me with a warm smile and we chatted briefly about my courses before he told me that a journalist wanted to write an article about me and my work in the villages. I told him that I was happy to have an opportunity to publicize the issues my community faced. He agreed, but before I left his office he cautioned me, in a fatherly way, that the interview was for a newspaper so I should make sure I was comfortable with what I said.

A week later, I sat with a Jewish journalist over a cup of coffee in the school cafeteria. I don't remember what she looked like, only that she was excited and that her excitement didn't really seem to be about me.

She wanted to know how my father had come to allow me to study at university and what the other people in my community had said about it. "Who supported your decision?" she asked.

"My father and everyone in the tribe," I answered.

"There must be some who opposed it."

I was used to this by now. In all my classes, I surprised people by being a Bedouin woman who was allowed to do something other than stay at home with my ten children while my husband was off with his third or fourth wife.

"It was something that my family encouraged me to do," I said.

She fell silent. That wasn't the answer she was looking for. A Bedouin girl whose father supported her education? No. That wouldn't sell any papers. She tried again: Why had I chosen to study social work? I spoke about my work in the village and the Laqiya Women's Association that I had helped establish. She scribbled one line. When I had finished speaking, she leaned forward and lowered her voice as if she were asking me the location of hidden treasure. "Are you telling me that you're a feminist?"

If she were a dog, she would have been drooling, but I couldn't understand why. What had she discovered in this magic word?

"What's a feminist?" I asked.

She squealed. "Feminists are women who fight for women's rights. You must be a feminist." Then she looked down at her notebook and wrote, "A Bedouin feminist," repeating those words to herself. "This is great."

I still couldn't figure out what was so great, but she was set on it. "Would you define yourself as a feminist?"

I had no other frame of reference, I had never spoken to a journalist in my life, and I didn't know anything about feminism other than what she had told me thirty seconds earlier. With the naivety of a shepherd from the desert, I answered: "If feminism is about fighting for women's rights then, yes, I am a feminist."

She slapped the table and said it again: "A Bedouin feminist." We wrapped up the interview and she explained that she would bring a photographer the following week who would take pictures of me on campus.

She got up to shake my hand, then said: "You should wear a scarf. I want people to see that you're a Bedouin."

"Of course," I said.

Why would I agree to wear the scarf? Coming from her it felt like wearing the scarf was a way to reveal my identity and not to hide myself in that tradition-encrusted box. When Jidee asked me to cover my hair, it was because he wanted to hide me from the public. This journalist wanted to present me to the public. Later I would come to understand that this was orientalism, plain and simple: members of ethnic minorities should look the way the majority expects them to look. The public wants to see a woman in a scarf so that their assumptions about how she lives and who she is remain unchallenged and intact.

A few weeks after my encounter with the journalist and our photo shoot around campus, I was feeding the sheep when I heard Ummi's voice calling me to go and see Abouee. I walked past her and she grabbed me by my arm.

"What did you do? Aboukee is furious."

By now this felt like her reaction to everything I did. "I don't know," I said and I tried to keep walking. She seized both my wrists.

"What did you do? Did someone see you do something?"

From the fear in her eyes, I caught the gist of what she meant, but I didn't have the patience for it.

"Like what?" I asked, taunting her. Her biggest fear was a report circulating at the *taboon* or the *diwaan* of me holding hands with a strange man in the big city. I had no time for such things. The fear of crossing that line shook me to my core. I yanked my wrists from her grip and walked towards the veranda where Abouce stood waiting for me. Ummi followed. Abouee turned to face me and I saw two red coals. *What can it be?* I racked my brain trying to remember if I had walked with a male student on campus and someone had seen me. Then I saw the newspaper folded under his arm.

Abouee held out the newspaper and pointed to the front page and shouted: "Is this you?"

It was a full-page photograph of me in front of the university campus under the title: "The First Bedouin Feminist". I looked fantastic, but this wasn't the time to celebrate.

He shouted again.

I took two steps back. "Yes, that is me." I started explaining, telling him that this was a good thing, but he cut me off.

"Don't you feel ashamed? You should be embarrassed by what you did. I fought against everyone to send you to university."

My poor mother. Standing a few feet behind me, she was biting her thumb, begging Abouee to tell her what was in the newspaper, and praying: "*Ya rab sitrak* [God protect us]."

Abouee continued. "You are shaming us. What should I say? Everyone now has wood for the fire to condemn me for sending you to university."

Ummi acted as if she understood the issue. She hit her face. She wailed. She moaned: "*Ya fathihitkee ya Hayjar* [What a scandal]."

I didn't cry, but I was worried about what was in the article that had unleashed Abouee's rage.

"What is the problem? I didn't do anything wrong."

He grabbed my arm and thrust the newspaper in my face.

"You said you are a feminist?"

"Yes."

"Do you know what that means?"

I shook my head.

"Well, they are American women who dance in the streets and burn their bras. Is this what you learned? Is this what they taught you at university?" He clicked his tongue. "Ah, this is my fault. I sent you."

This definition of that magic word shocked me. The journalist had lied to me. I wanted to slap her in the face, but I stood my ground. "That's not what my feminism means."

His red coals fired at me but behind them was something else: fear. Fear of how the community would react. He desperately wanted me to give him something he could use to protect us.

"What does it mean, then? *Your* feminism?"

I took a deep breath. I wasn't prepared for this question and saying that feminism was about fighting for women's rights was too radical. I had to find my own definition that would be true for me and acceptable in Abouee's eyes. The concept was new to me then. I didn't yet know about Virginia Woolf or Judith Butler or Nawal El Saadawi. All I knew was that my father was grasping for anything that would save us from shame or worse, and my mother was ready to beat me once his interrogation was over.

With the confidence that Abouee had taught me and the fearlessness that Jidatee had instilled, I made my case: "Feminism is about not stopping me from doing things just because I am a woman." I was surprised by what had come out of my mouth, but I kept going. "You know that I can do better than men and that I want to be treated according to my abilities, not my sex."

He loosened his grip on my wrist and let out a long sigh.

"*Shuufee, ya bintee* [Look, my daughter]," he said, more softly. "Your feminism is a tough one that requires time to be achieved but *Alhamdulillah* your feminism is not the American women's feminism." He took a few steps back and said, "Just don't burn it, that thing." He said those last words without looking me in the eye and I too averted my gaze. Although we would talk endlessly about politics and philosophy, women's personal needs were never part of our conversations.

Feminism and I started out our journey on the wrong foot, but this didn't make me walk away from her. On the contrary, I challenged myself to find my own definition, a definition that grew from the land where my feet were rooted. A definition that my people wouldn't feel threatened by and could even embrace. Burning my bra didn't fit into my world.

The article flung me even further into two different worlds. In my community, I received so much criticism that my daily walks to the highway to catch the minibus became unbearable. I couldn't walk to the station without groups of people jeering at me from their car windows or pointing at me from the side of the road, saying: "What does she call herself? Fimzim?!" and then howling with disdainful laughter. This article depicted me in a way people disliked. I wasn't just a girl in the village innocently running summer camps and teaching women how to read and write. I was now a young woman who was fighting against the patriarchy: a "feminist", that foreign and controversial title.

On campus, the article also drew attention to my presence, but in a different way. My professors stopped me after class to ask me about my work in the villages and the administration invited me to meet visitors to share my story – I was an easy sell to donors – but the interest in my work was genuine. I became a sexy attraction for Jewish journalists: "the Bedouin girl on the BGU campus who fights against oppressive traditions". Two weeks later, another article appeared, after I'd taken a group of journalists on a tour to learn about the programmes in my village. I tried to make them focus on our struggles, but they persisted with questions about my personal life. I would show them that our schools didn't have enough supplies or clean bathrooms and they would ask me things like: "Would your father allow you to marry the man of your choice?" These journalists were obsessed with telling a good story and too ignorant to realize how their approach jeopardized my position within my own community.

Another journalist accompanied me in order to report on my work in Laqiya and in the unrecognized villages where I had expanded my literacy classes for women. We became close friends, or so I thought. Never think that what you tell a journalist will be off the record, especially when they tell you it is. We spent two days together. She stayed at my parents' house, ate with us in the *Hoshi*, and slept next to me on the same mattress. The morning before she left, Ummi and my sisters prepared a fancy breakfast: eggs, cheese, fried cauliflower and *saj* pita with zaatar. We sat together around the fireplace. Everyone was very happy to be hosting "Amal's Jewish friend". When the journalist saw Ummi preparing the pita on the *saj*, she grabbed her camera and snapped a few photos. Jidatee intervened with the little Hebrew she knew, telling her to stop. I explained that taking photos of a family's private moments was forbidden. The journalist apologized and I tried to reassure Jidatee, but she warned me: "She will take our photos and show them to strangers."

Before saying goodbye, I asked the journalist not to use any of the photos except for the ones showing the work in the community and not to include any of my personal stories in the article. I told her that I felt comfortable with her, which is why I had shared so much. She promised to respect my wishes.

When the article came out, it was entirely about my personal life. My community work and the issues we faced were mentioned in a handful of sentences at the end. She even disclosed I wasn't going to marry my cousin because I was concerned about genetic diseases. No one in my family knew my thoughts on this, not even my sister Narjis.

It was expected that I would marry one of my cousins, but it had now been publicly announced, in one of Israel's largest newspapers, that I was rejecting this longstanding tradition. I dug my nails into my skin. I prayed that the printing press would break. I asked God to stop my family from seeing the article. I went to see my professor and told her that the article had put me and my family at risk. My professor immediately rang the journalist. She tried several times, but the journalist never answered. You could complain to the editor, my professor suggested. But the harm was done. There was nothing I could do.

The article contained many photos of me so anyone who knew me picked up a copy in Be'er Sheva or Rahat and brought it back to the *diwaan*. In a tribe, if the walls have eyes, then the stones have tongues. People conjured up terrible rumours: I was a traitor and Abouee a dangerous fool for trusting me. "Girls need a tight leash!" The article confirmed it.

I couldn't travel between my village and the campus anymore. Those seventeen kilometres of road became more and more treacherous. Every time I left and every time I returned, a hundred eyes watched me, all waiting to catch me in some terrible and shameful act. I also needed better studying conditions. Our generator switched off a couple of hours after I arrived home and my siblings and I had a single oil lamp between us to illuminate our schoolwork. Between the chatter and their constant demands for help with their homework, I could barely finish my own work. I would wait till everyone finally went to sleep, usually around ten o'clock, then take the oil lamp and study alone in the kitchen.

My sister Na'ama suggested that I stay with her in Beer a-Saba, where she and her husband had just moved into a small apartment. This was an acceptable solution to my parents and it solved the problem of Abouee needing to wait four hours for me during the winter to pick me up after classes. At Na'ama's, I had a small room which she fitted out perfectly for a student with a bookshelf, a desk and a chair.

My first night there felt strange. I missed Narjis's toes brushing up against mine and her breath warming my neck. It was my first time sleeping in a bed all on my own and the darkness felt infinitely larger. The next morning I awoke disoriented. I didn't have my usual tethers: the desert sun streaming into my window, the sheep braying for their breakfast, or the smell of the pita baking on the *saj*. The room was still dark, the blinds were drawn, and the roar of cars replaced the sounds that I knew. I got out of bed, flipped the light switch by the door, and the lights turned on. *That was easy.* "The Prisoner", a poster of a painting by a Palestinian artist, looked back at me, its vibrant colours a stark contrast to its grim subject. My privacy came hand in hand with solitude, but perhaps solitude was something that I could befriend. Wasn't it what I wanted? The opportunity to make up my own mind and to be myself away from the warring perspectives of the village and the institution. Here, in my small room, in the city, I could disappear into myself.

Hannah

THE FIELD PLACEMENT coordinator sent me to complete my first placement at a nursing home in Omer, a suburb of Be'er Sheva. Although it was only a fifteen-minute drive from Laqiya, I had never been there. First, because the services we needed – the hospital, the market, the post office – were in Be'er Sheva, and second, because Omer was and still is one of the wealthiest towns in Israel. In Laqiya and other nearby Bedouin villages, whenever we saw someone with a new piece of furniture, a dark-wood dining table or an almost new leather chair, we would joke: "Where did you get that? Is it Omer rubbish?" We would use the English word "rubbish" to mean the garbage dump where the residents of Omer took their trash.

The first day of my placement, I took the bus from the university to the main station in Be'er Sheva to catch another bus to Omer. I waited on the platform, not knowing if I was in the right place. One thing I still hadn't grown used to about the city was everyone's certainty about where they were going. Soldiers travelling between cities packed the square: young men and women my age in khaki-green jumpsuits belted at the waist, carrying an oversized backpack with an assault rifle slung over their shoulder. It was the details that humanized them: a pair of Nike running shoes instead of combat boots, a purple hair tie, a beaded bracelet. I sat on a bench outside the station, staring at the pavement, trying to be small. My nose caught the scent of Palestinian falafel coming from the eastern street corner. Tunisian fricassée wafted from the west. I sniffed and sniffed, picking up the scents of dishes that I knew. Turkish shawarma from this corner, Moroccan tagine from another. It was these familiar smells that told me that I belonged, despite the hundreds of soldiers around me.

I boarded the bus. Before I could pull out my wallet to buy a ticket, the driver started explaining to me how to get to the bus that would take me to the open-air market where I could catch a shared taxi to the villages. I tried explaining to him that I was trying to get to Omer, but he kept repeating the same instructions. We were speaking in Arabic since he had addressed me in Arabic. I couldn't tell where he was from. I switched to Hebrew. I explained that I was a student who was on her way to her field placement in Omer. Only then did he let me buy a ticket. Inside my village I was watched because I was a woman, outside my village I was watched because I was an Arab. I paid the fare and looked for an empty seat next to a woman, preferably a woman who looked like me, but there weren't any. I sat next to an elderly woman whose white scarf tied neatly under her chin made her look like one of those actresses I had seen in Egyptian movies. She had a short grey fringe and was wearing a long pink and grey dress. I couldn't help imagining how odd Jidatee would look in that dress.

The bus left the station shortly after I boarded. Once we were a few stops away, the traffic lightened. I looked past the woman and out of the window at the concrete buildings, the sidewalks, the expanse that lay beyond the city. We got onto the highway and, after only a few stops, turned right to take the exit to Omer. The bus came to a halt as it neared a large gate that slowly opened wide enough to allow the bus to pass. Why would a town have a gate? We never even used the lock to our shack.

I got off at the bus stop next to the nursing home. I scanned my surroundings for the entrance and noticed a large sign which read GANEI OMER (Omer Gardens). I walked past the sign into a luxurious garden. A perfect green lawn stretched out before me and magenta and yellow flowers kissed the path at my feet. Ahead I saw a two-storey building with floor-length windows and smooth, white-stone balconies adorned with tasteful planters. My eyes feasted on the radiance around me, but my ears starved. Save for the chirping of the beerds, the low hum of the bees, and a cough here and there, the place was completely silent. The Bedouin know the silence of the desert, so when we are among people, we make up for it by speaking a lot and speaking loudly. This place seemed haunted. I wandered around the garden until I saw a short woman with dark hair coming down the path towards me.

"Are you the student from BGU?" she asked.

"Yes."

"They didn't tell me they were sending an Arab student. Are you an Arab or a Bedouin?" She started walking back to the building without waiting for my answer.

I hurried to catch up with her. "I'm a Bedouin. It's the same thing, though."

She stopped and looked at me. "Really? I thought Bedouin were Bedouin."

I knew that calling myself a Bedouin would make it easier for everyone at the nursing home to accept me. "Arab" would immediately breed mistrust. The Bedouin have the reputation of being loyal to the state because some have always volunteered to serve in the army, even though they were not mandated to do so like the Druze, another Arabic-speaking community in Israel.

At the entrance to the building, a security guard eyed me suspiciously. The woman said, "She's with me," and he let us through. Her office was on the first floor down a hallway covered with abstract paintings. I had never seen much art so I wouldn't have known if they were Picassos or works by the residents. I remember thinking that each piece looked like a reflection of human thoughts and feelings.

She invited me to sit and told me that today would be about giving me a general overview of the residence. After I had formally introduced myself, she asked me where Laqiya was. I looked through her window and pointed in the direction of my village.

"Oh! So you are our neighbours," she said with a laugh.

I liked the concept. "Yes," I said. "Yes, we are."

"Why did you choose a nursing home for the elderly as your field placement?"

"I didn't," I replied. We were addressing the discomfort that we both felt at my presence in this place. A Bedouin Arab Palestinian spending time with elderly Jews. It was odd for everyone. "I was sent by my supervisor."

Her smile didn't slip. "Don't worry," she finally said. "I am sure you will learn a great deal here."

She took me on a tour of the building, including the dining room, the fitness room and the activities room. When we entered, there were a handful of people, men and women, sitting together doing handicrafts. They sat hunched over their work, deeply focused on the bits of string or scraps of paper they held between their feeble hands. I imagined Jidatee and the other elderly people from my village sitting in this fancy room, sewing or doing embroidery together. Their voices would have shaken the ceiling.

She greeted them in a singsong voice that was friendly without being patronizing. They looked up and smiled. I think they liked her. She introduced me as a social work student and told them my name. One of the men asked if I was an Arab. "She is a Bedouin," she quickly replied. "From Laqiya. Our neighbours." As we left, she

199

whispered to me: "It's better if you say you are a Bedouin. They'll be less scared of you." I didn't say anything.

The following week when I arrived at Ganei Omer, the social worker explained that today I would follow her and observe her work, then the following week I'd be on my own. She pulled several manila folders from her filing cabinet, some of which had names highlighted in yellow, others in blue. We went upstairs. There were beige doors along a long corridor. Without knocking, she entered the first room. I followed close behind her.

"*Boker tov hamouda* [Good morning sweetheart], it's a nice day today."

She walked past the old woman sitting in her wheelchair and drew the curtains. The woman must have been in her eighties. Frail and skinny, she sat slumped in her chair. A purple scarf was draped over her thinning hair and a few wisps fell about her face. She turned her head towards the light streaming through the window, but it was too much for her. She looked back down at her skeletal hands folded in her lap.

"This is Amal. She is a student and she will be with us for the next three months."

The woman didn't move and the social worker continued: "Let me know if you need anything," and slid out of the room as softly as she had entered it, without waiting for an answer.

In the next room, I was introduced to a man also in his eighties but who looked much younger. He sat on the balcony reading a book. The social worker greeted him and he saluted her enthusiastically. He waved his book at her and said, "I'm reading because the people I loved have already died." Later, when I took to reading Amos Oz's novels, I realized that he was quoting Oz, who wrote: "I am writing because the people I love have already died."

Room after room, we visited people who sat alone. I felt sorry for them. Illness wasn't killing them; loneliness was. I thought about Jidee pointing to the prayer rug and all of us children climbing over each other, competing to be the first one to bring it to him. My grandparents' lives didn't have fancy facilities or large indoor swimming pools, but they were rich with bustle and noise, rich with small hands grabbing at their cheeks, and rich with people, young and old, sitting near them, talking to them and keeping them company. We say *al-jadda edde*, meaning that our grandmother is like the *edde*, the chest where we store our most valuable items: knowledge of our history and our traditions. Where were these people's children? Had these people chosen to live alone? What was the point of having a beautiful garden if you had no one to sit in it with?

The next week, I was walking in the hallway when one of the nurses asked me to take a blanket to a woman sitting alone in the communal room next to the dining area. She was so thin that I could see her veins beneath the wrinkles of her skin. I didn't know where she wanted the blanket. She noticed my confusion and motioned impatiently that I should wrap it around her shoulders. I unfolded the blanket and placed it carefully around her tiny bones, just as I did with Jidatee.

She asked me to sit with her. I looked towards the door, wondering if this was allowed, but my culture dictated that respecting the wishes of my elders was more important than following the rules. I pulled up a chair and sat in front of her, our knees almost touching so that she could hear me. She asked me my name and where I was from. I answered, but she struggled to keep her head up. Every time she raised her head, her neck folded under its weight. Without thinking twice, out of respect, I slid from the chair to the floor to accommodate her. The corners of her eyes softened, and as in the moment when you notice the bright and perfect moon reflecting on still, dark water, something shifted. Whatever bitterness she had subsided and my small gesture transformed us from strangers to friends. She slowly reached her hand out towards me and I placed mine on her knee. I told her that I had twelve siblings. Her dusting of eyebrows disappeared into her hair.

"Do you have siblings?" I asked.

She strained to raise her head a couple of inches and looked towards the entrance of the room, perhaps seeing their ghosts in the doorway.

"I used to have two. One sister and one brother."

"Where are they?" I asked.

"I don't know. They might be dead or alive. I lost contact with them during the Shoah." She said that they were taken by the Nazis to concentration camps.

I didn't know what I was supposed to say so I just squeezed her hand.

She started crying. I was worried that I'd get into trouble for making her cry. I moved to get up but she held my hand so I sat back down and she continued. She said she was five or six years old when she was transported by a British ship from Germany to England with thousands of other children who were raised in foster homes all over the United Kingdom. She told the story with few details, sharing only the main events: the boat ride to England, meeting her foster parents, going to school, moving to Israel to live on a kibbutz, getting married to her husband. She told the story as though it was a grocery list, not a life's journey. Maybe she didn't remember the details. Maybe they were too painful. Maybe both. My supervisor's voice interrupted us. "Here you are!" She placed her hand on the old woman's shoulder. I stood up.

"Thank you for listening," she said, "and I'm sorry if I took up too much of your time."

"No, no, no," my supervisor replied. "That's fine. If you want, Amal can sit with you more often when she's here." She looked at me proudly.

We left the communal sitting room and I followed my supervisor to her office where she asked me to complete my reflection log. I sat at the area of the desk that she had cleared for me and picked up my pen, but the words didn't come. I was too confused. My feelings competed inside me, a battle of history, culture and identity. The words I had heard that day were familiar: "Holocaust", "Nazis", "concentration camps". I had learned about them in history lessons when we studied the founding of the country. We learned that the Holocaust was the reason that the Jews needed their own state, a safe haven to prevent these atrocities from ever happening again, but those classes never aroused my sympathy. What I learned was that their plight came at my expense. They took our land because they had suffered somewhere else and now my people had to pay for it. This was my first encounter with someone who had survived the Holocaust and it changed me, or rather, I should say, it opened me up to change. It was the first time I could put a face to all that suffering.

The next week I arrived late because the village minibus wouldn't leave before all the seats were filled. When I made it to my supervisor's office, she didn't even greet me, she just asked: "What did you do to Hannah?" – that was the old woman's name. I was worried that maybe I was in trouble.

"She has been asking about you all week. I think it would be very good for you and her to continue your conversation. Hannah doesn't open up easily. Just sit there and listen."

I entered Hannah's room and she greeted me with the same smile as the other day. The kind of smile that carries within it the magnitude of human sorrow. She told me to bring a chair: "I don't want you to sit on the floor. It's cold."

I carried a chair from the corner of her room and placed it in front of her.

"So, how is university going?"

"It's going well."

"How old is your grandmother?"

"I have two. My mother's mother is around seventy, maybe seventy-three, and my father's mother is around seventy-five. I don't know exactly."

"Do you know how old I am? I'm eighty-six. I have three children and seven grandchildren."

She smiled at me impishly. "I am sure your grandmothers have an army of children."

I nodded. "They do."

"This is my notebook," she said, pointing to a black, leather Moleskine sitting in her lap. "I used to write everything. Everything! But when my children were little and when I was working as an English teacher, I didn't have time to write. Do you mind if I read it to you?"

"Please!" I said.

Now she filled in the details of the journey she had only glossed over the other day: the bittersweet goodbyes when leaving one inadequate foster family, the fear that what came next might be worse, the excitement that it might be better, the promise of having your own bedroom, the frustration of never fitting in, and the struggle of never finding a place to call home. She was a rowdy child who never settled into her role as a good little girl in an English home. She moved from one foster family to another and finally, as a teenager, moved to Israel and lived on a kibbutz. She wrote that the kibbutz was the first time she ever felt like she belonged. I remember she wrote: "There you don't need a family. Everyone is family."

Over the next two months, I would arrive an hour before my shift to chat to her. She spoke almost entirely about the family she had lost. Each time she'd fill in the contours of their lives, always adding another detail, another memory. Sharing their stories with me acknowledged those lives and, in doing so, allowed her to put their ghosts to rest. Hannah showed me the human beings behind the history books. Her stories peeled away the layers of rage that caged my heart and forced me to confront the ideology I had been given, the one that I carried around like a badge of honour. I came to see that the truth wasn't so simple. We never discussed politics. We only told stories. But stories are the only way to see the human face behind enemy lines. History can't do that, only a story can.

Jidatee and Karl Marx

MY SISTER NA'AMA was expecting twins in March. I knew that keeping up with my studies while dividing my time between the Laqiya Women's Association – the organization I had established with other women in the community to run all of our community activities – and assisting Na'ama with her newborns would be impossible, especially since she had decided to go back to school. At the suggestion of one of my friends, Zahava, who lived in the dorms on campus, I applied for one without my parents' permission. My application was initially rejected on the basis that I lived only seventeen kilometres away from campus without acknowledging that I didn't have electricity or running water. After meeting with the dean and the dorm manager and threatening to set up a tent to have access to these necessities, they assigned me to a dorm.

At the weekend, Abouee was working alongside Narjis and me, filling barley sacks. I sealed one and said: "Do you know that the university gave me a room to live in? Usually they don't give it to people who live close to the city, but they gave me one." I spoke of it as an achievement to sway him in the right direction.

He stopped working and said firmly: "No. You can't live in the city by yourself. It's not safe out there."

He told me to fill up the remaining sacks by the mill, then left the factory. Narjis's eyes met mine, but she didn't say a word.

In the evening, Ummi confronted me. "What is this that you are bringing in? Aboukee won't let you live by yourself in the city. You have your sister's house. You stay there and help her with her twins. You can't leave her."

"I can't study surrounded by four children – two under seven and two newborns!" I protested.

"That's what you have. Work it out." She folded her arms.

"Why should I work it out when I have a better option?" I wasn't here to plead. I was here to win.

"A better option for you, not for us."

Maryam, bless her, the one you could always count on, stood up for me. "There are many Arab girls from the north who live in dorms. What's the problem?"

"These are the *felaheen!*" Ummi waved her hand at her. "We are not like them. We have our tradition." That enshrined, immovable tradition that we must never betray. "We don't send our girls to live by themselves. And you would walk around in the middle of the night and people would see you. Not everyone knows you are studying late. They will think that you are consorting with strangers." By "strangers" she meant "men".

She stormed out, not without calling to God, "*Emshi al-hayt al-hayt wit-gooli ya rabb ya saatir* [Walk next to the wall and pray, 'Oh God, hide us or protect us']."

I followed her out, my perseverance and sense of justice not allowing her exit to have the last word. "I don't want to walk next to the wall! The wall can't protect me."

She spun around. "Don't make Aboukee angry," she shouted. Her eyes locked into mine to bully me into agreeing that her words were final. "I wish these years were over," she moaned. "I am tired." She was saying this to God, her favourite tactic to trigger my guilt. "*Hamm al-banaat lal-mamaat* [The burden of girls lasts till you die]."

That phrase stabbed me like a knife. "*Hamm al-banaat* is only in your head!" I hurled at her all my fury and indignation of having made it this far only to be roped back in by exactly what I had been trying to escape.

"I will tell Aboukee to stop you from going to university."

"I don't want to go anymore," I said. "I prefer staying home to going and getting low grades."

"Well, stay home then. Who do you think you are?"

After I had missed almost three weeks of class, my parents still hadn't changed their minds. With each day, I feared my strategy wasn't working until finally, one night after dinner, as we sat around drinking sweet tea, I got up to help Maryam and Ummi clear the dishes and Abouee beckoned me to his side.

"Do they still have a room for you at the dorm?" he asked.

His eyes looked almost black in the firelit kitchen tent, like dark pools. "I don't know," I said, trying to hide my relief. "I might have lost it by now."

"Listen," he said. "I don't want you to miss your classes. Here is the deal: you stay over only during exam periods. Other than that, I will be driving you."

Inwardly, I cheered. I agreed to the deal, mainly because Abouee didn't know when my exams were so I could stay over as often as I liked. I don't know if he really expected me to abide by that agreement or if it was another way he navigated the minefield of his fatherly duties: his often competing responsibilities to a daughter hellbent on winning her independence and to traditions insistent on holding her back.

The dorm was a circular, two-storey building with an open-air courtyard on a small mound at its centre. My room faced the main thoroughfare and I could see the sports centre on the other side of the street. When I walked in, a girl with messy blonde hair sat at the dining table, eating a sandwich. She wore shorts and a tank top and one of her hands was deformed, the fingers curled in on themselves. She saw me, but continued eating. When she noticed my confusion, she pointed to the stairs and told me that was where the rooms were.

I carried my blue bag downstairs and found the room numbered 1. I pulled the key out of my back pocket and opened it. The room was even smaller than the one at Na'ama's. I dropped my bag on my bed and plopped down beside it. My eyes landed on the only colour in the whole room, my blue bag. I hugged it and burst into tears. I missed Narjis, I missed Na'ama, I missed Basma, I missed Maryam, I missed Ummi and Abouee, I missed all my brothers and sisters. I do not know how long I sat there crying. The smell of coffee and the sounds of my roommates pulled me out of my homesickness and back to practical concerns. I didn't have any groceries for breakfast, save for some dates that Na'ama had given me. I ate one and felt better. I wrapped my scarf around my head, organized my backpack for the day's courses, and left my room, noting the satisfaction of locking the door to a place that belonged entirely to me.

I entered the kitchen and the commotion I had heard ceased. The girls were huddled by the stove, pouring themselves coffee. I heard two of them whispering: "I heard she's an Arab." "No, she's a Bedouin." The girl with the messy blonde hair and the tank top who wasn't standing around with the others approached me. She had a limp. She thrust her non-deformed hand towards me with confidence. "I'm Ayelet," she said.

"I'm Amal."

"What do you study?" she asked.

"Social work."

"Oh, great," one of the girls by the stove chimed in, "we have a social worker." I didn't know what she meant by that, but the rest of them laughed. It didn't seem kind.

Ayelet didn't laugh. With the severity of an army commander she continued: "We're meeting tonight to discuss the house rules. Be back by 8 p.m."

On my way to the campus, my mind was spinning, paranoid that this whole "house rules" thing was a prank they had decided to play on me, the Arab. I went directly to the cafeteria to buy a coffee and then went searching for Zahava, my Ethiopian guide to Jewish society, to get her advice. She reassured me that the house rules were for everyone.

"They're to make sure you don't leave dishes in the sink, you clean the bathrooms, clean the dining table, that sort of thing. You can also tell them your rules," she continued. "It's your place, just as much as theirs."

In the evening we all gathered around the dining table. I sat next to Ayelet. She felt the safest. She began the meeting and each of us went around the table and showed everyone where we were keeping our food in the fridge and on the shelves. Some of the girls were friendly while others made a point of staring me down while they spoke. When it was my turn, before I could finish speaking, Reli, who was religious and Sephardi, pounced on me. "You can't put your food in the fridge! I keep kosher."

"We don't keep kosher," another girl retorted.

"Get your own fridge if you want to keep kosher," Ayelet shot back.

Reli didn't stand down. "This is a *Jewish* place," Reli yelled. "Kosher is one of the rules!"

"What is kosher?" I asked. Sometimes being the elephant in the room has its perks. My ignorance of the religious protocol about food preparation, which is a source of controversy for many, many Jews, stunned them into silence. I continued, "I have no problem respecting the rules so long as we all respect them."

"What are your rules?" Ayelet asked.

"I don't have any for now. I still don't know what things are like here. Once I see something that bothers me, I'll let you know," I said.

My diplomacy seemed to have satisfied Reli because she said more calmly: "I need to keep my food away from non-kosher food."

"Well," I said, "I'm not planning on bringing any food from home. My food will be from the supermarket, just like yours. I guess the food from the supermarket is kosher?"

"It is," Ayelet confirmed before Reli could say anything else.

Ayelet and I became close, perhaps because we were the two people in the margins or perhaps because we were both strong-willed and determined. This was my first exposure to the conflicts within the Jewish community itself. Before this experience, I had thought of Jews as one unified group, but Reli and Ayelet fought constantly. Another significant conflict in our dorm was around whether or not we should be allowed to bring boyfriends over. Ayelet was unequivocally for, Reli against. I supported Ayelet, but it was more out of loyalty than anything else. Truthfully, I wasn't comfortable with the idea of having men over, but it was easier to stand with the liberal Ashkenazi Jew who accepted me without question rather than the conservative Sephardi Jew for whom I was always an outsider, in spite of our shared respect for tradition, family and tribe. Needless to say, I wasn't very active in dorm life. I was too busy with my classes and my activism in the villages to pay too much attention to the petty conflicts that arose each week. I sat with Ayelet when she was there, but otherwise I kept to myself and only used the dorm as a place to sleep.

My first week back at university, I received a phone call from a woman named Dvorka Oreg who introduced herself as the director of Shatil's office in Be'er Sheva. She said she had read about me in the newspaper and she needed my help. *My help? What? A Jewish woman needs my help?* The next day I waited in the hallway near the cafeteria when a well-dressed woman in her forties came up to me and introduced herself.

"I recognized you from the article," she said.

Her beaming smile softened my guard and we went to the cafeteria where she ordered coffee for both of us. She explained that she had just started her job as the director of Shatil, a nationwide organization supporting the creation of NGOs which assist people in accessing their rights. She had read about my organization, the Laqiya Women's Association (LWA), in one of the articles, and wanted to learn from my experience how to better support communities in other unrecognized villages. Later that week, we drove down the main road in Laqiya to visit the LWA and see the activities we were involved in. Sara and Chesen, who ran the association's daily activities, met us at the entrance and we led Dvorka into one of our women's literacy classes. By now our programmes had expanded to include two levels of literacy classes, a summer camp for children, and a programme for teenage girls where they learned traditional skills such as embroidery and baking from their mothers to bridge the gap between the generations and allow the younger generation to see how their traditions still had a place amid the rapid urbanization of the Naqab Bedouin.

By the following month, I was volunteering with Shatil, advising them on how to expand Bedouin civil society, using the LWA as a model. We drove together from one village to another, meeting with the women, encouraging them to form committees and, from there, to run programmes and, eventually, to start an organization. My involvement with Shatil led to the establishment of tens of organizations that turned the Negev from the land that God and the government forgot into a hotbed of community work and social service provision.

Dvorka alerted me to the services and agencies that existed within the government to assist non-profits and civil society organizations. To provide financial opportunities for the women at the LWA, we started a jewellery-making programme, taught by a Jewish woman that Dvorka had recommended. Each week, the women in the village attended classes to create beaded bracelets that we decided to sell at the Bedouin bazaar on Thursdays. The first bazaar we attended, four women and I set up our stall and arranged the bracelets and necklaces on a woven blanket. Each time someone enquired about an item, the women scurried behind me. I got angry at them for being so shy. By the end of the day, we hadn't sold a single thing.

When I got home, Jidatee was sitting in front of our house. She asked me where I'd been. I told her I'd been at the bazaar in the city to sell the jewellery made by the women in the LWA programme.

"How much did you sell?" she asked.

"Nothing!" I was still exasperated. "They didn't want to talk! They kept standing behind me." I mimed the women's modest shuffle for the full effect.

"Hmm." Jidatee was in no hurry to comfort me. "Show me the stuff."

I produced a handful of bracelets from my bag.

"What is this?" She wrinkled her nose as if I was holding up a fistful of animal waste. "This is not ours."

"What do you mean?" I asked.

"This is not Bedouin jewellery. I wouldn't take it if you gave it away for free." She let out a hollow laugh. Then, she said something that illuminated everything: "Why do you want them to sell something that isn't theirs?"

"But they made it," I protested.

"So what! They made it because you asked them to make it. Would they wear it? No. If they won't wear it, they can't sell it."

Jidatee was right. If they produced something that they didn't feel belonged to them, something they didn't believe in, something that, in their hearts, they didn't own, how could they sell it? Jidatee had put Marx's mode of production theory into practice. I was excited because every day I struggled between the philosophies I learned at school and the practical lessons I learned at home. One time, when I was cleaning out the barn with Abouee, I spoke to him about social class and conflict theory, which we were studying in my sociology class. I tried to apply the theories to the dynamics within our community. I explained how tribal conflicts are class-based and how the Bedouin who own land lord it over those who don't and that they don't mix with other tribes because they fear losing the resources afforded to their class. Abouee didn't agree with my example.

"You have to be careful," he told me. "Don't take things for granted. Knowledge is like the market. Don't be fooled by the loudest vendor. You buy good fruit based on your own instincts, not according to how convincing the vendor is. You are the buyer. You get to choose."

Just because Western knowledge dominates the institution doesn't mean that it's necessarily the best. These words taught me to chew before swallowing the knowledge that was fed to me. From then on, I engaged with the material on my own terms, bringing my indigenous knowledge into the classroom and distinguishing between theories that served my worldview and those that didn't. From the moment I adopted the shrewd attitude I used at the souk, I fell in love with my classes.

Jidatee brought Marx's theory to life. All the factors that contributed to the way the bracelets were produced (the materials, the social relationships, the classes) alienated the women from the final product. To humanize the production process, the product and the process had to reflect the women's abilities and aspirations and the women themselves had to be included in the decision-making.

A week later, I consulted Jidatee about how to improve the programme.

"Start from where the women are," she said. "Start from their strengths. Let them feel proud. Once they produce things they feel proud of, they won't stop."

She suggested that we started with Bedouin embroidery. That challenged me to think how to use embroidery to empower women.

The other leaders of the LWA and I sat with a group of mothers in the building we were now able to rent after receiving our first grant from the New Israel Fund* as a fully fledged NGO. I explained that we wanted to create financial opportunities for women in Laqiya. The transition from a semi-nomadic lifestyle to a sedentary one had devastated their position within the community. Bedouin women have always been weavers. In the days when we moved with the cycles of the sun, it was the women who wove the tent. The process took time. The women gathered together with their looms and sat in a circle. Day by day, thread by thread, story by story, they wove intricate patterns, black and green diamonds zigzagging across a background of black, red and white stripes until they had a tent large enough to shelter a family of ten. Carrying water from the well to the village was also women's work. Ummi said that, although she sometimes thought the desert sun might scorch her to dust, what gave her strength was knowing that every part of her body gave the tribe life. At the well, the women from all the tribes in the region wove their knowledge together. They shared secrets of all kinds, recipes to heal and to feed, charms to cure any ailment relating to love or the land, and innovative embroidery patterns.

---

* A progressive fund working to strengthen Israeli civil society by funding organizations that promote civil and human rights, religious pluralism and closing social and economic gaps, especially between Jews and Arabs.

Forced urbanization displaced women's roles and uprooted the women from the earth where their knowledge was shared. Those in fixed houses lost the tent's open air. Water tanks replaced the wells and the men took over that sacred duty because they drove the tractors that laid the pipes to fill the tanks. Women now found themselves passive consumers relegated to the home, whereas previously the survival of the entire tribe had depended on them. The men, too, lost their status when we lost our land. A man would take a menial job that diminished him and then come home to a wife who needed him to have enough dignity for both of them. To make up for his loss of status, for feeling worthless, he often oppressed her and the cycle continued.

How could embroidery break the cycle of oppression? How could an old idea fuse with a modern need to promote the status of women? When I was nineteen or twenty, this question kept me up at night. Looking for answers in textbooks and lectures was no good. I needed to discuss it with Jidatee, with Ummi, and with the other elders in my village.

Bedouin embroidery is not purely decorative: each pattern tells a story. Some are social, like the "daughter and her mother-in-law", and others are political like "Begin and Sadat". Although the women didn't sit in the *diwaan* like the men and talk politics, they still had their opinions, only they expressed them with a needle and thread. They wove their feelings into the cloth, stitching together an idea they weren't allowed to articulate, a feeling they couldn't explain, or a vision so beautiful words wouldn't do it justice.

Each week the women gathered at the LWA for a lecture on women's rights and a lesson on a new embroidery pattern. They received the materials and the pattern for the week and went home to complete the work in their own time, when their children were at school and they could sit gossiping together in the tent. We invited the woman who had led the jewellery-making workshops to advise us on what kinds of pieces to create. Nobody was going to buy my mother's *thobe** covered in stitching, but people would buy a T-shirt with a small piece of embroidery on it. We wanted to produce things that would appeal to the global market, to merge the old with the new. Every month each woman would get paid according to the size of the embroidery she had created, regardless of whether or not the product had sold. The LWA had women on the production, marketing and sales side. We started with bazaars and slowly, slowly would end up opening a visitor centre where we showcased not just the embroidery, but the history behind it. Each component of the business provided the opportunity for a Bedouin woman to regain her traditional status as a bringer of life to the community. Her hands wove intricate patterns and her words inspired people from all over the world to invest in her wares.

Aisha's Tent

DURING MY SECOND year at university, Ghaalya, my classmate from high school, joined me at BGU. We wanted to extend the LWA's adult education programme to her village, Umm Bateen, ten minutes south of mine. The elementary school, which sits in the Wadi Al-Khaleel valley on the east side, is their only government-owned public building. It closes during the winter months because the flooding in the valley is too dangerous for the children to cross. Ghaalya and I met with the principal to explain the project: Friday evening classes for the women in the village to learn how to read and write in Hebrew and Arabic. He enthusiastically agreed and we organized our first class the following week.

That Friday, we arrived to find more than thirty women dressed in the traditional, brightly embroidered *thobe*, a white *shash* wrapped around their heads, waiting in front of the school gate, which was locked. The principal drove up in his car and let us in. When the

---

* Traditional ankle-length dress.

215

women saw him, they covered their faces. "Don't worry," I told them. "He is only here to open the gate and the classrooms. Then it'll be just us women."

We directed the women into the three classrooms to administer a language assessment exam, but the principal intervened and told them which classroom to go to based on what he thought their level was. I said nothing because I didn't want to make a scene.

"I'll be in my room, if you need anything."

What did he think he was doing? "No need," I said, trying to be diplomatic. "That's very kind, but we are taking care of this."

He ignored me and went to sit in his office.

After organizing the women according to skill level, I was greeting my new students when they all covered their faces and bowed their heads towards their desks. I looked over and saw the principal standing in the doorway.

He scanned the faces in the classroom and pointed to one of the women sitting in the back row. "You. You know how to read! Why are you in this class? Come to my office."

"I'm coming to your office," I said.

We argued over who had the authority to run the programme. "You are the principal from Sunday to Thursday and only for elementary school. Today is Friday and this is adult education. It is our project and we decide."

He didn't like that I stood my ground. "This is my school," he said much more forcefully, "and I decide."

The following Friday we went to the school but the principal didn't show up to open the gate. Ghaalya and I discussed our alternatives. She suggested we hold the class at the community mosque, the *masjid*, but I said that was too radical a solution. If we wanted to hold it at the mosque, we would need to consult the head of the tribe first. We didn't know what else to do so we walked back to the west side of the village followed by the women, who were cursing the principal and apologizing to me, their guest.

It was May and the wheat harvest was at its peak. The fields swayed in the evening breeze, the wheat brushing against the air, dancing as one golden mane. At this time of year, people live out in their fields for two to three months with their livestock. They build a simple summer tent with the basics they need to live on: a *saj*, a mattress, a fence to contain their animals. Some don't live there, especially if they have a shack close by. Sometimes it's just a place to find a moment of easy shade while the sheep graze on what's left over from the harvest.

We passed by a summer tent erected in the field beside the dirt road. An old woman sitting by her *saj* motioned at us to join her. The rumours about the adult education programme had already made their rounds in the village – some celebrated the programme, others condemned it. Her hands, with deep wrinkles like the cracked desert floor after rain, picked up a blackened kettle and poured enough tea for all of us. We sipped sweet tea from small cups coated in dust and the women told her the story of how the principal had locked us out of the school and, in doing so, halted the programme. The old woman, Aisha, shook her head and raised her hand.

"It's not his father's property," she said, her voice hoarse, as if it was full of dust. "It belongs to the government. Why didn't you stand up to him?"

"What do you want us to do?" the woman who had spoken on behalf of the others replied. "If our husbands find out about this, if they see we are causing trouble, they will stop us from going altogether."

While they were talking I looked around the tent. It was large enough to seat thirty women. There was room to bring in a metal sheet to use as a blackboard. The whole idea was cooking.

"Aisha," I said, my eyes full of wonder, "we don't need the school. We can do it here, in your tent!"

The women laughed and the debate began. Some agreed, others dissented, until Aisha settled the argument. She raised her hand to shush us and said, "You are welcome. It's my place. No one can kick you out. I will say that you are my guests."

It was settled then. We cheered and immediately got to work. I asked the women to sit in two circles. We dragged a rusted metal sheet we found in a pile of scrap behind the tent and leaned it on two barrels. For chalk, we collected coals from her fireplace. In no time at all, women were coming from every direction to join the class. Ghaalya and I hugged each other, overjoyed. We had even more women than the previous week. We learned that having the classes in the tent made it much easier for women to join. They were simply coming to Aisha's tent. There was nothing wrong with that.

When Ghaalya and I shared our success with Dvorka in her office at Shatil she suggested that we request a meeting with the Department of Adult Education in Be'er Sheva, a branch of the government's education department, to see if they would fund the programme. Ten days later, Dvorka, Ghaalya and I piled into Dvorka's car and went to present the project to the head of the Department of Education for the Negev, and his team.

At the end of my presentation, one of the officers said, "We know that Bedouin in some villages don't send girls to school and, if they do, they make them stop after elementary school. Are you telling me that Bedouin women who never went to school want to study now?"

"Yes," I said. "Why not?"

"But, according to your traditions, women don't go to school. They have children every year. I don't think this will work."

"Traditions are not fossils in a museum!" I said passionately, my hands grabbing at the air. "Traditions are dynamic, and if there's an opportunity, new traditions are created."

The head of the department was used to meeting with sheiks and mayors, but here was a Bedouin woman, a young Bedouin woman, coming to speak about political issues in her community. I was an exotic sight and in those first meetings people just came to watch. "Your Hebrew is fantastic!" they would say and I'd smile because for the next meeting they always came much better prepared.

The head didn't ask many questions. He watched me the entire time, his face maintaining a neutral look throughout. He closed the meeting by saying that they would take a look at our proposal and get back to me. Despite what I had grown up to believe about Jewish people, I didn't feel an antipathy from him or his officers. I did feel patronized by the assumptions they made about me and my culture, but there is a difference between being patronized and being humiliated.

A week later, we still hadn't heard back from them so we decided to ask for a meeting with the main office in Jerusalem. It was now nearing the end of June and one morning one of my roommates left a note by the phone for me. The note read: "The Adult Education Department would like to visit the programme on Thursday at 11 a.m. Call them." I didn't know what to do. It was noon on Wednesday. I immediately phoned Dvorka and told her about the visit. The problem, I explained, was that the class was on Friday, not Thursday. She told me that they would never visit on a Friday because they needed to be back before Shabbat and everything closed at the weekend.

The following day, Ghaalya and I were at Aisha's tent by nine in the morning. We had two hours to get the women to come to the class that morning in order to show the people in government that what we were doing was real. Sitting by her fire, Aisha waved her hand. "No problem, *ya bintee*. Send one of the children to call the women. Don't worry," she said with the absolute certainty of someone who lives according to the laws of nature and knows in her heart that God rewards those who are good. In her mind, that problem was solved so she moved on to the next one. "Should I prepare tea for them?"

I wasn't sure. She answered for me. "We have to. These are our guests and they will help us."

This wasn't the time for me to launch into my lecture about the difference between guests and government, privileges and rights. Dvorka was supposed to drive our "guests" to the tent, but she didn't know where it was. I asked one of the children to bring me an empty sack of rice and a marker. Ghaalya, who has beautiful handwriting, wrote on the sack: "Welcome to the Umm Bateen School of Adult Education".

Around half past ten we sent two boys to stand by the highway at the entrance to the village, which was a dirt road you would only notice if you knew where it was. The women dressed as if they were attending a party, wearing their black abaayas with colourful fabric peeking out from underneath. Not a single one forgot her notebook. Ghaalya and I started the class, but I couldn't focus on the lesson because I kept glancing towards the road to see if our "guests" were coming.

It had just gone eleven when a caravan of four cars slowed to enter the village. No one was paying any attention to what Ghaalya was writing on the board. The first car stopped next to the two boys and then drove behind them as the boys ran down the path towards the tent, the empty sack of rice waving like a proud flag in one of the boy's hands. We tried to continue the class, but couldn't, we were too excited. I watched for the cars and then saw the head of the tribe walking towards us. He must have seen the unfamiliar vehicles entering his territory.

"Hurry, hurry! The education office from Jerusalem is visiting the women's class and you have to greet them." I spoke quickly, conveying urgency and also making him feel important so he wouldn't cause any problems.

"What should I say? In Hebrew or Arabic?" he asked, as if this had been the plan all along.

By now he had reached the tent and the women exchanged worried glances, concerned that he had come to reproach them, but he greeted them in a very friendly way and immediately started practising his welcome speech.

The cars parked on the road by the tent. Seven people emerged from them and stood in a line in front of the tent. The head of the tribe shook their hands and delivered a perfect address, explaining why this initiative was important and thanking Ghaalya and me for bringing this programme to Umm Bateen. He looked at the women with pride. He wasn't just playing his role. He meant it. The delegation spent an hour with us, learning about our programme and taking pictures. Ghaalya and I translated between the women and the visitors so they could see for themselves the value of this programme in these women's lives and how these women were changing the traditions.

The visit was a success. In September, less than three months later, a policy was enacted which allocated a substantial budget for adult education classes in the Negev. We received a portion of those funds and were mandated to use the elementary school as the site for our programme. We left our beloved tent and moved back to the school. This time, when the principal came to open the gate, he promptly left the premises.

I loved teaching these classes and I did my best to make the programme not only about learning, but also about building confidence and community by organizing parties and events and excursions. One time, I took the women to Akka (Acre). For most of them, it was their first trip to a city. Two stories from that visit stand out in my memory. One demonstrates their cleverness, another their naivety. In the first story, one of the women refused to join us on the boat ride we had organized. There was nothing I could do to convince this desert dweller that God himself had made the sea and it must be trustworthy, so we left her ashore. Although these women were older than me, I sometimes felt like their mother, as if I needed to look out for them, especially here among the tourists and the city bustle, a world that was nothing like their own.

As the boat neared the shore after an hour-long joyride, I saw the woman sitting on a bench surrounded by a group of people. My heart clenched. Something must have happened to her. The boat docked and I rushed towards her only to slow down a few paces later when I realized she had become the main attraction: the town square fortune teller. She sat there with a queue of people lining up to have their palms read.

"What are you doing?" I shouted at her.

"You think I'm going to waste my time waiting for you? God's blessings are great, but life is short, *ya bintee!*"

Later that day, I took them to a restaurant for the first time. They found it very confusing. After I explained how it worked, showing them how to choose things from the menu and pointing to the waiter who would bring the food, the same woman, after a small fuss, ordered a kebab. The waiter took our orders and returned shortly with salads for everyone. She grabbed his hand. "Are you bringing me salad?" She was livid. "I ordered kebab!"

"I know, I know, but this is the first course," the poor waiter tried to explain, a young Arab guy, maybe seventeen, who didn't know what to make of these twenty women in their black *thobes* and white headscarves.

"I don't care about the first course. Bring me my kebab!" she insisted, pushing the salad aside.

I rushed over to explain to her that it came with the first course and that it was free, you didn't have to pay for it.

I think back on these memories with pride and fondness: the beauty of bridging worlds, especially when they are not oceans apart, merely a step or two. It wasn't every day that the people in Akka met their indigenous Bedouin neighbours and it wasn't every day that these Bedouin women faced the fact that there was a whole world outside the tribe. It was important for me to see how these women reacted to new situations. I developed a better understanding of peoples' differences and mind-sets. My focus on educating women made me accepted within the Bedouin community and outside it. I steered clear of the most volatile issues. I played it safe. I built my reputation among the Bedouin in the region and worked to restore women as equal partners in a society that, more than ever, needed them to reclaim that space.

Cover Up to Be Exposed

"YOU'RE NOT A child anymore. You have to cover your hair when you go to the city," Jidatee told me one afternoon.

I looked at the tight, dark brown curls that hung at my shoulders. "Abouee said that when I go to the city it's better not to look like an Arab."

"Aboukee isn't right about everything," Ummi retorted. "You have to cover your hair. You have to protect yourself."

"Modest clothes and the scarf are your protection," Jidatee agreed.

"But Abouee told me differently!" This conversation was driving me crazy. "He said that I shouldn't draw attention to myself, that looking different would cause trouble. The first day he drove me to university he told me to fit in."

Ummi and Jidatee clucked their tongues and shook their heads. Finally, something they agreed on. Ummi said: "Aboukee thinks about the Jews and how they will look at you. I think about the Arabs and what they will think about you going around the city with your head uncovered."

Jidatee nodded. "*Bazapt* [Exactly]."

When I moved to the dorms, I agreed to wear the scarf mainly because Jidatee had convinced me that my people were more likely to trust me if I did. "If you go around uncovered, how will our people believe that mixing with the Jews hasn't ruined you?" I didn't argue because I didn't want to lose my right to an education over a piece of fabric on my head. Nevertheless, she turned out to be right. During my work in the villages, the scarf conveyed that I hadn't completely assimilated and that I still valued our traditions.

One evening I finished my last class around eight and was on my way to the dorms. It was a cold night. The sky was changing from dark blue to black and the stars were brushed across the horizon. I had crossed the street and was headed in the direction of the dorms when a low honk startled me. It came from a truck driving on the road beside me. I picked up my pace, but the driver followed suit, and once he got close enough he told me to get in, told me that he'd take me wherever I wanted to go. I ran and he pursued me, yelling in anger: "Come! Come!"

I recognized his accent as one of our own, a Bedouin guy. I reached the intersection. The dorms were just on the other side of the street, but he turned right, blocking me from crossing. I ran into the street, in between the traffic lanes. He couldn't reverse because of the row of cars behind him heckling him to move. He left the truck, blocking the traffic, and started walking towards me. I dashed in and out of the cars and looked around, trying to decide where to go. The dorms were behind me and the campus was too empty at this hour.

When I was within earshot he yelled: "What are you doing out at this hour?" He swore at me for running into the middle of a busy street.

I ran back to the intersection.

"Where are you going?" he shouted.

I didn't want him to know where I lived. I turned left to the sports centre, which I knew he couldn't enter without a student ID. I pushed open the doors and flashed my ID at the security guard. A group of Jewish students, four boys, who were chatting nearby, noticed me: a girl with a headscarf at the sports centre at night. It was unusual.

One of them walked over and asked: "Are you all right?" He could see that I was trembling.

"Yes, I'm fi—" I couldn't finish the sentence. "No, no, no. I am not OK. There's a Bedouin man chasing me. I'm scared." I don't know why I specified he was Bedouin. Was I trying to get him on my side?

With a gentle voice, he told me to stay calm. While we spoke, I saw from the corner of my eye the truck park across the street. I hid behind the boy. His friends noticed and came over.

"What's going on?" they asked.

"There's a Bedouin guy chasing her. Can you guys check if he got out of his truck? Let us know if you see him."

A couple of them went out to check and returned shortly. "There's a truck by the bus stop but we didn't see anyone."

They told me to sit down and asked me where I lived. I told them I lived in the dorms and they said they would take me there. I told them that I didn't want to leave just yet. "He'll see where I live and come for me."

"He can't do that. If you see him again, take his licence plate number and call the police."

The idea of involving the police made me want to puke. I immediately heard the rumours: "He wouldn't chase her unless she'd done something." "They knew each other." "She just didn't want her father to know." The story would be woven together and I would be the villain, not the victim.

"No. There's no need for the police. I'll stay here until he leaves and then I'll go."

"OK. Do you know him?"

I shook my head.

"He's a Bedouin, right?"

"Yeah," I said, not feeling so good about having told them that. "I guess."

"*Ben zonah* [Son of a whore]."

Two of the students left while the other two waited with me for about an hour. I sat mostly in silence while the two of them chatted to each other. Finally, one of them looked out of the window and said, "The truck's gone. Let's go." They accompanied me to the door of my apartment, walking on either side of me like bodyguards. When we reached my unit, I thanked them. I don't even remember what they looked like, except that they were tall. I entered the apartment and Ayelet was still up, cooking. She saw my face was pale and my eyes red from crying.

"What's wrong? Are you OK?"

She placed her hand on my shoulder and I burst into tears.

"Are you hungry?" She pushed a plate of rice and schnitzel towards me.

I couldn't eat. I didn't want to tell her that a Bedouin man had chased me in the street. I didn't want to badmouth my people. I was their advocate. They were already stigmatized. I'd spent the last four months bringing our cause to light, trying to convince public institutions that there was a problem that required government intervention. I'd even had an argument with one student who called the Bedouin thieves. She gave the example of the Tarabeen tribe who had been caught stealing cars from residents of Omer. I defended their actions, saying that the people in Omer had stolen their land and left them without electricity or running water.

"They see the people in Omer with their fancy houses and big parks. How do you expect them to feel? They're angry," I said. "And angry people do angry things."

"Oh, so you justify their actions?" She wasn't really asking.

"No. I don't, but I can understand," I said. "Do *you* understand what motivates them? Have *you* ever asked yourself why these people are living in such conditions?"

I knew Ayelet would understand, but I found myself saying that I had failed an exam.

"Amal!" Her hand that had been rubbing my shoulder now gave it a sound smack. "You're killing me. Are you serious? You're crying because you failed an exam?" She got up to clear my untouched schnitzel. "You have a second chance, right?"

"Yeah," I said.

"Then what's your problem?"

I forced a smile. "You're right. I should be realistic. It's only an exam."

I wished her goodnight and walked down the stairs to my room. I sat on my bed, pulled the scarf off my head and held it between my hands. *Yes, there is a problem. Who are you afraid of? The Jews or the Bedouin? A man from my own community threatened me and who protected me? My enemies.*

I paced around my room going through the facts as if I was solving a maths problem. Jidatee had assured me that the scarf would protect

226

me from the men in my community. She had assured me that they would respect me because I respected the traditions. She said if I walked around without it, they would harass me. But, that's not what had happened. The scarf drew attention to the fact that I was a Bedouin woman walking around at night. The scarf didn't protect me, it exposed me. This man must have thought that a Bedouin girl walking around at night was easy prey. It ran through my mind like a broken record: *Jidatee cautioned me against the Jews, but this guy was a Bedouin. A Bedouin tried to hurt me. One of my people. The ones who protected me were Jewish. The ones that Jidatee warned me against. And it was the scarf. The scarf that was supposed to protect me gave me away.*

Was it my scarf or my people? Abouee didn't like the idea of my wearing a scarf. He said that it would expose my identity and that I would be harassed by Jews. As a woman, I was harassed by Bedouin men, but never by Jews. The Jews harassed me as an Arab, calling me "terrorist", "savage", "dirty". I never disclosed this to my parents because I didn't want them to worry about me.

It wasn't a maths problem. There wasn't a clear answer. All I knew for certain was that no place was safe. I needed to learn how to protect myself and be prepared to be singled out. The next day I bought pepper spray and kept it tucked in my pocket when I walked home alone late at night. But that was the easy step. The others would require years to perfect. I needed to be even more careful with my words and my actions to navigate between being a woman in a patriarchal society and being a Bedouin in a Jewish state. Neither identities could walk in the middle of the road without glancing over their shoulder.

Switching Gears

WHENEVER I REACHED the Shoket junction, where highway 60 from Beer a-Saba meets route 31 to Laqiya, I switched gears from Amal, the student at Ben Gurion University, to Amal, a daughter of the a-Sana tribe. As the minibus pulled into the village, I was prepared to weather Ummi's lecture about respecting our traditions, marrying within the tribe and fulfilling my responsibility as a woman to put the tribe's success over my own happiness. But when I crossed that junction on my way back, I switched gears again. I sat in lecture halls where my professors spoke about a woman's right to her body and mind, individual responsibility and her right to live her life on her own terms. They said that we belonged to no one but ourselves. Sometimes I forgot to switch and I would end up arguing with Ummi about women's rights, talking about things like agency and patriarchal oppression. These confrontations never ended well. Ummi would ask me to leave, saying that she couldn't understand all my *kalaam faadee* (empty words).

I used feminism to my advantage, taking ideas from one context and dropping them into another. When I spoke about it to Abouee, I made sure to mention that feminists hate men and that men fear them. I knew Abouee would like this definition. He wanted me as far away from relationships as possible and felt reassured by my activism, organizing protests against the state where I'd take charge of women and men alike. He'd say, "*Bint ar-rjaal ma alayha khof* [A daughter of a strong man we don't have to worry about]."

One morning, one of my colleagues, Ibraheem, a Bedouin from another tribe, came to my house to pick up the signs for a demonstration we had organized for later that day. I told all my male colleagues to see me as a mother, or as a sister. I didn't want to be seen as a sexual object, but as a comrade, a soldier in arms. The boundaries needed to be clear so that we wouldn't lose sight of our goal. Even though he was a few years older than me, Ibraheem called me "mama". He said it jokingly, but beneath it was the respect and admiration a man has for his mother, for all her hard work and ferocity. He parked his car outside our *hosh* and was greeted by Jidee, who was on his way to see Abouee.

Jidee assumed the man was there to see my brother. "Do you want Salmaan?"

"No. I'm here for Amal."

According to Ibraheem, Jidee's face darkened slightly, but he maintained his composure until he saw Abouee standing under our grapevine, tying the vines to the trellis. Then, he lost it.

"What is this *maskhara* [farce]? Since when do strange men come asking about our girls!"

"He is studying with Amal," Abouee said calmly.

I listened from behind the door, waiting for the men to resolve the issue of my respectability.

"So what!" Jidee's voice was full of anger. "He is a stranger. He's not even from this village. What *fauda* [chaos]."

Abouee didn't react. He called me to tell me that Ibraheem was there and to bring the signs.

I walked out carrying a stack of hand-drawn poster board signs in my arms. I looked straight ahead to avoid Jidee's glare, incredulous and disapproving, and quickly left.

On my way out, I heard Abouee say, "Don't worry. Amal is a feminist. You know, feminist women fight against men. They are not interested in them. They are like men." I tried to stifle my laughter from outside the *hosh*. I could tell by Jidee's silence that he wasn't sure what to make of all this. Abouee continued in a way that he would understand, "*Ya'ani, ma biyjeeb lina aar* [She won't bring us shame]."

I attended my first feminist conference in June 1994 at Givat Haviva, a non-profit organization in the north of Israel, at the invitation of one of my professors. This was the tenth conference for all women's rights activists, academics and organizations – Jewish-Israeli and Palestinian-Israeli – from across the country to come together to speak about promoting the status of women. I didn't ask my parents' permission to attend. My professor had invited me to speak about the challenges facing Bedouin women and to talk about my work in the villages organizing adult education and youth leadership programmes.

I stepped out of the bus towards a field of women sitting on the grass, passionately engaged in conversation, and immediately felt a sense of belonging, of sisterhood. I scanned the faces trying to find one that looked like mine, but I didn't see any. I was the only woman wearing a headscarf, but that didn't bother me. I felt I belonged because I was a woman. We were all women.

I went to sign in at the registration table and heard someone call my name. "Here you are!" I turned around to see Naomi Chazan. This was our first meeting since I had started university. I hugged her and she asked me about my studies. I shared everything with her, the progress we were making with Shatil and how more and more villages now had women's organizations and literacy programmes. I wanted to show her that her trust in me had paid off. She beamed when she heard about my progress and introduced me to the women around her, who commended my good work sincerely and enthusiastically. "We need more women like you," one of them said, and they all agreed. I felt hugged by all of them.

When it was time for the opening proceedings, a group of three women standing near the front of the room shouted at the MC, bitterly denouncing the conference organizers as oppressive hypocrites. "You are exactly like an Ashkenazi institution!" they shouted. Women left their seats to step in, some of them joining the women at the front, others forming an opposing camp on the other side of the stage. I saw a group of Palestinian women standing on the sidelines. One of them smiled at me and I walked over to her to ask what was going on. "It's not our fight," she said. This woman turned out to be Nabila Espanioly, a prominent Palestinian-Israeli activist. "We have enough to deal with. This is about Mizrahi and Ashkenazi women fighting over representation." She explained to me that the Mizrahi women – Mizrahi refers to Jews from North Africa and the Middle East – were angry because they felt that their issues were not as well represented as those of the Ashkenazi women at the conference. When the conference finally started, each panel consisted of an Ashkenazi woman, a Mizrahi woman, and either a woman from the Palestinian minority or a representative of the queer community.

The panels sought to provide as broad a representation as possible and to make space for the intersectionality of ethnicity, religion and sexual orientation. I would later learn that this event was the catalyst for the beerth of a Mizrahi feminist movement, distinct from Ashkenazi feminism. The Mizrahi women's cause spoke to me because they cared about reclaiming their Arab identity from Israel's "melting pot" policy which had attempted to unify the country by erasing cultural differences that pervaded institutions and society, all dominated by the Ashkenazi hegemony. Our otherness united us.

This conference made me aware of the incredible diversity within Israeli society, within both its Jewish and Palestinian communities. Each group has its own hierarchy of pain and exclusion, which determines its position, social construction and identity politics in relation to others and played by the system. It was generally agreed that I came from the most excluded group – a Bedouin in a nationalist state and a woman in a patriarchal society – and I felt that way too until I met a black Bedouin woman at the conference, who, like Nayfa, Jidatee's slave, had a history of oppression that exceeded mine.

These hierarchies of oppression must be acknowledged but not used against others in a pageant of suffering. It is not a competition. Your suffering does not negate mine, nor does it give you more legitimacy in this competition where there are no victors, only victims. When you start understanding that the personal is political and that everyone has suffered some sort of loss, we begin to understand that there are two goals: the first is to recognize the individual experience of each woman. No woman can be a representative of her entire community. I can't speak on behalf of all Bedouin women, a Palestinian woman can't speak on behalf of all Palestinian women, and a Jewish woman can't speak on behalf of all Jewish women. Our experiences are personal and it is only from these personal experiences that we can move to the second goal: the goal of understanding our shared sisterhood. If women are not united, how can we fight for a world where each woman, and every shade of her identity, has a voice?

The Mobile Library

I BECAME THE go-to person for organizations which wanted to work with marginalized communities in the Naqab. While I was still studying at university, Dr Majid Al-Haj, a professor of sociology at the University of Haifa, approached me to extend the work of his NGO, Insaan (Arabic for "human"), to the Naqab Bedouin. In an attempt to increase the number of Arabs at universities, the programme provided scholarships for students who created initiatives that supported their communities. Arab students often could not afford to attend university because their exemption from army service meant that they had few opportunities for subsidized education. The programme was a way to promote community engagement among Arabs, who, as a result of urbanization, tended to leave their communities and find work in the cities after completing their education.

My job was to recruit the students for the programme, coordinate their projects with local communities, and supervise and mentor them. Our cohort consisted of twenty-one students between the ages of nineteen and twenty-nine, all from different Bedouin villages and all studying in different departments at BGU. On top of their individual projects, the entire cohort banded together to create a mobile library for the unrecognized village of Awajaan, an impoverished shanty town across the road from Laqiya. Saleem from Awajaan and Yasmeen and Nahal from Rahat led the project. We refurbished an old wooden cart, lined it with shelves, and filled the shelves with books. Sitting atop a donkey, one of our students drove the cart from shack to shack, bringing the gift of knowledge to the children in the village. The children marvelled at the books, their colourful pages and stories of untold wonder, and soon the demand for books exceeded supply. Not having the funds to purchase more books, four students – all men – and I borrowed a minibus and drove two hours north to Nazareth to collect donations from Arabic bookstores. Surrounded by hills, Nazareth is an ancient city lined with cobblestoned-streets and stone facades. The first bookstore we entered was a modest storefront with dark, mahogany shelves from floor to ceiling. When I told the bookseller about our programme, he couldn't believe that children in the unrecognized villages wanted to read, but if they did, he would do everything in his power to help them. He sent his assistant to put together a pile of books for all ages and started phoning every bookstore in the city to help us.

I walked down the main street in Nazareth, four men by my side, without giving a second thought about who saw me. This was the Arab capital of Israel and a place where Arab women were free to live how they pleased, so it wasn't unusual to see an Arab woman accompanied by men. In each bookstore I was the one who brokered the deal and one bookseller even said: "I guess what my father told me is true: Bedouin women are strong."

We left the store, which was right next to Mahroum sweetshop, a small bakery renowned for its *knaafa*, a famed Palestinian delicacy: a melted mozzarella-style cheese sandwiched between two toasted semolina angel hair cakes, soaked in sugar syrup, sprinkled with pistachios and served warm with a dollop of *eshta*, Arab-style clotted cream. I recalled our first school trip when the bus driver drove past Mahroum and the teachers insisted we stop and pick up some *knaafa* for our families. It was back when pastries were rare in the Negev. For the Bedouin, dessert is the sweet tea we drink after each meal. On holidays or special occasions, Ummi would spread olive oil on hot *saj* pita and sprinkle it with sugar, and sometimes, as children, we'd steal fistfuls of sugar from the brown paper bag in the corner of the kitchen. We sat at a plastic table on the street and enjoyed the *knaafa*, scraping our paper plates for every last crumb. When it was time to pay, the men began arguing, each one jockeying to foot the bill, while I slipped into the store and paid. The men blamed each other the whole ride home. Letting the woman pay went against everything they'd been taught. I'd had enough of this false chivalry. I told them that if they wanted to work with me, I wanted to be treated equally. If they each took turns paying for things, I should too.

The next day, Saleem and I stood at the entrance to Laqiya flagging down cars to collect donations for the mobile library. We wanted to collect money from the locals to raise awareness of the project and to encourage the wealthier tribes to support those who were less well off. Each car that drove by stopped when I waved them over. Everyone I asked gave money. Saleem was not so lucky. Few cars stopped for him and even fewer gave. Of the cars that did stop, most of them listened for only a few seconds before rolling up their windows and driving away. By mid-morning, Saleem stood with his hands in his pockets, head down. I told him that it wasn't personal. That our work was for the common good. "We shouldn't be ashamed," I said. "The ones who should be ashamed are those that didn't give." I explained that raising money in this way was very new for the community. It was common to ask for donations at the mosque, but I wanted to differentiate between giving to the poor and giving to a community project. I wanted people to understand that their donations sustained a larger system: they weren't giving to feed a family, they were giving to feed the community. The return on investment wouldn't be immediate but donating to support the education of Bedouin children would bring changes that none of us could predict.

After sorting all the books according to age, language and subject, we discovered that our donkey-drawn cart wasn't big enough. We went to the garage in Awajaan, where the owner pointed us to a beaten-up white van he was willing to offer us in return for the cost of outfitting it with shelves. A week later we returned with our books, but after arranging them on the shelves, we still weren't satisfied. The van was old and rusty, with a cracked windshield and several dents on the sides. The beauty of community projects is not only the end product, but the process of engaging the entire community in their implementation. I remembered that my tenth-grade teacher was an artist and we invited him to repaint the van. He spent a whole day on it, surrounded by children who sat patiently, eager to see the library come to life. The whole village took part in the opening celebration of the mobile library. Saleem's family staked a tent large enough for fifty people. The desert floor was as well dressed as anyone, covered in red camel-hair rugs and embroidered cushions, and music pounded through a pair of old speakers. We had guests from all over the region and speeches from the staff from Insaan's office in Haifa as well as a member of Knesset.

A week later, Abouee was praying at the *masjid*. It was a Friday, the day when the residents of Awajaan also prayed at our mosque. He finished and snaked his way through the crowd of people standing in the courtyard outside the mosque. A man tapped him on the shoulders and Abouee turned around, recognizing the man as a leading figure in Awajaan.

"You have a great son," the man said. "We are very grateful for what he is doing to help our people."

At first Abouee didn't understand what he meant. Then it dawned on him. Abouee smiled. "You mean my daughter." The man shifted uncomfortably, not wanting to disrespect Abouee by mentioning his daughter in public.

Abouee noticed and gently squeezed the man's hand. "My daughter," he repeated. "Say 'daughter'."

Three years later, I organized a tour of the unrecognized village of Awajaan. One of the attendees, a woman by the name of Gaie Scouller who was invited by the New Israel Fund, noticed the van and asked me about it. I told her it was a mobile library and that we would visit it later in the day. When we got around to it, there were dozens of children lining up to borrow and return books, with a student managing the entire operation. Gaie was so taken by the project that her foundation donated $90,000 to upscale the operation into a truck, which, to this day, not only provides a larger selection of books, but is also a mobile storytelling theatre and cinema. The mobile library was the first of its kind and was later duplicated by organizations and communities in the north of Israel and in the West Bank.

While I headed Insaan's projects, we transformed the programme from having an impact on individuals (through tutoring programmes) to having an impact on communities. I remember being up at four in the morning with men and women working together to paint the lines on a soccer field we had built for the unrecognized village of Umm Bateen. I remember Professor Al-Haj's surprise at coming to the Negev three times in three weeks. In those days, we were sowing the seeds of social change in this part of Israel. We wanted to show the rest of the country that, although we were desert people, we were not desolate. Our hands knew hard work. In our hearts and on our land, an important social movement was beginning to sprout.

The Massacre

EARLY IN THE morning of Friday, February 25th, we woke up to Jidatee and Ummi crying. It was the month of Ramadan and we usually slept late because of the *suhour*, the meal you eat a few hours after midnight to prepare you for the day's fast. I sprang from the mattress. The fear that someone I loved had passed away gripped my body. I made my way to the kitchen. My parents and Jidatee were sitting around the fireplace. The light was new, the sky grey and the air was very cold, so cold that Jidatee sat with a thick grey blanket wrapped snugly around her and Ummi had covered her shoulders with the prayer rug. The fire illuminated their faces, the light glinting on their tear-stained cheeks. My siblings and I stood around them, gravitating towards the warmth of the fire, but fearful of the heaviness that surrounded it. Finally, Abouee spoke. "There's been a massacre," he told us. "Palestinians were killed by a Jewish settler while worshipping at the mosque in Hebron."*

---

* Baruch Goldstein, a Brooklyn-born doctor who lived in the settlement of Kiryat Arba, dressed in his miltary uniform, walked into the Cave of the Patriarchs in Hebron and killed 29 Palestinians praying there, and injured more than 125. It was Ramadan and hundreds of Moslems were in the midst of morning prayers. Goldstein was beaten to death by survivors of his attack.

31

32

33

34

31 With Anwar in Italy, 1996

32 With Professor Jean Panet-Raymond and Noga Porat on the McGill Middle East Program in Civil Society and Peace Building, 1998

33 With my fellow MA students at McGill, 1998

34 My twins Moad and Adan, 2003

35 A student and Azoulay her tutor in our video and photography programme, 2004

36 First playground in the unrecognised village Khashem Zaneh, 2005

37 With my family at Yousef's wedding, 2005

38 Adan and Moad, 2006

39 With Moad

40 With Vivian Silver at a presentation in Khashem Zaneh, 2006

41 With Cherie Blair and Vivian Silver (*second from left*), at the inauguration of the catering programme in Hura village, 2007

38

39

40

41

42   Teaching the AJEEC approach, 2006

43   Adan and Moad, 2007

44   Inauguration of mobile library, 1999

45

46

47

45   With my mother in Istanbul, 2007

46   Moad and Adan with their classmates on a Hajar school outing, 2007

47   With my father on his first trip abroad at the Van Gogh Museum, Amsterdam, 2008

48

49

48 With the Dutch ambassador and the Mayor of Hura inaugurating the Women's social enterprise for catering, 2007

49 Moad riding a donkey with other children in an unrecognised village, 2007

50 Anwar, Moad and Adan in Beersheva, 2009

51 With Moad and Adan in Beersheva on Palestinian Land Day, 30 March 2009

52 With Anwar in a playground

53 Visiting Wadi an-Na'am with the head of the tribe, 2009

54 With Vivian Silver on Human Rights Day March in Tel Aviv, 2010

55 Attending a conference in Belgium on the role of women in peacebuilding, 2010

56 With Palestinian Ambassador to France in EU Parliament, Brussels, 2010

57 & 58 At the Knesset talking about Bedouin women's employment, 2010

"How many were killed?" I asked, my fear now turned to fury.

"You are not leaving the house today," Ummi warned. "They will arrest everyone who demonstrates."

I ran over and turned on the radio in the corner of the kitchen. Those faraway voices spoke on every channel about the massacre. In Arabic and Hebrew, I heard the reporters' descriptions of the bloodshed, the gunman and the senseless violence as a call to arms.

We didn't have any phones in the village so I dressed quickly and went directly to the Laqiya Women's Association to write a press release to call for a demonstration. The building was empty. The solitude didn't bring me peace, but it brought me focus. I took the megaphone and walked around the village, insisting that people stand with me. Chesen and the other women from the LWA joined me as we marched through the village shouting for justice. Abouee's van drove past me, but I continued to shout into the megaphone, calling on all those who stood against the occupation to join our side. Abouee stopped his van to chat with my uncle, who gestured at me, telling Abouee that I should go home. I shouted louder and marched on.

By the time I walked back to the centre, we were a group of men, women and children, a hundred strong. My uncle Talab el-Sana, who was a Knesset member at that time, arrived in his car and found me in the crowd. There was an urgent meeting of the High Follow-Up Committee for Arab Citizens of Israel. Did I want to join? I asked for five minutes to change my clothes and told the younger ones to continue handing out flyers about the protest as I hopped into my uncle's car. He asked me if I could mobilize students from the university and Bedouin in the villages where I worked. I borrowed his cell phone and as we flew down the highway towards Rahat or Beer a-Saba – I don't remember which – I made two calls: one to the student union at BGU and another to my sister Na'ama in Beer a-Saba and asked her to drive to the villages and spread the word about the demonstration.

We arrived at the meeting at noon. Tens of people from all over the country representing the Palestinian minority in Israel – Knesset members, mayors of primarily Arab towns, leaders of every major Palestinian-Israeli civil society organization – sat around a large oval table. I was the only woman. This was during Rabin's second term as prime minister and it was the first time that the head of the country had formally approached the committee for advice on how to handle a crisis. Everyone was waiting for us to arrive; my uncle Talab was chairing the meeting. In his opening remarks he condemned the hateful acts wrought by the Israeli occupation and we stood for a minute in silence, honouring the victims who drew their last breaths on their knees, not in subservience to the state, but in service of the prophet.

Anger broke the silence. Men's voices saying the same thing, calling all Arabs to unite for justice. I said nothing. I felt ready to sit at this table, but not confident enough to share my thoughts. My friends from BGU trickled into the room. One by one, I caught their eye, and they came to stand behind me. My uncle interrupted the discussion and put his hand on my shoulder. "Laqiya is already hosting demonstrations. The main protest should be there. Amal is the leader of the student union and can mobilize students from all the universities and colleges in the region."

I looked back at my activist corps. We were willing and able. The committee unanimously agreed: the main protest for all Palestinians in Israel would take place in Laqiya the following day. The meeting adjourned and our preparations began. We needed to source enough Palestinian flags, prepare a flyer to distribute across the region, and select the slogans that would be our battle cry. A couple of hours later, two of the students and I drove through the city of Rahat: they distributed flyers and I shouted through the megaphone, my voice echoing through the streets, a *salaa* that called for civil disobedience. Passersby looked at me with surprise. Rahat, although a large city, did not participate in politics. It was a nationalist success story: an almost entirely Bedouin urban centre that had put aside most of its traditional practices. Luckily for me, the news of a woman representing a political cause travelled fast.

I arrived back in Laqiya late in the evening to find Ummi and Jidatee sitting in front of our television, cradling each other and sobbing. They were calling on Allah to take revenge on the Jews. "They have no heart," they cried. "They've rebelled against God!" Images of the massacre flashed across the screen. "Twenty-nine men dead and more than a hundred others wounded," the newscaster repeated. Nothing else he said stuck, but the images stayed with me for years: the dissonance of a holy site stained with blood. Bodies strewn about the floor. Bare feet. Grace violently dominated by will. I had no words and no tears. Only rage. That big, unholy rage that glosses over so much grief.

I went to the kitchen where Narjis and Maryam were cleaning up after the iftaar. I asked them to come to the centre early the next day to help me prepare the flags. I told them to wear black. I was so focused that I didn't notice at first that Narjis had been crying. She asked me if I had seen the people and the blood. I nodded. She held my gaze for a moment before bending down towards the floor, planting her hands on the ground as if the soil could console her. Maryam, always the strong one, continued scraping burnt lentils from the bottom of the pot. We stood there until Ummi's voice broke the spell.

"Amal, Aboukee insisted that I tell you that he doesn't want you to participate in the protest tomorrow. You will be expelled from university. You still have two years to go!"

Narjis looked up at Ummi, her eyes red and wet. "That's what you care about? Our people are slaughtered and you care about Amal finishing her education? How can you call yourself a Palestinian? You don't deserve to call yourself one. You eat and sleep. Like a cow. Your life is easy. There are people fighting for our freedom every day."

I had never heard Narjis talk like this before. She stood up and took Ummi's black abaaya from the cupboard next to the sink and handed it to me. "Here. We'll need more for tomorrow."

Ummi left the kitchen. I assumed she had stalked off as usual, but she returned a couple of minutes later with another abaaya folded in her arms and thrust it towards me. Her actions spoke louder than any apology.

The next day, the police were everywhere. A helicopter circled the village, its sole purpose to instil fear, to discourage us from assembling. On the ground, my sisters and I were busy at the centre, sewing Palestinian flags and inscribing our battle cries on large sheets of poster board: FREE PALESTINE, they said. AL-KHALEEL GABAL AL-JALEEL HEBRON BEFORE THE GALILEE, and GOLDSTEIN IS A TERRORIST.

By the afternoon, I stood at the head of over a thousand protesters marching from the entrance of the village to the centre, police officers ushering us off the highway. The women outnumbered the men three to one. Our black abaayas formed one thick black snake, a symbol of mourning, but also an act of defiance against the stream of red blood that was etched into everyone's memory from the night before. The protesters waved flags, carried signs and shouted slogans. With Ummi's abaaya draped around me, I held the megaphone at the head of this beast and called on everyone to repeat after me: "*Alfashiy lan taami a-sha'ab al-falasteenee huur* [Fascism doesn't stand a chance. Palestinians are free]. *Men al-lgyiya li-bayruut sha'ab hi ma bemuut* [From Laqiya to Beirut, one people that will never die]." One thousand hearts united for one great cause. Similar demonstrations took place across the region and beyond, in Jaffa, in Hebron and in Nazareth. Palestinians protesting the right to pray in their own land. The demonstrations garnered much coverage in the international press and it was the first time that Rabin recognized the legitimacy of the Follow-Up Committee by calling on the Arab leadership to settle the unrest.

In the evening, my family and I sat around the television to see footage of the protests throughout the country. It wasn't the solidarity that floored us, but the news of a single death from the neighbouring city: Mohammad Abu Jaame, a twenty-year-old from Rahat, was killed by the police while demonstrating. This was the first time since the Nakba that a Bedouin had been killed during an act of civil disobedience. Despite the housing demolitions and lack of access to resources, we had always believed that our Israeli citizenship granted us the protection that a state owes its citizens. This event was proof that it didn't. The hand holding the gun didn't differentiate between the Palestinians living under occupation in the West Bank or in Gaza and those living inside Israel itself. Mohammad's death prompted another wave of protests, these much more violent, with people running in the streets and burning tyres on the road. The women in Laqiya hired a bus to take us to Mohammad's funeral in Rahat. As I left, Abouee tried to stop me from going, but my oldest brother, Salmaan, defended me.

Our bus of women pulled into Rahat where fifteen thousand people had taken to the streets. We were the only women. This was a defining moment for women's participation in political protests. People must have been thinking: *Where is their fear? And where are their fathers?* We climbed on top of the bus and raised the Palestinian flag while shouting together in unison: *Al-fashia lan tamoor* (Fascism won't stand). Journalists swarmed around us and locals handed us a megaphone to magnify our presence. The media loved the Bedouin women who rose from the desert sand to protest against the state. We fulfilled their idea of strong women who were as harsh as the arid lands we lived on. Women had attended rallies before, defending social causes such as the rights of children or the right to education, but no one had seen women stand up for a political cause, for a crisis where our nationhood was at stake.

A week later I was called to meet with the security department at the university. I was waiting for them to call me, since they had brought in all the students who had participated in the protests. Before I stepped into the office, I remembered that I was wearing a necklace adorned with the territory of Palestine and a bracelet with the flag on it. I removed them and placed them in my jacket pocket.

I was worried. In the aftermath of the previous week's events, I thought they might expel me. I didn't truly believe that these protests would solve anything, but I did want to be able to express my views and my anger without paying for it with my future.

The security guy sat behind a desk with a folder open in front of him. His blue eyes motioned towards the chair in front of him.

"I see that you are very active. How is your studying going? You study social work, right?"

"Yes."

"Your grades are good except for microeconomics."

"Yeah. I registered to take it again. I don't like maths."

"It's not maths," he said. "It's human behaviour in the market: at what cost are people willing to act?"

I knew what he was getting at and I knew better than to bite back.

"Why can't you just focus on your studies and stop with this *balagan* [mess]?"

"It is not *balagan*!" He had goaded me into a fight. "To stand up against injustice is not *balagan* and why should I choose between the two? Do Jewish students have to choose? Do you call them when they get involved in politics?"

"Listen," he said. "This is an academic institution. We are not political."

"Really? The fact that you invited me is proof. If I was protesting against car accidents would I be here?"

He wasn't expecting so much heat. He stood up. "Listen. You know that I know who your friends are. I know what you have hanging on the wall in your room. How do you think I know all of this?"

It was a scary thing to hear, but I stayed strong. "I'm not impressed. That's your job."

"It's also the job of your friends. The ones that you trust. How do I know what's in your room?"

I didn't answer. I wanted this conversation to be over.

"We know everything." His blue eyes held my gaze until I said, "OK."

"It's better for you and for us to make a deal here," he said, closing the folder in front of him. "Focus on your studies. You're helping women. Do that. Why get involved with politics? Don't destroy your future. This is a warning. I don't want to hear more of this *balagan*."

He stood up and I picked up my bag from the floor by my chair. When I put it on my back, he noticed the keychain in the shape of Palestine. "Take that off," he said. I unclipped it, but as soon as I left his office I clipped it back on.

Why Open the Wound if You Can't Heal It?

The doctors at Soroka Hospital couldn't understand why Bedouin children, once taken to hospital by their parents for one ailment or another, were left there, often for months on end. The administrators approached me and my cohort of students from the Insaan programme and asked if we could do something about it. We visited the children's families and found out that in each case the family had an impossible choice to make: bring the child home knowing full well they didn't have the resources to provide the necessary care (electricity for respirators or refrigeration for insulin) or leave the child in hospital in the hope that they would have a greater chance of survival. The administration understood that children who required long-term care couldn't be sent back home and that without adequate public transport it was impossible for their parents to bring them in for regular treatment.

We decided that if the children were going to be a fixture of Soroka Hospital, then the hospital needed to provide a space where they could feel like children, not patients. In the library, we established an Arabic section with several shelves stacked with books and games in a language that felt like home. When the parents did visit, doctors and nurses referred them to the library and very quickly a warm community flourished, an oasis of compassion in the sterile hospital, a space that reflected all of Israel's citizens.

This initiative received much attention from the press and the administration asked our cohort to assist other departments at

Soroka. That was how I met Dr Rivka Carmi. Back then, she directed a unit specializing in genetic diseases. She asked me to help organize workshops within the Bedouin community to raise awareness of the transmission of genetic diseases through marriage between cousins. Her request aligned with my personal belief that such marriages were risky so I invited her to Laqiya to speak at the Laqiya Women's Association.

I met Rivka in the hospital parking lot. She stood next to a fancy red sports car which purred blissfully along the highway until we turned onto the road towards the village and the paved surface changed to uneven dirt and rocks.

"How long until we get there?" she asked me.

"We're nearly there," I said, not realizing that, as far as she was concerned, each metre of unpaved road was devastating for her car.

I pointed to the centre that sat atop a hill.

"Are you serious?" she said. "That's all rocks. There's no other way in?"

"No," I said. "That's how we get there."

She didn't like my answer. With the body of the car close to the ground, she manoeuvred the wheel from side to side, attempting to avoid the rocks – which was impossible – and winced each time there was a thud. I didn't feel sorry for her. What had she expected? It wasn't my fault the government hadn't paved our roads.

We finally arrived and she parked next to the gate. Fifty women had already gathered in anticipation of the event and Rivka's anger evaporated when the women swarmed her with hugs, kisses, and excited greetings of *"Shalom, shalom!"*

We all walked together towards the largest room, where the women sat on a motley assortment of plastic and wooden chairs, arranged in five rows. I stood with Rivka at the front of the room, next to a blackboard. I introduced her as the head of the genetics department at Soroka and explained that she was going to talk to us about genetic diseases. Up until this point, the women had no idea what any of this meant. Disease, sure, but "genetics" wasn't a concept commonly thrown around in the Bedouin community. Rivka began her presentation and I translated. When Rivka said that marriage between close relatives was one of the causes of genetic diseases, I could tell that some of the audience members understood, but I wanted to explain it in a way that might make them more receptive to the idea. I used the hadith where the prophet Mohammed says, "*Qa rbu alnikah* [You should marry a stranger to avoid having weak children]." Some say these are the prophet's words, others credit them to his companion, Umar Ibn al-Khattaab. What mattered to me was to bring this knowledge closer to them. I wanted the women to see that this knowledge wasn't foreign, that it existed within our own tradition.

But each word pulled me further away from them. I had broached an untouchable subject, one that underpinned the tribe. A practice so essential that we routinely said, "The girl is for her cousin." Criticizing this practice was as reprehensible – and as inconceivable – as wiping my soiled hands on a prayer rug, but here I was, standing in front of a room of fifty women and telling them that everything they believed about how they should live their lives and how they had lived their lives was wrong. And not only was it wrong, it was harmful. The faces that had been so eager a moment before now winced as if there was a foul odour in the room. I avoided Ummi's gaze. The sound of people shifting in their seats grew more and more audible until one woman left. Then another. Then two at once. Then half a row. On her way out, an old woman shot back: "Don't destroy our girls' lives with your fake stories. Are you blind? Look around you! It's the strange women who gave us dumb children." At the time, the three children suffering from disabilities were the offspring of three women from a different tribe. "Put your brain back in your head, *ya bintee*. It looks like you lost it."

Her anger gave permission for the other women to leave. Some looked at me apologetically – Rivka was our guest after all – but most of them stormed out, humiliated and upset. Rivka didn't understand exactly what was going on, but she knew the women weren't taking the lecture well. I said to her: "They're not ready to talk about this. This practice is very rooted in our tradition and we can't address it in just one lecture."

Rivka looked down at her notes and apologized for putting me in an awkward position. She glanced back at the empty seats and noticed seven women, all seated in the front row, who were waiting patiently for the lecture to continue. "But these women haven't left!" She looked hopeful.

"These women are my mother, my sisters and my aunts."

Rivka still hadn't caught my drift.

"They're here out of respect because you're my guest."

As we headed back to the car, one of my cousins who was engaged to her first cousin looked at me with tears in her eyes: "Why would you tell me this?" she cried. "You know there's nothing I can do. Don't open the wound if you can't heal it."

Open the Jar

IT WAS DECEMBER. Winter in the Naqab. Dvorka and I were driving back from one of the unrecognized villages east of Beer a-Saba where we had just met with a group of young women and one man to discuss starting a community organization there. Dvorka was at the wheel, her eyes fixed firmly on the road, but her right hand motioned towards me as we debated whether or not we thought they were ready to establish their own organization. I had my doubts. It wasn't the women who had invited us, but the man. He had dominated the conversation – which wasn't unusual – but something about the situation seemed off. I worried that he was trying to take advantage of the women; use the organization as a front to receive funds from Shatil and then use that money for his own aims. Dvorka's lips curled into a smile.

"I think he had other intentions."

I didn't get what she was trying to say. She turned down the volume on the radio. I took it as a sign that we were about to have a serious conversation. Dvorka and I had become close friends, we spent hours planning community projects, writing proposals, pitching campaigns. We relied on each other yet we maintained a professional distance. Dvorka had never intervened in my personal life. Until now.

"Well," she said, "I think that guy is more interested in you than in starting a women's organization."

I gulped.

Either she didn't notice or her intuition told her to keep pushing into this topic of conversation that, until now, had been off limits. "I think he's a good guy, but I understand the tribal barriers. Which tribe is he from? Is it one of the 'OK' tribes? Would you fight this?"

She stared straight ahead, but her words tapped against the glass jar where my heart was locked away for safekeeping. I had no intention of letting them in. I had sealed my heart in that jar during my conversation with Abouee after Basma's wedding and so far had not regretted it.

"I don't think so and I have no plans to marry any time soon," I said quickly.

"But one day you'll have to think about it."

"That's what my mother would say," I said defensively. She dropped the subject. I could tell I had made her feel awkward.

Shlomit Aharoni came on the radio, singing *"She'tavo ehbek"* ("When You Embrace Me"). I stared out of the window. The sun was setting over the desert plain, seeking a place to rest. Dvorka's questions, the words of the song, the sunset. I said softly:

"I have a very close friend, but I'm not sure if it's love or friendship."

Sensing my vulnerability, Dvorka proceeded cautiously. "Hmm. How do you know him?"

"I've known him for years. We were in the same class from elementary school to high school."

"And where is he now?"

"He's in Italy studying law."

"Is he from your tribe?"

I turned to look at her. "Dvorka! What's happened to you? You're as bad as my mother."

"No, no! I just want to make sure you're not getting in over your head."

I let the silence make itself felt, then said: "Honestly, I hadn't thought about any of this until twenty minutes ago."

Dvorka drove me to the dorms and dropped me off. We waved goodbye and she smiled at me with a look I hadn't seen before, the tender look of a mother. Maybe she was right. Maybe it was time for me to examine what was in that jar.

I entered the room that I now shared with another Palestinian-Israeli student, Zaakya. This apartment had six students, two per room. Zaakya wasn't home yet. I pulled off my brown leather boots, which were caked in mud from walking on the dirt roads of the desert, and left them outside the door. I took my old blue backpack from the cupboard and emptied it on my bed. Tens of letters fell onto the bed, each one bearing those unmistakable red and blue airmail stripes: greetings from Italy.

Anwar and I had been classmates since first grade. He belonged to the group of students who came from Awajaan, the village next to ours. While Laqiya is a recognized village with utilities and resources, Awajaan is unrecognized and destitute, but Anwar's pride never stopped him from being involved in the activities in our village. When we were thirteen, the Sons of Laqiya Association trained us all in *debka* and Anwar was the only person from Awajaan who joined us. He had the charm to navigate the tribal boundaries and the wisdom to know what to resist and what to accept.

In high school, during one Hebrew literature class, I pulled the textbook from my bag and flipped through it till I landed on the text we were studying: the Book of Ruth. Sitting there, wedged in the spine of the book, was a folded piece of paper. I trembled. A note like this meant that someone loved me. A note like this could also jeopardize my reputation and even my place at the school. Girls had been expelled for notes like these. And that was just the beginning. First you were expelled and then the rumours would start. Some girls were so severely bullied that they never returned to school again. I hoped that the teacher hadn't seen anything. My aunt Aalya was sitting next to me. She moved forwards to cover me as I slid the paper into my bag. I knew the note was from Anwar. The teacher called on me to read and the story came alive in me. I described the way Ruth offered herself to Boaz, placing her shawl at his feet. Ruth's vulnerability softens Boaz's heart. I imagined myself in Ruth's place and Anwar receiving me. My face flushed a deep red and I immediately rejected the whole idea. We were friends and that was it. It was too dangerous. Too complicated. Too impossible even to think about.

After class, Aalya and I agreed to open the letter in the barn next to my house. There we'd be safe. I arrived home, gobbled down my lunch, and ran to the barn where Aalya stood waiting for me. The letter beckoned to us like a rare artefact which offered a glimpse into another world. The world of boys, of which we had no real knowledge, only fear.

My fingers delicately unfolded the note to reveal a single sentence: "I love you and I know that you don't like these things and I am sorry but I had to tell you."

Aalya looked at me and blinked. She had expected more.

"What do you want to do? Are you going to write back to him?"

"No way!" I said. "Are you crazy?"

Aalya whacked me on my shoulder, called me stupid, and left the barn, perhaps feeling that the whole episode hadn't been worth the anticipation. I took solace in the sheep. I separated the lambs from their mothers and coaxed them into their pen. Rereading the letter in my mind, I was planning how I would hide it. I wanted to keep it, but that was too risky. I decided I would rip it into small pieces and burn it in the fireplace. I would have to be patient. Wait till after dinner, until everyone had left the kitchen, then toss my prized love note into the flames. For the rest of the day I walked around as if I was hiding a bomb. My fear was great, but the feeling of being loved was greater. I stayed out in the field and savoured that feeling for as long as I could because I knew that the feeling couldn't last.

The next day, Anwar tried to exchange looks with me but I avoided him.

After a couple of weeks, he understood my answer and he dropped the subject. Our relationship returned to normal. We continued to be friends and volunteer together in the summer camps and other community activities. He used to drive his father's blue van into our village and park it next to the well. He would sit there and watch me walk back and forth between my house and our barn.

A few years later, in our eleventh-grade biology class, Anwar asked me to be his partner for the class research project. I accepted, although it was unconventional. It was the first time that a girl and a boy worked on a project that required them to spend time together away from the watchful eye of the school. Our project looked at how three desert animals – camels, goats and dogs – coped with the heat. For two weeks, under the blinding noonday sun, we would go to my house to watch the goats and the dogs and then drive to Anwar's village to observe his neighbour's camel.

Once my grandfather saw him coming to our barn and asked what he was doing there. Ummi explained that he was doing homework with me. My grandfather wasn't happy with that answer, but Anwar didn't put too much stock in how people reacted to him. His skills on the soccer field eventually won my grandfather over, but I still had trouble deciding whether Anwar's actions were bold or reckless. Did he not understand our traditions? Did he just not care?

Another time, after our high school graduation ceremony, while I was walking towards the girls' bus, Anwar tried to speak with me. I walked straight past him and had taken my first step onto the bus when I heard something hit the ground beneath my other foot. I looked down. There was a cassette tape lying on the asphalt. I turned to see Anwar darting towards the boys' bus. I picked it up and stashed it in my bag. It was Umm Kulthum's "Amal Hayati", a clear message that, despite everything, he had not given up. *Amal hayati* means "hope of my life". I didn't see Anwar once that whole summer, but I'd see his blue van, every day, right before sunset, the exact time when I'd leave my house to feed the sheep.

During the year when I volunteered at the school in Um Mitnan, I was out in the schoolyard playing with the children one morning when I saw someone walking towards the school. He was too far away for me to recognize, but something in my bones told me that it was Anwar. As the man drew closer, my eyes confirmed my intuition. I ran to the gate to stop him before he entered the schoolyard, worried that this was another one of his "to hell with tradition" antics that would get me in trouble. What would the principal say if he saw us? That I used the school to meet with men? That I did this behind my family's back? There were endless ways the story could be spun. It was noon and Anwar was drenched in sweat. He had walked the length of the rocky dirt road from the highway to the school and he stood there catching his breath. I was livid. I didn't even greet him, I just shouted: "What are you doing here? Are you crazy?"

He smiled, trying to calm me down with his confident charm. It didn't work.

"I don't want anyone to see us," I hissed.

"I just came to say goodbye," he said. My heart jumped at the word. Anwar leaving? His presence in my life felt as easy and as certain as the sand beneath my feet. I lowered my gaze, avoiding his eyes so they wouldn't draw my emotions out of me. "I want you to know that you are the one and that you will always be the one." I kept looking down, not letting myself feel or take in any of it. He continued: "I am travelling to Italy to study. I still don't know what I'll study but I'll start with Italian."

"That's great. Good luck." I forced the words from my mouth. "You know my brother Salmaan is there if you need any help," I continued, falling back on courtesy to pull myself together. Anwar was used to it by now. He seemed to understand that I was resigned to keeping my heart locked away.

The voice of one of the children asking to go to the toilet freed me from the charade. We shook hands. It was only for a second. My hand clasped in his, his other hand gently resting on mine. Time froze. Time flew. The moment lasted an instant and forever all at once.

Over time our relationship weakened. I'd see him during summer vacations when he came to volunteer at the summer camp in the village but he didn't visit every summer. We used to write to one another. He got my uncle Abd al-Rahman's postcode from my brother Yousef, knowing that my uncle was open-minded and wouldn't betray our secret. I'd pick up the letters from my uncle's house. The letters were formal. Anwar would tell me about his work and end them by saying that he missed all of us in Laqiya. They weren't particularly moving or poetic, but short and to the point, more like a laundry list than a love letter. I'd reply just as formally, never crossing any lines, but providing wordy accounts of my community work, news about my family, and short anecdotes about riding into town with Anwar's father who used to drive a minivan between Beer a-Saba and Laqiya. "My Dear Brother Anwar" they'd start, just in case the letters fell into the wrong hands.

The evening I returned from my drive with Dvorka, I picked the letters off my bed and read them one by one, trying to unearth something I had buried. Something that I had never even given the chance to breathe. I wanted the words to fight me. I wanted them to tug at my heartstrings so forcefully that I wouldn't be able to stop the jar from crashing open.

I heard Zaakya before I saw her. She made a light-hearted jibe about the mud caked on my boots: "Oh God," she said. "She's brought half the village with her!" She entered the room like a breeze. True to her name – zaakya means "delicious" – she was pure magic. You couldn't help but feel good around her.

"Hello soldier," that's what she called me, "what battles did you fight today and which village did you invade?" She pulled off her jacket and tossed it on her bed.

I was carefully putting the letters back in my bag. "I went to a new village and met with a new group of women and—"

"Wait, wait, wait." She walked over to my bed. "Did you start working abroad without telling me?"

I placed the last one in the bag. "No, these are from my friend, Anwar. I told you about him."

Zaakya was too smart to believe that that was the end of the story. "*Taayeb*," she said through pursed lips. "Why would you get them out now? Are you looking for something?" she asked, teasing me gently. Her warmth softened me. I felt something shift: the key to the rusted safebox where I had abandoned my heart.

"I am," I confessed. "But I don't know what I'm looking for ..."

Zaakya looked into my eyes. "You are looking for something that you're afraid to find."

We sat there in silence. She let out a deep breath. "Let me get something to eat and I'll tell you what you're looking for." She ruffled her long dark hair. "Have you eaten?"

I shook my head.

"Well, come then!"

Zaakya visited her family once a month and returned with what seemed like an entire Palestinian kitchen bursting from her luggage. She truly was a roommate sent from heaven. We would sit together gossiping over homemade kofta or diwali rashta or zucchini stuffed with meat, everything drizzled with tahini, served with a dollop of baba ganoush and plenty of fresh pita on the side for dipping. Zaakya warmed up a container of stuffed grape leaves, knowing they were my favourite, and called me to the dining table. The dark green, almost black, leaves glistened with olive oil. I picked one up and plopped it in my mouth. I felt Zaakya waiting for me to speak. I had sat with her countless times, listening to the latest episode of her love story, which alternated between comedy and tragedy every other week. We had lived together in the same room for nearly a year and I had only ever spoken to her about my activism, what she called "my craziness". Her complicated love affairs and ever-changing emotions were just as crazy to me. Love was a battleground where, until now, I had dared not go. She didn't need to push. I was ready for her to guide me there.

I told her about the conversation with Dvorka that had got me thinking about Anwar. "You know," I said, "my friend, the guy who is studying in Italy."

Her dark eyes widened and she let out a victorious and knowing "yessss!", an invitation to me to continue.

"I don't know," I said. "We are friends and I call him a brother."

"You call him 'brother' because you are afraid to call him something else. I knew there was something going on." She spoke with the certainty of someone who finally had the evidence to back up her intuition. The kind that feels especially satisfying because the person she was talking to had everyone around them fooled, even herself.

"I noticed how you react reading his letters, and even when you go to Awajaan for the mobile library you come back full of excitement."

It all made sense to her, but I wasn't willing to see my love as anything more. "I get excited because we're long-time family friends," I said.

"Amal, stop it. What are you afraid of? Look at you." She leaned in. "You're a strong activist who enpowers women to stand up for themselves but you yourself are a slave."

"What? I'm not a slave! I do everything I believe in. I move freely. I do what I want. I am a free woman."

I was free to work, to think, to act, but was I free to love?

"You're lying to yourself. You are a free woman who's locked up her heart so it won't get in her way!" She pushed her plate towards me and stood up.

"Look at us. Sheep in a lion's skin. We pretend we are strong, but we oppress ourselves. This is not courage. Courage is being yourself, doing the things you want. Not giving up." Her eyes gleamed. "You are afraid to be in love." My stomach jolted. "And you know what?" she continued. "The one who doesn't have it can't give it. You will never be able to free women if you limit yourself. I mean, us. Us, Amal."

The jar smashed open. I heard my forgotten self in her voice. Shards of glass lodged in my chest, the tears poured from my cheeks. We sat together, hugged tight, sobbing. The salt cleansed the wound, the pain lessened, and my heart throbbed: cautious, raw and tender.

Who Wronged Yasmeen?

I ENTERED MY supervisor's office at Soroka Hospital where Bedouin woman sat waiting with her young son in her arms. The boy's face was nestled into the fabric of her black *thobe*. He turned when he heard me and I suppressed a gasp: brown doe eyes, a short little nose, and white gauze where his mouth should have been. The gauze covered a terrible and tragic monstrosity he had afflicted upon himself: he had chewed off his own lips. The boy suffered from a rare genetic disease that meant he didn't feel physical pain.

This was my supervisor's first meeting with the mother. Each case was different, but the clinical social work interventions followed more or less the same formula: focus on creating a nurturing parent–child relationship, help the mother navigate the complex challenges of her son's medical condition, and support her in seeking services. I was there with two hats: managing the case as a student under supervision and as a translator.

We sat across from the woman. Her white shawl framed fine features. Her eyes were large and innocent, just like her little boy's. Where she clasped him to her, it was clear how thin she was and how loose her garment, as if she was wasting away. The boy's fingers had also been wrapped in white gauze to protect him from hurting himself.

The supervisor introduced us, explained that I was also Bedouin and that we were social workers.

"Are you a doctor?" she asked me.

"She is not a doctor. She is a social worker. Every time you come you will see a doctor and a social worker," my supervisor explained. "Amal," she turned to me, "you will need to explain what a social worker is."

I told the mother.

She blinked. "I want the doctor."

"You will see a doctor, but I'll also be here to help you," I said.

"I don't need help. I need the doctor to heal my child."

"The doctor will help your son and I will help you."

My supervisor excused herself and told me in Hebrew that we would reconvene at the end of the day. When she left and closed the door, the real conversation began. "*Men ay arab inti?* [Which tribe are you from?]" the mother asked me.

"Laqiya village," I told her.

"Are you married?"

I shook my head.

"Why not?"

"I haven't had the chance yet."

"Do you have brothers and sisters?"

"Yes. I have twelve brothers and sisters."

She smiled. "From one woman?"

"Yes," I replied. "Abouee is married only to Ummi."

While I was answering her questions, the guidelines that forbade the relaying of personal information to the client sounded in my head. But my gut instinct told me that what was happening was right. I needed to establish trust. Why would she open up to me without knowing anything about me? In the tribe, we define ourselves by our relationships. The son of, the daughter of, the wife of. Trust is built on identifying who you are and where you come from. Then you can get to talking about what you want.

I asked her the name of her son. I knew it – it was in the yellow folder between my hands – but I wanted to build a relationship with her. To start from where she was.

She lifted him to her lips and planted a kiss on the part of his cheek not wrapped in gauze. "Ahmad. I named him after my father."

"That's beautiful. How old is he?"

"The doctor told me he is three years old, but I don't count. He was born the same month that my father died. Not long ago. I'm still wearing my mourning *thobe*."

I glanced at the green and brown embroidery covering her shoulders and chest.

"During my pregnancy, I was very sad and my mother said that the baby was sick because he absorbed all my sadness."

"*Allah yarhamaha* [God will help you and your son]."

"*Inshallah*. Is there a cure for this?"

"What has the doctor told you?"

"He said *inshallah* but I'm afraid. I can't sleep at night. I'm very worried."

"I'm here to help you be strong so you can take care of him."

"Social work", in its institutionalized form, was a foreign concept to the Bedouin community. We had no concept of the extent of our dispossession or of the processes and services that existed to help us reclaim our rights. We lived away from it all, trapped by our own ignorance, by a staunch refusal to seek help, and by the systems in place to keep it that way. Academic social work made no sense for people who lived in self-sustaining communities with an entirely different culture. It made no sense because it was about providing services to people who lived on the margins, but still within the system. How do you provide services to people who live entirely outside the system? Entirely outside any frame of reference?

The mother still didn't understand what our meetings were for. My intuition told me that speaking about "resilience" and "attachment theory" would create yet more distance. I tried something else.

"If you made a salad in a broken plate," I asked her, "what would happen?"

"The juice would run everywhere," she said.

257

"You are the plate," I explained. "If you are not strong, you will not be able to support your son through this. I'll be here for you at every step."

When I told my supervisor about the meeting, she scolded me for my openness, for answering personal questions, and, worse, for inviting the woman to come by on Wednesdays without specifying a time. "You have other clients," she said sternly. "You should set the time so that she arrives on time."

What was I here to do? Support the mother in managing her son's disease or teach her to be punctual? My supervisor didn't understand the circumstances. How was she supposed to arrive on time when the very notion of time was a reminder of one more thing about her that didn't belong? Even the most basic requirement – scheduling appointments – was a sign of an inherent othering of the Bedouin way of life and a disregard for this woman's particular circumstances. Time was not hers to command. She rose and rested according to the sun, acted according to her children's needs, and moved from one place to another according to her husband's motivation to drive to work.

My supervisor lectured me on boundaries. Setting boundaries and respecting boundaries. Boundaries related to my role, my profession and my time. The word irritates me to this day. Although they are meant to protect, boundaries assume a sterile relationship between social worker and client. They're a hallmark of Western helping traditions (psychology, psychotherapy, psychiatry) that create an artificial space where problems are tackled in isolation. Do any problems exist in isolation? This case validated my hunch that they did not. To act according to my supervisor's boundaries, to the profession's boundaries, would have been like cutting off my arm. My identity and knowledge of the culture made me useful, so useful that, to help the mother, I'd end up breaking every rule in the book.

In the space of two months, I saw the mother at least six times. Sometimes she would come to see me even if she didn't have a doctor's appointment. If I was busy, I'd ask her to wait. She always did. One session, I explained that her son's disease was genetic and recommended that, if she planned on having more children, she should get tested. She said that she'd had three children before Ahmad and that they were all fine.

"*Al-hamdullilah!* If you decide to have more children, you should tell me or the doctor."

She agreed. Before leaving, she turned to me: "Can you come and visit me? As my guest?"

I didn't know what to say. I told her that we weren't supposed to visit our clients, but that I would ask my supervisor and get back to her.

When I asked my supervisor, she all but rolled her eyes. "You know she lives in the Bedouin *pzura*. I can't take responsibility for sending you there."

Until the mid-nineties, no one called them "unrecognized villages". They used the word *pzura*, which loosely translates to "sprawl". They saw us like a fungus that had spread in every direction.

I insisted. By now she had already experienced my stubbornness and didn't have any interest in arguing with me. "If you want to do this," she said, "inform the hospital. They have a minibus that takes doctors to the *pzura*."

The following week, I pulled up in a minibus, driven by a Bedouin. The mother emerged from her shack, her brow furrowed, and her mouth in a small but arresting half-moon. "Why did that man come with you? My husband is not here. What will people think? I told my mother-in-law that you are a friend. She doesn't know that you are a . . . what is it called . . . ?"

"Social worker," I said.

"Yes. That."

I asked the driver to leave and come back two hours later.

We entered her shack. Four walls made of metal sheets, streaked with dark, orange rust. A thin mattress lay on the thick rug that covered the dirt floor. On top of the mattress were two plump pillows resting carefully against the wall. Every Bedouin's single luxury: a place to sit and have tea. I removed my boots and sat down. She disappeared and returned with a tray of tea and oranges and placed it on the rug in front of me. She sat on a cushion on the other side of the tray, filled a small glass from the silver *buraad* and handed it to me. Her small hands picked up an orange and began peeling it.

"Drink your tea," she urged me. I thanked her and brought the glass to my lips. Her eyes fixed on the orange flesh between her fingers, she said quickly: "If my mother-in-law asks, say you're a friend from the hospital."

I still didn't know why the mother had invited me. This visit was a risk for both of us. Receiving visitors from other tribes was uncommon and raised suspicions. My appearance in this woman's home could spur any number of rumours and, as a social worker, it was my duty to protect her.

"I'll say that we met at the hospital and that's it."

"But if she keeps asking?"

"Don't worry. I'll handle it."

"Please. I don't want her to know that you work there."

No sooner had I taken the first sip when a large woman entered the shack. She carried herself like a rooster, welcoming me with a gregariousness that was meant to ward off predators.

We shook hands and kissed on both cheeks. She sat down next to me and ordered her daughter-in-law to bring lunch. The mother I had come to visit looked uneasy. I sensed she didn't want to leave us alone. I smiled at her to convey my confidence. "Don't worry," my eyes told her. She left the shack.

The mother-in-law played nice, but she suspected something.

"Which tribe are you from?"

"I'm from Laqiya."

"*Amm ahlan wasahlan* [Welcome guest, this is your home and your place]." We use this phrase frequently with our guests. To avoid the discomfort of silence, whenever the conversation stalls, the host reignites it by repeating the guests' blessing.

"Are you married?"

My presence in the tribe may have been odd, but our etiquette prohibits interrogating a guest.

"Are you Bedouin?" I teased.

She looked stunned. "*Badawiyya men asil alhado!* [I am original Bedouin!]" she declared, pointing to her chest.

"Since when do Bedouin ask their guests so many questions?" I asked with a laugh, but she got the message.

"*Wallah*, I am not questioning but *al-ma'arfe zayne* [knowing people is always a blessing]." She quickly changed the subject. "Here, take this orange. Eat. Eat."

I didn't want her to ask me something I couldn't answer without lying. In our tradition, the guest determines the topics of conversation. For three and a half days, the guest shares what she wants to share. The host provides food and shelter, along with a generous ear and a disciplined tongue. Suppose you arrive feeling angry with your mother, but, after a day or so, your anger subsides. The three and a half days gives you the chance to leave with your mother's name unstained and your dignity intact.

The mother-in-law chose a more suitable topic: the burden a daughter-in-law brings to her family. Every second word was her daughter-in-law's name, Saleema, followed by *inshallah*. *Inshallah* Saleema would bear no more sick children, *inshallah* Ahmad would be well soon, *inshallah* her son wouldn't have to miss any more work to drive Saleema to the hospital. *Funny,* I thought to myself. *I didn't know he drove her.* I had never seen him.

Saleema returned with a heaped platter of rice topped with chunks of stewed lamb and placed it on the rug in front of me. "He drops me at the hospital and then goes to work," she explained. "I wait around until he finishes and then he picks me up. At least it's not hot in the hospital. Here we feel like we're in an oven."

"I told you to sit in the tent! It's much better but you insist on hiding yourself in here," the mother-in-law chirped. I could tell that this criticism wasn't new. "There's nothing better than a tent. It brings you the best air."

Saleema glanced in my direction, that displeased half-moon on her face again.

The mother-in-law tore a hunk of lamb to pieces and pushed them to my side of the platter. I pinched the rice and lamb together, pressing the warm morsels into a ball before putting it in my mouth. We ate almost in silence, save for the few pleasantries exchanged every few minutes: my gratitude, Saleema's welcome, the mother-in-law's complaints.

When I moved back from the platter to signal that I had finished eating, the mother-in-law protested: "Eat, eat. We made it for you!" "Thank you," I said. "I am really full." She insisted again. "*Amaar!*" I said, using this common phrase to both convey my sincerity and my wish for their home to always have an abundance.

"*Sahhtayn!* [To your health!]" they both replied.

The mother-in-law pulled the platter away from me and reorganized it in the usual way. She piled the lamb in the middle and patted down the rice, so it was level. "Come," she said, slowly rising to her feet. "I'll take this to the children. We'll eat in the tent."

When the mother-in-law turned her back, I saw Saleema cobble together a small plate of rice and hide it in the cavern of her scarf. We all started walking towards the tent, and Saleema called the children to follow their grandmother. "I am taking her to wash," Saleema told her mother-in-law. I didn't know why she said that, but I followed her in the opposite direction.

We walked down a dirt path, Saleema carrying the plate in one hand and the *ibreeq*, the pitcher for cleaning yourself, in the other. The sun bore down on us and I swatted at a persistent cloud of flies. They were the big ones, the ones that swarm rotting flesh and animal waste. Saleema said nothing to me as we walked. We passed the barn and stopped a few minutes later when we arrived at a storage container that looked like it had been abandoned. Warped metal sheets so rusted that the lightest scratch left a clear and enduring sign. "Mary plays with Nuri" was etched on the front, a reference to the textbook all first-grade children in the Negev had.

Saleema entered the darkened room and signalled to me to follow her. Quickly. She gripped my hand and spoke her first words to me since we had embarked on this mysterious errand.

"Please. Promise me you'll help me with this. If you tell anyone that I told you, they will kill me."

The light from the sky outside peeked through holes in the roof. The horns of the half-moon on Saleema's face pleaded with me.

I started to worry. "What is it?"

"First promise." Even in that dim room, I could see tears staring at me in her eyes.

"I promise."

She held my gaze a moment longer to make sure I meant it and then led me to a corner of the shack where a large plank of wood was propped against a metal sheet. She put down the *ibreeq*, lifted the wood out of the way, and slid the metal sheet open a body-sized crack. The smell of human waste nearly choked me. I held my breath but could feel that the air emanating from that part of the room was awful and damp. She beckoned me to follow her. I was about to tell her I didn't need to use the bathroom when a soft whimper emerged from the dark. Another whimper was followed by the dragging of a chain, rubbing against the foul, wet earth. Two brown eyes peered out at me from that man-made prison. Two eyes, a deep gash across her nose, and warped, scarred flesh surrounding a gaping black hole for a mouth. She had no teeth, no fingernails, and, on some fingers, no fingertips even. I wanted to run from what I'd seen. To run and forget.

Saleema sat down on a wooden crate beside the girl, pinched together some rice from the plate tucked under her scarf, and fed her like a baby lamb, carefully placing the food in her mouth and making sure she had swallowed it before handing her another fingerful. The girl moaned gratefully. I didn't run. I didn't shut out Saleema's reality. I sat down beside her and put my arms around her waist as if I was holding Narjis between my arms. Saleema cried. Maybe she always cried when feeding the girl, or maybe my presence heightened the tragedy of the circumstances. It's devastating what we can learn to live with.

"She is my eldest," she explained. "Her name is Yasmeen. I called her that dreaming of a flower and here she is sinking in her own waste. *Khara* [Shit]." Yasmeen lived in a cell no larger than a bathroom stall and one of her legs was chained so that she couldn't escape. "I can't do this again," Saleema continued. "When I see Ahmad, I am terrified. You have to help me."

Yasmeen was trying to catch her mother's shawl, but she didn't have enough of her fingertips left to clasp the delicate fabric. Saleema kissed the girl's cheek and told her she'd be back. Yasmeen nuzzled her and looked at me. There, against a decrepit backdrop of a mother's worst nightmare, of a father's desperate acts, and of a family secret so shameful that to whisper it meant death, I saw Yasmeen's disfigured mouth greet me with her version of a smile.

We left the storage container and Saleema told me to pretend I was washing my hands. When we returned to the shack, the mother-in-law was preparing coffee over the fireplace in the tent.

"Drink your coffee before you leave," she barked at me.

I walked over, my thoughts still with Yasmeen. *Why would she smile?* I sat on an empty wooden crate by the fire and took the *finjaan* she handed to me. I don't remember what we spoke about. I felt as hollow and empty as the space inside the crate I sat on.

Finally, it was time to go. Saleema accompanied me in my absent-minded state to the car and talked to me about Yasmeen. "I have to get her out of there. My husband doesn't want her in hospital. He doesn't want anyone to know about her."

"How long has she been in that place?" I asked, afraid to hear her answer.

"Once she started crawling, we noticed that she'd get hurt but would never cry. She'd burn herself, but still she wouldn't cry. We took her to the doctor, and he told us she needed to be in hospital, but my husband decided to keep her at home. She ate her lips, her fingers. Her father took out her teeth when she was six so she wouldn't hurt herself."

We said goodbye and I got into the minibus. All the way back to the hospital, I pictured Yasmeen in the darkness. Her brother, Ahmad, had been taken to hospital and was receiving treatment for his condition. Yasmeen, because she was a girl, was treated worse than any animal. She was hidden away, a mark of something so evil that her own father had chained her up like a dog. Her face haunted me the whole way home. Those eyes, that mouth. But, more than anything, what I saw looking back at me was her smile, her smile that sent a clear message: "Don't give up on me."

My supervisor had already gone by the time I got back to the hospital. It was half past four. I asked the nurse how to contact my supervisor in the case of an emergency. She gave me an answer that made me want to throw my bag in her face. She suggested that I wait until the next day because the supervisor didn't like it when people didn't respect her time. "She is very clear when it comes to her boundaries."

What did boundaries mean for someone like Yasmeen? I stormed out and made my way back to the dorms where I found a telephone directory in the lobby and looked up hospitals in the north. Yasmeen needed to go to hospital and I wanted her to be as far away as possible. I settled on Akka. I had just got my driver's licence that month and had never driven that far, but there wasn't any time to think.

The next day, I skipped class and went directly to my supervisor at Soroka. I entered like a sandstorm. I blurted out that we had an urgent case and needed to act immediately. She didn't flinch. "Calm down," she told me. "Sit." Whether it was the shock of not having processed what I had seen or the cold manner in which she defused my energy, I sat down and burst into tears. She went to fetch me a glass of water. In those brief moments alone, I let myself feel the horror of what I had seen, but when she returned, I pulled myself together and told her about Yasmeen.

"We have to call the police," she said bluntly.

I jumped at the word. "No! No. Police intervention will ruin everything. I promised Saleema that I wouldn't harm anyone in her family."

"What? You can't promise something like that. You should have come to me first. I can't be guided by your judgement. You're a student." This woman's ignorance felt like a slap in the face. She was older than me and tradition dictated that I should respect her, but everything she stood for felt at odds with what I knew to be right.

"I know. But I know what should be done. I have to take her to hospital."

"The police will take her to hospital."

I finished her sentence: ". . . and her parents to jail."

"Maybe. They have to take responsibility for their actions."

"Please," I was begging now. My voice had seldom sounded so desperate. "This is not the right way. We save the girl and destroy the entire family?" I all but shouted that last phrase, hoping that she would hear the truth in it. A truth she couldn't have understood since she hadn't grown up there, in the Bedouin *pzura*. Even the word reinforced her belief – not just hers, but the mainstream belief – that the lives of the Bedouin were as haphazard and disorganized as our tents and shacks dotting the desert skyline. But behind that appearance of chaos existed a very real system of boundaries. Boundaries that had nothing to do with the tidy world of time and client-patient relationships. Boundaries whose transgression bore the very real penalty of exile, violence and even death. Two lines: God's and the tribe's. Going to the police was a severe offence against the tribe's own system of justice, and the repercussions for everyone involved, even for me, would be severe.

"We have to get the police involved," she repeated. "This is what we have to do as social workers. We can't cover up something like this. If the girl dies tomorrow, we'll be held responsible."

I didn't know what to say. She was right, but she wasn't right. I told her I wanted to consult the mother because I had promised I would help her.

She lost patience with me. All of this deliberation didn't sit with her neatly delineated boundaries. "Look," she said. "I have to go and see another patient. We'll talk about this later."

She left the office and I walked in the opposite direction, that meeting only reinforcing my determination to rescue Yasmeen myself.

I rushed out of the hospital and was hurrying towards the university when I saw Saleema, Ahmad in her arms, walking towards the hospital entrance behind a man who I presumed was her husband. She hadn't told me she was coming. Her appointment was the following week. I intercepted them and asked her why she was there. She explained that she had come for herself, not for Ahmad, but that she couldn't leave him at home: her mother-in-law couldn't deal with him and she didn't trust the other children to look after him. Her husband stood to one side, allowing us to speak. He was tall and gaunt, looking older than his thirty-plus years because of how thin he was. She told me that he had been at home the other day, he had cooked us the meal, but he had stayed away from the house to allow us our privacy.

I told him that I would take her to the doctor and drive them home. It took some insisting, but finally he agreed, reaching into his trouser pocket and handing his wife some money before turning to go. I accompanied Saleema to her doctor's appointment and an hour later we were in my car, driving back to her village. The village wasn't far from Beer a-Saba, but it was far beyond the paved roads that ran through the desert. Off the highway and into the dust we drove, speaking little. I had only one thing on my mind. When we arrived at her shack, that's when I told her.

"We need to move Yasmeen to hospital."

She protested. Her husband would be angry.

"I'll explain it to him. He will understand," I said.

It wasn't that I had a plan, it was that I knew what needed to happen right now. We had to get Yasmeen out of there. The other steps would become clear once Yasmeen was in the right hands.

The half-moon on Saleema's face pleaded with me for another

option, but I was resolute. Yasmeen's treatment had been weighing on her soul and I think my certainty gave her the confidence to take the risk. She placed Ahmad in my arms and went to prepare Yasmeen. I sat in the car and the nosy mother-in-law came by to ask why Saleema had returned so early. I gritted my teeth and lied. "She forgot Ahmad's medicine, so I drove her to pick it up."

That satisfied her. ""*Allah ya'tikei al-aafya* [May God give you health]," she answered before waddling back to the tent to lie down in the shade.

Saleema emerged from behind the shack, carrying Yasmeen's emaciated body in a blanket. We placed both children in the back of the car and I started the engine. I reversed the car, kicking up thick clouds of dust as I drove towards the highway. My heart raced, but I was careful not to drive too fast on these untrustworthy desert roads, where rocks are bigger than they seem and ditches appear out of nowhere. When I reached the highway, I changed my mind. Akka was too far and I didn't know the way. I took her to Soroka and within half an hour we were in the emergency room.

I introduced myself to the staff, but when the nurse saw Yasmeen, she stopped asking questions and took action. They put the girl on a stretcher and took her into another room. I stayed behind with Saleema and helped her fill out some forms. Twenty minutes later, I was talking to Yasmeen's doctor, having the same conversation I had had that morning with my supervisor. He was insisting that we needed to report the case to the police. I didn't have the patience to go through this again, to plead my case to someone who would refuse to understand. I asked to speak to his supervisor.

I entered the supervisor's office and explained the whole story, stressing that involving the police would make matters much, much worse.

He understood, but said that Yasmeen's father had done something wrong. "He left her in that shack to die. This is serious." The hospital was duty-bound to report it.

"But jail is not the solution for everything," I protested.

His hands lay folded on his desk in front of him. They barely moved as he spoke. Steady and firm. There was nothing he could do. He had to report it. But his eyes told a different story. "I can see you are a strong social worker," he continued. "You can make the case to the police."

I left his office deflated. Now I had to tell Saleema that my actions had jeopardized everything.

I sat down beside her. "Saleema, they will call the police. I tried to convince them not to, but they said they have to. It's the law." I knew this wasn't right, that involving the police would only cause greater harm, that Saleema would pay the price for my indiscretion, but it didn't matter anymore. What was done was done. Saleema's face darkened, the repercussions of what I'd said so overwhelmed her that she slapped her chest and her face, again and again, repeating, "*Ya khrab diyaarki ya Saleema* [You've destroyed your life, Saleema]," like a punishing prayer. I tried to interrupt her, but she was now crying with the abandon of a neglected infant, her tears spelling out her regret at having shared such a dark and terrible secret with me. I sank lower in my chair and felt consumed by shame.

Twenty minutes passed. Two police officers arrived and I saw the doctor escort Saleema and Ahmad into the examination room where they had taken Yasmeen. A few minutes later, the doctor called us in. We stood under the harsh fluorescent lights which now reminded me of an interrogation room. The only difference was that I wasn't going to let anyone bully me into submitting to a process that didn't serve my client. Saleema and her husband were symptoms of a deeper problem. I looked at Yasmeen sitting on the examination table. The same doe eyes as her brother, her mother's frail hands recognizable despite the mutilated digits. She craned her neck to look at everything she had never seen, not agitated, just curious, as if a lifetime spent in darkness gave her access to some untouchable calm. A jail sentence wouldn't give Yasmeen justice. Why liberate one family member only to imprison another? Yasmeen didn't deserve more deprivation, she deserved abundance.

The doctor spoke first addressing the policemen. "Look. This case is not for you. We reported it because we had to," by the grace of God, the doctor had heard me, "but we have a very good social worker," he continued, "and she can work with the family."

That one instant restored my hope.

A police officer asked me my name.

"Ah, it's you," he smiled. The same cohort of officers dealt with issues in the Bedouin community. My role in organizing and leading demonstrations had got me something of a reputation by then. "It's nice to see you in real places where you can actually help people," he said.

The interview with the police lasted about an hour. I gave them my observations and then they spoke to Saleema, who assured them that her husband never beat the girl. He had chained her up to protect her from injuring herself and the other children, who were afraid of her. She was unpredictable and didn't have any awareness of her own strength. They agreed not to arrest the husband, but protocol obliged them to open a file on him, and he would need to give a statement. I told them I would speak to him.

We drove back to Saleema's village. When we reached the crest of the hill leading to her house, I slammed on the brakes. Her husband, Younes, was waiting for us. He stood in front of their shack wielding a threatening metal rod. "He'll kill me!" Saleema shrieked. She started hitting herself again. My trembling foot eased on the gas. Their mother's distress set off Ahmad whose scared sobs reminded me of my duty to protect both of them. I didn't know what to do. We were getting closer. I tried to control my shaking leg when Jidatee's wisdom came through. "Even if you're afraid, don't show it," she would say. "Act like you are the strongest person on earth. Make the other person scared of you."

We pulled up in front of the shack and I told Saleema to stay in the car. I opened the door and slammed it with all the fury of a bull released from its cage.

"What do you want?" I shouted. "Tell me." I didn't hesitate. I didn't flinch. I advanced, allowing this show of anger to take me over completely. "She was about to die!" I yelled. "Do you want to kill your daughter? She is your daughter."

We would have been standing nose to nose if he hadn't taken a few steps back. My strategy was working.

"Where did you take my daughter?" he shouted. He raised the rod to try to regain the upper hand, so I leaned in again. "Hit me," I said. "Hit me. You can." He took another step back and waved the rod in front of my eyes. Again, I came closer. "Hit me," I said. This time I didn't shout. I said it staring straight into the black wells of his eyes, straight into his soul where all his pain stared back. "If you think this will solve the problem, do it." For that instant, we met on another plane, a world away from Yasmeen, from Ahmad, from Saleema, from the Bedouin *pzura*. It was only for a second, but in that second I seized the rod from his hand and continued: "Do you really want to kill your daughter? Do you want her dead? She is yours."

The man crumpled to the ground. He sat in the dirt, holding his head between his hands, and shook with quiet, ashamed sobs. Saleema got out of the car with Ahmad. I motioned to her to get inside the shack. At that point, I think she was more afraid of me than of her husband.

Saleema left us alone. Younes let himself cry. I stood beside him and waited for him to speak.

"She is my daughter," he said finally. "Do you think I want to kill her? She is my flesh and blood. I love her, but I can't help her." The words were lodged in his throat along with his pride. He had no more fight in him, nothing left to hide behind. Carrying the weight of that secret had been like holding a serpent to his own veins. His humiliation and shame cut deep, but his soul lifted a little at the respite from the venom.

"Younes, I believe you love Yasmeen. I know you love her. I understand that you wanted to help her but didn't know how. This is normal. Yasmeen's situation is very, very hard. You are not supposed to find the solution alone. I am here to help you."

He wiped his face with his sleeve. "Where did you take her?"

"She is in hospital. The doctor said it will take some time for her wounds to heal, especially the one on her right leg where the chain cut her flesh to the bone."

He broke out again in tears.

"I also want you to know," I continued, "that the police are involved because any case of abuse should be reported to the police."

Younes jumped like a startled animal. "Are they coming to take me?"

"No. I told them that we will both go to the station in Beer a-Saba to give your statement there. You will come with me, right?"

"Yes," he said. "I need to resolve this."

We met the next day in the parking lot of the police station in the old city of Beer a-Saba. When he stepped out of the car and walked towards me, I could hardly believe that this was the same man that I had confronted yesterday. He was like a wilted plant that had been revived. He had shaved and wore a flattering shirt and a pair of dark blue jeans.

"Thank you for being here for me," he said.

We entered the police station. This is not a place anyone wants to visit unless absolutely necessary. All eyes were on us, especially all Bedouin eyes. I heard people whispering obscenities. "He knows her," fluttered across the room like a tidal wave. I didn't feel comfortable waiting there. I told the woman sitting behind a computer screen near the front of the room that I wanted to see the police officer, Ronen.

She barely glanced at me before looking back at her screen. "Wait there and we'll call you," she said.

"No," I said. "Tell him that Amal el-Sana from Soroka Hospital wants to see him."

Now she looked at me. "He is busy. You can wait outside."

"No, I can't wait outside," I said with authority. "If he is busy, I need a place where I can sit and talk with my client."

She scoffed and raised an eyebrow. In her eyes, I was supposed to be either a victim or a criminal. My confidence and sense of what I deserved didn't fit with who this woman thought I was based on the colour of my skin, and my wearing a scarf. Nevertheless, she picked up the phone and called the officer. A second later, she put down the receiver and said through pinched lips: "You can go in."

Ronen greeted me and told us to wait in his office while he retrieved Younes's file. I told Younes to relax and to explain to Ronen what he had told me: that he had had no intention of hurting Yasmeen. That he hadn't known how to help her. That he had locked her up to keep her from hurting herself and the other children who bullied her. Ronen returned with the file and the interview went smoothly. Younes told him everything.

"Why didn't you bring her to hospital?" Ronen asked.

"I was ashamed. I didn't want anyone to see her," Younes said.

"Did you ever hit her?"

"No. Never."

"Did you deny her food or water?"

"No. Her mother served her meals. I didn't want to see her. It was too hard for me."

At the end of the interview, Ronen asked Younes to sign the statement. Now the secret was out. The story was official. Years of trying to hide from his conscience spelled out on a few sheets of paper. Younes looked at me for the go-ahead before picking up the pen and signing his name at the bottom of the page in Hebrew. I asked him to wait outside and Ronen and I continued the conversation.

"Younes wants to cooperate with me to find the best solution for Yasmeen," I said.

"You know that hiding her doesn't absolve him of his duty towards her," Ronen said.

"Not having these villages on the map doesn't release the state from their duty to provide for them. It doesn't mean that these villages don't exist," I shot back.

Ronen waved me away. "I don't want to get into this. You're a good advocate and I appreciate the work you are doing, especially this work. Not the demonstrations." He smiled, and we shook hands. "Good luck with the family," he said.

I walked out of the office, but in my heart I bounced out of there.

"*Yalla,*" I told Younes, "the police won't charge you. We will work together to make a plan for Yasmeen."

When we reached the parking lot, we stood face to face, just as we had stood the day before.

"Yesterday you wanted to hit me. I was very afraid," I said.

He opened his arms wide and smiled. "I am very sorry."

We shook hands. He walked towards his car and I to the bus station.

He rolled down his window as he passed me. "Just for the record, I was the one who was afraid of you."

I saw Saleema and Younes the following Wednesday at the hospital. They both looked different, younger but also older: more rooted, more at peace. The couple had decided to put Yasmeen in an institution where she could be cared for properly. When Saleema and I visited, she whispered to me, "I wish we could all move in here."

At the end of the term, I sat with my supervisor to review the case. The meeting didn't go well. Facing me, arms crossed, she listed the ways I hadn't just strayed across some boundaries but had violated the very ethics of the profession. "You weren't supposed to take further steps without telling me," she shouted, raising her voice to convey how badly I had acted. "You put the entire family at risk."

I didn't say anything, but that meeting told me that clinical social work wasn't for me. To help Saleema and others like her, I would need to tackle the policies outside the community and the practices within it, to help create solutions that addressed the problems on a systemic, not individual, level. The university was training me to promote people's well-being, but it wasn't teaching me how to address the issues that created the problems in the first place.

Graduation

IN JUNE 1996 my parents entered the university for the first time in their lives to attend my graduation ceremony. Abouee wore a blue button-down shirt and blue jeans. Ummi came dressed in her fanciest Bedouin *thobe*, embroidered from top to bottom, and her black *qunaa*. I walked with them feeling that the world was too small to contain my happiness. We passed the university president, Avishay Braverman, who bowed when he greeted my parents. Out of propriety, Ummi wrapped her right hand in her *shash* before shaking his hand briefly and Abouee shook his hand with both his hands and held onto it.

"*Mabrouk*," Avishay said. "You should be proud of her."

"I hope she didn't make any trouble for you," Abouee replied, grinning.

"I won't say that," Avishay winked at me, "but they were good troubles. We are very proud of her and I believe that she'll take her community to the next level."

The university photographer followed the president, taking photos of him greeting all the happy families. This was the same photographer, Hertzel, whom I had invited to photograph all the projects and events I had organized during my time at BGU. He snapped a photo of Avishay with my family, then one of my parents and me. It's funny how one click encapsulates so much effort, so much determination and so much change. We walked around the quad, bumping into my friends – Jews, Ethiopians, Palestinians, Bedouin, boys and girls – who all greeted me and my parents with the same jubilant enthusiasm. Ummi was the only woman in a traditional dress, but I didn't feel out of place.

My sister Abeer ran across the grass, beaming, one arm waving at us while the other gripped a large bouquet of flowers. She had just started her first year in the social work programme, and everywhere she went, people called her "Amal's sister". This infuriated her so she had taken to introducing herself with the words: "I'm Abeer and Amal is my sister, not the opposite."

She handed the flowers to Abouee and instructed him to give them to me at the end of the ceremony. He bowed towards Ummi and playfully held the flowers out towards her. "For you, *sa'idaati* [my lady]. Who is Amal? You are my life." Abouee knew how to flirt, but Ummi never knew how to respond. She would sometimes say, "We're not children anymore. Behave yourself." One day I asked her why she refused to enjoy his games. She told me that she never felt as though she deserved them. All her life, people had said that Abouee should have married a prettier woman than Ummi, whose dark skin made her undesirable. It was a common refrain even among her own sisters who said, "We never knew what Abd al-Kareem saw in you. Never." She would laugh with them to protect herself, but it stung.

After the graduation, we went to a restaurant in the city, a Moroccan Jewish place I had been to many times for celebrations over the past four years. When I entered wearing my black cap and holding my flowers, the owner rushed over to congratulate me and the *zagareet* sang out from his wife's mouth. They seated us, but Ummi's rigid movements told me that she wasn't comfortable. She hardly ever ate out in public and, if she did, she never let strangers see her. She held her *shash* over her mouth or sat facing a wall, like the few times we went to eat falafel in Beer a-Saba with her as children. Biting, chewing, licking and swallowing are actions considered too sensuous for public display; the mouth is a private place.

When I asked her what she wanted to eat, I again put her in an uncomfortable position. *She* did the serving. No one served *her*. No one asked her what *she* wanted. They had couscous with meat, chicken or fish, I told her.

"How come they have couscous? They're Jews."

"Yes," I explained. "They are Jews who are Arabs. These are Moroccan Jews. They have the same food as us."

"What, Jewish Arabs?" She looked at me bewildered.

"Remember Aliza whom you spoke Arabic with in hospital?

She's an Arab Jew!" Remembering her fondness for that old lady brought a smile to her lips.

Abouee joked with the waiter, while Ummi made up her mind.

"I'll have the couscous with meat," Ummi said finally. "I want to see how they do it."

When the waiter came around to our side of the table and I said couscous for Ummi, Abouee warned him that she had ordered it just to test him. Ummi nodded without knowing what Abouee had said. The waiter bent down towards Ummi and said, in a Moroccan dialect, "*Inshallah mezian* [Delicious]."

"*Inshallah*," she answered, playing along with the joke, but also somewhat doubtful of these Jewish Arabs and their couscous.

Moments later, when he placed the couscous in front of her, she didn't even look at it before pushing it towards the centre of the table.

"This is what you ordered!" we shouted at her.

"It's too much! I can't eat it all," she said when I pushed the plate back towards her. That heaped plate of couscous made her self-conscious. When we sat on the ground sharing from the same plate, no one focused on how much you ate or how fast. We shared everything and there was a communal rhythm to eating that discouraged greed. I dug my spoon into my own mountain of couscous and took large, slow bites, my tongue caressing the buttery kernels. Ummi barely touched her plate. She dipped her spoon into the dish and cautiously brought it to her mouth, keeping her lips as close together as possible as she scraped barely a thimbleful into her mouth. Abouee was busy with his steak while Abeer and I hovered around Ummi, showing her how to enjoy her food as if we were teaching a baby. We opened our mouths wide and closed them again, bringing our lips together with a delighted smack.

She threw up her hands. "I feel naked!" She refused to eat another bite and decided that she would take the food home. When we arrived back at our house, Ummi sat with Jidatee on the floor of the *hosh* and they enjoyed the meal together.

"*Mabrouk, ya bintee*. These days, knowledge is the best weapon," Jidatee said to me in between mouthfuls of couscous.

Over the weekend, my aunts and uncles from both sides came to our house to congratulate me. Abouee slaughtered a lamb. For the first time, it wasn't to celebrate a woman's relationship with a man but to celebrate her relationship with herself, her relationship with the world. Whoever had disagreed with Abouee's decision to send me to university faded into the background of the children running around, the ecstatic *zagareet* and the intoxicating smell of the lamb that had been braising all afternoon. The women sat together, six or seven of them around a large platter, eating with relish.

Abouee called me over. He stood with the head of the tribe.

"*Mabrouk*," he said and he shook my hand. "May you always be strong. We still have a long way to go in this country and we need people like you to get our dignity back before they take it all."

Abouee's pride radiated from his body into mine. "They may take the land," he said, "all the land, but they will never be able to take what we have here." He pointed at my head.

That night the girls' room was busy with happy noise. We gossiped before going to sleep, Narjis, Abeer, Wafaa and I, squashed together on one mattress, and Maryam neatly tucked in her cot on the other side of the room.

Although closeness epitomized my sense of home, after one week back, I was beginning to feel suffocated. I missed my privacy and the freedom that it afforded me, not just with regards to space, but with regards to time, with regards to the private rituals I had created for myself. But now that I had graduated, I no longer had a valid reason to live in the city on my own. Since we still didn't have a landline, being home meant being isolated from the world. My mobility was also restricted. Every minute after sunset that I was out was a transgression: good girls don't hide in the dark. They come home early. But still, I never asked Ummi permission to leave the house. I didn't want to reverse any of my hard-won independence.

One day, Ummi and I stood together at the entrance to the *hosh* singing along with a passing bride caravan. In the past, the bride would have ridden on top of a camel adorned as elegantly as she was: gold jewellery, red garlands, ribbons. Today, the bride is often driven, the cars decked out as fancily as possible, but, since this bride and groom lived close by, the family accompanied her with balloons and drums, walking her from her parents' house to her husband's home, where she would start her new life.

Weddings were the best part of summer. Everyone made peace with each other because no one wanted to miss a wedding. The women's tent with its red and white flag fluttering in the distance became for me an emblem of female power. For seven days, women from the entire village flocked to the tent to celebrate not only the union but also their own freedom. Our songs expressed our joy and our frustrations, and we played games where women in fake moustaches pretended to be controlling husbands who were outsmarted by their wives at every turn. We indulged day after day, dancing until the stars came out to join us, and every night, the men would cook and serve dinner. As the caravan passed, we sang, "*Ya um al-khedoud al-mehmaara ma yom telati labara,*" which means "respectable women are always in the home". Tears leaked from Ummi's eyes. "I can't sing this song for you," she moaned. "You're always outside the house."

One day while everyone was either at school or at work, I was sitting on Maryam's bed when Ummi barged into the room and announced that a neighbour was here to see me. "Amal's here," she yelled before I had a chance to say anything. The woman entered, passing Ummi who not-so-subtly motioned that the woman wanted to speak to me privately before closing the door.

"I need your help," the woman said. My first social work case in the village.

"Please," I gestured towards the cot, "sit." The woman told me about one of her children who suffered from a disability. I nodded and, following protocol, asked her probing questions while giving her enough time to "ventilate". After a few minutes she broke down.

"My husband is using drugs and sometimes he beats me to get all the money I have and if I don't give it to him, he threatens me by beating my children . . ." Her voice trailed off into sobs. I got up and reached for the doorknob to bring the woman a glass of water. The door flew open and Ummi rushed in, glass of water in hand, mumbling, "*Beseer khayr wahdi Allah* [Don't worry, it will be all right, drink, drink]." She handed the woman the water and rubbed her back.

Ummi must have been listening from behind the door. I pulled Ummi aside and told her that she couldn't be part of this. She wasn't the social worker. I was. Ummi's blank stare told me that I was from another planet.

"She came to *my* house," she said. "If you hadn't been here, she would have talked to me." She paused as if checking that I understood, surmised that I didn't, and continued, eyebrows raised: "You think I don't know her problems? You think women didn't help each other until you came in with your social work thing?"

She marched right past me and sat down on the cot beside the woman to console her. I stood there, stunned but corrected. Ummi was right. Who was I to underestimate her knowledge and the indigenous means of providing support and solving problems? I would end up helping that woman, but not by providing a sympathetic ear. She needed me to tell her how to access financial support for her disabled child. The best way to listen to communities is not to impose. Let them tell you what they want so the solutions are based jointly on community and professional knowledge. The social support was already in Ummi's hands; filling out forms was in mine.

For the four years while I was at university, Basma moved back and forth between her husband's house and ours. Every other week, I'd see her in our kitchen, her usually bright complexion grey from crying. They'd fight, she'd leave, and so it went on until, one day, she stormed into the *hosh* and swore that she wasn't going back. Abouee built her a two-room cabin next door where Basma lived for a few months until she caved in to the pressure to return to her husband.

Those two rooms remained empty until I decided that having my own room wasn't self-indulgent, it was necessary. My brother Nasouh, who was starting university, and I renovated the two rooms and when we had finished, my room felt like my very own mansion. In a society that constantly reminded me that it owned me, my room reminded me that no one owned me but me. This was where I lived and where I started my private social work practice. A tent is good when you want everyone to come, but sometimes a tent doesn't work. My room became a place where women and girls could share their problems. The contents of their hearts found safety between those four walls, there, in that room of my own.

The Smoke Closest to Your Eyes is the Harshest

AFTER GRADUATING, MY first job as a paid social worker was at one of the Bedouin municipalities in the welfare department. It took only one month for me to earn the title of troublemaker. When one of the clients confided in me that the manager had sexually harassed her, I encouraged her to report him, but she refused, afraid that both she and her family would suffer. In an interview I gave on the radio, I exposed this terrible truth: that Bedouin women who faced sexual assault in the workplace refused to speak up to avoid further violence. The next day the guilty manager called me into his office and fired me. On my way out, he told me to close the door. "Leave it open," I shot back while walking down the hall, "people like you can't be trusted behind closed doors."

I then found two part-time jobs: one as the social worker in the high school in my village and the other as the coordinator for the Galilee Society Organization. No one at the high school understood the role of "social worker", so they assigned me to the class where all the students considered intellectually challenged had been lumped together and they told me to teach them sociology. These children had lots of energy so I arranged for them to start a garden at the school. I was also appointed disciplinarian for students who arrived late or didn't do their homework. Much to everyone's disappointment, I didn't punish anyone. I did what any good community social worker would do: I helped them fight for their rights. I found out that the late students were mostly from Awajaan, and that they walked to school every morning, traversing the dusty roads and difficult desert terrain. The local municipality had a budget for transport, but corruption stopped them from providing it. I gathered the students and together we staged a protest, marching from Awajaan, our fists in the air, shouting "from Awajaan to Laqiya, we demand a bus". When we approached the school, the teachers, the principal, the mayor and his staff stood at the gate to prevent us from entering. "Don't stop," I commanded them, "continue walking. Don't use violence. Just keep walking."

As I passed the principal, he smiled at me. "I think you're confused," he said. "You are supposed to be on our side."

"I believe I'm on the right side," I said. I was fired a few months later.

Working for the Galilee Society exposed me to other issues that my people faced: disease contracted from drinking from rusty water tanks, home accidents which accounted for almost all hospital visits, and a child mortality rate that was twice the national average. The organization equipped me with a white pickup truck which I drove from village to village, learning about the health issues faced by the Bedouin in the unrecognized villages and helping them to access governmental services.

The October after I graduated, I brought a delegation of Jewish North Americans to tour the unrecognized villages. The tour was organized by The New Israel Fund, and by BGU's School of Social Work. Dr Jim Torczyner, a professor of social work from McGill University who was teaching for a term at BGU, led the delegation. Jim was a lively middle-aged man with dark hair and a matching beard. In the same breath, he would exhaust you in a relentless argument and delight you with his charm. Some of those on the tour adored him, others found him irritating, but they all respected him. He is the kind of person who has spent his life fighting for what he believes in. For Jim, there is no neutral stance and the intensity of his conviction forces others to find theirs.

The tours were intended to give its participants an understanding of the issues faced by minorities in the country. We were loaded onto a bus and driven from one village to another. In each place, I introduced them to the men and women I knew and showed them how the government failed to provide for a people who had lived on this land long before Israel existed. It wasn't easy. I was showing these people, all of them strong supporters of the state, the ugliest parts of this country. People's ears shut down when they feel attacked, so, as Abouee taught me, I spoke to their hearts. "Here is a father who lives without electricity." "Here is a mother who lives without running water." I showed them how we struggle to survive without access to basic things. But they still didn't understand. "Why does this father keep living here if he doesn't have electricity? Why doesn't he move to the townships that the state built for him?" they asked me, as if it was a simple matter of primitive people refusing to change. They interpreted the reality through their own lens, often unwilling to criticize a government that gave them the story of their birthright, the salvation from the unimaginable horrors of the Second World War. But must the salvation of the Jewish people come at the expense of Bedouin claims to the same land? The participants of the tour saw only the leaves while remaining oblivious to the roots. These injustices couldn't be rectified by relocating us to townships that we weren't even consulted on. I did my best to field these questions without resorting to victimhood. I didn't want any of them to feel sorry for me. To hell with their story about the poor Bedouin woman. I wasn't asking for pity; I was seeking justice.

The last station in the tour was the *diwaan* in Umm Bateen where the head of the tribe sat with us and discussed what we'd seen that day. I translated using the little English I knew. When I didn't know a word, I said it in Hebrew and Jim threw in the English. At the end

of the tour, I walked with the delegation along the dirt road back to
their bus when Jim caught up with me and asked me what I did. I
told him I had just finished my bachelor's at BGU and had applied
to do my master's there as well.

"Don't go there," he said. "I have a better idea."

I cocked my head.

"I'm developing a master's programme at my university, McGill,
that would bring together a group of students from Israel and
Jordan." He explained to me the central thesis of his work, that peace
treaties without strong relationships between people on the ground
are empty political acts.

I nodded along, but I still didn't understand his better idea.

"I want to nominate you for the programme," he said. "You
would come to McGill for a year to do your Master's in Social Work
and then you could come back here and implement what you'd
learned."

I barely grasped what the programme was about, but Jim's energy
told me that this was a special opportunity. While he spoke, I tried
to imagine how far McGill was from Laqiya. If the world seventeen
kilometres away was entirely different, where would thousands of
kilometres take me? Abouee's face appeared like a dark cloud,
poisoning the promise of this new adventure.

"What do you think?"

Abouee's face faded, but his stern eyes remained. "Yes," I said
instantly. "I would love to join. It will be very difficult to convince
my father and my whole family, but I will work on that. You tell me
what I need to do to apply."

After I had left Jim and the tour, I travelled to Beer a-Saba,
where I met Mary Ann Stein, the president of the Moriah Fund, to
present a programme I had put together that was intended to prepare
Bedouin women to apply for a degree in social work. Mary Ann loved
the programme and agreed to fund it. That day must have been
blessed. I flew back to the village that night with wings broad enough
to embrace everything and everyone. Love radiated from me and I

felt pride in my bones. My horizon had expanded beyond anything I could have imagined and the same was now true for ten Bedouin women who would start the programme the following year.

"Abouee," I said, sitting down beside him under the caress of our grapevine, "you won't believe what happened!" I decided to start by telling him about the social work preparation programme and build up to my bigger request. His face opened into a soft smile, admiration flowing freely from his eyes, but his body shifted. He put the pillow he had been leaning on onto his lap and sat up straight. He was preparing to say something important.

"I am so proud of you," he began. "I wish you were a boy. You are so successful, but I can't share your success in public. I can't say anything about your great achievements in the *diwaan*."

His words hit me like an arrow to the stomach. After all these years of trying to prove to him that having a girl was worth more than having a boy – my work in the factory, my projects in the community, my degree from the university – it still wasn't enough. I could take this from Ummi, but not from him.

Ummi came over with the tea tray. "When did you come home?" she asked me. "Have you eaten?"

Abouee rubbed his temples. "*Shuufee*," he said, "if she were a boy, she would lead everyone. She would be the perfect leader."

Ummi placed the tray down in front of us. "*Wallah, al-banaat* [girls] are also good! Why can't they lead? There are girls who are smarter than boys." She clicked her tongue. "Ah, they have no luck in this world. They can work like donkeys but still won't get recognized like the men." She shook her head and waddled back to the kitchen.

What was going on? Was Ummi starting to change? Once Ummi had left, I felt it was the right time to bring up the second piece of news. I wanted to test the water without her usual melodrama. But I first had to let Abouee know how much his words hurt me.

"I thought you had already broken the shell and that you were no longer afraid to tell people about me," I said.

"I was never afraid," he answered quickly. "I am very proud of you and I talk about you, but not everywhere and not to everyone. I have to choose the right people. The ones who understand." The knot in my chest loosened.

"What I am saying," he continued, "is that I long for the moment when I can bring you up with anyone – you know, with the people who were against my approach, with the people who blew up my truck, with the ones who tried to hurt me."

"That day will come," I said, the hope overcoming the pain in my voice, "everyone can change."

I moved my pillow and inched closer to him. "There is a new opportunity that I want to tell you about."

I could tell he was hoping that I wouldn't say something that would stretch his skin even more.

"I received an invitation to do my master's."

"But you are already starting your master's here."

"No. It's a master's in Canada. They have selected me for this special fellowship programme. I won't be alone. I will be with another Jewish student from Israel and Jordanian students and—"

"I don't know where Canada is," his eyes searching for something in mine. "The only thing I know about that place is that it is very far away and that in the late sixties the Israeli government offered us ten thousand dollars to emigrate there. They wanted us to leave this land and go live on somebody else's land. Jadek [your grandfather] refused. We didn't even ask about this place. But, listen, no matter where it is, I want you to be smart and not push any further. Don't break the elastic. Even if it's flexible, it has its limits. I am fifty-eight years old and I'm tired of these fights. Your mother also can't take any more. We brought you to this point. It's a good place to be in. You are already doing great things. You are successful and people admire your work. Please, *ya bintee*, don't put any more weight on my shoulders."

Abouee had shielded me from the hottest flames, but I wasn't a little girl anymore. I grabbed the cushion and held it firmly on my knees.

"There is always better and you know that I can get to those better places. Why limit myself?"

"I know you can, but I can't." He let out a long sigh as if he had discovered something for himself. His face looked worn. There were wrinkles I had never noticed before and his strong body appeared hunched under the enormous vine. "If you can convince your brothers," he continued, "then I have no problem. I am no longer *abu al-banaat* [the father of the girls]. Your brothers are grown men and they must be part of the decision."

I couldn't believe what he was saying. This injustice was one I had always fought. I had dealt with countless cases where a brother prevented his sister from going to school or marrying her beloved. A boy as young as fourteen could decide his sister's destiny, believing that exercising this power made him a man.

I leaned into the pillow for support. The pride I felt from the day's achievements evaporated when I reflected on where I thought I was and how much further I still had to go. Abouee was the one person I wouldn't have expected to do this, to pit me against my brothers. The harshest smoke is the one closest to your eyes.

"I don't want this fight," I whispered, placing the pillow next to him on the mattress.

I went to the barn where I sat and sobbed. One by one, I conjured up my brothers' faces and I cried harder with each one. Salmaan, the oldest, was already working as a pharmacist, Yousef was about to finish his law degree at Tel Aviv University and had enrolled in an accounting programme, Nasouh was in his last year of high school, Ibraheem was in tenth grade, Ousaama in ninth grade and Muntasir, the youngest, was in kindergarten. My brothers were the best souls on earth, but would they stop me from pursuing my dreams? Would they have the strength to withstand the pressure from the rest of the community?

In my desperation, I began searching for reasons not to go on the fellowship programme. What if I lost my family in my fight to go, only to fail the programme? Was it really worth the risk?

Narjis appeared in the doorway. "Abouee told me you were here," she said.

I wiped my tears and adjusted my shirt, my hair and my scarf.

"What happened?" she asked, half-smiling because she correctly guessed that I was trying to hide that I'd been crying.

I told her about the tour, but she knew that wasn't it. She nodded and looked at me as if to say, "OK, what else?"

"I got a fellowship to do a master's in Canada."

"Wow. That's great." Her voice changed. "Did you tell Abouee? He said no, right?"

"I wish. He told me I have to get our brothers' permission."

Tears spilled onto my lap as Narjis came and sat beside me.

"Don't worry. They always say no in the beginning but you always get what you want."

"Yes, if it's up to Abouee."

"They love you, they'll agree. If not, you don't need it. You're already established here."

"Why do I have to explain why I'm entitled to do this? Why do I have to convince them?"

It wasn't about whether I needed it or not. My desires, a woman's desires, have equal standing to those of men. Her lack of sympathy came from her ignorance. Narjis couldn't see how God's will had been tainted by outdated rules governing who decided what we could or couldn't do. After a short pause she changed the subject as if what she had come to say was much more important.

"Actually, I came to tell you that there is someone from our tribe who is interested in you. He wants to know if you are interested."

I noticed the smell of musty barley that permeated the room. In that moment, my conversation with Abouee, my brothers, Jim, Canada, all vanished.

"How do you know?"

"He spoke to our uncle. He told him that he will support you in whatever you do. He knows that you're crazy and that you have big dreams."

Our uncle entered the barn and called out to us: "Ah, this is where you share secrets. Did Narjis tell you?"

"Why didn't he speak to me directly?" I asked.

He sat down on a bale of hay across from Narjis and me. "He has never spoken to you before and besides, who would speak with you directly? You are like a *goula* [monster]."

With my wild hair that was like an extension of my wild ideas, I felt like one.

"He has money and he is well established. He'll support your work. He knows what he's getting into and he said he still wants you. What should I tell him?"

"Well, *you* don't need to tell him anything. *I'll* tell him."

"So, you'll see him?"

"I think he deserves an answer, no?"

The very next day my uncle and my potential suitor showed up at the entrance to our shack. I had seen him before, but we had never spoken. He was neither tall nor short, neither handsome nor ugly, and his clothes told me that he had money but didn't flaunt it. In his face I saw a man who was hardworking, reserved and serious.

He barely looked at me when I arrived, which I attributed to his being shy. My warm smile eased the tension and I asked my uncle to leave us alone. He hesitated at my untraditional request, but finally nodded and walked away.

"Why would you marry someone like me?" I asked him.

"Because you are strong," he replied, his words quiet but clear. "You have no fear. I like women like that."

"Are you looking for a bride or a soldier?" I teased him.

"No, no," he said with a laugh and his body relaxed. Without the stiffness he seemed more sweet than serious. "I think we need strong women like you."

"I think you deserve a good woman but not me," I answered. "I am not ready for this adventure. I want to continue my studies."

He straightened up again to make his case. "Don't worry. I will support you. I have money. I have everything."

"I know you have money and you are a very nice guy. It's not about you, it's about me."

He nodded gently and then asked me why I had agreed to meet him if I wasn't ready to marry. I told him it was out of respect. "You don't need a middleman," I said. "Now we can become friends." I reached out to shake his hand. He wasn't sure what to do but I left my hand there until he shook it and left. My eyes followed him through the window and I waved goodbye.

I don't know the real reason I agreed to meet him. Maybe I wanted to be sure that there were men who would marry someone like me. Every other day, Ummi told me I was crazy. *Majnoona*. "No man can handle her. She runs around everywhere. She walks with men. She's already in trouble with the police. Who would bring this *thing* into his house?" Aspiring to be an activist, I thought that I might sacrifice being a wife and mother.

I decided to apply for the Master's in Social Work in Canada without getting permission. It was only an idea so why fight it? Why make noise and lose my brothers for nothing? But a month later, Jim told me that I had been accepted and that the programme would start in September. I received the news with mixed feelings, secretly hoping for the programme to be cancelled so I wouldn't have to confront my family. I had to proceed carefully, to plant the seed slowly, targeting the soil that I knew was the most fertile. I told Yousef first. He supported me, but knew that it would be hard to get everyone on board.

From then on, I brought up the subject every night at dinner. We would sit huddled in a circle in the kitchen and as soon as Ummi finally took her seat, I would start. "I still don't understand what's wrong with me getting an education abroad. You sent Salmaan. You sent Yousef."

"It's not the same thing," one of my brothers would say.

Basma supported me, Yousef rephrased my argument to make it more appealing, Ummi and my other sisters admonished me for wanting to go abroad when I already had a good opportunity in

Israel, Salmaan mounted the loudest resistance, Abouee threw up his arms in defeat, and finally, once we were all worked up, Ummi shouted, "*Khalas!*" over and over again, all of us ignoring her, until I got up and left, a mess of tears, to seek refuge in the barn.

My sisters and brothers hated me for this. One night, the arguing had begun and I had burst into tears, as they were used to by now, and I was about to leave when Muntasir, who was five at the time, grabbed Abouee's hand.

"Because she is a woman you are not letting her go?" He turned to me. "Don't listen to them. Go!" His innocence dissolved our shouts into laughter. Everyone begged me to stay and eat.

After the meal, Salmaan came over to sit with me. He never liked arguing with me and was searching for the right words. After a long pause, he finally said: "Listen. You are smart and will get wherever you want in Israel. What do you need this for? You think it's easy to study abroad by yourself? Trust me. It's really hard."

We argued over whether or not studying abroad was harder for girls. I interrupted him at every turn, not wanting to hear another word about how I couldn't do something when I was stronger than all of the boys combined. Finally, he got up. Both of our faces were flushed.

"I'm tired of you," he shouted. "You want to shape the world according to your own views. It won't work. You don't live here in isolation. You have to consider society and what society would say about you living abroad by yourself."

"Exactly." I stood up and stuck my face into his. "I want this society to be different. On what basis were you allowed to study abroad and I'm not? Even Islam tells us that pursuing knowledge is for men *and* women."

"Forget about it!"

With a mother's instinct, Ummi rushed over and stood between us. "Who do you think you are? We're tired of talking to you." She pushed her finger into my chest with each accusation. "You are upsetting us all with your plans. You turn every meal into a battlefield. We respect you, but you don't care about us. You only care about yourself."

"Why are you crying?" I retorted, refusing to fall for her tears. "You are the ones making it difficult. It's easy. Let me go."

Salmaan puffed out his chest, taking his place as the real man of the family. "It's not that easy. You won't go. That's it."

"You think you're going to decide for me? Who gave you the right?" I shouted back.

As our shouts in the kitchen tent grew louder and louder, our arguments made less and less sense. No one dared interrupt us. My brothers and sisters sat frozen on the sidelines, praying that things wouldn't escalate, but neither Salmaan nor I were about to back down.

Ummi tugged on Abouee's arm, urging him to intervene before we crossed a line. My relentlessness had overtaken Salmaan and mine was the only voice that reverberated off the cold stones of the *hosh*. My anger coursed through me and I turned my hands against myself, hitting my head over and over again until Salmaan spat: "Over my dead body. Forget it." His mouth was white, his body shaking. He walked out.

Ummi cursed me on her way after him. "I wish I never had you."

I looked around at the damage I had caused. Narjis and Maryam glared up at me as though I was an evil stranger. No one said anything as I walked off towards the barn where I sat the entire night trying to shake off what had happened and strategize my next move. But I couldn't. Every time I remembered Salmaan's face and his words "over my dead body" I felt hopelessly alone. Just thinking about his death destroyed me. I would never tread on anyone's body to achieve my goals, not even my enemies'. There had to be a peaceful way. I had to use diplomacy to lobby for myself, the same way I used diplomacy to fight for the rights of so many others.

Later that week, I called Jim and asked him to come and speak with my parents, thinking it might help. He arrived at my parents' house the same day with his wife and stepdaughter and my parents prepared a big traditional meal to greet him. Thankfully, Jim spoke Hebrew, which meant he could communicate with my father directly. Everyone in the family knew that this was part of my plan and that Jim wasn't just a guest, but a guest with an agenda.

Jim explained about the programme and told Abouee that I would be safe in Canada and that he would take good care of me. Ummi and Abouee weren't convinced but they acted respectfully. They responded with "*inshallah*" to everything Jim said, which as an acknowledgement of God's will means "maybe yes, maybe no"; with a daughter like me, who knew what God had in store.

At the end of the evening, when Ummi handed Jim a parting gift of hard Bedouin cheese, I stood behind her and shook my head to signal that the issue was not resolved. Jim got it and walked with Abouee back to his car. "What if I give you my stepdaughter for a year and I take Amal?" They both laughed and shook hands, but Jim's humour wasn't enough to overcome the obstacles that stood in our way. I watched his car disappear over the hill and sat in the sparse grass under the soothing canopy of the olive orchard. I welcomed the silence. I rested against the bark of one of those enduring trees. *Just sit*, the tree told me. *Let the dust settle.*

The day after Jim's visit I went to see Na'ama's husband Aamer in Beer a-Saba. We had become close when I lived with the two of them during my studies. He knew about the issue because Na'ama had told him that I was making my parents' life hell.

We sat together at the kitchen table with small cups of black coffee with sugar and cardamom in front of us. I had recounted everything that had happened and looked like a deflated version of myself when he sat back in his chair and asked: "What do you want?"

"I want to study abroad. I want this opportunity." I wavered between exasperation and rage, but here with Aamer my exhaustion conveyed that at the root of it I felt hurt, betrayed even.

"This is for your own future, right?"

"Yes."

"Why would Aboukee pay the price for something you want?

293

Something not urgent, not essential. He has already fulfilled his obligation. More than fulfilled it! Far more than you would expect from people in our society."

"I know. I know!" I wanted to push away the accusation my sisters threw at me: that my desires were selfish and unreasonable. "But why should I give up on my dreams?"

"No one is asking you to give up on your dreams," Aamer continued. "Follow them. But you need to pay the price or have someone who would benefit from your dreams pay it."

He gestured with his hands while he spoke, waving his fingers in the air to underline his certainty, but my blank stare told him that I didn't know what he was getting at.

"I think it is time to transfer the responsibility from Aboukee's shoulders to someone else's shoulders—"

I stood up from my chair. "Am I a burden?" My anger resurfaced and prevented me from deciphering the message Aamer had been trying to get me to figure out on my own. "I don't need anyone to take responsibility for me!"

He took a sip from his coffee and continued, "Do you want to fight the vineyard owner or get the grape?"

"I want the grape, but I care about how I get it! I won't compromise my principles to get it."

"It's time to stop hitting your head against the wall," he said softly.

I melted into my chair, nestled my head in my arms on the table, and cried like a child. Aamer moved his chair closer to mine. He placed one of his large caring hands on my head and whispered in a voice as precious as a prayer: "Call Anwar."

The Silences of the Palazzo

STUDYING ABROAD SEEMED like an insurmountable obstacle that could only be resolved by creating an even bigger problem. My uncle, Abd al-Rahman, the one who worked as a doctor and had an

Italian wife, was the only one with whom I had shared Aamer's idea. "Anwar is a good man," he told me, "and you need a strong man like your father to accompany you on the rest of your journey." The trip to Turin arrived like a gift from on high. I had been eating dinner one evening with my uncle, his wife and Paola, an Italian researcher who'd been studying Bedouin culture for a few years, when she mentioned that she would be attending a conference there. I heard myself asking if she would be able to get me an invitation? Yes, she would.

After dinner, I dialled Anwar's number from my uncle's office. My stomach churned with every beep until finally I heard his voice. It had been difficult to call him after I moved back to the village. We hadn't spoken in six months. He was thrilled to hear from me and spoke as if it was business as usual, asking about my work in the village, my brothers, if I saw his mother.

"I'm coming to Turin in two weeks with Paola for a conference," I blurted out.

He didn't hide his excitement and pressed me for details. "I want to see you," he said.

After I had hung up, his words lingered, soothing my troubled soul. At the other end of that line, there was hope.

The next day I went with Paola to buy a plane ticket. When I returned home, I told my parents that I was going to Turin, then headed to the bedroom without waiting for their reaction. From there, I heard Ummi say, "Let her go. We don't want to break her. It's only two weeks. And it's with Paola. She's a good woman, and her uncle will call his friend to also take care of her." Ummi imagined Italy was like Laqiya: every Italian was a friend of my uncle who had studied there and when he married an Italian woman, he had become part of the Italian tribe. Minutes later, Ummi appeared, her white scarf coiled authoritatively around her head. "Aboukee agreed," she told me, "but you must take care of yourself and whatever you have in your mind, you should get it out," by which she meant Canada.

Salmaan suggested that I contact Anwar if I wanted to see the main attractions. I nodded innocently, but inwardly I cheered. Not all shepherds lead from the front of the flock.

The night before I left, I packed a copy of the Tunisian film "The Silences of the Palace", the first film I ever saw in a movie theatre. The story of Tunisia's independence is told through the lives of the palace servants, namely Aalya and her mother Khadeja, the extravagant Ottoman-style palace walls providing only an illusion of safety. The occupants, those upstairs as well as downstairs, are victims of French colonial rule and repressive social conventions, and behind closed doors everything is permitted. Aalya witnesses one transgression after another, but the palace has only one rule: silence. The film has long scenes with the female servants washing clothes, baking bread, chopping vegetables – testament to how their bodies do not belong to them but to someone else. Without a voice, they have no safety, no freedom, no future. When Aalya finally runs away we see that her liberty is still constrained by the world of men. How do we make sense of our independence as women when the world we inherit requires us to heal the untold wounds of countless women who came before us? I brought the movie to test Anwar's stance on the issues facing women in our society. If I was going to fight to marry him, it would have to be the right fight.

Later that evening, a car light beamed through our window. Anwar's father had come to see me. He handed me two envelopes: one for Anwar's studies and another to allow Anwar to show me the country. Abouee stood a little way off to give us privacy in case Anwar's father wanted to deliver a private message to his son. If Abouee had been within earshot, he wouldn't have told me about the second envelope. His smile told me that our hearts shared the same plan. The darkness saved me. Had it not, he would have seen me blush.

Paola and I arrived in Turin at night. Stepping out of the airport and into a taxi, I was astonished by the cold. It was a week before Christmas and the buildings were lit up like ancient Christmas trees. The apartment building with its stone walls was also cold and Paola's husband showed me to my room where I bundled myself in blankets and basked in the hushed magic of what was to come.

In the morning, when we made our way to the university, a new world revealed itself. Streets lined with history. Towering stone buildings with impressive white facades, narrow alleyways with alluring mystery, and the smell of espresso everywhere. Distant blue snow-peaked mountains cradled the city, making Turin seem even more exquisite. How could something built by humans live up to the natural wonder around her? There are no words to describe my experience. I knew sand and dirt, mountains and grass, where we built humble tents, shacks and farms. I'd seen the luxurious homes in Omer and the ancient cities of Jerusalem, Beer a-Saba and Akka. But here was an enduring beauty whose forms were as foreign to me as the new tremors in my heart. I peered out of the taxi window, spellbound and breathless.

The university was just as impressive; in comparison, my campus had all the aesthetic appeal of a football stadium. Simply standing there made you feel intelligent. We entered a lecture hall where Paola and her adviser started speaking in Italian. I picked up that they were talking about me, Canada and Anwar. I don't remember much about the lecture I gave because my mind was busy with the real reason for my visit.

Back at the apartment that evening, Paola's husband told us that Anwar had called and that he would be arriving shortly. I felt dizzy. What if he had changed? What if I wasn't attracted to him? What if I was? What if this was it? The bell rang and I felt like I was in one of those American Christmas movies I'd seen on TV. My heart beating frantically in my chest, I was too scared to move. Paola called me and I tried to force my legs to carry me to the door, but I got no further than the living room. She told me to let Anwar in. I refused so she went instead.

"Ciao."

My heart danced out of that jar. Anwar appeared in the hall, his thick black hair tied back in a long ponytail. He flashed me a sexy smile. He wore fitted jeans and a black pea coat, a dark blue scarf tied around his neck. He looked like the man of my dreams. But what would my parents say about his hair? We looked at each other not knowing what to do. I'd never felt like this around him before. Was he different? Was I? Maybe this place had enchanted me, maybe it was the first time I felt it was safe to let myself feel what women are so afraid to feel.

We shook hands. It wasn't just my fingertips that sang: his touch coursed through my whole body and I retracted my hand as quickly as if I'd placed it on a hot stove. I needed to give him the money from his father. Yes. Practical things. I reverted to my task-oriented nature to save me from this first brush with sensuality. I handed him the envelopes and we stood there awkwardly. We both knew he hadn't travelled several hours to pick up a couple of envelopes.

Paola gracefully invited Anwar for tea. The two of them chatted in Italian. I brought the cup to my lips, but I couldn't drink. Paola suggested that we go for a walk to get to know the area.

I was desperate to be alone with him, but my accomplishments would mean nothing if I lost my reputation. Even here, the community had eyes: the ones they had transplanted inside my own head. Don't let men see you, don't let them speak to you, and, God forbid, don't let them touch you. My family expected me to maintain my honour and I intended to respect their wishes no matter how much I believed that women had the right to express their desires. Now that the most delicious fruit sat in front of me in a long ponytail and blue scarf, I couldn't let my self-control slip. When we left the building, the cold wind was a welcome distraction. I looked straight ahead, trying to quell my feelings of desire and take in his presence beside me. Turin at night, with eyes coloured with love. The city was alive and everyone looked happy.

Our conversation was formal. We spoke about my presentation and his studies. He confessed that he had changed universities because he had been too busy working with socialist groups advocating for workers' rights instead of studying. We walked without knowing where we were going, until Anwar pulled out a map and directed us to the river close to Paola's apartment.

The air near the river was even colder. It swirled around us aggressively, biting my face, but I didn't complain. I didn't want to ruin my first experience of love. We climbed a small hill that overlooked the river and sat on a bench that appeared to be waiting just for us. We nestled together, shoulders touching shoulders, thighs brushing against thighs, warmth mingling with desire. We stared out onto the black water, illuminated only by the light from orange street lamps: the perfect excuse to maintain the intimate silence of hot breath. When the tension felt too strong, I reminisced about the past, joking about teachers and events. But a long pause followed each story, a shy glance became an extended gaze in which we shared our unspoken astonishment at what was happening: two children from the desert sitting alone together across the Mediterranean with no shame to haunt us, a blazing emblem of the free world at our backs and a tempting abyss before us.

At midnight we walked down the hill and Anwar's fingers attempted to clasp mine. I disappeared onto another planet and a car crossing in front of us jerked me back to reality.

"I'm here because my parents trust me," I said, placing my hand firmly in my pocket. "They know I'll never dishonour them. I want to keep my promise."

He pushed a few strands of hair out of his eyes. "I knew this lecture was coming," he said gently. "I've loved you since we were in eighth grade but I never pushed. I respected your way of thinking. I know that for you to fulfil your ambitions, you need to protect your name, your honour. I get that. I will never stop you from being the woman you want to be, even if I sacrifice our love." He took a breath. "But," he said, "I believe we can do it. If we don't push at these obstacles, they take root, they take hold and they become walls that later become impossible to move. We must push."

I had never heard Anwar give a speech. He listened more than he spoke, but he said these words with the conviction of someone who had been rehearsing them for a long time. We stood outside Paola's apartment and agreed to meet the next day to see if it was worth pushing. I wanted a love that filled more than my heart. I wanted a love that lifted my hands and extended to my head, a love that could carry the weight of my ambition and the scope of my dreams.

The next morning over breakfast, Paola mentioned that Anwar had already called. I needed to do everything by the book so I called Salmaan before making any plans.

He laughed. "It's cold, right?"

"Yes! Freezing."

"Do you need money?"

"No, no. I have some. I just wanted to tell you that I would love to see the main cities, but can't go by myself."

"Go with Anwar," he said. My heart skipped a beat. "I have another friend who could take you, but I don't trust him as much as I trust Anwar."

We said goodbye and Paola could read by the look on my face that I had got "permission" as she called it. I didn't agree with her use of that word because I saw myself as free. I was just beating Salmaan and the rest of them at their own game.

When Anwar called me back, I gave him the news, and within an hour we were sitting in Paola's dining room with a map of the country spread out across the table, sketching out our plan in Anwar's notebook. Anwar wanted to take me everywhere but we had only one week so we decided on Milan, Venice, Bologna and the town where Anwar was studying, Macerata, near the Adriatic coast. We'd promised each other that he would act as my guardian throughout the trip, which meant no touching.

The day we arrived in Macerata, he invited all the Bedouin who also studied there, all men of course, for a New Year's Eve gathering. I had planned to show the film that night – the real test to see if Anwar was the one. We gathered in the kitchen and prepared a big meal. They had all heard of me and jokingly remarked that if they didn't support women's rights, they wouldn't be allowed to eat. We crammed into Anwar's living room and sat in a semicircle on the floor with our plates at our feet. I felt at ease among all the noise and shouting, but grew irritated when they refused to quieten down for the film.

"This is serious," I said. "This movie is very challenging. We need to take this subject seriously."

That only made matters worse in a "who is this young girl telling us how to watch a movie?" kind of way.

"I'm just here for the food," one of them said, grinning around for approval, "nothing more."

The others laughed, but Anwar set them straight. "If that's the case," he said, "I'll give you some food to take away with you so you don't need to sit here and bother us with your empty words."

I liked that.

The movie opens with a close-up of Aalya's face singing at a wedding. We can read her pain and are quickly brought into her present struggles with her boyfriend who wants her to have another abortion and her past life in the palace where she and her mother lived as servants to the bey. The work is hard, but the load is lightened by their jokes, gossip and song. Their personalities in the kitchen are in stark contrast to their unquestioning obedience of the demands of their social class and men's desires. At one point, the women in the kitchen are no longer laughing. Hot tears run down my cheeks every time I see that scene. They are seated, two of them scrubbing rags, the others kneading bread. Their labour is the only sound we hear as the camera pans from one face to another, each telling a story of unspoken torment.

When the movie ended no one moved. The discussion began slowly, with a few neutral remarks pointing out the similarities between the tools that Bedouin women used for domestic work. Then one of them turned up the heat.

"She didn't have to sleep with him," he said. "She has no honour."

"Why don't you say anything about the man who raped her?" Anwar fired back. "Why is it always on the shoulders of the woman to keep her honour?"

The discussion flared into a passionate debate about a woman's right to choose her husband. The more conservative among them argued that women shouldn't have a say. Others shrugged the whole issue off as a matter of tradition. "This is how we grew up," they said. "It will be hard to change things." Anwar was a lone voice calling for change. "How do you want your wife to raise great children if she lacks the tools? She needs to be educated so she can educate her children. She needs to be strong so her children can be strong." I watched from the sidelines, but the checklist in my mind was going tick, tick and tick. He passed.

On New Year's Day, Macerata was enveloped in fresh snow. We went for a walk despite the cold and I told Anwar about the fellowship. He immediately encouraged me to go.

"My parents won't let me go and I would never do it against their will."

I listened to the quiet crunch our footsteps made as we traversed Macerata's gritted cobblestones.

"Do you think if I ask for your hand, they'll let you go? As your husband," he reasoned, "I'd be the only one to have a say over you. I'm ready to do everything for you to be a happy and successful woman."

By now I knew that this was the man I wanted. Everything in that week had shown me that Anwar was a partner worth fighting for, but even so, I knew the fight wouldn't be easy. "We have to test the water," I told him.

"I'll do whatever it takes, but I won't humiliate my father. He doesn't deserve that."

Anwar wouldn't stand for his father coming to see Abouee only to be refused. If Anwar's father came to Abouee's *hosh* to ask for my hand, the *zagareet* would need to serenade him back to Awajaan.

I cried the whole flight back to Israel. Leaving Anwar behind felt like breathing from a heart that had been poorly stitched together. Love wasn't only emotional, I discovered. I felt the pain of my longing through my entire body.

When I arrived back at my parents' house that evening, I waited until Ummi and my siblings had gone to watch our favourite series on the Jordanian TV channel before entering Abouee's room. He was lying down on the mattress where he and Ummi slept. I sat down by his head and told him that I wanted to discuss something with him, but that I wanted him to listen before he decided.

"What is it now, *ya saatir* [God protect us]?" The frown lines on his forehead told me that he knew he wasn't going to like what I was about to say.

"I've decided to get married. I think it's time to lift the burden from your shoulders—"

"Have I ever complained about being responsible for you? You're my daughter."

"I know, but my dreams are getting bigger and I need to find someone who will support me. I don't want to lose you or my brothers over my choices."

"I thought feminists didn't get married," he said, half hoping that he had a point there.

I smiled. "Not all of us are that extreme."

"Who's the guy?"

"Anwar Alh'jooj."

He shot up from the mattress. "Are you crazy?" The coals in his eyes lit up. "Get out!" he shouted, slapping the mattress as he did so. "I don't want to see you."

My sisters had overheard us and were shocked to see me speaking so openly with Abouee about these issues. These aren't the types of conversations daughters have with their fathers.

Ummi came running in. She demanded to know what had happened.

"It's your daughter. She is making more trouble. Tell her to forget about this."

Ummi grabbed my arm. "Are you out of your mind? Yesterday you wanted to go to that place and now you want to marry outside the tribe?" She pushed me out of the room. "Allah," she pleaded, "take her."

I stood next to the *hosh* like a wretched outcast whose only support was the rough, grey stones. Ummi continued, "Why does she always put me in these situations! Her heart is like stone. What if she's a Jew?" Ummi threw up her hands. "She could have been switched at the hospital! Maybe she isn't my daughter."

My sisters stared at me, squinting as if trying to see if I was really their sister. My feet carried me away towards my refuge, but Ummi's words chased me even there. "The world does not run according to your choices. I'd rather kill you than have you marry outside the tribe."

The smell of sheep waste and fresh hay filled my nostrils. I inhaled more deeply and the smell grounded me in the truth of past, present and future. Ummi's words rang in my head, but she couldn't penetrate my leathery crocodile skin. I had known this would happen. I asked myself: "What next?"

On the Menu, but not at the Table

A NWAR HAD A good reputation in my tribe and I counted on that to persuade the men who held my future in their hands. I went first to Salmaan and Yousef, who both knew Anwar very well. Yousef immediately supported me, but Salmaan was more difficult to convince, and as the oldest brother, his decision mattered the most. He knew that Anwar was the right choice for me, but he feared societal repercussions. My uncle Abd al-Rahman, the open-minded one, supported me completely. He spoke openly in favour of the marriage, not only for personal reasons, but also to set a precedent for abolishing cousin marriage and to support the right of women to decide who to marry. My brother Nasouh, who was in twelfth grade at the time, was against. The rumours had already crept into the soil. She must have slept with him in Italy, otherwise why would she insist?

Late at night, Nasouh appeared in the *hosh* and berated me. We shouted at each other, Ummi swore she would kill me, Abouee told Nasouh to get out, and Ummi chased me with a broomstick. I ran out to look for Nasouh and Ummi shouted after me: "If you don't change your mind, I'll throw myself down the well."

"You've lived your life," I shouted back. "You can't control mine. If you want to throw yourself down the well, go ahead. It's not far from here." I hated myself for saying that.

I walked through the olive grove calling Nasouh's name softly so as not to alert our neighbours to the chaos in our house.

"Go away," he moaned. "You see how you are destroying our family."

I sank down next to him and started to cry.

Nasouh put his arms around me. "I know that you are doing the right thing," he said, "but our society is not ready. People will talk badly about you and I can't have that."

I asked him if he had anything against Anwar.

"No. Anwar is a good guy. But he's not from our tribe."

"Who in our tribe do you think I should marry?" I enumerated the men we knew. One by one Nasouh discarded them like olive pits.

"People will talk no matter what," I told him. "I know that your heart knows what's right. I'm asking you to follow it. You have to be strong," I said. "People need strong leaders."

We sat there a little while longer, returning to ourselves. He stood up and offered me his hand. We walked back together to where Ummi stood in the doorway, wailing about her sorry fate. "You threaten your son for the girl?" we heard her shout to Abouee. "You forgot that my eyes rolled in the back of my head until the boys came and now you're condemning them to support these . . . these vaginas!"

Nasouh and I broke into laughter, a moment that told us our bond was the most important thing in the world. I left Nasouh in the *hosh* and went to sit out in the barn until the morning. Abouee had got up early to tend to the olive trees and noticed me. "Go inside and rest," he insisted. "God will bring only good things."

That fight with Nasouh was a wake-up call for Abouee. He realized that he needed to remain *abu al-banaat*. The boys were not ready to take his place as the breadwinner in the family or the representative in the tribe and, especially, not ready to take responsibility for their sisters. Abouee assumed that his open mindedness had been transmitted to his children, but what happened with Nasouh showed him the strength required to hold your own in a society that constantly tells you that you are in the wrong.

One afternoon, an uncle from Ummi's side showed up and told Abouee that if I wanted a lawyer, one of his sons was a lawyer. "*Bintee* is not a pot to add to your kitchen. She will marry with whom God pleases."

My uncle stormed out, and warned Ummi that my father deserved what would come to him.

Abouee's resoluteness wasn't without recognition of the potential consequences, but his love for me overcame his fear. "What Allah chooses for us," he said to Ummi's tear-streaked face, "we will accept. I have faith that Allah will do his best for her and for us."

Finally, the day came when my brothers and uncles crowded into Abouee's *diwaan* to discuss my fate. They accepted the small teacups Ummi placed on the ground in front of them. I was with Basma, complaining about feeling that I was on the menu and not at the table. She held me in her big, beautiful eyes. "To win the war, you don't have to fight in every battle." When the meeting was over, Abouee walked over and informed Ummi of the verdict. She came towards me as though she was making her way to a funeral. With each step, her frame shrank, anticipating the humiliation she would have to endure for yet another of my crazy desires. "Are you happy now?" she asked. "None of your cousins redeemed you."

I called Anwar immediately and asked him to cut his hair.

"Please," I said, "I don't want to start the whole process all over again because of your hair."

"I love my hair," he said, "but I love you more. I love you."

A week later, tens of cars were parked outside our shack. The *jaaha* – Anwar's father, along with other elite members of the Alh'jooj clan – filed into the *diwaan* to request my hand. The *jaaha* is a delegation of notables sent to secure an agreement and a large one is a sign of great respect. Half an hour later, Abouee left his guests to consult with Ummi. You never accept the *jaaha* on the first visit, but must tell them to *lko alena radet kher* (wait to hear from us). A daughter is too precious to part with right away; it requires three or four visits to be persuaded to hand her over. Ummi said they should come back in the summer, and I shoved myself between them.

"No! Everyone is in agreement. You can't!"

"Get out of my face! You want to do everything your way!" she shouted. "Tell them we need time to think."

"No! I need to be in Canada by August."

Their eyes met in tacit understanding of my whole plan.

"I'll tell them *lko alena radet kher* in two weeks," Abouee said.

Ummi hit her face. "Marrying outside the tribe and only two weeks to think about it? Girls marrying *inside* the tribe take more time! Shame. Shame! Shame on you for embarrassing us."

Every day of those two weeks, another aunt showed up to revel in Ummi's misfortune. They hurled insults at her until her tears no longer satisfied them. Then they stirred up rumours. "We know she is good," they would start, "so why is she doing this?" There had to be a reason for a *bint irjaal* from a strong clan to marry into a smaller, less powerful one. Ummi allowed these women to tear into her flesh day after day. With a daughter like me, she would have to grow a thicker skin.

Two weeks passed and this time an even larger *jaaha* arrived. Only a short meeting later, my brothers slaughtered two fat sheep and we feasted, the Bedouin signal that a deal has been closed. Anwar called me from outside his shack and the *zagareet* carried me even higher. The two of us met the next day in the city to celebrate with some friends and buy wedding rings. Anwar had no money so we bought the cheapest ones we could find and he promised to bring me one from Italy. I didn't care. We went to the Moroccan restaurant where I'd taken my parents for my graduation and the waiter shook Anwar's hand with evident respect. "I never thought she would find a guy who could handle her. Hats off to you for your courage."

The ring didn't go unnoticed. As soon as Ummi set eyes on it, she slumped deeper into her resignation. "Nice," she said, her tone thick with irony. "*Mabrouk*, but I am not coming to your wedding."

God's Works

A NWAR HAD GONE back to Italy to complete his law degree and things had returned more or less to normal. I was still working for the Galilee Society when one morning a soft knocking on my door drew me from my bed.

Abouee's voice telling me to wake up launched nightmarish thoughts that something terrible had happened to one of my family members. He pushed the door open and held my shoulders. "It's your pickup truck."

Thick, black smoke spewed from the engine like a hateful warning. Bad girls get punished, it said in evil ink. I needed to call the police. This truck was on loan to me from the Galilee Society.

Abouee cautioned me not to do anything that could escalate things further. "I was expecting worse," he said. "Breaking the rules of the tribe is not an easy thing and there is a price. This is cheap, believe me. You should keep a low profile in the tribe this month. Let's get to the wedding with minimum harm."

The smoke drew Jidee towards our *hosh*. He didn't comment on the destruction other than to say, "These are weak people. Cowards. They have no dignity," then he walked over to his prayer rug and laid it out for the morning recitation.

His head kissed the ground and his voice recounting the magnitude of God's works was like relaxing magic: the abundant plains, the glowing fields, the blessed mountains. An incantation to conjure up an appreciation of our insignificance and our foolish grasp of destiny.

Delivered to a Stranger

PUTTING ON A festival a month before my wedding was a stupid idea, but the project was the first of its kind: two weeks of some of the best Palestinian musicians, actors and artists flocked to Laqiya to reaffirm our Palestinian heritage. When the festival ended, I had ten days to plan the wedding. Bedouin weddings are not a one-day event; they last an entire week. The celebrations would begin with the henna, which is the party at the bride's house for all the women. Then there would be a farewell party at my parents' house in the morning and the official marriage at Anwar's in the afternoon, and, although it was unusual, we would also have a party in the city for our friends outside the community. One week before it was all scheduled to begin, Basma demanded to see the wedding dress.

"This is disgusting," she said picking at the glossy, ruched sleeves.

"What? It's nice!" I had rented it in all of twenty minutes while on a lunch break in Ramallah.

"C'mon. In the car," she snapped. "Let's go."

She drove me to a bridal salon in Beer a-Saba owned by Orna, a Moroccan Jewish woman with whom Basma shared a casual friendship.

Basma got straight to the point. "She's getting married in one week. She has three parties. We need three dresses, make-up and hair for three parties." The situation seemed more serious now.

Orna looked from Basma to me, examining my burnt skin, calloused hands and filthy fingernails, assessing the scale of the task. She picked up my hand. "Have you been working on a construction site?" It's possible I was the roughest bride she'd ever seen. "You think I'll be able to fix this in a week?" Her pencil-thin eyebrows disappeared into her sleek updo.

"Orna, please. People will be coming from all over the country for this wedding."

I stood there like a donkey being argued over in the market.

She went to her desk to pull out her calendar. "When is your henna?"

"The evening of July 30th, at eight."

"OK, that's a Wednesday."

"When's the wedding?"

"August 1st. Friday."

Basma explained that I would have to be ready by noon. She told Orna that I was marrying outside the tribe. We would serve lunch to the groom's family and then they would take me right after lunch. I shuddered at the words "take me".

Orna ploughed on. "And the next event?"

"Saturday evening. Eight o'clock."

Orna pushed the calendar aside. "Basma! That's Shabbat! I don't even drive on Shabbat!"

Basma held one of her finely manicured hands. "Orna, I know, I know, but she's already rented the place and sent out the invitations."

"Look. For Saturday you will need to find another salon, but I will rent you the dress for Saturday. You take it on Friday and I won't charge you for the extra day."

Orna took me to a cosmetic bed and went to work. She expressed her shock with disapproving "tsks", followed by outbursts of "*Elohim yishmor* [God save us]", playing up the melodrama of providing a makeover at such short notice for a bride who had never even groomed her eyebrows. I pulled out my phone and started making a few calls to make a dent in the infinite to-do list, but Orna stopped me. "I told you to relax," she said sternly, "not work."

Anwar returned to Israel a week before the wedding. According to Bedouin tradition, the groom's family has to take the bride and her mother to choose *el kiswe* – new clothes, usually lingerie and silk robes, and extravagant gold jewellery – and his family pays for them. *El kiswe* is displayed at the henna in two suitcases for all the women to see what a pretty price they paid for the precious jewel that is the bride. I didn't agree with this tradition, but didn't want to deny Ummi all the customary things mothers do with their daughters. Anwar, his parents, Basma, Ummi and I all piled into Anwar's father's minivan and drove to al-Khaleel. The groom doesn't usually come, but Anwar is as crazy as I am.

Ummi asked the goldsmith to show her his latest collection. She picked up the heaviest pieces and asked Anwar's mother for her thoughts. Anwar's mother is the complete opposite of mine. She is shy and gentle. She quietly told Ummi to choose what she thought I would like best.

"Don't ask her!" Ummi scoffed. "This generation of girls don't understand the value of gold. This is their savings account!"

I didn't say a word and let Ummi select whatever she liked. She chose large, ostentatious pieces that I would never wear.

When Ummi asked about the clothing, I told her that I didn't need any. She squeezed my arm. "You can't not buy any clothes!" I tried to explain that Narjis had bought some for me in Ramallah the week before and that Anwar and I weren't buying any because we knew we'd need warm stuff for Montreal, but she was resolute.

We entered a store and Anwar's mother picked up a white shirt and black skirt and showed them to me. I didn't know how to buy clothes with all these people watching me so I just nodded. The seller told her the price was one hundred shekels. She was about to hand him the money, when Ummi stepped in. "What? For these simple fabrics!"

"How much do you want to pay?" he retorted.

"Fifty is more than enough," Ummi said.

"You'll see," I whispered to Anwar, "in ten minutes, she'll get it for what she wants." Just as I predicted, ten minutes later, Ummi was telling Um Anwar that they double the price knowing that you ask for half.

"If you guys weren't with me," she added, "I would have argued until I got it for 25!"

"Now I know how you became so strong!" Anwar teased.

My henna evening felt like a continuation of the festival. Women from all the villages I worked at arrived in buses or husbands dropped off their wives and returned late in the evening to pick them up. We had levelled the area between our house and the barn and set up chairs and a DJ booth to accommodate the six hundred women who attended. I don't remember much because I felt like I was playing the role of the bride. I remember Ummi's sad eyes when my sisters asked her to dance with me. She moved slowly, like someone who was very sick. Was she really not happy for me or was she just not allowed to show it? I also remember when they picked a song to describe me: "Ghajariah", the wild woman with her crazy hair.

Jidee worried about the DJ – the Islamic Movement was gaining strength in our community and its supporters opposed having a man in front of hundreds of women and the playing of popular music in public – and asked that we finish the henna before ten o'clock to avoid any problems. Once all the guests had left, Abouee and my brothers joined the party. My whole family came together, forming one dazzling circle. Yousef brought Ummi into the centre to join me, and we held hands, her eyes still full of sorrow. I felt like crying. I wanted to apologize for everything: for all the trouble I had caused her, for not making her proud of my choice, for making her look weak in front of her friends.

Salmaan had been shuffling around the circle, reminding us to wind the party down. Now, he stood by the DJ, arguing with him, until he turned off the music. I rushed over, and asked him angrily why he had done that, but I didn't want to start a fight. When the whole family sat down together afterwards, my glare told Salmaan that his actions weren't acceptable. He prodded Na'ama with a loving elbow and she hugged me. He explained that Jidee had seen teenagers throwing rocks outside the party and he didn't want any strangers to get hurt. "Besides," he added, "you have your whole life ahead of you. You'll dance all around the world."

In the morning, when I went to the salon to return my dress, Orna asked me if I had found a salon for the Saturday. I had, but I wasn't happy with it. She told me to come back on the Saturday afternoon and that she would lock the door to make sure no one saw that she was working on Shabbat. "You see," her eyes gleamed, "I'm sacrificing Shabbat for you."

I returned to my parents' house at noon. The sun was very hot and my relatives milled about in the living room chatting and drinking coffee. This party is called the *taala*, the leaving party. I joined some women sitting on the couch. Others danced while everyone sang special songs. Songs to give thanks to the parents who raised the bride, songs that tell the bride how to act as a married woman, songs about obeying your mother-in-law, and songs that praise the bride's good qualities – that she obeys, she is polite, that she never goes out – qualities that I didn't have. Ummi placed a heavy gold necklace around my neck and slid equally gaudy rings on each one of my fingers. None of the pieces of jewellery went with my dress, but I didn't resist. I wanted to give her the chance to enjoy these traditional things.

Her sisters stood next to me while I reminisced with friends of mine who had come from the north. One of my aunts leaned over my shoulder and hissed at me to cry.

"I don't feel like crying," I said, turning to face her.

"Try." She pinched my hand hard.

My aunts stood around me in a circle and tried to provoke my tears with singing. They sang about the loneliness of being a stranger in a strange tribe and grew more distressed with every refrain. Everyone's eyes were wet and shining. I couldn't help but remember Basma at her wedding: the red contour of her eyes offset by her ghost-white face. No one cried at her wedding, except her. Now, everyone was crying. Everyone, except me.

"They're coming!" someone shouted, meaning that the relatives from Anwar's side were coming to take me. I turned from one wailing face to another, seeking a reassuring smile, a gaze that could give me strength, but I found none. Na'ama stroked my arm, taking the seat next to mine. "You still have time." The voices praised the safety of the parental nest and I quivered like an uncertain flame. Basma and Na'ama pulled me back into the circle and it was the first time in my life that I wasn't dancing to express joy but to chase doubt. I waved my arms and clapped to "*Ya Um al-Hudoud*" [You, the beautiful woman with red cheeks], the song I had promised Ummi to rewrite, and caught a glimpse of her broken smile.

Basma pulled me back onto the sofa. Then, a haze of strange faces appeared in the crowd: Anwar's aunts who had come to take me. How could I leave the familiar faces for these unfamiliar ones? Na'ama begged to accompany me to the other side, but of course she couldn't come. Two of my oldest aunts – elderly women who would not catch the attention of any strangers – would accompany me. Standing between the women I knew and the women I didn't, my heart quickened. Abouee's voice requested entry, Na'ama shrouded me in the white and gold abaaya, and the tears that everyone wanted me to shed finally came. Abouee and Salmaan stood beside me to deliver me to my husband and my tears turned from delicate sniffles into loud, ugly sobs. The two men pushed through the crowd towards the car, the singing now a cacophony of wailing. With each step, my sobs grew louder until I too was wailing at the top of my lungs. Hertzel, the Jewish photographer I'd hired, caught up with us and said to me in a concerned whisper: "It's OK to change your mind, Amal. It's not too late!"

I didn't know whether to laugh or cry harder. Abouee had also started to cry and Salmaan begged me to stop. "People are watching! *Khalas!* Do you want this to be what they remember?"

I heard the driver say: "Too bad about all the money she spent on her make-up." I heard Anwar try to calm me, but I wasn't listening. It really felt as though I was leaving my family forever. I squeezed into the car with my two aunts and through the window watched everyone crying and slapping their faces in despair. At birth they had welcomed me into the tribe with tears and now they were sending me off, once again in tears.

Crossing the Ocean

W HEN ANWAR AND I landed at Dorval airport, a guard briefly examined our documents before handing them back, saying: "Welcome to Canada." Those words made all the difference. When I had returned to Israel from visiting Anwar in Italy, I had been taken aside and questioned like a criminal. I was returning to my own country! Retrieving our bags from the conveyor belt, I felt light and free. We disappeared in the crowd of different skin tones, languages and styles of dress. No one looked at us as if we were guilty just for existing.

This freedom followed me throughout the city. We had arrived here only a few weeks after our wedding party in Beer a-Saba, when we had celebrated with our friends from work and university. Many prominent figures from Israel's civil society attended and we danced not to your typical wedding songs but to songs about revolution and peace. The easy joy of this party stood in stark contrast to the bittersweet farewell I had endured the day before, but our pleasure did not go unpunished. All the cars in the parking lot had their tyres slashed and their windows smashed – another blow from my tribe.

The tension that pervaded every aspect of my life in Israel now seemed very far away. Anwar and I held hands and walked slowly, lovingly, along the promenade in Montreal's old port. We had time to ourselves and we savoured it: admiring the eclectic displays of fashionable boutiques, allowing ourselves to be carried away by the excitement and confusion of crowds of tourists, and basking in the feeling of being completely alone. In our studio apartment on Durocher – a five-minute walk from the university – we prepared coffee in our tiny kitchen each morning, marvelling at the abundance that surrounded us. Montreal in the summer is electrifying and we drank in her magic with the appetite of new lovers. Our life as a couple felt like paradise on earth.

The day Anwar left to return to Italy, he told me that I was strong and that I could manage without him, but having to give up the good life now that I'd had a taste of it was terrible. It was the first time I had allowed myself to surrender to the bliss of companionship. After I dropped him off at the airport, I cried until I couldn't cry anymore and fell into a deep sleep. When I woke up all by myself in the studio apartment, the freedom I had felt turned to fear. When we are with those we love, we feel at home. Without them, things that were once familiar seem strange, even menacing.

Thankfully, college started a week later, which helped me to settle in. In the third week, my professor sent me on a field placement to a women's shelter. She gave me the address and told me to take the bus from Sherbrooke Street – the main thoroughfare that runs east–west on the island. I got on the bus and tried to hand the money to the driver, who pointed to a box beside him where I should drop the coins. I asked him in my very basic English if this bus would take me to my destination, holding up a card with the address on it. Without even looking at the card, he said something in French. I tried again, and again he replied in French, sounding more impatient. My face felt hot. I tried a third time. Again he replied in French. The man was visibly irritated and I despaired until I heard familiar words from the back of the bus, in Hebrew, "*Ima, ima, tekanhi li et ha'af.*" A little girl was asking her mother to wipe her nose. I ran towards the voice and bellowed back, "*At yechola la'azor li.*" The woman stared at me and introduced herself. "You are new here?"

I told her I was from Israel and that this was my first time in Canada. Would she happen to know this address? She did. I needed to take the bus in the opposite direction, but she graciously offered to show me the way. Speaking Hebrew, a language I had always thought of as the language of my enemy, I had found a friend. At that moment, this language became my own. It wasn't my mother tongue, but it was a language that I too could claim.

There were five of us in the programme: two Jordanians in their forties, Mohammed and Humoud, and two Jewish Israelis, Merav and Noga. Merav had been my field placement supervisor during my undergraduate degree and was doing her PhD in the programme. Noga was a proud lesbian who had grown up in a religious moshav. I occupied a weird position in the group as the Arab, the Palestinian, the Muslim and also one of the Israelis. During our conversations, I switched back and forth between Hebrew and Arabic without even thinking about it. The Jordanians didn't trust me. How could I speak their language and be friends with Noga and Merav? As a Palestinian, how could I forgive them for what they were doing to me and to my people? The Jordanians were also reluctant to discuss controversial topics – the settlements, the two-state solution, the Nakba – whereas Merav, Noga and I debated these topics passionately. One day, Mohammed pulled me aside and asked why I wasn't afraid to speak out against the government. "How is it that you fight with Noga and later I see you eating together in the cafeteria and playing guitar and singing?"

The programme, a master's in social work with the International Community Action Network (ICAN) at McGill University's School of Social Work, is about training social workers in rights-based practice, a methodology that allows people to access their rights and change systemic injustice from the ground up. More than that, the programme is about creating a network of coexistence, using social workers to build peace on the ground. But how would we do that in the Middle East if we didn't trust each other? "You can't be afraid to say what you think," I told Mohammed. "Real relationships can only be built on real conversations."

That changed things. From then on, Mohammed and Humoud joined in our arguments and it transformed their relationships; they relinquished the politeness which masked their prejudice against

Noga and Merav and were able to see that the two women really did care about the suffering of Palestinians and wanted to hold the government to account. McGill and Montreal became neutral spaces where we could discuss difficult issues.

In October, Jim introduced me to my mentor Sheila Goldbloom, a professor at the School of Social Work who had been lauded for her heroic efforts to establish community organizations in the city. When Sheila invited me to her house for a Shabbat dinner, I called Abouee to ask his advice. I'd worked with Jews, but I hadn't really spent time with them in a social setting. "By the way," he added at the end of the call, "it's Rosh Hashanah so bring an apple and honey and wish her *Shana Tova*." I had never participated in a Jewish new year before.

I arrived at Sheila's imposing home in an upmarket part of the city and checked the address five or six times before ringing the bell. My heart pounded. The door swung open and there stood a tiny, well-dressed woman with perfectly coiffed white hair. When she saw the apples and honey resting in my arms, she smiled at me with so much love that whatever fears I had vanished in that instant. She gave me a hug.

Sheila and her husband Victor were my doors to understanding the Jewish community outside Israel. I remember our arguments about Israel's policies regarding the occupation. I asked them what they thought about the Bedouin. How was it that we as citizens were deprived of basic rights and recognition? Sheila was quick to challenge her biases, but Victor was torn between his love for Israel and his commitment to human rights, justice and equality.

Being away from the conflict gave me the opportunity to zoom out not only from the gender issues within my community, but also from the political conflicts within Israel. I had always thought that the Palestinian conflict was the only conflict that existed on the planet, but my master's exposed me to how conflict between majority and minority communities plagues every society. In Montreal's own front yard, I saw the tension between the anglophone and francophone communities. We learned about the struggle of indigenous people in Canada and the shocking history of residential schools. I began to see how members of the free world had built their wealth at the expense of those already living there. The indigenous struggle in Canada resonated with my struggle as a Bedouin indigenous to the territory now called Israel. Once when I asked Abouee's uncle about the Israeli policy of land confiscation and the policy of settling as many Bedouin as possible into the smallest area of land, he said, "You know, it's as if my friend comes to ask to borrow my cow for a few days because he needs the milk to feed his starving children, but when I come to ask for my cow back, he tells me: 'It's not yours, it's mine.' And when I tell him that my children are also starving, he tells me there is hardly enough to feed his own children." They took our cows and are now depriving us of milk. What is the lesson for us as indigenous people? Don't host? Give up on our tradition of hospitality so that others don't take advantage of us? Or educate the greedy in our ways of sharing and hosting?

The first Palestinian refugee I met was Nabil, who came up to me after a talk I gave at the McGill Faculty of Law where I presented the need for Arab–Jewish partnership to fight for justice and equality. Nabil rejected my approach. "When they apologize for what they did, when they return our houses and our land," he would say, "then we can talk." Nabil was originally from a small village next to Haifa. During the Nakba, he was expelled with his family to the Ein el-Hilweh camp in Lebanon. In the seventies, Nabil's brother joined the Fedayeen, a group of Palestinian freedom fighters, and was killed. His body was never returned to the family for a proper burial. He was twenty-two. Nabil was twenty-four.

I became good friends with Nabil and his family. I would stay over at his house on the weekends and for a whole week during the ice storm when I lost electricity in my apartment. We spoke mostly about Palestine and he raved about a future when his homeland would be free. Like many refugees who bemoan the horrors of the past, he clung to the narrative as if his life depended on it and in some ways it did. His family had been dispersed: one aunt in Italy, others in Chile, Kuwait, Jordan, Lebanon, and him in Canada. Our histories form our identities but sometimes we become so entangled in them that we can no longer imagine another way forwards. He showed me the key to the house that had been stolen from him. He used to sit around the map with his children and they would point to all the destroyed villages. His children knew their rights, and they spoke with anger, with rage.

"I'm not angry at the Jews who are native to Palestine," Nabil would say. "My problem is with the Zionist movement. On what basis can they kick people out of their houses, these Europeans, come and kick people out of their houses and take their land?"

I too would be infected by his rage and would leave resigned and defeated and unwilling to talk peace with Jewish Israelis. Then the following week I would meet with Victor and Sheila who would talk about the right for Jews to have a safe haven and not be exposed to another Holocaust. Nabil's family and Sheila's lived only a few neighbourhoods apart, but their two perspectives seemed impossible to reconcile. I felt that my role in life was to bridge the gap, to shed light on a path forward that was founded on acknowledgement of the past and the promise of a just future. That year in Montreal determined the work I would go on to do. It gave me the freedom to see, for the first time, that Jews were not my "enemies" but my neighbours; that diversity is not only possible, but preferable; that justice and equality have nothing to do with which side is right, but is about bringing people from all sides to work together.

Professional Activism:
Roads Through the Cracks of Citizenship

Politics versus People

WHEN THE PROGRAMME ended, I joined Anwar on a two-month tour of Italy with less than a thousand dollars in our pockets. We slept on the beach, camped in the woods and ate pizza from small stalls. We felt like we were the wealthiest people on earth. A month after Anwar and I returned to Awajaan, Anwar's parents granted us permission to leave the village. We exchanged our shack, where we lived in fear of one day finding nothing but a pile of rocks courtesy of Israeli demolition trucks, for a small apartment in Beer a-Saba.

I started my field placement at one of ICAN's rights-based practice centres which was nestled in the centre of a bustling market in one of the more disadvantaged neighbourhoods in the city. In between stalls of fresh vegetables and the Tunisian pilaf place on the corner, residents could come into our centre to be informed about their rights and receive help in accessing them. We were five community workers. I was the only Arab. The manager, Hadas, a Yemeni Jew with thick, dark curls that fell softly around her face, stood at the head of the table as we drew a map of the neighbourhood – mostly impoverished Mizrahim and recent Russian immigrants – and planned our outreach efforts.

Map in hand, I walked towards the dilapidated apartment buildings on Rehov Avraham Avinu: sad concrete buildings with fans whirring in almost every window and clothes lines weighed down with rags. I checked the map: Efrat, the other community organizer, hadn't been there yet. The dimly lit entrance smelled of boiled cabbage and garbage. I stood in front of my first door and knocked without thinking twice. An old woman appeared. She wore a scarf that had once been a deep blue and a shapeless black dress that fell to her calves. She stared at me. I held the brochures and my clipboard in my hands and smiled, but before I could say anything she held out her finger and walked back inside the apartment only to return a moment later to place a single shekel in my palm. She closed the door. After a few seconds, it dawned on me: she thought I was a beggar.

I knocked again. She opened the door with an exasperated: "*Ze ma yesh!* [That's all I have!]"

"I'm a social worker," I said gently, "and I'm here to ask if *you* need any help." I handed her a brochure and explained that our centre was at the Gilat shopping centre, beside the bakery, near the Tunisian fast food place. "You can come any time Mondays and Wednesdays between nine and twelve. We're there to help *you*."

She glanced at the brochure and handed it back to me. "I don't read Hebrew," she said.

"I'm sorry," I said quickly. "Which language do you read?"

She repeated, "I don't read Hebrew," and had moved to close the door when I thrust the Arabic brochure at her.

"You are Arab?" she asked after her eyes had scanned both the brochure and me.

As soon as I said, "Yes," she slammed the door.

I moved on to the next apartment, another elderly woman, this one named Sara, but my experience was no different. Doors shut in my face as soon as they identified me as an Arab, or because they thought I was the one asking for help. It didn't occur to them that I was there to help them. To my surprise, a few days later, I passed by Sara sitting in the waiting room clutching the Arabic brochure I had handed her.

"*Boker tov*," I said warmly.

My fellow community organizer Efrat, an Ashkenazi Jewish woman, finished with a client and asked Sara to come into her office.

Sara didn't budge. She pointed at me and said: "I want to talk to her."

"She's busy. I can help you," Efrat said.

"I want her," Sara repeated.

When I had finished with my client, Sara sat in front of me and began to explain her housing situation, but her Hebrew was clumsy and slow. Would she prefer to speak in Arabic? She glanced around her as if to make sure that no one was watching and then asked if we could sit in another room. We didn't have one, I told her, but we could sit outside if she wanted privacy. We left the centre and sat on the stairs beside the Tunisian kiosk from where the delicious smells of cumin, harissa and grilled lamb joined our conversation. As soon as she started to tell me the story in her Iraqi Arabic dialect, this timid old woman was transformed into a lioness. She spoke loudly and made very clear demands. We returned to my office to fill out some forms and agreed to meet the following week.

When she arrived that week, she marched right past the waiting room straight into Hadas's office. Hadas calmly asked her to wait in the waiting room until one of us was ready to speak with her. That wasn't acceptable to Sara. She would only speak to the Arab social worker. Hadas, in her gentle way, said that whoever was available would see her.

Sara refused. "I only want the Arab social worker."

Hadas reiterated the organization's policy more firmly and Sara took a seat in the waiting room, tapping her cane impatiently on the floor.

Later, a Bedouin woman wearing a traditional *thobe* and white *shash* entered the waiting room and Hadas directed her to my office.

"I was here first!" Sara shouted.

"Yes," Hadas said, "but she doesn't speak Hebrew. You do. Any other social worker can help you."

Sara rose to her feet and slammed her cane against the floor. "I'm also an Iraqi Jew and I don't speak Hebrew. It is my right to receive service in the language that I know."

My heart made a victorious leap when I heard her stand up for herself. She'd kept her Arab origins hidden for years. God forbid someone confuse her with an Arab in a Zionist country. This was the first time she had had the courage to acknowledge her heritage.

At last, Hadas waved Sara into my office. I waited for her to speak. I knew she would have something to say about what had just happened.

"You know," she began, "we Iraqi Jews were very successful in Iraq. My father was the minister for public health. Everyone respected him. I studied economics at the university in Baghdad and worked in a big company until my parents decided to make *aliyah* [settle in Israel]. They told us that if we didn't leave for Israel that the Arabs would kill us. We left everything and we came here to be treated like illiterates. I got married to an Iraqi guy and never worked outside the house. We felt bad about ourselves because our culture was Arab but Arabs were the enemy and we didn't want to associate ourselves with the Arabs. But I always missed the songs, the language and my childhood back in Iraq. Everything about Iraq reminds me of myself, of being a strong woman and a proud Jew. Here, I'm the immigrant who comes from an Arab country. A Jew who speaks Hebrew with an Arabic accent."

When Sara finished her story, I asked her what she needed today. She looked up at me and a slow, satisfied smile spread across her lips.

"Nothing. I just wanted to speak in Arabic without feeling ashamed."

We hugged, and on her way out of the door, she looked at the Bedouin woman in the waiting room and said, in Arabic, "*Tifadali* [Your turn]."

The centre was mostly frequented by Jews. Why would I expect a Bedouin to travel to our centre in a residential Jewish neighbourhood? On the twentieth of each month, Bedouin flocked to the city centre and waited under the baking hot sun for their welfare or child benefit payment. I made use of this existing infrastructure and got permission from those government departments to set up a table on their premises or on the street nearby where I could offer our services. My table became a watering hole where I'd offer assistance with bureaucratic processes and the filling out of government forms; I would even accompany people to their appointments to translate for them. Soon I had to train volunteers to set up more tables providing the same services. One day a week, I'd pack the table into my car along with my flyers and brochures and set up in Umm Bateen and al-Grin, two unrecognized villages that I had identified as having serious social problems and limited access to services.

Salha, a large woman in her late thirties, approached the table I had installed at the National Insurance Office and I helped her fill out forms to claim single-mother benefits. She had five children of elementary school age and her husband, her first cousin, had left her for another woman. Single mothers in the Bedouin community are doubly condemned: their husbands abandon them for a younger wife and a nicer shack, and they are unable to claim the benefits afforded to single mothers because the Israeli government, on the basis of cultural sensitivity, rejects the notion that a polygamist community even has single mothers, while at the same time not enforcing the law that prohibits polygamy. When the husband officially divorces his first wife and registers the second, he receives the benefits for each set of children, under the term "expanded family". Back in the community, he remarries the first wife under Sharia law, but it's a marriage that serves only his ego.

Salha mobilized sixteen other single mothers to advocate for their rights. We called the project "The Unrecognized Single Mothers" because, like the unrecognized villages, these women didn't officially exist. They were easy to ignore, until they weren't. Using the rights-based community practice methodology I had learned during my master's, we held weekly meetings for three months, moving through the stages from awareness to empowerment until we finally brought our case to the Supreme Court. Fifteen of the seventeen single mothers received official recognition, and it was a victory for all Bedouin women. We sent a clear message: *You may not see us, but we are here. You may push us to the ground, but we will stand and fight.*

During our farewell session, Salha gripped me in a tight embrace, our hearts bound together by pride. She handed me a piece of embroidery whose message perfectly described the battle we had won: *Where there's a will, there's a way.* As she left, she said: "We have a big problem in the village, but I don't know if there's anything we can do about it." As soon as those words had escaped her lips, she walked back into the room and settled into the chair beside me.

She told me that the central water point in the village had been closed for some time, which she thought might be because the bill hadn't been paid. I suggested we call the company to find out why they had cut off the water. I dialled the number and put the phone on speaker. Even though Salha barely understood Hebrew, I wanted her to see that calling the authorities was as easy as baking *saj* pita. The fear of being rejected is a major impediment to marginalized people, one that stops them from taking the first step. Sometimes the fear is real and they need to learn how to deal with the issue; other times the fear is perceived and they need to work on their own mindset to build their confidence. Salha was right. The company hadn't received their monthly payment. The head of the tribe who was responsible for the account had collected the money but hadn't paid the company. And this wasn't the first time. I asked Salha why the company had chosen him to be in charge of the account.

She shrugged. "Because he's the head of the tribe."

I suggested we arrange a meeting at the company with the manager of the account.

"We can't do that!" She feared the head of the tribe would think that we were undermining him.

"We won't do anything," I reassured her. "We just want to know the criteria for being in charge of the account and if there is a way for you to pay to get the water."

We role-played the scene – a method I had often used with women to overcome their fears. Facing Salha, I played the manager and Salha played herself. Then we switched.

The day of the meeting, we sat down with a company representative and Salha launched into a passionate explanation in Arabic. He completely ignored her and spoke to me in Hebrew. I kept my eyes glued to Salha while I translated for her, forcing the representative to speak to her. He told us that the only criterion for being the account holder for a water point was that you needed to represent at least fifteen households.

We left the office, our minds working. "Do you think you can organize fifteen families to create a new account?" I asked her.

She smiled. "Yes. And I'll be the new sheikh of those families."

I knew that for this to succeed she couldn't just list a group of fifteen families. We would need to create a community process which ensured accountability. More than that, we would need to create a forum to build trust. Salha was taking on a role no woman had ever played before: managing a crucial resource, navigating the government system, and taking leadership out of the sheikh's hands. Salha and I sat in the tent in front of her shack and ran through names of families. We divided them into the ones we thought would join and the ones we thought wouldn't, addressing the reasons for each scenario, and we created an action plan. Salah selected single mothers and elderly couples. We visited them and explained our idea and invited them to meet in Salha's tent.

The day of the meeting, Salha saw the sheikh's car snaking its way towards us and in her face I read her fear of how this might get her into trouble with her ex-husband. The sheikh wanted to see me. I told the women to stay in the tent and walked towards him.

"Are you here to create problems?" he shouted from his window.

"Actually, I'm here to solve a problem," I answered lightly.

"When you incite the women against me, what do you call that?"

"I didn't incite the women against you," I said. There was no place for hesitation. If I stumbled or seemed uncertain, I would lose.

Only a lion can fight another lion. "We said nothing bad about you. We just want to open another account. Your account is still yours and you can continue to run it. This one is for the people who can't pay. These are the people who are creating problems for you, right?"

"Yeah," he said, stroking his beard. "I never pay on time. I have to go back and forth begging them like I'm asking for myself."

"You don't need to deal with this," I said. "Let Salha do that."

"Salha! You're joking."

"You don't lose anything by letting her try."

"Do whatever you want but don't come near my family." He drove off. This wasn't an empty threat: half of the village were his relatives.

When I told the others, they panicked, since we only had ten families, but the manager at the company agreed to let Salha represent the account with only ten families and we created a water fund into which each family deposited a hundred shekels on the twentieth of the month when they received their social security cheques.

When the first month's bill arrived, the ten families gathered in Salha's tent and her daughter, who was barely twelve years old, read the invoice because she was the only one who knew Hebrew. The cost was 647 shekels. I remember the number because the group had to figure out how to subtract 647 from 1000. The rest of the money stayed in the fund to cover the monthly fee if anyone couldn't afford that month. I followed Salha for eight months and she paid the bill each month without delay. A year later, I ran into her at a Hebrew language class offered by a Bedouin women's organization.

Both Salha and Sara faced barriers accessing basic rights. In some cases, people and laws impeded these women from accessing their rights; in others, it was the voice in their head telling them that they didn't deserve them. Arab, Jewish, this was the beginning of my understanding of a shared humanity that transcended ethnic identity and the ways that politics are used to turn us against each other. When working with women to address their daily needs, such as paying their rent or sending their children to school, there's no place for prejudice. When we speak about political issues, that's where prejudice plays a role and, in large part, it's because it is in the interest of politicians to pit people against each other, "us' versus "them" so we don't turn our attention to fixing the problems in our daily lives. People all want the same things: they want to be happy, they want to feel free to express themselves, they want to create a better future for their children. When we leverage the things that we all want, we see very different politics. But instead we tell Salha that she lives the way she does because Sara took it from her and there's nothing she can do. I chose to see it differently. Salha's life is in her hands. Nothing can change the past, but what we learn from it helps us change the present and shape the future.

Ordinary People

IN THE UNRECOGNIZED village of al-Grin, I couldn't go door-to-door the way I did in the Jewish neighbourhoods of Beer a-Saba. Being a guest or requesting help granted you access to people's homes. Given that I was the one offering help, I had to be invited as a guest. I sat at the office with Hassan, a volunteer from al-Grin whom I had trained, and asked him if anyone had given birth lately.

He cocked his head.

"I'd be a guest," I said, "and they'd have to welcome me."

With my brochures under my arm, a sturdy pair of boots and a long skirt, I trudged across the desert road towards the house where Um Khaled had given birth one week earlier.

I was almost at the shack when an old woman appeared in the doorway and greeted me. I removed my boots and entered a room full of women sitting on a mattress placed against the wall. To one side of the room, the woman who had just given birth lay on another mattress beside a wooden crate where her baby slept swaddled in a light blue cloth. The only light came from the open door and the warm glow of the *kanun*, a large stove where tea and the bachor sat warming on the hot coals. The aroma of the bachor – a thick date and nut mixture which the new mother eats for forty days after she has delivered – wafted through the room, blending with the familiar aroma of black tea spiced with cardamom. The place buzzed like a happy hive until I entered and their eyes fell on the colourful brochures I clutched over my chest.

"*Ya ahlaan foti* [Take a seat]."

They squashed even closer together to make space for me. As I sat down, I became aware of having no plan to disarm the uneasy glances demanding to know why a stranger had shown up in their tribe.

"*Mabrouk ma jaaki* [Congratulations for what you have received]," I said, opening with the traditional greeting for these occasions.

"*Allah yibaarik feekee* [May God congratulate you for what you will receive]," they answered in unison.

"I thought it would be better to come here first to say *mabrouk*, but also to meet all of you. I was sure that I would find you hiding here eating maktoum [wrapped sweets] before the new mother can have any."

They all giggled. My traditional dialect set them at ease. The Bedouin are not a homogenous group. The ones in the urban centres have mostly abandoned the traditional ways of life and these Bedouin were delighted that I was knowledgeable about the old customs. The happy hum resumed and they tried to guess where I was from. After a few guesses, another woman appeared in the doorway and pointed at me. "I came back for you. My son told me you were here and I came running." With her chin lifted a little higher in the air, she bragged to the others that her son, Hassan, worked with me. "She helps people know their rights and get them."

Um Hassan squeezed in next to me as if I was now her responsibility.

One of the young women looked at me and asked: "Are you

Amal a-Sana? I heard you on the radio and saw you on the TV. You're a social worker."

"A social worker!" another woman shrieked. "You people destroyed my daughter's family. She came to ask for her and the social worker had her betray her husband. She reported him to the police and then her husband's family threw her out, back to my house, and the husband's in jail."

Thirty heads bobbed up and down in agreement, murmuring, "Yes, they destroy families."

"No!" Um Hassan cut in. "She's not like them. She works with the people to get them water and services from the government."

"I'm a community organizer," I said, knowing that this title meant nothing to them, but as long as I wasn't a social worker, I would be accepted.

"What do you have?" Hassan wanted to know. "*Yalla!* Tell us." She asked as if I was selling something at the souk.

I had come to raise awareness about genetic diseases. Al-Grin had an unusually high incidence of deafness due to inbreeding. I wanted to raise the topic in the right way, to weave it into my agenda with their "here and now" issues. I looked at the little pink baby, breathing soundly in the box.

"What's the name of your baby?" I asked the mother.

"Khaled," she said, picking him up and placing him on her lap.

"*Ashat al-asaami* [May God give long life to this name]," I said warmly. "This is his father?" I pointed to the framed photo behind her. "He looks like him. Handsome."

The grandmother, sitting next to her daughter, remarked: "He's handsome like his father, but we hope he won't be deaf like him."

"Shhhhh," erupted across the room. "Spit it out!" "*Inshallah!*" The women cast out deafness as if it were a curse.

"How close are you to your husband?" I asked.

She said they were first cousins.

"This has nothing to do with your relationship with your cousin," her mother interjected. "It is from Allah!"

"Yes," the room agreed. "Allah decides and we must accept our fate."

They clearly didn't want to hear another opinion, so I didn't push. Instead, I told the mother that she didn't have to wait until her son grew up to find out if he was deaf, but could take him to the doctor to find out sooner. A woman sitting on the mattress across from me asked what she should do. She had two children at home who were deaf. I asked her why her children were at home.

"What can we do with them?" she said. "We send them to school, but the teachers say that we need to send them to a special school in the city."

"You know," I told her, "if you have enough deaf children, we can ask the government to provide a school here. You don't need to go to the city."

"We have tens of them!" several women said at once. One started counting on her fingers the names of the fathers or mothers of deaf children and the others corrected her. Each one chimed in, adding her expertise, until a consensus was reached and Um Hassan stood up to proclaim that her son would make a list.

That is how we formally documented this community knowledge and how I gained access to the village. Every Wednesday morning, I would visit Um Khaled's shack from ten till twelve to discuss community issues with whoever showed up. We sat together on those mattresses, with little Khaled asleep in his crate or suckling from his mother's breast. I never imposed my own agenda, but asked open-ended questions such as: "How are you?", "What's been going on?", "What are the issues you would like to change?", and, once we felt more comfortable with each other, "What are your hopes and dreams?" This led to discussions about the school, children with disabilities, polygamy and lack of access to basic services. I would say, "This one we can tackle," or "We need more resources for this one." As the first outsider to intervene, I had to proceed carefully. It's important not to promise anything and create expectations that could destroy trust in the next generation of people who come to provide support. I listened more than I spoke, and guided them when I felt they were ready to move forwards.

I was on my way towards our usual meeting place when one woman rushed over to tell me that we would be meeting at Sabaha's house. She had given birth the week before and there were many women gathering there. On our way to Sabaha's, a blood-curdling scream cut through the dust and diverted our attention to a woman in the distance, running barefoot, her hands clasped together and pressed to her chest. I hurried to my car and drove towards her. Blood dripped down her fingers where the tear in her *thobe* revealed a gash in her breast. I told her to get in and I would drive her to hospital.

She refused. "No. Take me to my parents."

Instead, I drove her to my uncle's clinic in Laqiya. He was used to dealing with cases where women couldn't risk reporting their injuries to the police. Blood was gushing from the cut, but it wasn't deep. He sewed it up and gave us our privacy. She'd heard of me from the meetings at Um Khaled's, but had never attended them. "I wanted to see you and tell you about my problems, but I was worried the other women would tell my husband." Now her pale face displayed more pride than distress. On the examination table lay what she'd been holding onto for dear life: her ID card, smeared in her blood.

Her story is that of thousands of women from the West Bank and Gaza who left their families to marry a Bedouin from Israel in the hope of a better life. After the Six-Day War in 1967, Israel's occupation of the West Bank and Gaza – territories previously governed by Jordan and Egypt – gave Palestinians within the country the opportunity to reunite with their relatives there. There were no checkpoints and women from the West Bank and Gaza married Bedouin from Israel to reunite with their families and, in doing so, obtain an Israeli ID. The women without any relatives in the Bedouin tribes sacrificed everything they had for this privilege. Joining the Bedouin community without anyone to protect you – no *jaaha* to advocate for you – meant that they faced their struggles entirely alone. Among the single mothers, these women were the most disadvantaged, invisible to both the community and the government.

Her husband wanted a second wife, but he needed his first wife's ID in order to officially divorce her before registering the second one. How was her ID sufficient proof of her consent? She was a person, not a piece of property. The policy – again, in the name of cultural sensitivity – permitted the husband to hand over his first wife's ID, as proof that she agreed to the divorce, and then present his new wife's ID to register the marriage, as if he was trading an old horse for a new one.

Her husband had hit her again and again and again, but she wouldn't give up that small piece of plastic. When he lashed at her with a jagged plank of wood that cut her across the chest, she ran. Her legs carried her with a will that saved her life.

"You know why they have deaf children?" she said. "It's because God is angry at men and the way they treat women."

This woman joined the Unrecognized Single Mothers project. We attempted to put the child benefits in her name, but in order to meet the criteria she would have to move out of the divided shack she shared with her husband. I argued with the officer from the social security office, explaining that she had nowhere to go. If she left the shack she wouldn't be allowed to take her children. The officer refused. Without separate households, she wasn't eligible, but in Jewish Israeli society a divorced couple could live in the same apartment so long as they had independent household expenses.

We went back to the officer and he agreed to visit the shack in order to make a decision. The metal sheet delineating the two separate spaces seemed to satisfy him and he was about to sign off on the papers on his clipboard when he noticed a thick, black cable beneath the sand.

"What's that?" he asked.

"This is electricity from the generator which is over there." I pointed to it.

He asked if they received electricity from the same generator.

They did. "Well, then they share a household," he concluded smugly.

"But she pays for it," I protested.

"How would we know? There's no meter."

I lost my patience. I didn't want to argue the case all over again. "She doesn't have electricity like you have in your house. Why does a single mother, a citizen of the state, have to run the risk of getting her electricity from a generator in the first place? You know how many children are electrocuted each year. Why doesn't this bother you?"

He stood there, mouth open, looking even more out of place than usual. His unwillingness to look at the reality was evident when he said: "That's not my job. Ask the government."

"You *are* the government," I shot back.

The woman noticed me shouting. She didn't understand what we were saying, but she walked towards us, knife in hand. With one swift cut, the cable lay lifeless in the ground.

"There," she said, "now we no longer share electricity."

The officer approved the documents and left.

Each day, I learned new things from these people. We weren't able to open a school for the deaf children in al-Grin, but we successfully lobbied the government to provide transport for the children to attend a special school in the city. Every day, the women in al-Grin braved evil just to exist. These women epitomized the word Bedouin: they navigated the wilderness of their lives with a fierceness in their hearts whose fire never went out. They inspired me to believe that ordinary people can change the world.

"I'm Not Going to Talk to a Woman"

IN SEPTEMBER 2000, Anwar passed the bar exam and started a law firm with my brother Yousef. We left our apartment and bought one closer to the city centre, and while we waited for the renovations to be completed, we moved into Dvorka's house in Omer to keep her company while her husband was on sabbatical in the United States. I never thought I would live in the wealthiest Jewish town in the country, but after we had worked tirelessly together for several years, Dvorka had become more than my mentor: she was another mother. We took possession of a room with a large bed and window that opened onto the tidy streets lined with palm trees and gladioli. One day the phone rang and I answered.

"Are you the Bedouin family living with Dvorka?" a woman's voice asked me. I laughed and she told me that everyone was talking about it. "You know," she said, "this is so unusual."

What was unusual to me was living side by side and not knowing one another. What was unusual was to be questioned by the security guard at the gate every single time just because I was an Arab. What was unusual was living in a country for my entire life and being reminded that I didn't belong. Dvorka was an Ashkenazi Jew who saw beyond my ethnicity. She saw my expertise, my intelligence and my commitment to my cause. We lived with her for seven months as her Bedouin children. It was in those seven months that Anwar became fluent in Hebrew. Dvorka and Anwar made a deal: she corrected his Hebrew; he corrected her cooking.

It's difficult to describe what it felt like to be living there during the first days of the second intifada. Four days after Ariel Sharon's visit to the Al Aqsa mosque in Jerusalem*, Palestinians all over rose up in protest and Israeli bullets killed twenty Palestinians, including

---

* In September 2000, the controversial politician and future Prime Minister, Ariel Sharon, made a provocative visit to the Al Aqsa Mosque on the Temple Mount, the third holiest site in Islam. This was widely seen as the trigger of the second intifada which lasted approximately five years.

a twelve-year-old boy, Mohammed al-Dura. Television cameras caught the murder of this young boy who fell to the ground, hiding behind his father during the raid. Ummi couldn't understand how I could work with Jews. How could I trust them? I tried to explain that there were Jewish mothers just like her who cried when they saw this, who understood that the occupation was unjust, but she chose to believe the headlines which told her that the Jews were our enemies, full stop.

The tension was at its peak. Everywhere I went, the sense that a fight could break out at any moment lay heavy in the air. Riding the bus, walking down the aisle of the grocery store and passing strangers in the street now involved glancing over one's shoulder, avoiding eye contact or staring someone down. It's in the details that fear smothers a population.

Whenever Yossaleh, Dvorka's husband, was back home from his sabbatical, their two sons, Shaul and Yoav, would drive down to visit their parents for Shabbat dinner. These dinners shared the most important qualities of any Palestinian family dinner: good food and good debate. Fighting about who was right was the main dish and Dvorka's children were as loud and opinionated as I was. Those dinners were a microcosm of the political atmosphere that engulfed us every single day. We couldn't ignore the tough questions: Who was here first? How can the state be Jewish and democratic? What happened during the Nakba? Why did the Palestinians refuse the '47 division? Dvorka always tried to find common ground, but we would yell until in good conscience we could no longer ignore her pleas for us to shut up and eat. At the end of the meal, we would kiss goodbye until the next time.

But when thirteen Palestinian Israelis were killed by Israeli police in a pro-intifada demonstration, I asked myself: *Was I betraying my family by living with Dvorka?* I sat in my family's *hosh* one weekend and listened to Ummi, my aunts and my sisters speak with mistrust and rage. The talk was hateful, the voices full of pain. I looked at my aunt and thought to myself: *How many things do I have in common with her? How many things do I have in common with Dvorka?* The answer was clear. Dvorka and I didn't share a bloodline, but we shared the same values – as activists and as women. Our belief in a future where people of all cultures could live together connected us beyond kin. I wasn't ready to give up on my relationship with Dvorka, which meant that I wasn't ready to give up on my relationship with Jews.

In the early 2000s, Shatil hired me to lead the campaign to advocate for equitable budget allocations for the education of Bedouin children. At the time there was the Authority for Bedouin Education, a special government department, distinct from the Ministry of Education, and our goal was to have this department absorbed into the Ministry to ensure it was efficiently and equitably run. Our main concern was the pitiful budgets for education in the unrecognized villages. For example, some 40 million shekels were spent transporting Bedouin children to schools in the recognized villages when a school could have been erected in their own villages for a fraction of that cost.

I formed a steering committee of Bedouin leaders drawn from civil society organizations, established professionals in the community, members of local municipalities and members of the Regional Council of Unrecognized Villages.

My team for the campaign consisted of a field coordinator, a lobbyist and a media coordinator. We organized protests and demonstrations: several times a week, thirty to fifty people showed up outside the Authority's office to demand equal access to education for Bedouin children. Once a month, we marched alongside hundreds of protesters, making the same demands at Beer a-Saba's main junctions, attempting to attract as much media coverage as possible in order to bring the issue into public discourse. When we learned that the children in the unrecognized village of Tarabin still used donkeys and carts to travel to their school in Tel a-Saba, we thought this would serve as a powerful way to show how Israel, the only democracy in the Middle East, provides for its non-Jewish citizens. We toured the villages with Israel's main news channel and

I showed them the appalling state of the village schools. The journalist asked a seven-year-old boy riding back from Tel a-Saba in his cart why he insisted on making the long journey every day.

"Because I want to study," the boy replied.

"Why do you want to study?"

The boy patted the animal's bristly forehead. "Because I don't want to be like this donkey."

This story finally brought our cause to the public. Even Haim Yavin, a leading news anchor, commented on the situation. "The kid wants to learn. What's so hard to understand?" Yavin's words on the evening news placed the Authority for Bedouin Education under tremendous public scrutiny, but the next day the steering committee called an emergency meeting. They were furious. I should have consulted with them before bringing the media to Tarabin. I explained that they had approved the work plan, which stipulated that it was my job to initiate strategic media coverage to bring the issue of Bedouin education before the public.

"Yes, but you must ask our permission before you take any action," one of them told me. This dynamic was getting to me. If they wanted someone who wasn't going to think for themselves, they shouldn't have hired me. "We want you," the chair conceded, "but sometimes you have to consult us, especially when there are considerations. Tensions."

Tarabin wasn't represented by the Regional Council for Unrecognized Villages (RCUV) – a council to which many of the steering committee members belonged – because they communicated their issues to the government directly. This harkened back to the days when sheikhs had personal relationships with government officials, something that was going out of fashion as the governance of Bedouin villages was formalized and had bodies like the RCUV that spoke on their behalf.

I chose my next words carefully. "The campaign calls for Bedouin education. These children are Bedouin and I will serve them whether they are part of your organization or not."

"Then we do have a problem with you." He stared me down as he adjourned the meeting.

Later that evening, while I was preparing for the next day's protest, my field coordinator informed me that my steering committee was talking about firing me. "They think you might be working for the Shabak [Shin Bet]," he told me, "which is why you're not following their orders."

I told everyone to keep working while the field coordinator and I got into my car. My foot trembled on the gas pedal, not from Beer a-Saba's cool winter air, but from the anger coursing through my body. This accusation was dirty play. They couldn't dispute my honour, so they questioned my loyalty – the blow typically reserved for men. The RCUV offices weren't far from Shatil. I parked the car and ran up the stairs, with the field coordinator running behind me. I pushed the door open and stood defiantly face to face with a roomful of men sitting around a large table. Each pair of eyes was on me.

I pointed at the man who had made the accusation. "I want to talk with you. Now. You can continue," I told the others. "I'm sorry to interrupt."

The man left his seat and we walked into an empty office. For my safety, I left the door ajar before tearing into him. "Why would you do that? I didn't follow your orders so you smear my reputation? You felt hurt that a woman said no to you? And what is this Shabak thing? You know who I am. You know my family has been fighting against institutions since the beginning."

"Listen," he said, in a treacly voice. "Lately you've been doing things that we don't agree with and I'm worried about you. The Shabak bullied you to work for them and you couldn't say no. Sometimes they make us do things we don't want to do."

"So you're saying I'm working with the Shabak?"

"Yes. Otherwise, how do you explain the fact that you're confident not doing the things we ask of you. They're backing you up. And we all know that you're living with a Jewish woman. She might have a photo of you in the shower which they're blackmailing you with."

I couldn't believe it. Not only was I a traitor, but I was a traitor who couldn't even think for herself. I was just the helpless puppet caught in the claws of the state, that tyrannical puppet master. His patronizing tone made me sick and his delusions made me angry. My arms reached for the electric heater next to me and I hurled it at him. I showed him what a woman taking charge looks like in the only way he could understand. The metal box flew across the room and grazed his coffee cup, which spilled onto his shirt, leaving a dark brown stain.

The men in the other room appeared in the doorway and the head of one of the tribes hurried over to try and calm me down. I brushed him off and made for the door, but before leaving, I turned to all the men.

"You let this happen. You are Bedouin. You know the price of ruining a woman's name and none of you were brave enough to stand up for me and say that you've known me for the last ten years. How do you expect our community to trust you to fight against the government if you don't have the courage to speak your mind?"

When I returned to Dvorka's later that evening, she sensed something was wrong and asked me if I was all right. I tried to imagine her stealing a photo of me while I was in the shower, but I couldn't. What a crazy, paranoid idea. I told Anwar what had happened and he held me in his arms, grounding me in his endless sea of calm. "Go back to work as usual. This story will be buried," he said. "You've shown them that you're not to be played with."

About three weeks later, I was in Jerusalem, leading a demonstration next to the Knesset, where men and children chanted, "We want education. We want a future," – a simple, uncontroversial request. My cell phone rang. The voice on the other line said he was a sheikh from one of the unrecognized villages who wasn't represented by the RCUV. He told me to stop this *maskhara* (circus). "You're not representing us. You're ruining our relationship with the government. Nothing good will come of this."

"I don't know who is speaking," I replied, "but I'm not fighting for you, I'm fighting for a solution to a social problem. If you don't suffer from it, then it doesn't concern you."

"Listen," he said, "I'm not going to talk to a *hurma* [a woman]. I'll call your father and talk man to man. He'll find a way to deal with you." The line went dead.

Quickly, I dialled Abouee's number and told him that I was demonstrating in Jerusalem and that one of the sheikhs was going to call him to complain about me.

"Did you *wasakhti lesankee*? [Did you dirty your mouth? Is your side clean?]"

"Abouee, you know me. Have I ever done that?"

"I know, but I needed to ask so I know how to handle this."

Later that day, Anwar called me to say that the sheikh had called Abouee, but Abouee had told him to call my husband. Had Anwar received a call? No, no one had called him. The sheikh knew that if he called Anwar he would have told him that I was doing my job and that he was not my boss.

The campaign roused conflict with the members of my community who didn't want things to change. All this obscured the real issue we were fighting against: money was being mismanaged to maintain the political narrative that the unrecognized villages were illegitimate settlements that didn't merit proper investment in education and infrastructure.

During one protest in front of the Authority's main office, the members of a counter demonstration, also Bedouin, walked towards our faction. One of the Bedouin from the opposing group started calling me names, trying to turn the fight into a tribal struggle. If something were to happen, he threatened, my tribe would pay the price. We marched on, calling for the dissolution of the Authority.

When the protest was over, I was walking towards my car when I noticed that a member of the Authority was also leaving the parking lot. I looked away, but he drove up to me and said: "*Ya bint el-Sana*, don't cause yourself more problems."

342

"It's not between us," I told him. "I have nothing against you and I know you have nothing against me. This is a governmental office. You're not fighting for your tribe. You're fighting for the government. It's not personal."

"Soon it will become personal." He drove off.

The same day my cell phone rang and a man told me that they would kill me if I continued with the campaign. I hung up and felt nothing. This was part of my journey. If I wasn't ready to pay the price, why would I have started down this path?

Our weekly protests continued, with one taking place next to Prime Minister Sharon's farm in the Negev. People held banners demanding better schools and photos of children riding their donkeys with the words: Education in Israel in 2001?

A security guard appeared at the farm's gate and asked for the organizer of the protest. Of course he approached one of the traditionally dressed men and asked him to follow him, but the man pointed to me. The security guard looked surprised. He walked over to me. "Are you the organizer?"

"Yes," I said.

"Are you sure?"

"What do you mean?" I asked. He shrugged and signalled me to follow him.

After he had searched my bag and my body, we entered a building a few paces from the gate and the security guard led me to an office where a secretary invited me to take a seat. I saw on her desk the Katz report, a document outlining ways to improve the Bedouin education system that no one had yet bothered to read. Staring at her computer screen she said: "I see here that you sent us a letter concerning Bedouin education. I understand that the purpose of the protest is the same as what you wrote here."

"Yes," I said and pointed to the report.

"Yes. I've already asked for an update on what is happening in response to the report."

As she spoke, I heard movement in the other room and two

security guards entered. She stood up and I saw Sharon walk out of his office. Without thinking, I stood up too. I don't know why, but it wasn't out of respect. He saw me and laughed, then with intrigue and surprise in his voice said: "What happened to the Bedouin tribes? Where is the sheikh?" He was referring to the old guard.

"Things are different now. I'm the sheikh," I said.

"I'm sure this will be good for the Bedouin," he said and left with his security guards.

It was strange seeing him in the flesh. In Palestinian memory, he is the butcher who oversaw the Sabra and Shatila massacre in Lebanon, and the puppet master of the October events, the one who allowed thirteen Palestinian citizens of Israel to be killed. I couldn't separate him from these atrocities and was too shaken by the collective memory, by the narrative I'd been told, to form my own judgement. I left the farm very confused. I chose not to tell my steering committee that I'd seen him. First, because we didn't speak about anything, second, because I knew they would find a way to use it against me – I'd be accused of consorting with the enemy – and third, my media consultant would have a field day with Sharon's ignorant comments on meeting me and that would totally eclipse the issue we were fighting for.

After more than a year of campaigning, we finally won. The Authority for Bedouin Education was absorbed into the Ministry dealing with the education of all Israel's citizens. The issues surrounding Bedouin education in the unrecognized villages was now part of the public discourse and we had succeeded in generating a sustainable movement to fight for equal rights for Bedouin children.

Fresh Blood Under the Stars

THE FIRST TIME Ummi visited us in our apartment in the city she came with Maryam. I knew this was more of an inspection than a visit. She toured the apartment, wiping her finger along the dining room table to check for dirt, and opening closets to make sure my clothes were nicely folded. I'd been preparing for this visit all week, cleaning the apartment after my long hours at the office, but when she stepped into the kitchen she jumped as if she'd seen a snake. Anwar stood in front of the stove, stirring something in a large pot. He asked her if she liked spicy food.

She didn't answer but the scowl on her face spelled trouble. She left the kitchen and walked over to me. "What is this? You are letting your husband cook like a woman! Shame on you."

"He wanted to do it. He likes cooking."

"What's this bullshit! He *likes* cooking? Get up and take over from him."

Anwar came into the living room with a spoonful of rice for me to taste. Ummi found something interesting on the carpet, to make it clear that she wasn't complicit in how poorly her daughter had been raised.

"Come on," Maryam whispered. "This is their life."

"God take her," Ummi muttered, "I wish I hadn't come." Her hands made small bewildered gestures towards the invisible patriarch. "Why did I come?"

I set the table and Anwar appeared from the kitchen to announce his big achievement: he'd made the best maqlouba ever. I carried the dish through and presented the steaming platter of chicken, rice, onions, cardamom, cumin, eggplant and tomatoes neatly packed into an upside-down loaf to Maryam and Ummi. The dish looked perfect and Maryam complimented the chef on his skills. Ummi's dirty glance in her direction indicated that her comments were only adding salt to a very infected wound.

"Let's see if you like Anwar's cooking better than mine," I said light heartedly. Ummi glared at me. She couldn't have looked more upset, or so I thought, but then Anwar began serving. His question "leg or breast?" didn't reach her ears. Her veins bulged from her neck and I signalled to Anwar to let me serve.

Ummi turned to Maryam. "I can't breathe," she gasped. "Take me out."

Maryam looked at me, and we both understood that Ummi's discomfort was so extreme that it wasn't the time to educate her about gender roles. After all, I had invited her and I wanted to make sure that she would come back. I followed Anwar back into the kitchen and told him that Ummi had reached her tolerance quota for untraditional behaviour for the day and he should pretend he needed to pick up drinks from the grocery store.

As soon as he left, Ummi took a deep breath and removed her black abaaya.

"This will be the last time you do this to me. Do you understand?"

"But he's used to this," I tried to explain.

"I don't care. You do whatever you want inside your house, but I don't want to see it. When I come here, you cook and you serve."

We resumed our seats around the table and Ummi placed a spoonful of rice in her mouth. Her eyes widened. "If I weren't your mother and knew that the only thing you can do in the kitchen is boil an egg, I would have said this was a woman's cooking."

On our very short weekends – Friday afternoon to Saturday – I had no choice but to visit both my parents and Anwar's. Even if my weeks were packed, leaving me no time even to wash my clothes, I was expected to prioritize nurturing my relationship with my two families. The biggest issue in the relationship with both Ummi and my mother-in-law was that Anwar and I didn't have children on the agenda. They left us alone at first, but after three years they started to push. Not in a casual "Oh, wouldn't it be nice if . . ." way. Ummi explicitly ordered me to get pregnant.

"Why do you think women get married? Do you think the man will keep you if you don't bring him children?" she would shout only minutes after I had walked into the *hosh*.

My mother-in-law was more sensitive. Every Saturday – Anwar's family's day of the week – after the *ahlan wasahlan*s, the questions would stream in from Anwar's aunts and brothers' wives. "Is there anything new? Any news?" they would ask, pointing to their bellies. "What is going on? Did you check?"

At the end of the day, we would get into our car and Anwar's mother would give me some kind of parting gift. One time it was a Coca Cola bottle filled with the blood of a sheep they had slaughtered earlier that day. She handed it over with careful instructions: "Early in the morning, before sunrise, clean yourself in the shower with salt water. Then, pour the blood all over your body and massage your belly." I nodded reverently as if she was revealing the secret I'd been waiting for all my life, but once Anwar and I were a safe distance away, we'd toss the bottle somewhere on the road. Another time she gave me a cloth bag containing seven stones. "Every day put one stone in water and leave it under the stars. In the morning, drink the water." Again, I took her gift and tucked it safely in my bag – and that's where it stayed.

Over time, the questions became more aggressive. No one ever asked me about my campaigns or my advocacy, my opinions on recent political events, or ways to address pressing social problems. I was a woman and having children was the only thing that counted. One Saturday all the women sat in the *hosh* outside Anwar's parents' shack and they chatted pointedly about women who had married the same month as me who now had four or five children. "What are you lacking?" Anwar's aunt asked me. "No one keeps a cow that doesn't give milk."

"The only thing you gain from the man is children," another chimed in. "And men want children. Don't believe them when they say they don't. One day, he'll leave you without warning."

I thought a short answer like *inshallah* would be enough, but it was never enough. In fact, it had the opposite effect: not providing them with an adequate explanation gave them licence to ask more questions. That said, I understood them. Having children was the only thing they received credit for. My life was very different. My fulfilment didn't only come from what I produced in my womb. On our way home that day, I told Anwar I'd had enough.

347

"I'll take care of it," Anwar said. I knew that he could be direct and was worried that he would offend his mother.

"Please, if you're going to hurt her, I would rather you didn't speak to her."

"Don't worry," he said and he left it at that.

We stopped by my parents' house on our way back to the city and I was happy to see Jidatee sitting in the *hosh*. I kissed her forehead and sat down beside her. She wrapped her hand in her white *shash* before shaking hands with Anwar, who went to sit with Yousef in the other room. Jidatee tilted her head questioningly. "What's going on with you? Is it from you or from God?" She was asking if I was taking birth control pills, which I didn't want to admit to and open the door to that storm.

"I follow you in the news and I'm very proud of you. You are like *Jaddatki Jidaa* [your grandmother, strong] and *bint rjaal* [the daughter of strong men]. Keep going and God will protect you." I hugged her tightly. Being seen for what really mattered to me felt like a golden ray of sunlight warming my face.

She opened my palm and scanned its long dark lines. "You know that the main place for a woman is her house and her main role is to bring forth someone to carry on her husband's name. I'm not telling you to give up on what you do, but balance it, *ya jiddi*. Time is passing so quickly and it won't wait for you to complete your work. The work is constant. It will never finish so long as we humans are living here. There will always be problems: oppressors and oppressed, rich and poor, strong and weak." She let go of my palm and caressed my shoulder. "I want you to stop the pills if you are taking them. You're poisoning your body. Besides, the Jews invented them to stop us from having children so that we disappear."

The following weekend when we were sitting having lunch with Anwar's family, Anwar stood up and started helping his mother clear the plates. Coming from a family of eleven – eight boys and only three girls – Anwar and his brothers were used to helping their mother, not least because the girls were born much later. He stood next to her saying a few quiet words. I saw his mother place her hand over his mouth, then hug him. I was dying to know what he had said, but it was not the right time to ask. After lunch, Anwar's nosy aunts came by to say hello and drink coffee. One of them said: "My children saw you on TV at the demonstration. How long are you going to waste your time? Why haven't you got pregnant?"

Anwar's mother cut in, her voice louder and more assertive than I had ever heard it. "There are plenty of women who bring children. She's busy. She doesn't have time. If you want children, you bring them."

I couldn't believe my ears. This polite, soft woman championing my decision to choose my work over children? The topic didn't come up again for the entire visit.

On the drive home, I asked Anwar what he'd done.

He smiled mischievously. "I told my mother that *I* was the one with the problem."

Now I understood. She didn't want anyone to know that her son, her prize and joy, was the cause of our "child troubles". Anwar's little lie bought us time.

A New Horizon: AJEEC

THE OCTOBER EVENTS and the second intifada left a deep rift in the relationship between the Jewish majority and the Palestinian minority. In order to rebuild trust within society, significant effort was made to foster "coexistence". We used to call these meetings "hummus and falafel" dialogue because they were about getting to know each other's cultures rather than talking about the real issues – the occupation, the Nakba and our contradictory narratives – that prevented us from working together. In spite of these efforts, though, there was a pervading belief that working together just wasn't possible.

After a protest I was leading against housing demolitions, I noticed that none of the Bedouin I had spoken to had shown up. I stood by the Knesset feeling frustrated and thought to myself: "What if one of the ministers does come out and asks us what we want? We could describe the problem, but have we given any thought to the solutions? And, even if our advocacy does succeed in changing the law, do my people know how to implement those changes and make the most of them?" I needed answers so I went back to the same people who had told me they would come in order to find out why they hadn't. They told me: "The palm can't fight the needle," meaning that Israel was a strong country and we were a weak people and there was nothing we could do. Some accused me of using them to build my career and others justified their victimhood by quoting our community's suspicion of women: "*La khayr fee umma etgoud-ha emra'a* [a society led by a woman has no blessing]."

At the same time, I heard a radio show where ordinary Jewish citizens were expressing their anger at the Bedouin residents in Rahat who had burned down a bank and vandalized streetlights in protest against Israeli violence in the West Bank.

"I don't understand them," one guest said. "We built banks and roads and gave them houses and jobs and cars. They drive better cars than us, but they burn everything."

"Who gave me this car?" I thought, shaking with anger. Ordinary people believed that they had given us what we had. Our neighbours knew nothing about our culture, our history and our struggle. We knew their history, their language, we even knew their prayers and poems and songs. "If the Jewish majority only knows me through their media," I thought to myself, "that means I haven't presented myself properly. If I want the Jewish majority – ordinary people – to know and understand our struggle, it is our responsibility to educate them. We can't leave this to the government, which benefits from maintaining the rift between us. Change comes from people and it is for us, the people, to find common ground to work together."

While many called for separation, I decided to reimagine the relationship, to create an Arab-Jewish organization – to bring Jews into the process, not as the "enabler", as with most NGOs, but to invite Jews to see how things are done in our community, and for them to learn from us in order to support a more egalitarian pluralism. That's how I came to establish AJEEC, the Arab-Jewish Centre for Equality, Empowerment and Cooperation. AJEEC, in Arabic, means "I am coming to you". I put "Arab" before "Jewish" because the work is led by the minority in order to establish equality between all citizens. I decided to change the paradigm from "coexistence" to "partnership". Co-existence is between two equal parties, but partnership is built between unequal parties, knowing what each side brings to the partnership and acknowledging the inequality of the relationship. It would be an organization that served people's immediate needs and tackled structural barriers at the same time, simultaneously aiding service provision and advocacy, since marginalized communities don't have the luxury of doing one over the other.

I didn't read about different projects in the world. Instead, I spoke to the people in my community. In one conversation with Jidatee about women's freedom, she said: "Our liberation is in here," pointing to her head, "not in how we dress." She echoed the Brazilian educator, Paulo Freire's conviction that oppression begins in the mind and that transcending our marginality begins with freeing ourselves from an oppressed mindset. From these conversations, I understood just how much of our indigenous knowledge we'd abandoned in response to the daily reminders that our way of life was primitive. I spoke to people about what they saw, whether they believed it could change and how. I observed four main mindsets in my community: the defeated, the victim, the oppressed and the proud. These observations became the basis of my model for community development which focuses on mapping these mindsets as part of an assessment of the needs and strengths of a community.

The defeated believe that only Allah can change their fate. They are passive and they submit, content to walk next to the wall in the hope that God will protect them until they die. The victim is angry, but they blame others for their situation and don't want to change things. If the bus arrives late, they blame the bus as though it has arrived late on purpose; it is as if the entire world conspires against them to extend their suffering. The oppressed understand that the situation is not right. They're angry and aware of the external factors that contribute to their problems. These people want to change things, but they don't know how. They are usually the target population for extremists because their anger is ripe for converting it into action. The proud are the ones who believe in themselves, the ones who link their hope to their strength and who want to change society from within. Their belief in their agency comes from the pride they feel about their identity and they use that pride to leverage community resources and create change.

I established AJEEC as a department within the Negev Institute for Strategies of Peace and Development run by Yehuda Paz and Vivian Silver. Yehuda was more Zionist than the people I typically worked with. One of our first arguments was when he compared the Bedouin of the Naqab to Turkish immigrants in Germany. "We are not a minority who immigrated here," I countered. "I was born here and all my great-grandfathers were here. The one who immigrated was you. We are an indigenous minority. We don't struggle for equal rights, but for collective political rights and recognition as a national minority."

Early on we needed to be clear about what we agreed on and what we didn't agree on. It was much easier for me to join forces with an Anti-Zionist, but the views I wanted to change were those of Jews in the mainstream, Jews like Yehuda, not the ones on the margins.

I remember once Vivian and I were making coffee in the small kitchen in our office. We were arguing about whether she was aware that she belonged to the majority and that her daily actions were encoded into the power relations between the groups. She poured the coffee into her mug and was about to move mine when she asked sarcastically, "Is it OK for me to do that? Is there a power relation in this act?"

We were both exhausted from scrutinizing everything. We weren't just working to promote projects, we were working to change our mindsets. We'd been arguing constantly, expanding our awareness in an attempt to reach real partnership.

"Yes," I answered. "Language, daily behaviours – everything reflects the power relationship."

Yehuda and Vivian had both emigrated to Israel from North America and their lived experience of being a minority in their home countries gave them the ability to critically assess their behaviours and values. It was a challenge for them to work with me and a challenge for me to work with them, but we were all brave enough to meet that challenge.

The Gatherer-Based Approach

ONE EVENING I was at a wedding on the outskirts of Rahat, dancing in the women's tent. The bride was one of the women I had helped during my work with the rights centre. I was always happy to attend weddings and revel in the beauty of women in all their glory. The bride and I sat together on plastic chairs and her eyes were fixed on something on the other side of the tent. Her long lashes fell when she asked: "Why is it only the men who have someone taking photos and videos?"

At that time, the only photographers in the Bedouin community were men and therefore they weren't allowed in the women's tent. Instantly, I had an idea. What if we trained Bedouin women to be photographers and videographers? It would create jobs for women, and it would allow them to have their side of the wedding documented. I invited twenty women from different villages between the ages of eighteen and forty to discuss the idea. This was an opportunity to put my grandmother's wisdom into practice. In the past, the men, the hunters, looked outside the tribe for resources and means to survive whereas the women, the gatherers, used what we had around us and under our feet. The women and I came up with a whole programme that would start with empowerment, then photography and camera training, and, finally, business training. I looked to our past as hunter-gatherers to reclaim women's traditional roles as gatherers by looking for targets for social change that were close at hand.

I approached the Authority for Small and Medium Enterprises within the Ministry of Labor to request support for the programme. They said that they could provide the business training, but that another department within the ministry would provide the vocational training. It seemed obvious to me that vocational training without business acumen would do little to change people's situation. Thankfully, the head of the Authority for Small and Medium Enterprises, Dani Matzliach, a Mizrahi Jew, agreed with me. It took two years from the moment I approached the women to the launch of the first programme. The bulk of the work consisted of conducting conversations within the community. Community outreach is not a stage, it's an ongoing process. Finally, in 2004, the project started with twenty-seven women out of the forty who applied. At the end of the course we provided loans to the graduates to buy equipment and they worked in teams of two: one did video and one did photography. We held an impressive graduation ceremony to which we invited the press, and published the names of the women in the paper. Within three weeks all the graduates were booked for the entire wedding season. The mayor of one of the Bedouin towns who was a member of the Islamic Movement thanked me for respecting the traditions. That wasn't my vision. I had in mind a future where Bedouin women took photos in the men's section or fixed electric cables when none of the men around her knew how to, but to navigate resistance to change it's important to start by planting seeds.

The programme was even covered in the national news. The day after it aired, I received a call from a woman in Jerusalem who worked with the Haredi community – ultra-Orthodox Jews – asking me to bring the model there. They too had separate spaces for men and women during weddings. I ran an empowerment session with the Haredi women, explaining the relationship between income and influence. When I told them how much the Bedouin female photographers earned, they were amazed that they could make a decent income without breaking community rules, which would give them a say in decision-making in their families. I looked at these Haredi women in their scarves and saw my sisters' faces staring back at me. Our challenges were the same: we lived in societies run by men and were forced to play according to their rules.

Soon after the female photographers' programme, we identified another need: female DJs. We used the same model, combining vocational training and business training, to train Bedouin women DJs, but this time the teachers were Jewish youth-at-risk. Fourteen-, fifteen- and sixteen-year-old boys, graduates from a DJ-training programme in Sderot that was intended to give them an alternative path to a life of drugs and crime, taught Bedouin mothers aged thirty to forty how to DJ a party. It was an unlikely partnership between two sets of underdogs brought together by their passion for music and their desire for a better future: the women hugged and fussed over the boys as if they were their own sons and the boys benefited from the affection of such doting mothers. Everyone shared their favourite music and was wowed by what they heard. The conflict couldn't have entered that room even through the tiniest crack.

Both these projects were first steps in changing not only people's realities but also their mindsets. The International Society for Small and Medium Enterprises presented me with an award for these two projects, which showed my community that the world was watching, that our suffering was not a given. A field of dreams can blossom from one simple idea.

If This Succeeds, We All Succeed

I N 2006, YULI Tamir, the Minister for Education, passed the "Feed All" proposal which aimed to provide hot meals to all Israeli children living in under-privileged communities. One morning, I was driving back to Beer a-Saba when I saw a big white truck with the words "Gush Etzion Catering" written on the side. Something in my gut told me to follow it. Sure enough, it turned into Hura, a Bedouin town. I followed the truck, certain that this was a trial for the "Feed All" proposal. The truck pulled into the school's parking lot and I watched employees unload hundreds of little white boxes. Why did a Bedouin town need to get food from a Jewish settlement in the West Bank?

An idea sparked and I dashed out of the car towards the school. One of the teachers called out to me: "*Allah youstor.* [What brought you to our school]?"

"I want to taste the food," I said.

He thought I was joking.

"Seriously, I want to see the food."

He accompanied me to the principal's office where the principal invited me to have a seat.

"No, really, I would like to see the food," I told him.

"Do you want to complain to the Minister for Health?" he asked.

"No. I want to build a kitchen where our women can cook and provide food."

He fixed his eyes on mine. "I like the idea, but this is a big adventure. Do you know how many meals a day you need? Thousands."

"Let's go and see the food."

We entered one of the classes and noticed that most of the small white containers were still half-full. "The children are not hungry, I guess," the principal said.

I scooped up some rice and put down the spoon. "Our children are hungry," I said, "but the food has no taste. Who would eat

Ashkenazi food? It reminds me of what they serve in hospital. Where are our spices? The children are used to our food."

Thirty minutes later, I was sitting in the office of the newly elected mayor, Dr Mohammed al-Nabari. He had been elected under the Islamic Movement and I was aware of their position towards my activism, but the Moslem values Abouee taught me were not to judge someone before getting a chance to know them, so I decided to give the mayor a try. Before entering his office, I visited my friend Yousef al-Ataawne, the Director of Education at the Hura municipality whom I had known since my days as an activist at BGU. I wanted him to introduce me to Mohammed to smooth things over.

Yousef and I entered Mohammed's office, a fancy room with wooden panelling and old-fashioned lights that were at odds with the T-shirt and casual trousers Mohammed was wearing. He stood up when he saw us and I knew not to extend my hand. I explained the idea: Yuli Tamir's department was subsidizing caterers to provide hot meals to students. Why couldn't we build an industrial kitchen in Hura and employ women, ideally single mothers, to cook meals for their own children? I made it clear that I had no real business experience and no money. Mohammed put aside everything he'd heard about me and listened intently. He didn't see me the way people painted me, as a crazy feminist; he remembered me from BGU, a fellow student activist fighting the government's policies.

After I finished, Mohammed nodded. "I have 50,000 shekels. I know it's nothing, but I'm in."

On my way back to AJEEC, I wondered what I had just done. I had no money and no experience of setting up a business of this size. But I had raised sheep and sold grain and made enough money to buy Ummi an extension to her bedroom and give Abouee some rest. I took the elevator to our offices on the ninth floor and went directly to Ruth, Yehuda's wife, who was our grant writer. Seventy-five years old and a Holocaust survivor, Ruth always dressed elegantly and wore her immaculate white hair short, with tasteful earrings that stood out against her pale skin and blue eyes. I loved sharing my crazy ideas

357

with her because she always managed to transmit perfectly my vision in writing.

An hour later, she sent me a first draft. I read it and walked back to her office, draft in hand.

"Ruth, the problems of the Bedouin community are not because of the transition from a traditional way of life to a modern one. It's not an issue of adaptation. Besides, I don't believe in the dichotomy between tradition and modernity. You can be very modern and maintain some of your tradition. The Bedouin problem is political. This needs to be explained in the proposal."

Ruth acknowledged my feedback then purposefully returned to her typing.

Three hours later, she entered my office and placed a new version on my desk. I was busy with something else and she waited for me to finish. I never liked making her wait. I treated her like Jidatee, and I never made Jidatee wait. I always told her to call me and I would come to her office, but she liked to get up and move.

"What do you think?" she asked.

I started reading and noticed she hadn't incorporated my comments, particularly the ones that criticized Israel in the language of systemic discrimination and structural barriers.

"Ruth, the issue is not transition," I told her again, "it's political and social and the proposal must reflect that."

Ruth was known for her temper, but she usually treated the Arab staff with a bit more restraint. Her painted lips pursed tight, she struck my desk with her fist. "I will *never* criticize Israel the way you want me to. This is my country. This is the place where I feel safe and secure."

As she stalked off, I shot back: "Ruth, the proposal is in my name, not yours. I have to be true to myself. If it is difficult for you to write it, I'll find someone else."

Her shoe skidded across my desk. "I'm not working for this fucking organization," she screamed before walking out of the door. Sarit, my assistant, who was sitting in the other room, ran over to me and apologized. I took a deep breath. Ruth refused to see herself as part of the oppressive state apparatus. She saw herself as a victim who had been through the worst that can happen to a human being. We were fighting over whose suffering mattered more. When working with Jewish Israelis, I did my best not to see them as representatives of the state but I didn't always succeed.

I bent down and picked up Ruth's white leather shoe from the office floor. Sarit had turned a dark red. "It was my mistake," I said. "Once she calms down, I'll go and apologize."

"It's Ruth who should apologize," Sarit said. I didn't answer and Sarit quietly walked back to her office.

Two hours later, I took the shoe to Ruth, whose office was four away from mine. She shared her office with Liora, a soft-spoken woman who had trained as a social worker but had decided to work as an accountant. When she saw me, her face pleaded with me not to escalate things. She knew how I could be. I gave her a reassuring smile and moved towards Ruth's desk. Ruth avoided looking in my direction. I bent down at her feet.

"I am sorry, Ruth. I know how hard it is for you. I am sorry that I wasn't sensitive."

Her face softened. She stood up and the three of us, Liora, Ruth and myself, all had shiny faces where tears of forgiveness had washed away the pain.

The next day, Ruth entered my office with a new copy of the proposal. All my comments had been incorporated. "It's your proposal," she said. "It's your people. I'm here to help. To make sure things are not visited on anyone ever again."

At that time, Shimon Peres was the Minister for the Development of the Negev, Galilee and Regional Economy, and one of the major plans under his mandate was the development of the Negev. His plan focused on the Judaization of the region, which viewed the Bedouin as an obstacle to that plan. In general, it is very difficult to raise money from the government, and doing it under the leadership of

Peres was very tough. Mohammed and I requested a meeting with the CEO of the ministry, Joha, to present our idea for this social enterprise. We were empowering Bedouin single mothers, feeding children with their food, and reinvesting all the profits back into the community to support other Bedouin initiatives. Joha's eyes sparkled with excitement.

"Are you sure you're a Bedouin?" he asked. "You don't look like one and your Hebrew is fluent."

I patted him on the back and said as sweetly as I could: "Yes. I am a Bedouin. In fact, my camel is in your parking lot."

Mohammed glared at me. I'm not sure what happened – whether it was my comment or the bureaucracy – but we didn't get the grant. We didn't give up. I believed that taking a risk with this enterprise was worth it. I had every reason to believe that it would succeed: first, a law had been passed to ensure that an enterprise would be chosen to supply the meals, the people in local government were on my side, and, most importantly, I had a group of single mothers who were looking for jobs which relied on the skills they already possessed.

Within AJEEC, not everyone was as thrilled with the idea. It posed a huge financial risk to the organization and many of my colleagues thought the whole project was crazy. Vivian was very sceptical because of our lack of experience. Yehuda, on the other hand, loved it. It's good to have an idea but you also need a good plan to translate it into reality. Mohammed and I presented the project to Yuli Tamir, the Minister for Education.

"I like it," she told us, "but it's only an idea. I can't sign any contract with you before you have a kitchen."

"I can't build a kitchen without ensuring the market. This project will cost a lot of money. I need to make sure you're in," I said.

"I'm in. You have my word."

Her word inspired us to hold our course and our commitment found a string of other supporters: the New York Jewish Federation and the Dutch Embassy, which funded the single mothers' training in an industrial kitchen on a kibbutz, and a resident of Hura who converted his property into an industrial kitchen on the condition that we would rent it from him.

As the project progressed the challenges grew. I ran ahead, fuelled by a blind hope that the details would take care of themselves. Vivian, however, was a very practical person and the more she knew, the more worried she was, and the more we would fight. I decided to work more closely with Atef, the project coordinator, and spare Vivian our daily struggles.

To protect AJEEC from the financial risk, we established a separate legal entity for the project. Dr Mohammed al-Nabari and I were the co-directors of the enterprise and the single mothers whom we planned to hire were on our board. During a meeting with our lawyer to create the best legal model that would allow us to generate income as an NGO but that would also protect AJEEC if the business failed, Yehuda suggested we nominate Raffi Goldman to the board. I jumped down his throat. "This is a Bedouin enterprise! Why should we have a Jew in it?"

"To help you." Yehuda believed so strongly in the project, but my stubbornness was wearing him thin. He wanted the enterprise to succeed and begged me to accept help. "He has a lot of business experience," he said, almost crying.

"We're learning as we go along," I snapped back.

Yehuda thought I didn't want Jews involved with the project at all, but that wasn't the case. I was concerned that the one Jew would be given all the credit, not by external voices, but by my own community. I wanted them to feel that they could succeed on their own, that it wasn't only Jews who could succeed. I'd witnessed how a young Jewish secretary in a local municipality had more authority than an Arab mayor – not because she wanted it, but because the mayor himself internalized his inferiority despite his position of power. I wanted to challenge this by showing examples of success and power created by the community's hands.

"You need him," Yehuda told me. "It's your decision, but I'm afraid you'll fail without him."

We stood in front of the elevator doors. They closed softly. "If we succeed, it will be the community's success," I replied, "and if we fail, it will be lessons learned by the community."

Yehuda hit his cane against the door before marching off. I rushed to meet Mohammed and Atef to decide our next steps and register the social enterprise with Bedouin members only.

Four months before the kitchen was due to open, Atef informed me that the electricity company still hadn't provided power to the kitchen, claiming that Hura wasn't under a jurisdiction that received industrial power. I called Mohammed to get his input and he told me he had never heard of this. I was certain this was a political decision to limit economic production in the region.

I knew that Fouad Ben-Eliezer, the Minister for Infrastructure, was the one responsible for electricity. He was an Iraqi Jew who knew the Bedouin through the lens of the sheikhs, the tent and the mansaf. That's what he knew about the Bedouin and that's what he loved about them. I contacted one of the sheikhs who was very close to him and asked for Ben-Eliezer's personal phone number. Then I called the minister and introduced myself. He immediately asked me which tribe I was from, who our sheikh was, et cetera. I felt like we were in the 1960s, but I didn't want to lose him by objecting to his patronizing questions. I told him about the project and ended by saying, "Would you believe that in 2006, Hura, a planned town, has no electricity for industry? I haven't asked the government for any money for this project, but the least they can give me is electricity."

He was shocked. "Are you saying that Hura has no electricity for industry?"

"Yes. We need to change that immediately, otherwise we can't open the kitchen before the start of the school year and that is a great risk. We have to provide meals to schools."

"Consider it done. I like the idea of cooking Bedouin food. Who would eat this Ashkenazi food?"

"Exactly." We both laughed at that.

By August we had everything: the kitchen, the women, the

contract with the ministry to provide meals. We had everything except . . . the ingredients. I'd managed to pull everything together with nothing but belief and, of course, a major detail had fallen by the wayside. I called Mohammed and we did two things.

First, we sourced ingredients from Bedouin suppliers, requesting to pay them in six months' time. "We have to make this project reliant solely on Bedouin energy," I told them. "If we succeed, we all succeed."

Second, Mohammed and I met with the director of the bank to request a loan. He explained that he couldn't give a loan to a social enterprise. "You're not a proper business. There's no guarantee that you'll be able to pay it back."

"Can we personally be the guarantees?" I asked. Mohammed looked at me, trying to understand where I was going with this.

The bank director nodded.

"Then you have my apartment," I said.

His jaw dropped. "Are you aware that you're risking your own apartment?"

"Not only her apartment, but also my new Nissan van," Mohammed said.

"We know. We believe it's worth it," we said in unison.

The bank director signed the loan and Mohammed and I both signed the agreement.

Later that afternoon my cell phone rang. It was the bank director. "I can't stop thinking about you two. About your commitment. I feel very small next to you." He was so inspired by us, he said, that he would do his best to find donors for our enterprise.

Through immense effort, unflinching belief and God's grace, we opened the social enterprise on time. The project became a model for the whole country and was duplicated in both Arab and Jewish communities.

Through these projects – teaching women how to be photographers, videographers and DJs, and building this social enterprise from the ground up – my people saw what they were capable of. Pain shakes you, but hope pulls you up. Pain can push you to change your location, to run, to hide, to leave, but hope makes you fix it. Pain can fade and become part of the past, the forgotten past, but hope can always be ahead of you. In the long run, we can't be motivated by pain. We must be motivated by hope.

Our New Project

A JEEC WAS GROWING and, as usual, work didn't leave me much time to focus on my personal life. I was happy that Anwar's mother was not talking to me about children, but I had stopped taking the pill after Jidatee's nagging, and after a year of not getting pregnant, I went to see Dr Levitas, a fertility specialist at Soroka hospital.

I remember running late to the first appointment. I pulled up at the clinic and my brother Nasouh also happened to be there parking his car. I tossed him the keys and asked him to park my car while I sprinted to the office. I uttered a breathless apology when my phone started ringing. I ignored it, not wanting to answer it after arriving late, but Dr Levitas encouraged me to take the call. It was Nasouh. "I'm fine," I told him. "I can't talk. Put the keys under the front wheel." I closed the phone.

Dr Levitas placed his hands in front of him on the table. "Are you sure you want children?"

"Yes, yes. Why are you asking?"

"Because children are forever and when they call you must answer." He paused. "Do you have the time?"

"I will make the time."

"When?"

I looked at him as if he was the one who needed convincing.

"I suggest you go home and sit with Anwar and decide. For now, what I see is that you will need to undergo IVF, which requires time and patience."

59   Discussing the Prawer Plan at Sapir College, 2011

60 & 61   Speaking on creating a shared society at the Israeli Presidential Conference
        "Facing Tomorrow", 2010

62 Moad on a donkey next to my family's house in Laqiya, 2011

63 With Na'ama in Rawabi, 2012

64 Presenting the catering programme in Hura, 2009

65 At a conference on "Building Israeli-Palestinian Partnership" organised
    by the French government in Lyon, 2010

66 Moad and Adan at the Demonstration for Gaza, Montreal 2012

67 With James Wolfensohn former president of the World Bank, 2012

68 With Moad and Adan at Ousama's wedding, 2012

69 Village demonstration against revenge killing, 2012
70 Receiving the Solomon Bublick Prize for Community Involvement
     at the Hebrew University, Jerusalem 11 June 2012

71 Discussing peace-building with Queen Noor of Jordan, 2012
72 In the library at McGill researching my PhD, 2012
73 At the Harvard Early Childhood Conference, 2013

74 Speaking at a *Haaretz* Conference in London on: A Jewish Democratic State or Democracy for the Jews? 2016

75 Discussing human rights issues in the Bedouin community with Bernie Sanders, 2014

76 With Anwar celebrating my PhD at McGill

77 Celebrating with my parents

78 (*left to right standing*) With Moad, Na'ama, my mother, my father
(*sitting*) Adan, Anwar

79

79 (*left to right*) With Maryam, my father, Na'ama and Basma

We started the process a few weeks later. I juggled the appointments in between my daily meetings in Haifa, Tel Aviv, Jerusalem and the Negev, hosting delegations from abroad, speaking with donors, supervising staff and training volunteers. I ran from traipsing through a dirt road in an unrecognized village in the morning to a meeting at the Knesset in the afternoon, changing in public facilities or in the car. Where exactly would being a mother fit into my busy calendar? I loved my projects and I never felt like a career as a mother was on my horizon. But being me, someone who didn't want to disappoint and who needed to prove I was capable of doing everything that could be done, I had to go through with it.

My fertility journey started with daily shots to stimulate my ovaries to produce more eggs. It became increasingly difficult to make it to the clinic, which opened at eight, when I needed to be in Jerusalem for nine, so the nurse taught Anwar and me how to administer the shots ourselves. The first time Anwar tried it, his hands were shaking. I ordered him to hurry up. Anwar closed his eyes and pressed the needle into my lower abdomen. I pulled my shirt on, grabbed my bag and ran out of the door. Anwar's voice followed me to the elevator: "She's crazy. If this was a project or a donor, she'd have spent more time doing this right."

Several weeks later, we went early one morning to the fertility clinic at Soroka for my eggs to be extracted and fertilized. Our chances of conception were around 25 per cent. After Dr Levitas and his colleague finished retrieving my eggs, they told me that they got twenty healthy ones. They gave me some painkillers and told me to contact them if I didn't feel right. The big day – the day of the embryo transfer – would be on the Monday. I took the rest of the day off and sat in bed with Anwar trying to enjoy the delicious pasta he had prepared. The pain in my abdomen was extreme, but worse was my shortness of breath. I clambered to the window to get some air, but I felt so nauseous that I had to sit back down. The pain grew more intense and each time I inhaled, the air wouldn't reach my lungs. I started to get worried. *Maybe we should return to hospital.* When I went to get dressed, I noticed a rash on my skin, mostly around my upper legs.

We drove to hospital, where, after several examinations, Dr Levitas admitted me. This was my first experience as a patient in this hospital and things felt much more disempowering on this side of the fence. Anwar brought me my washbag and the book I was reading and I asked him not to mention my hospitalization to anyone. In the evening, Dr Levitas informed me that I had ovulation hyperstimulation syndrome and that we would need to delay the embryo transfer until my body recovered.

There were six of us in the room, both Bedouin and Jewish women, separated by curtains. Some moaned from the pain, some shouted instructions to their husbands over the phone and others lay staring at the ceiling. I devoured my book to make the time pass. It was the Hebrew translation of *Feminism Is for Everybody* by the American feminist bell hooks. That night, with the IV and other needles in my arm, I hardly slept.

The following morning, around half past seven, a group of four doctors greeted the patients, and the supervising doctor explained each case to them. When they reached the woman beside me, the supervising doctor greeted her by her name. He then explained that she was an unmarried Bedouin who had just delivered and that her baby had already been put up for adoption. "The staff brought her to this department to cover up the real reason for her visit. Her family thinks she has appendicitis," he said.

His indiscretion shocked me. Suddenly my curtain was pulled open and, seeing my book, the doctor said: "Oh, what have we here? An educated Bedouin woman." He read the title and waved his finger. "And she's a feminist." One of the other doctors with him, a Bedouin, knew me well. Later, he told me that he was praying that I wouldn't attack that doctor for patronizing me. I wasn't interested in teaching him manners; there was something more serious that needed his attention. He began explaining my case and I cut him off. "I understand that this is a university hospital, but I think you should ask permission first. I will explain what I have."

He was surprised, but he considered my request, and nodded. "You are right. Can you tell us what you have?"

I explained, using the same academic terms that Dr Levitas had used with me, his diagnosis, my symptoms and the treatment plan. I answered their questions with the confidence of someone who knows their stuff, not with the helplessness of a patient. They were there to cure my health, but I took the opportunity to cure their stereotyping. When we finished, I asked to speak to the supervising doctor about something unrelated.

"Listen, you're lucky that it's me sitting next to that woman. I am a social worker and bound by confidentiality, but do you realize that you completely exposed her? You brought her to this department to protect her, but you are putting her at risk by using her name. Everyone can hear you. I know her personally. Imagine if it was another Bedouin woman. She'd be killed today."

The four of them who had looked so confident a moment earlier now had fear in their eyes. The supervising doctor asked one of the other doctors to find out who else in the room was Bedouin. He returned shortly and informed us that the only other Bedouin was in the first bed on the other side of the room. "I'm sure she didn't hear anything," he added. The supervising doctor wasn't convinced and asked me to speak to the woman they were trying to protect. If she didn't feel safe, they would move her to another department. Before he left, he shook my hand and thanked me. He glanced once more at the book by my bed and said: "Sorry about my comment. I didn't mean it."

When the team left, the young woman beside me walked heavily towards my bed. I tried to get up, but remembered the drip in my arm. "How are you feeling?" she asked.

"*Al-hamdulillah*. How are you?"

"You know how I am. You heard the doctor and I heard you. I know you won't tell anyone." She started to cry.

I reached out to hold her hand. "No one will hear from me. I promise."

She kept crying, sentences falling out of her mouth, justifying what had happened.

"You don't need to explain yourself to me. You need to learn from this experience. You are aware of the consequences of such acts. You risk yourself and your family."

"I know," she said, wiping her tears with her hands.

I examined the belly protruding from her gown. "Was it your choice or were you raped?"

"He promised he would ask for my hand and then he disappeared. I tried to call him, but his phone was out of service."

While we spoke, I heard my sister Na'ama asking the nurse which room I was in. I told the girl to go back to her bed. I didn't want Na'ama to see her.

Na'ama pulled open the curtain and gave me a big hug. "Why didn't you tell me? You don't have to go through this alone!"

"I didn't want to bother you. I was planning to. If it all worked out, I was going to tell you and Ummi and everyone."

"I called you twice, but your cell phone is off. I called Anwar, who told me but asked me not to tell Ummi."

"That's good. I'll be released in a couple of days. There's no need to tell her. I'm feeling better."

She came closer. "Are you doing IVF?"

"Yes."

She hugged me again, happy that after five years I was finally thinking about having children.

The day of the embryo transfer, Na'ama and Anwar accompanied me back to hospital. It's very hard to keep a secret in my family, but Na'ama enjoyed knowing something that the rest of them didn't and was waiting for the success of the transfer to boast that I had chosen her as my confidante, ironical when we all knew that Na'ama was the worst at keeping secrets.

The doctors waited for me inside the operating theatre and the fertility nurse, Lillian, a plump woman with vibrant ginger hair who was always smiling, wished me luck. The doctor played classical music and told me to relax. "Breathe calmly and think only about good things. Don't think about the unrecognized villages," he teased. "Relax your body and prepare to welcome your baby."

After the operation, Anwar, Na'ama and the two doctors stood around me. Dr Levitas was explaining the post-op protocol, when Na'ama interrupted him. "She has to lie down. She can't move. Tell her," she pleaded with Dr Levitas, "otherwise she'll go back to work!"

Dr Levitas laughed. "She doesn't need to lie down, but she does need to rest. She can do simple work."

Na'ama knew that "resting" wasn't part of my vocabulary.

For the following two weeks, Anwar gave me an injection every morning, prepared breakfast, then left for court. I stayed home, but, as Na'ama had rightly pointed out, I couldn't rest. I hated losing control and living in the unknown. My work grounded me and I continued to work from home in spite of everyone telling me to relax. On the Monday morning we went for the pregnancy test. Lillian, the nurse, asked us to call her at noon to find out the results. Rula, my high school classmate who lived next door to me with her husband Yousef, made maqlouba and showed up at our place at noon to receive the news – whether good or bad.

Noon struck and Anwar announced it was time to call the hospital. I ran to our bedroom to hide.

"No," he said, pulling me towards him. "We will hold hands and call. I have a good feeling."

Anwar called. I gripped his hand. It was moist. My heart thumped loudly in my chest. I heard Lillian's voice answer the phone.

"Hi Lillian, this is Anwar and Amal."

"*Mabrouk! Mazal tov!*"

Anwar shouted and jumped, overjoyed. He surprised me. I hadn't known he wanted children so badly. Lillian told us to celebrate. "We are at a good beginning," I heard her say.

Rula embraced me and Yousef embraced Anwar and they both went to the kitchen to serve the maqlouba, turning the round pan upside down and tapping it with an extra flourish. They returned to the dining room, the maqlouba in their arms, and they serenaded me as if they were leading a bride to her seat. I rang Na'ama and told her to share the news with Ummi and our sisters. Less than ten minutes later, Ummi called. "Lie down. Don't move. If I hear you went to work or that you've been working from home, I'll come to take you to stay with me." After barking, her voice turned sweet. "Don't tell your mother-in-law that it is IVF. She doesn't need to know. Tell her it's a normal pregnancy." Then she went back to her usual style of ordering me around: "Give me Anwar. I want to talk to him."

"Don't worry. I won't let her leave the house, I promise. I'll tie her to the bed," he told her. I could hear her laughing.

Slowly, slowly I went back to the work that I had never in fact left. By that time, I had a driver, Peretz, a Moroccan Jew who'd worked with me for almost ten years. We had become very close; he and his wife and children had even dined with my parents in Laqiya. Whenever he drove me to the airport for an early flight, he'd always bring me a breakfast of hot chocolate and boreka. When I became pregnant, he took good care of me. Once, on my way to a morning meeting in Jerusalem, I yelped when I realized that I'd forgotten to inject myself. "Don't worry," he said. "Do you have them with you?" I did. He parked by the side of the road and got out, giving me the privacy to inject myself in the car. This became routine until we no longer even stopped the car. I'd just say, "Don't look in the mirror, I'm going to inject myself!"

It was in week eight, during the ultrasound, that Dr Levitas told me I was expecting twins. It still hadn't registered that I was going to be a mother, but this news made me as happy as if he'd told me that a donor had doubled his donation. When I found out the twins' sex – a girl and a boy – I thanked God for such a perfect gift. I thought: *God knows that I'm too busy for another pregnancy, but also that I'm capable of raising two children at once.*

Given the twins' position in my womb, I'd been informed that a C-section was the best course of action. I carried the twins until the thirty-third week, Sunday, February 23rd. Anwar and I took everything I needed, including our video camera, and drove to hospital. Abouee called me on my way there to wish me luck and I told him that I had the video camera to document the whole thing.

"This isn't a project that you're going to launch and then leave behind. This project's going home with you," he teased. I laughed, but even as we neared the entrance of Soroka Hospital, the reality of how my life would change still hadn't registered.

When I arrived, Dr Zlotnik, a huge man with a very heavy Russian accent, asked me if I wanted a full or half epidural.

"Half," I said.

"Full," Anwar blurted out at the same time.

"Why would you want half? It's better for you to sleep and wake up when it's over," he said.

"No. I want to see them coming into this world," I insisted.

We were disappointed when they told Anwar that he couldn't be in the room with me and the orderly offered to film the procedure. After Anwar left the room, the anaesthetist injected me with the epidural and sat beside my head, the nurse obstructed my view of my belly with a green sheet, and Dr Zlotnik said in his heavy accent: "Are we ready?" When I heard the clang of the metal tools being placed on the tray, I asked if I could change my mind about the half anaesthesia, but before it could be administered, I heard a cry. "We got the boy," Dr Zlotnik confirmed. A moment later, another cry, this one more shrill. "And here's the girl, the leader of the choir." They placed the two of them – Adan, my daughter, and Moad, my son – on my chest. Adan was covered in blood and Moad was covered in a white liquid like buttermilk. I was excited about having them, but even with their two warm bodies sitting on my chest, I didn't feel "motherhood". It was only in the evening, when Ummi came to visit me, that something changed. She sat beside me on the bed and recounted the story of my birth, but this time, she spoke like a woman who was free to speak her truth. Every other time she had recounted the story, she made sure that the listener knew that she had never wanted me. But that version of the story, Ummi told me, was a charade that she played for self-preservation. The truth, she continued, was that she had wanted me and had wanted me all along. We sat together for a long time, and as the sun peeked into the window, I noticed a new feeling arise in my belly. The cord between Ummi and I was beginning to heal: in becoming a mother, I finally felt like my mother's daughter.

I was released with Moad, who was a healthy 2.2 kilos, but Adan was underweight and was placed in an incubator. I hobbled towards her, this tiny human with lots of black hair just like her father, and tried to feel something, that feeling of motherhood and natural connection, but I only felt sadness that we were leaving her alone. The guilt at not having the right feelings made me cry and Anwar hugged me. The other women around me reassured me she would be OK. I whispered to Anwar: "I'm not worried about her. I'm worried about me. I still don't feel this motherhood thing."

He clasped me more tightly in his arms. "Motherhood is not one thing. No one can tell you how to feel. There's no recipe for it. It's not a button you press and hop! you're a mother. It grows with time."

We arrived home. Anwar carried Moad into the twins' room and asked me to follow him. Na'ama and Abeer sat in what looked like a baby paradise. They'd surprised me by preparing the room: yellow sheets and onesies for Adan, blue ones for Moad. They immediately apologized. They had known pink was out of the question, but Ummi had forced them to use blue.

"The commander is coming in the evening," Na'ama told me. She meant Ummi. "Let her do things her way," she advised, "don't argue."

In the evening the doorbell rang. Ummi and Yousef entered and sat next to me on the couch, crying happy tears. "I don't know how you're going to be a mother," Yousef confessed. "Are you capable of staying at home?" While everyone had been saying that, when it came from Yousef, my sensitive younger brother, I heard it differently. I didn't take it as a joke, but as a sincere, tender enquiry. I looked at him, my tears seeping into the creases from when I'd been smiling, and told him the truth: "I don't know, Yousef. I really don't feel anything yet except pain and excitement."

Ummi, who'd been caressing Moad, now placed him on Yousef's lap. Yousef pulled out something from his pocket which Ummi fastened onto Moad's pale blue onesie. "This gold Palestinian lira and blue bead were with all my brothers for their first six months to protect them," she said with pride.

"Do you have one for Adan?"

She slapped her knee. "Girls don't need it! They are strong. They have resistance against the evil eye."

Anwar's mother arrived the next day. I worried that her presence might create friction since Ummi was acting as if she owned Moad. Um Anwar didn't have the energy to interfere with her, so she sat idly on the couch and let my mother retain control of what she now saw as exclusively her domain. When Anwar prodded his mother about why she wasn't helping, she casually replied: "*Rabuna wahna bnaaref ahalina* [Let Um Amal do all the work. I'm not worried. She can raise them, but they'll know who they belong to. They'll know they're Alh'jooj]."

She asked Anwar to take her home the next day, not because of Ummi's possessiveness, but because she couldn't sleep "hanging in the sky", as she called it – our apartment was on the sixth floor. Ummi changed, fed and massaged Moad. I slept most of the time and ate whatever she ordered me to eat. For breakfast she served maktoum – mixed dates with roasted almonds, black sesame seeds and cinnamon cooked in olive oil. All day I drank tea with cinnamon. Lunch was freekeh soup with chicken from her farm and dinner was lamb with yogurt and rice. "Your body needs to recover," she said, "you have to eat."

Anwar and Yousef joined us for dinner. They had a running joke that "by the time Amal's body recovers, we will both be elephants".

Every morning, I pumped my milk and took it to Adan in hospital. Despite the pain I still felt from the surgery, I would visit her so that she wouldn't feel lonely. Anwar went in the evenings to bring her more milk and to bathe her, the way the Black Bedouin woman who was staying in hospital with her newborn had taught him. Whenever he showed up to care for Adan, the other Bedouin mothers said in hushed tones:

"Is he really Bedouin?"

"*Aysh, aysh.*"

"But look at his long hair!"

He greeted them in his Bedouin accent and asked them to keep an eye on Adan for him.

A couple of weeks after the birth, I woke up one morning and all the air had been sucked out of the room. My skin felt too tight for my body. I fled my bedroom for the living room couch, flopped down and started to cry. I heard Ummi in the other room feeding Moad and changing him. I walked over to the fridge.

"What do you need?" Ummi asked, bouncing Moad lightly in her arms.

"Milk," I croaked. I stood in front of the open fridge. "There's no milk, Ummi," I sobbed.

She put Moad back on the mattress and rushed over. "*Smallah alayki ya bintee* [what's happening to you]?

I closed the fridge. Still crying I told her I was going to buy milk.

"What! You can't walk like this. It's too cold outside. It's bad for your womb. Call Anwar. He'll get you milk on his way back from the office."

"I'm going to buy milk. Now." With bags under my eyes and my hair knotted and unkempt, I slipped on my shoes. "You're not going," she protested. I ignored her and wriggled into my jacket. She followed me, begging for an explanation. "All because of the milk! Are you a child? Grow up!" When I got to the front door, my exhausted eyes met her bewildered ones and I said: "I'm going and I'm not coming back."

Her face changed from confused to betrayed. "Go! Go and never come back." She continued to shout at me as I inched down the hall. "I knew you wouldn't be able to be a mother. You don't understand this."

I hardly noticed when she slammed the door. My mind had left my body far behind, but I carried myself out of the building and sat down on the front steps where I watched people walking on the street. Children stepped off the bus, neighbours waved to each other, cars drove by. It dawned on me that things were continuing as usual while my life had stopped. I didn't know what was happening to me, but I felt like I didn't belong to this world anymore. My apartment felt more like a jail than a home.

The day we had signed our lease and got the keys, we had parked our car and seen our neighbours exiting theirs: an ultra-orthodox Jewish couple, the woman's head wrapped in a scarf and tzitzit (ritual fringes) dangling from her husband's shirt. Anwar and I looked at each other as if to say: "Oh God, what have we done?" We hadn't asked about the neighbours. We had known it would be mostly Jewish tenants, as in most cities in Israel, but we trusted ourselves to build a good relationship with just about anyone.

Anwar sighed. "Who wants to live with Haredim? No lights on Shabbat, no elevator. Oh no."

When we entered, Benny, the man, was standing in his doorway to greet us his new neighbours. We eyed the stickers supporting the right-wing, religious Shas party, and winced inwardly, before saying: "*Shalom.*"

"*Bruchim habaim* [welcome]," he replied smiling and waving. "I'm here if you need any help."

When Anwar and I closed the door behind us, we both let out a deep sigh of relief. Benny was a nice guy.

I saw Benny's wife Edna, who was also nice, walking towards the building. I didn't want her to ask me why I was sitting outside so I hurried back upstairs where Ummi was massaging Moad with olive oil and salt.

"Why did you come back? You said you weren't coming back."

I started to cry again. Collapsing on the chair beside her, my eyes drifted over to Moad and I felt sorry that he had a mother who wanted to run away. Anwar called me and told me that Abeer was on her way. I knew she was at work and asked him why. "I don't know," Anwar said. "She called me just now and said she had to see you."

Ummi knew why. "I called her and told her what happened and she said that you might have something that women have after labour. I don't know what it is and what this *kalaam faadee* [empty words] is all about."

I returned to my bedroom. Everything made me cry: a bird on the windowsill, thinking about my work, the misshapen pillow I'd been cradling for the past two weeks. Everything looked very sad.

When Abeer arrived, I heard Ummi saying: "I don't know what happened to her. She has been crying all morning and hasn't eaten. If she continues like this, I'll leave. What is this?"

"Ummi," Abeer said gently, "Amal might have what is called postpartum depression and we need to help her."

"What depression? This is stupidity! That's what you get from social work! *Kalaam faadee!*"

Abeer hugged me. "Don't worry. You will be a great mother. It just takes time. Soon you will feel like yourself again."

"Even Ummi said that I can't be a mother," I blubbered, "and that I won't be a good one. She's right. I don't feel anything towards the babies."

"You know our mother. She didn't mean it. She said it because she got stressed when she saw you like this. When she called me, she said, 'Amal is the strongest woman I know and she's crying because there's no milk in the fridge. *Haraam.*' She was worried and she also loves you."

Ummi came to check on us, bringing cinnamon tea and dates. "What happened to your sister?" she asked Abeer, trying not to look at me. "What's this thing you said on the phone that your sister has?" She sat down on the rug. "I don't understand why she would have it.

She presses the wall and there's hot water. She presses the wall and there's light. She presses the stove and there's fire. What are you lacking? Why do you feel depressed?" She continued: "What would someone like me say? I gave birth to Salmaan and an hour later I was at the well getting water and collecting wood and *jalle* to start the fire and cook. I wasn't depressed. I stood strong. I said I have to be strong for my daughters."

She finally looked at me: "*Al-wahdi laazim itkoun guweeye* [The woman must be strong, otherwise she can't survive]."

Abeer, who unlike me always had endless patience with our mother, said: "You know, Ummi, some women feel that they won't be good mothers so they feel guilty and sorry for their children. They become very sad because they want to be good mothers."

A week later, after daily visits from my sister, I felt much better. I was lying next to Ummi on the mattress when she asked me what was the thing that Abeer said that I had.

"Depression."

"You know, I think I had that after I gave birth to Abeer. People weren't educated. They didn't know what it was. They used to say that the mother is *naafre ya haraam*. That's why we have forty days for people to be around the *nafasa**. We don't want bad thoughts to drag her to bad actions."

Once we were able to bring Adan home, Anwar and I brought the twins to the village for Moad's circumcision. After the ritual, I stayed with my parents that whole week, sleeping in the same room as my sisters Abeer and Wafaa. By that time, the room had dwindled from seven sisters to two. Narjis had married the year after my wedding, and Maryam married the year after that. The

---

* It's a tradition that for forty days after delivery, a new mother will be looked after by women in her family and community. They will bring her food, clean her house, look after the baby and generally support her. The term *"nafasa"* is understood as a state of post-natal impurity indicated by continued bleeding. Women visitors are screened by the women attending the new mother in case they are undergoing bleeding (menstruation, cuts, wounds) as this might invalidate the vitality of the birth.

house had started to empty and a place that once looked crowded now seemed quiet. For the week I stayed there, I woke up twice a night to feed the twins. One night, Moad had been crying non-stop and I'd tried everything. Abouee came to tell me that he would wake up Ummi.

Moments later, Ummi marched into my room, picked up both babies and asked for Moad's bottle. He pushed it away and continued to cry. Abouee stood in the doorway, barking at her to do something.

"Leave us!" she snapped. "I raised thirteen. Go back to bed."

Ummi put Moad's bottle in her mouth. "The milk is coming out so slowly! Where did you get this?"

"Ummi these are the best bottles with soft nipples that are graded according to age. The nipple has two holes—"

"According to age? What is this generation? How could this generation raise thirteen children? Ouuuuf!"

She tore the nipple with her teeth and placed it in Moad's mouth. He downed the bottle in less than two minutes and fell into a deep sleep.

In the morning Ummi picked a fight with Abouee over the previous night's events. "Why did you get involved? Don't you trust me?"

"I heard the baby crying and Amal trying, but I didn't hear your voice. I thought she was all alone, that's why I came."

"You think I'm deaf? She needs to learn how to deal with this by herself. You're not going to live with her. She can't be good at everything and not that. If you're good, you're good at everything. It's just a different task, but the skills are the same."

From then on, I saw the real power relations between my parents. I saw then that Abouee had no problem relinquishing power and that Ummi had no problem taking it.

Our Polish-Jewish Mother

AFTER I RETURNED TO the office, Anwar quickly learned that he couldn't rely on our mothers to care for the children. His mother couldn't sleep "hanging in the sky" and Ummi's interference in how we ran our house was more than he could take. Once he'd arrived home to find her on a militant cleaning spree while the children were crying in the other room. She was folding one of the rugs she'd given us for our wedding when she noticed a small hole in one of the corners and had a meltdown. Anwar called Yousef. "Yousef, can you please come and collect your mother. And bring a truck. I want you to take her and her rugs."

One evening, Anwar was carrying the groceries from the elevator when Benny, our Haredi neighbour, came out from his apartment to help. He knew we were looking for a nanny and suggested that his wife Edna take care of the children until we found a more permanent solution. A Jewish nanny raising Arab children? When Anwar told me what Benny had suggested I didn't know what to think. We had become friends and we saw beyond whatever political party they supported on their front door. On Sukkot we'd give up our parking spot so they could build their sukkah. We'd visit them and sit with their children, who were very polite and well behaved. Benny often consulted Anwar on legal matters. I felt comfortable leaving my children in their care which we did for a couple of months. It was much more common to have an Arab woman who babysat Jewish children, but nothing about my life was common.

We interviewed more than five women before we met Paulina. My brother Salmaan recommended her. She was the cleaning lady at his pharmacy, but he sensed that she'd be a good fit. She was fifty-two years old and had just made *aliyah* from Poland. She had a master's degree in finance. We invited her to interview and asked her the questions we'd asked all the other candidates, questions we had found online from searching "how to select the best nanny". Mid-sentence, her grey eyes noticed a blob of snot dangling from Adan's nose, and she pulled down her shirt sleeve and wiped it clean. I shuddered. When she left, I told Anwar: "She hardly speaks Hebrew. She doesn't speak Arabic. She smokes. She's never worked as a nanny—"

"I want her. I think she's the best one so far."

"What? Why?"

"The minute she used her sleeve to clean Adan's nose, I knew she'd be great. She wasn't grossed out. She was authentic. Like a real mother."

He convinced me. Anwar's intuitions about people are always right.

We invited her back and set some ground rules: she wouldn't smoke during work hours and we'd prefer if she spoke her mother tongue instead of broken Hebrew.

Her first day of work, I returned to the house at noon as we had agreed to find the floor covered in Ummi's precious rugs. She'd placed the children in several layers of clothes, including two pairs of socks, and toys were strewn all over the living room. She saw my puzzled expression and took me by the hand. "Your house is not a museum; it is a place where you raise your children. It has to be free from unnecessary restrictions. The children are at the centre. The walls, the floors, these are all secondary."

Moad and Adan rolled around on the floor, drooling over their toys, happy and free. Anwar was right. Paulina was the perfect fit. Whenever the twins were sick, Paulina brewed tonics, gave them teas and used other natural methods to cure them. Caught between a Polish nanny and a Bedouin mother, I had very little say in the way they were raised, but I couldn't complain. One grandmother rooted them in their Bedouin heritage and their nanny opened them to the world and taught them how to be part of a strong and proud minority. These two women led the way in raising children who would never shrink near the wall, but would take large strides in the centre of the road.

We were Paulina's only family in Israel. She was divorced and sent a portion of her monthly salary to her only daughter who lived in Italy where she studied medicine. Paulina celebrated our holidays and attended our weddings, and we celebrated Rosh Hashanah and Pesach with her. I found her a subsidized apartment in Shekhouna D in Beer a-Saba where Paulina became a very active member of the community. Whenever we brought her food on our way back from dinner in Laqiya, she would introduce us to her friends, new immigrants mainly from Russia.

As a child in Poland, she'd been tormented for being the only Jewish child at her school. She lived there until she lost everything that tethered her to that place – her husband, her parents – and came to Israel to find the home she had never had. But the Holy Land wasn't what she had been promised.

"I ran away from exclusion to experience another version of it," she told us. "There I was excluded for being a Jew, here I'm excluded for being an immigrant." Despite her degree, she could only find work as a cleaning lady and was at the mercy of the turf wars between Moroccan and Russian Jews, whose hatred for each other ran deep.

We adopted her and she adopted us. She devoted her spare time to supporting her neighbours, with the help of her adopted daughter – me, the social worker – and her adopted son – Anwar, the lawyer. Like us, she believed in relationships that transcended identity while simultaneously recognizing the importance of being rooted in your heritage. One day, I returned from work early and saw Paulina walking with the twins. They were three years old by now. I parked the car and joined them. Adan commanded me: "Get in line! Follow Savta [Granny] Paulina and repeat after her."

I was the last in line, Paulina at the front, Adan and Moad in the middle. We stepped in time like soldiers and proclaimed in Hebrew: "*Ani Aravi gaeh, ani Aravi gaeh* [I am a proud Arab. I am a proud Arab]."

My heart swelled. This Jewish woman who had herself experienced exclusion because of her identity was teaching my children how to be proud of theirs. At the park, I had noticed that my twins didn't hide in the corner or defer to the Jewish children in the line for the slide. They played freely and although they were the only Arab children in the park, everyone treated them the same – Paulina made sure of that.

I remember attending the same park with my sister and her children. Moad and Adan were already tearing through the playground when they noticed their cousins clinging to their mother's dress.

Adan tugged at her cousin's hand. "*Yalla, yalla!*"

Her cousin pointed and hid her face. "*Yahud* [Jew]."

"We are Arab!" Adan shouted gleefully. "*Yalla!*" She grabbed her and the two girls ran into the playground together.

"Why are they afraid?" I asked my sister.

She shook her head. "It's the news. They see how Jews kill Palestinians in Gaza. They hear people talk. I can't keep them in a bubble. This is reality."

"That's true, but we are here not only to protect our children from guns, but also from learning prejudice and hatred."

The twins were around six years old and it was a couple of days before Pesach when I received that crushing phone call.

"Are you with the children?" Anwar asked. I moved into the other room. "I'm at the hospital. Paulina's dead."

We had known for a while that she had cancer, but we didn't know it was stage 4. When she had refused chemotherapy, we thought it was because she was healthy enough not to need it.

I sat on the edge of my bed, my elbow digging into my knee. "We saw her on Sunday! Please, please don't say this."

Paulina had never shown any signs of weakness, not even when she spoke about her daughter, who only visited her once the whole time that we knew her. We were listed as next of kin and the doctors had asked Anwar to identify her body. The nurse asked Anwar what her relationship to him was.

"She's my children's *savta*," he told them. They gave him a form to sign and called the *chevra kadisha* (religious burial society) to take care of the funeral rites.

When Anwar got home, we sat in the bedroom, discussing what to do next while grappling with the shock and heartbreak. In Israel, only Jews can be buried in Jewish cemeteries. Paulina had left that line on her ID blank.

I wasn't familiar with Jewish burial rites, so I called my assistant, Sarit, at AJEEC. She explained to me that since Pesach was starting on Sunday and she had passed away on Friday, we only had to sit *shiva** on Saturday. I went to see Paulina's neighbours to let them know about the funeral. Anwar filled in all the paperwork and even though the officer saw that her ID didn't identify her as a Jew, he assigned her a plot anyway. Then Anwar went to Rahat, the largest Bedouin city, to select a tombstone and have it engraved. He gave the stonemason Paulina's name in Hebrew.

"You're burying a Jew?" the mason asked dumbfounded.

"Yes. She's my children's *savta*."

About forty of us attended the funeral: Paulina's neighbours and some of AJEEC's Arab and Jewish staff, including Sarit. This was my first time attending a Jewish funeral and my first time accompanying a body to the cemetery – in my village the women don't. We stood around the coffin and the rabbi read the final prayers. They placed her body in the ground and I moved away as everyone took turns to shovel earth in. I couldn't watch her disappear under the earth. At the end, Sarit placed a small stone on the grave and I did the same. A couple of her friends and I said a few words. Paulina came to the promised land to find a home and she made *aliyah* into a Palestinian-Israeli house.

From there, we all went to Paulina's apartment to sit *shiva*. We sat on the floor. I recited from the Quran and a few paragraphs from the Tanach (Hebrew Bible) that I had committed to memory from high school. Her neighbours brought food. Paulina's dog, Pitza, sat

---

* A week-long period of mourning in Judaism following a burial. If a festival occurs within the week then the number of days of mourning is shortened.

next to me and nuzzled his warm nose into my belly, the two of us consoling each other. Her neighbours had always thought that I was her daughter until the day when someone mentioned that I was a Bedouin and that Paulina was our nanny. The news of this unheard-of arrangement spread quickly and by the evening the entire neighbourhood had packed into that tiny apartment to celebrate such a glorious relationship.

Later that day, I entered Moad and Adan's room with a stack of photos and placed them on the carpet. They were photos from the park, photos of Paulina laughing or looking stern, photos of dinners Paulina had joined, photos of her holding a tiny Moad in her arms. We sat around them on the floor.

Moad, always the observant one, said: "Yuma [Mom], you are going to tell us something bad about Savta Paulina." Adan looked at me to see if this was true.

"It's not bad," I said gently, "but it is something that will make you sad because you won't see Paulina in real life anymore."

Adan stood up. "She's dead!" She buried her delicate face in my chest.

I hugged her. "Yes, *habibee* [sweetie], she is."

Moad didn't cry, but he took one of the photos of him and Pitza playing. "I'm sad for Pitza. Who will take care of her?"

"We can bring her here if you want."

"But then Jidatee won't pray in our house," Moad said.

"There's nothing in the Quran* that says that and if your Jidatee won't pray in our house, she can come in between the prayers."

The next day, we visited Paulina's neighbour, who'd been caring for the pup. She met us in the lobby, her face spelling more bad news. "Pitza couldn't make it without Paulina." The children ran upstairs and found the dog lying dead on the floor. Now Moad's tears came. We had lost Paulina and Pitza only three days apart.

---

* Dogs are regarded as unclean in Islam, consequently many Moslems will not pray in a room if a dog has been present. This is not specified in the Quran but is an interpretation.

Hope's Ashes

IN MAY 2005, when my organization was in its growth stage, criticism of my work reached another level. Articles in the press criticized me for fraternizing with the enemy and turning women against their community. I understood why. Hisham Sharabi, Paulo Freire and Saad Eddin Ibraheem, scholars of the psychology of the oppressed, state that marginalized groups internalize their inferiority, refusing to believe in the ability of their leaders. Any success must be a mistake. We aren't able to accomplish anything unless someone is using us as pawns in their master plan.

At four-thirty one morning, my cell phone woke me up. It was my sister Na'ama, who was running the Desert Embroidery Centre in Laqiya.

"You have to come," she said, "they've burned the centre."

I didn't need to ask who "they" were. "They" weren't Jewish people from the neighbouring town, "they" were our own flesh and blood.

It was still dark when I entered the village and the men were leaving the mosque after the *al fajr* (dawn) prayer. When I saw my uncle Ahmed, I rolled down my window.

"They did it. They burned the best thing in this village."

"God shall punish them," he replied solemnly.

"No. We should punish them. You men have to say something. Do something!"

He shook his head. "*Beseer khayr* [All will be good]."

"We need to bring the *khayr* [the good]! I'm not going to wait. The *khayr* has no legs to come by itself!"

I turned into the parking lot and saw the smoke rising from the windows. My brother's house was only metres from the centre. He ran over to me, his son in his arms, and shouted: "I don't want to lose my children because of your work!" I let his words wash over me, knowing they arose from fear.

Na'ama sat on the floor with Chesen and a small group of women who worked in the centre and lived nearby. Na'ama's face was covered with black ash, as were her hands and her tears. "We built it and we will build it again," she said hugging me. Chesen cautioned against my plan to call the police.

"If we do that, we'll gain more enemies. They'll be angry that we're airing our dirty laundry."

"The news is already out! Can't you see the smoke? That dirty, dirty smoke." I convinced them that we had to make the call in order to claim the insurance.

I had always received criticism but this was the first real threat. The centre stood on a piece of land Abouee had gifted us. We'd constructed a first-rate workshop, a showroom and a library that drew international visitors to buy Bedouin embroidery crafted and designed by our women. Not only was it a source of income for the village, but the centre told our story, as Bedouin, as women, as Palestinians.

We sat in the tent next to the centre's scorched concrete, grieving our loss, grappling with our disbelief. When the police came, a crowd gathered around to monitor us and collect evidence to use against us if we misspoke. We told the officer that we didn't know who was responsible, but that some men in the community didn't like it that their wives worked at the centre.

"Can you give me some names?" the officer asked.

"No. We don't know who specifically, but you are welcome to start your work," I said.

"You know that if you don't tell us we won't find out. You have to cooperate."

"We gave you that bottle. You can check it for fingerprints."

"If you don't give us any names, we can't do anything."

I snapped: "Would you say that if this happened in a Jewish town? It's your work to find the names. Don't put the work on our shoulders."

I drove back to my office in Beer a-Saba and wrote a position paper in Arabic condemning the arson as a violent act against women.

Women were equal members of our community and their work fed our joint future, I wrote. I sent a press release to the media, then returned to Laqiya and asked my uncle if I could use the mosque microphone to spread my message to the whole village. He refused. As a woman my voice was *haraam*.

"If you don't want me to do it, then you do it. You have to read this. You have to take a stand. God and our prophet are not just waiting for your prayers. What are prayers if they don't translate into good actions?"

By noon there were several reporters at the centre, including one from the main Israeli news channel. As she started to interview me, the call to prayer sounded and the men passed behind me, not even bothering to look in our direction. When the reporter asked me about them, I spoke the truth that was in my heart:

"They're going to the mosque. We don't need a prayer that doesn't help people to do good or to stand up against wrong-doing."

In the afternoon, we built a stage on the main road so that cars would have to stop and look at the desecration that had taken place. One hundred and sixty women, all employed by the centre, stood on the stage and spoke – using a microphone that we weren't supposed to use because our voices were *haraam* – about how working at the centre helped them and their families. Cars gathered and people watched from their parked cars. My uncle read my statement in the mosque, adding, "These are our daughters and we must support them."

In the evening, I watched the news on our living room TV while Anwar put the twins to bed. For once, the issue – not our exotic lifestyle – was the focus of the report. They showed footage of the fire and the proud women who worked there. I watched my interview, nodding along, until the last thirty seconds when I ran to the bathroom and threw up in the toilet.

"What is it?" Anwar yelled.

"They'll kill me."

"Who? What happened?"

"They broadcast the interview but they shortened one sentence. I sound like a heretic."

The channel had reduced my sentence to: "We don't need prayer." I paced in front of the TV and started to cry. My cell phone rang, but I was afraid to answer it. It was probably someone who wanted to threaten me for saying something against our religion. I had crossed one of Jidatee's red lines.

I frantically called everyone I could until I reached the reporter who had interviewed me.

"What have you done?" I shouted. "You've endangered my life by not conveying my message correctly to my people. You have to fix it in the next broadcast."

She promised she would, but it wouldn't appear again until the midnight news. Who would still be awake to see it? Who would still have electricity to watch television that late, given that the generators in the unrecognized villages shut down at 10 p.m.?

My legitimacy in the community was already hanging by a thread and now this had put me in real danger. Anwar suggested that we put the full interview on a tape and make fifty copies to take to the mosques, otherwise the *khotba* (Friday preaching) would incite violence against me.

I called Abouee. I didn't need to explain myself. He knew that my approach was never to insult our religion or our traditions. I'm a Muslim. I follow Islam. And yes, I'll always challenge those who use religion to justify unjust actions, but this interview didn't represent what I believed in.

Anwar and Abouee distributed the interview to the mosques and only two of them publicly denounced me as a traitor, but the media still erupted and I received death threats. Now that I had two babies, I was paralysed by fear. I didn't want my children to be casualties of this hatred.

A few days later, I was driving on the highway from the village to Beer a-Saba with Moad and Adan in the back seat when I noticed a car following me. It flashed its headlights and I put my foot on the accelerator, turning up the music to spare my children the sound, God forbid, of gunshots.

The car put its lights on full beam and drew parallel with me. I whispered a prayer for my children. "Please God, please God." I had driven this road a thousand times and knew there was a police station up ahead. I turned in, but the gate was closed, and I slowed to a stop. The car braked beside me. The window rolled down. I couldn't breathe. A pair of dark eyes, peering at me from above a white scarf that hid the rest of his face, shot me a look of pure rage.

"*Ya kafaar!* [Infidel!]" he cried. "It's not over yet." He veered around and sped back to the main road.

I glanced back at Moad and Adan who were sleeping peacefully in their car seats. My head collapsed onto my steering wheel; fear released its grip and my tears with it.

"Is everything OK?" I looked up to see a policeman standing by my window.

"Yes," I lied. "I'm just adjusting my children's car seats."

How could I ask a police officer, the hands of the state, to protect me from my own people?

Confiscating Women's Voices

IN 2002, I had established Ma'an, meaning "together", to bring all women-led initiatives under one organizational umbrella so we could stand together to change policy. Fighting for women's rights is never easy. Our dispossession takes many forms. We're denied freedom in the name of God, in the name of protecting our honour, and in the name of defeating our oppressors. By formalizing our initiatives and uniting under one association, we used the confidence we had built through delivering social programmes to start tackling the most challenging social issues we faced: our right to vote freely in our community, polygamy, gender-based violence and murdering women in the name of family honour.

Elections in the villages weren't run the way they were in the rest of the country. The men collected the ID cards of all the women in the tribe and the candidate recruited a small group of women to vote on behalf of them. We women treated voting as though it was a task at a wedding. On election day, the women waited in a minibus outside the polling station. A man handed her an ID and she voted. When she returned, she got another ID, put on a different coloured *thobe*, and voted again.

This is what happened to me the first time I could vote. Some Arabs voted for Zionist parties and the men in our community wanted to make sure the votes went to Arab representatives – at least, that's how they convinced us to hand over our cards. But how could this practice be justified at a local level when all the candidates were from the village? It was a tribal race, not an election based on platforms and social agendas. And why weren't women allowed to have their say? During the local election in Laqiya in 2005, I wrote an article exposing the practice, but what would that do? I decided to sign up for the committee that monitored the election and I convinced my aunt to join me.

On election day, I arrived at the elementary school – our polling station – and took my seat at the front of the gymnasium. People entered and I heard them swear under their breath when they saw me. Everyone knew I wasn't going to let them play their usual game.

As the women arrived, I made a point of greeting each one by name so the committee knew who was voting and matched the ID to the face. One woman showed up with her face completely covered. I noted her shoes and her ring. Women rarely cover their faces in our community, but on election day some women showed up in a full burka.

"I know you," I said, "you've already voted. If you don't leave now, I'll call the police." She ran out, passing a group of men standing in the hall. "She has no right to control the elections," I overheard one of them say, talking about me. "Who put her there?" another one asked angrily. "It must be the Shabak."

I emerged from the gymnasium. "Anyone can do this job," I shot back. "You just need to fill out a form. You don't need to serve in the Shabak to have this honour." Nasouh and Salmaan were among the sea of men. Their worried glances were telling me to shut my mouth. They didn't want me to get hurt.

As the day progressed, I sent more and more women home. In the afternoon, my aunt pointed out of the window. "Look! Since when do we have so many women?" Once people realized that I wasn't going to let them play this dirty game, they ran home and brought their wives, mothers and daughters out to cast their vote themselves.

Shortly after midnight, we were sitting in the gym counting the votes, when I smelled smoke. We all ran to the window. Everyone turned their eyes to me. I knew that something had happened to my family. I knew that my parents and my brothers and sisters were paying the price for my actions.

An aggressive black cloud spewed from the barn where Abouee's hay was stored. I arrived at my parents' house to find my brothers standing in the debris, their faces smeared with ash. No one made me feel guilty about what had happened. It was, thank God, a small price to pay for a leap towards our emancipation. The guilt belongs entirely to those who confiscate women's voices.

Polygamy and Sisterhood

POLYGAMY PERSISTS IN the Bedouin community despite a law against it passed in 1977, and is punishable by up to five years in prison. Some figures suggest that as many as 30 per cent of Bedouin marriages are polygamous, a number which has been increasing over the past two decades, prior to which it was only practised by the very rich. Through Ma'an we decided to tackle this issue on every level: by raising awareness among women, by advocating for policy change, by encouraging the implementation of the law and by advocating within the community so that religious leaders would help limit the practice. We organized an impressive conference at BGU, with a panel comprising a renowned social worker, a leader of the Islamic Movement and a representative of the police force. It was a landmark event for BGU – to have hundreds of traditionally dressed Bedouin women streaming across the campus – and an even bigger achievement for women in the Bedouin community.

We showed the religious leaders and the state representatives that we had had enough. The closing message was about holding both the state and the community accountable, and it emphasized the role of religious leaders in educating the community in Islam which does not sanction polygamy, except in rare cases. No one was happy with my concluding remarks and the conference resulted in more threats against women's organizations. The Hebrew media reported that we were promoting women's rights; the Arab media – especially the religious outlets – criticized us for serving the Zionist agenda. The state wanted to fight polygamy because they saw its outcome as creating a demographic threat whereas the Bedouin upheld polygamy with a tribal mindset that equated having more boys with greater strength and wealth.

A week later, Aamne, an instructor in AJEEC's early childhood education programme, invited me to her home to discuss the possibility of opening a day care centre in her village. I arrived at her *hosh*, where three women were sitting at a wooden picnic table in the shade of a green canvas awning, at the centre of four identical shacks. The three Bedouin women waved when they saw me and flashed me three beautiful smiles.

"You will be angry and won't support our initiative if we tell you that we are all married to the same man," Aamne teased.

My mouth fell open and they burst out laughing. I didn't respond for a few seconds, then let their laughter carry me into their loving energy. Aamne told the story. She had married Musa, her cousin, when they were both eighteen years old. Ten years later, Musa was working in a factory when he met a man from Hebron who introduced him to his second wife, a woman from the West Bank. Three years later, Musa married this man's cousin from the Nuseirat refugee camp in Gaza and, after the peace treaty was signed with Jordan, he married a fourth wife from Irbid. Musa pitched in: "The last one was done for the sake of peace!" Their laughter tickled my ears. I hadn't noticed him before. He looked even darker in the shade of one of the shacks, where he sat comfortably in a chair. "If anyone is suffering," he said, "it's me. Can you imagine four against one?" They laughed again.

"Was this a free choice or were any of you forced?" I finally asked them.

Aamne answered first. "This is my cousin. It was my first choice. I didn't know any other men. I didn't go to school. I was at home. This is the man I knew."

Layla from Hebron told her story next. "My brother convinced me that the living conditions in Israel were way better than Hebron and he paid my brother a very high *maher*. I had never seen him before and I was surprised that he was black, but all people are equal. After all, Bilal, the first muezzin, was black."

The family of Suad, the most recent wife, had had to flee twice: first in 1948 to the village next to Jenin in the West Bank and then again during the Six-Day War to Irbid. She married at thirty-three and was afraid that she would never be a mother.

"We live in solidarity and sisterhood and we don't think this hurts anyone. We don't feel that we are doing wrong," Suad said. They told me how close they were. Since the three of them were cut off from their families, they had formed an alternative family.

While the women shared more stories, Musa moved his chair closer. He sat quietly and let them speak, not even interrupting to defend himself when they blamed him for something.

"We support each other, we take care of each other's children, and we always unite against Musa if he treats one of us unfairly." Layla glanced around at the others and they smiled as if to say, "Oh yes, *ya bintee*."

"See?" Musa said gently. "I have done something that no one has been able to do: I've united the Palestinian people under one roof."

We all laughed at that.

Listening to their story made me reflect about who is entitled to define the problem. The issue is complicated. We can't judge women if we don't provide them with an alternative. If we don't make space for single women to be accepted in society, if we don't provide options for women who come from poverty and are illiterate, then polygamy is their only option and it isn't necessarily a bad one. Sometimes as activists we run around thinking that we know the truth and that we know what's best. But who owns the truth? Who owns the truth about this problem? It's important to remember that what we are really fighting for, above all else, is choice.

In the Name of Honour

I WAS PREPARING dinner for my family. It was summer and Beer a-Saba let out a long sigh after the oppressive morning heat. My cell phone rang. The voice at the end of the line was breaking under the weight of what he was telling me. "I can't. I can't protect her. You have to come and take her to a shelter. You have to save her life."

These calls were not uncommon. This time it was Jaber, one of the community leaders I was working with on an early childhood education programme, who was calling to tell me about a girl in his village we needed to rescue. The more we progressed as a community, the more these issues came to light. I brought many girls under Abouee's protection until we could provide them with a safe alternative to going back home, where they risked being killed. One girl lived with my parents for seven years until she got married. Each story told the same tragedy: a woman on the run from her own family. Some ended up leaving the country, others married and some sought refuge in a shelter. The ones who weren't saved were killed. Whether by fire or acid, each suffered unimaginable horrors.

I was aware that Jaber was protecting Ghazaale from her family, who threatened to kill her in the name of what they called "family honour" – an honour that has nothing to do with honour. An evil that has slaughtered too many women.

Jaber said that the girl wanted to go to a shelter. Her life was in grave danger and she was afraid. I told him that we would get her out, but that first I would call Abeer, my sister, who was the social worker in charge of the girls-at-risk unit in the region, so that she could report the case and prepare the girl to be moved.

Moving to a shelter meant she could never come back home. She would be an outcast. An exile. A shameful woman who had stained the family name even further by sharing her dirty secrets with strangers. Being under the protection of another family guaranteed the girl's safety because the dispute shifted from her shoulders to theirs. It was no longer between her and her family, but between her family and the one protecting her.

After putting our twins to bed, I sat on the balcony and phoned Abeer. Ghazaale was going to be moved to a shelter in the north. Abeer, accompanied by the police, would meet her in the city the next day.

"Do you think that's safe?" I asked.

"I don't know, but this is the only option. Her relative made it clear that every second she stays in that house she may be killed."

I asked if we could bring her to our parents to buy time. Abeer suggested that to Ghazaale, but she wanted to get as far away as she possibly could.

The next day, on my way to one of my meetings in Jerusalem, the dust shrouded the road in a red cloud. My phone rang. I saw Abeer's name on the display and slowed the car. Abeer calling me meant something bad. I was almost at the entrance to the city. Abeer was screaming words I couldn't make out. I pulled over and cupped the phone in both hands, as if it would bring Abeer closer.

"Ghazaale is dead," she cried. "They shot her in the head. I saw it. I saw it. I saw the blood. I saw her hair soaked with her blood,

Amal. They killed her. They killed her. They killed her. I couldn't save her . . ."

Abeer's voice tailed off in her sadness. I tried to get back on the road, but the traffic was very bad. Cars honked at me and shouted insults in Hebrew: "Dirty Arab!" "*Bat zona*, move!" Another voice joined in, this one in Arabic: "Who gave you a licence, *ya ihmara*!"

I was numb to their words. I needed to turn around and go back to my parents'. When I made it back onto the highway, I heard myself say: "You dirty *hmar ben zona* [You dirty son of a bitch]." Tears blurred my vision. A drop for Ghazaale and a thousand more for every woman like her.

Ghazaale's sister had taken part in one of AJEEC's volunteering programmes. I knew the family very well. Her mother and I had gone to high school together. I ran into her twenty years later, her almond eyes a little less bright, her face imprinted with a map of her life, a life that had dragged her feet behind her. The corners of her eyes lifted when she saw me. "Amal, you always had a fire in you. I couldn't do it. I had to leave school in tenth grade." She looked at the group of female students who were volunteering to organize AJEEC's event and said: "I want my daughter Ghazeleh to join your programme next year. I want her to fulfil my dream. I want her to complete her education." Um Ghazaale had been a smart, strong and vocal student. She used to sit at the front with her long, black hair tied in a perfect braid that peaked out from under her scarf. Now we had reconnected, she would call me during the holidays and invite me to spend time with her family and remind me to keep a spot open for Ghazaale the following year in AJEEC's gap-year programme. That spot was never filled.

I snaked through the village roads and even the stones deafened me with their silence. It wasn't a holy silence, but a suffocating one: those who cannot scream condemned by those who refuse to hear. I parked next to my parents' house. I knew Abeer would be there, taking refuge.

I opened the main door slowly, quietly, as if I was complicit in the silent crime that no one dared to mention. My parents were taking their midday rest when they saw me. They sat up, concerned about what would bring me here in the middle of a weekday. Ummi covered her curly braided hair with her *shash* and leaped out of bed.

"What happened?"

I didn't answer and walked into our old bedroom. She followed me. "Tell me. Are you OK? Your children? Are they OK?"

We found Abeer hiding under the bed sheets. I scooped her trembling body up in my arms. Her face was soaked with her tears.

"What happened? What happened? Your brothers and sisters are OK?"

"Everyone is OK, Ummi. It's the girl that Abeer was trying to save. She was shot and killed."

Usually, Ummi would say: "*Allah yarhamaha* [God will help her]. We can't do anything. It's their girl and we can't do anything." She'd ask us not to intervene and I'd fight her. This time, Ummi took Abeer's hand in hers and kissed it. Her eyes glistened. "Why, God, why? Why are women shot for no other reason than they are women? Women are miserable. Where is Allah to see this? Where is the justice?" She wept, her soul finally permitting her to feel for all the women she hadn't allowed herself to care about.

Ghazaale was eighteen years old, pretty and full of life. The men in her family accused her of desecrating the family honour. Their words killed her even before a single shot was fired. These cases are buried in the dark and that's where they stay: no questions asked and no information offered. It's done. The family "cleaned its name", burying the rumours together with the body. Our daughters, sisters, nieces, aunts and mothers shut up in a prison called home and murdered by men heralded as champions for defending the family name.

I hugged Ummi and told her that Abeer had seen Ghazaale being shot. Ummi pulled Abeer onto her lap and held her between her arms. My sister's face was blank, her breathing shallow. After cradling her for a few minutes, Ummi went to get Abouee. He sat on the bed and placed Abeer's head in his lap while his mouth recited the At-Takwir surah. At verses 8 and 9 – "When the baby girls, buried alive, are asked for what crime they were put to death" – the grief resonated in Abouee's voice.

In a half-whisper, Abeer repeated the details of what she'd seen: "Her hair was soaked in her blood. She fell onto the concrete like a sheep slaughtered, her wool soaked in blood." She covered her eyes to shield herself from the memory. Abeer was too traumatized to return home and stayed with my parents for a month, sleeping in between them, like a little girl. Every night, Ummi caressed my sister, while reciting from the Quran. The guilt Abeer felt at knowing she could have saved Ghazaale if only she'd arrived an hour earlier wore my sister down long after the image of Ghazaale faded.

The hardest part for me to understand was how a father could kill his daughter, how a brother could kill his sister. How anyone could kill the person they'd spent their entire life raising and protecting. I wanted to understand the family so I visited the mother two weeks after the killing. I went in the morning to avoid being seen. We aren't supposed to visit, especially if we are from outside the tribe.

I parked my car some distance down the road, and walked for twenty minutes along the dusty path. I hid behind my Bedouin *thobe*, white *shash* and the *quona* (big, black shawl worn from head to toe) so that no one could identify me. I entered the *hosh* where some hens pecked at a bowl of warm water. They dispersed, creating a commotion that sent a middle-aged man with a beard out to see what had caused it. I covered my face and he ran back to tell his wife that a woman was there to see her. After she had invited me in, I sat on the rug and glanced at the forlorn objects around me. Everything looked as if it had lost its life. When I removed the *shash* from my face, Ghazaale's mother gasped. She hugged me and put her head in my lap, crying the tears she had been denied. I wiped her tears with my *shash* and rocked her in my arms.

"My girl was well raised. She would never betray the family

honour. You know me. I raised her well. She was a good student at school," she sobbed.

She stood up and came back with Ghazaale's report cards, flipping through the pages until a tissue fell on the rug between us. She snatched it up and sniffed it, kissed it, breathing in every last trace of the daughter she had lost. I thought of my daughter Adan. If this were to happen to her, I would destroy everything that had taken her from me, especially the silence.

Neither the community leaders nor the religious leaders ever spoke out against honour killings, although they are not condoned by Islam. Honour killings date back to pre-Islamic times, but the practice is so rooted in our traditions that instead of using Islam to quash it, our community uses religion to defend it. Until Ghazaale's murder, these crimes were committed behind closed doors. Girls were thrown into wells, set on fire, or locked in a room and gassed to death. We were told that these were family matters, but not this time. Ghazaale's killers shot her in a public lot, next to Abeer's office. Her killers had no fear. They had no shame. Because she was killed in public, honour killings and crimes against women became a public issue. Later that year, AJEEC brought together women's organizations, Jewish and Arab, to discuss how to deal with gender-based violence and murdering women in the name of family honour, not least since government institutions did not treat them as crimes. Why were they considered an ethnic practice? I argued this point with a police officer on one of our steering committees. "This is one of your traditions," he said, just as I'd heard countless officers say, "and we have to respect that."

"Traditions evolve. They are dynamic. They are not fixed," I answered. "We can change traditions. We abandon some, we create new ones. It is you who wants to keep our community from evolving. And why, if we tell you that we don't respect this practice, do you insist that we do unless it suits your agenda?"

That meeting incited the Bedouin leaders against me even more. How dare I ask the police to intervene in our customs and traditions?

These leaders saw my actions as cooperating with the enemy against the community. When I fought the state about housing demolition, I had these leaders' support, but what good is a house if it doesn't protect the women who live in it? What rights are worth fighting for if not the right to live? When women are oppressed, they become mothers who raise an oppressed generation. Free women and you free the world.

A Free Woman has Nothing to Fear

JIDATEE FOLLOWED MY work closely by sitting out in her *hosh* next to the LWA Embroidery Centre and listening to the presentations I gave at least once a week. She spoke neither Hebrew nor English and when my voice faded into the fabric of the tent, she would come down and ask me what my talk was about. Jidatee always had something to add or correct, and she always told me to take better care of my voice. "It's all you have," she would say. "I understand that you speak from your heart, but nobody is chasing you. Slow down. Breathe. Let your brain get the air it needs."

She understood the importance of my voice and the power of my mind. "*Al-huura ma betkhaaf* [A free woman has nothing to fear]. A woman who knows how to think freely and act responsibly is never afraid to face anyone," was another of her great lessons. Whenever I spoke about women's freedom, my community would accuse me of having been co-opted by Western ideology. Weaving together "women" and "freedom" threatened the very fabric of our community. But how could this be? Jidatee never went to school. This phrase didn't sprout in her brain from Western seeds. It came from her own indigenous knowledge. I'd heard her say it my whole life. For her, "freedom" meant more than physical freedom. "Freedom" meant the ability to think freely: to ask, to doubt, to deconstruct a question and to reconstruct the answer. In short, to imagine a new reality. And, when a person can reflect and ask questions, she is free from fear. No free mind can exist when the mind is jailed in fear. The saying *"Al-huura ma betkhaaf"* proved that the concept of women's liberation wasn't bestowed on me by the West. It was handed down to me from my very own Jidatee.

In the afternoon of Sunday, April 30th, 2006, Salmaan called me. I had finished my final presentation in New York City after a ten-day speaking tour and was in my hotel room, slowly packing my small suitcase. Calls from Salmaan meant something serious. He is the calm one in the family. He wanted to know what time my flight was.

"You know Jidatee is not young, and—"

"Salmaan, Jidatee died. She died right?" Chills invaded my body. My tears were ready to flow.

"No," he said. "She's in hospital. Amal, just tell me when your flight is."

I sobbed that I was leaving for the airport right away and that I was due to land at seven the next morning.

"I promise you that you'll see her to say goodbye. Just take care of yourself."

She had been at our uncle's house, chatting and feeling fine, until she felt something in her stomach. Salmaan took her to hospital, where she was now on life support. She had told my uncle that, were this to happen, they should disconnect her and let her go.

"Promise that you'll let me say goodbye, Salmaan, promise me, promise me." My hands were pleading with him, clutching the phone with a desperate love.

On the plane, Jidatee's face stared back at me from every cloud. I breathed her in: cinnamon and cloves. The tea she drank every morning and the spices that hung from her henna-dyed braids. I closed my eyes and conjured up our last meeting. It was the week before I left for New York. I was at my parents' house with Adan and Moad. My sisters and their children were there too. It was one of those weekends when we had gathered together for a taste of the old days. We had all slept over, snuggled in a heap on the floor, laughing and chatting in between shushing our children and telling them to behave. But there was no chance of that. At their grandparents' house, there were no rules and we quit our parenting roles the moment we got together.

That afternoon, Moad and Adan were being impossible. After my stern reproach, they followed me to Wafaa's room, dragging their feet away from the games their cousins were playing.

"I wish Narjis was my mother, not you," Moad whined.

I sat with them on Wafaa's bed and explained why they couldn't throw mud onto their grandmother's rugs.

Adan pouted. "But everyone is doing it."

"I'm not asking you who is doing it," I said. "I'm asking you if it's right."

Adan straightened up. "No, it's not right, but Jidatee didn't say anything and you and my other aunts can wash it before you leave." Her small hands mimed how the problem could be solved.

"That is not the solution," I said firmly. "If you play, you don't throw mud onto Jidatee's rug. Clear?"

They both looked at me with puppy eyes and scurried back to rejoin my sisters in the *hosh* where the rest of the children were still throwing mud. I asked my sisters to intervene, but they told me to relax and let them play.

Five minutes later, Moad was at it again, throwing mud, like the other children. I grabbed him by the hand and brought him to Wafaa's room. Jidatee was sitting in the living room, braiding her hair.

She raised an eyebrow. "Again?"

After admonishing Moad, I was on my way back to the *hosh* when Jidatee stopped me.

"Look there," she said, pointing to Abouee's photo hanging on the wall. "What do you think of this man?"

I knew she was testing me. "I think he is the best human being I've ever met."

She smiled. "And is he polite? Is he respectful?"

"Yes, Jidatee, but why do you ask?"

"I have never shouted at him or sworn at him. Never humiliated him or hurt him. There is a way to raise your child without hurting his feelings. When you hurt his feelings, you make him weak, you make him blame himself."

"But Jidatee, you saw how twice I told Moad not to throw mud on Ummi's rugs and he still did it."

"He did it because everyone is doing it and he is young. What do you want him to think? Everyone is playing except him. He will think that something is wrong with him. Go and fetch your sisters and explain, all of you, that this is not acceptable and they need to find an alternative before you stop their game. Never punish your child in front of his friends, or in public, because that way you break his eye – *la teksiri eine*. In your own home, talk to him privately and explain why he shouldn't throw mud on his Jedda's rugs."

I don't remember Jidatee ever shouting at us even though she was often surrounded by tens of grandchildren, screaming and crying, tugging at her *thobe* or thrusting their sticky hands in her face.

When the pilot announced the weather in Tel Aviv, some invisible force pushed me to my feet. Far away it was just news; soon it would be reality. Anwar and Yousef met me at the airport and when I saw Yousef, I knew that Jidatee was gone and that I wouldn't be able to say goodbye. Yousef walked towards me, head bowed, and we nestled our wet cheeks together in silent heartbreak. On our way to the car, I was afraid to ask if they'd already buried her, since according to Islam *ikraam al-maayet dafne* (bless the dead by burying them fast), even at the expense of some relatives not being there, but Yousef read my mind. "Abouee asked our uncles to wait for you to bury her. You're lucky. You'll see her."

The surah from the *masjid*'s loudspeaker wrapped the village in reverence. Hundreds of people stood at the entrance to Jidatee's house, gathered together in submission to the harshest truth of all: the truth of death. Ummi met me at the entrance and accompanied me inside where the women were gathered together like a black sea. Ummi's weight on my arm reminded me of the ground beneath my feet. "This is how she wanted to go." She pulled me in closer. "She always said: '*Ya rab, khothni w-ajaaja a-tareeg a rejlayee* [God take me while the dust is still stuck on my feet].'"

I thought that when I saw her I would shatter like glass. I approached her bedroom, where the weeping from my sisters and aunts was muffled by the camel-hair carpet beneath their feet. Only Narjis's sniffling was audible. But as soon as I stepped inside, their sobs washed over me, a wave of despair, receding with time and returning with every new mourner who entered. I tiptoed towards her body. I knew we would only have a few minutes together before the men came to take her. The faded tattoo on her chin was the only part of her that looked worn. Elegantly shrouded in a cotton veil, she was still proud, even in death. The waxiness of her skin made her look like a marble statue. There was a distance to her, but the familiar blanket that enveloped this formidable woman reminded me of each moment we'd spent together. I didn't cry. I sat beside her and kissed her hand. The blood that had coursed through her veins was fire, family and faith. She lived like an olive tree with her feet rooted deep in the earth and her face held high against the desert wind, so connected was she to the land. The things she knew are the things that need to be remembered for all eternity.

"Jidatee," I whispered, "I'm not angry that you left. I just know I will miss you. I will need you and you won't be there. I will try to touch you and I won't feel your hand. I will call you and I won't hear your voice. I will sit next to you, but I won't feel your warmth." I kissed her again.

Abouee and my uncles Abd al-Rahman and Ahmed entered and asked us to make room for them to carry her to the *masjid*. The only thought in my head was: "Won't she be lonely? The only woman accompanied by all those men." Abouee and his brothers bowed their heads, basking in her majesty for one last time. "No," I thought. "All these men are marching in this woman's honour. In honour of this woman who has always been free."

Not My Flag

WHEN THEY WERE three, we decided it was time to send Moad and Adan to day care. Paulina was still with us then, but we wanted our twins to interact with other children on a daily basis. We were among a handful of Arabs who lived in the city and had no other option except Jewish day care centres, so we sent them to Gan Orna around the corner from our apartment. We didn't know what to expect. Would this be my children's first exposure to the discrimination I worked so hard to protect them from? The day we met Orna was another lesson about making assumptions. We showed up with big smiles to win her over, but her heart was already open. She ushered them into the class and invited them to play with the other children. For her, Moad and Adan were just two more adorable children in her centre and we were two friendly and helpful parents who volunteered our time whenever we could. Our friend Rula sent her daughter there too, so now Orna's class of fifteen had three Bedouin representatives.

Orna, a Mizrahi Jewish woman, was also the product of Israel's melting pot approach. She taught the curriculum she had learned – the one that emphasized a national story over individual identity – and when I drove up to the nursery one day, I saw Moad and Adan gleefully waving Israeli flags in celebration of Israel's Independence Day – our Nakba. My heart sank. It was easier for me to explain our religious differences than our political ones. I pretended not to notice the flags, but when Adan wanted to hang them out of our window like our neighbours, it was time to have our first conversation about identity and citizenship.

"You know that we have our own flag," I said.

"This isn't our flag?" Moad asked.

"We have another one."

Adan shouted: "This is our flag. The teacher said it's our flag."

"Yes," I said calmly, "but we have a different flag. The flag of your Jidee in Laqiya."

Now that excited them. They hopped up and down asking to draw Jidee's flag.

I got out a piece of white paper and three crayons and drew the flag. "This is the Palestinian flag. Do you want to colour it in?" Yes, they did. I showed them where to put the green, the red and the black.

When Anwar came home, he saw the Israeli flags on the table together with the Palestinian ones. They ran to show him and asked him to hang them out of the window. I shot him a look and he immediately said: "No," and then saved himself. "We'll hang this one on your Jidee's window in the village. He'll love it."

Our neighbours knew we were Bedouin, but hanging out a flag in those days could pose a real threat to our safety. It would be read as an act of resistance and our neighbours wanted to believe that we were Israeli Bedouin – Bedouin who wanted to fit in.

After they had completed their pre-kindergarten year, Anwar and I were torn between two unappealing options: to send our children to a Bedouin school in the village where they'd receive an inferior education, or to send them to a Jewish school where they might be treated as inferior and be cut off from their identity. Our existence in the city needed to be institutionalized. We had to be part of the public space. We needed representation.

I was first introduced to joint Arab and Jewish schools in Israel in 1999 through a model school called Hand-in-Hand. Amin Khalaf, the co-founder, had asked me if I thought this model could be expanded to the Negev. At that time, I was more concerned with rights and hadn't yet developed my solutions-oriented approach to activism. Now, having been exposed to bilingual schools in Montreal, I contacted Amin and asked him if he would help us establish a joint Arab and Jewish school in Beer a-Saba.

Our first meeting was held in our living room. We invited Arab and Jewish friends from AJEEC and from Anwar's work with Ta'ayoush, a grassroots organization working towards co-existence. Our small but committed group comprised of Neev Gordon and his wife, Eyfat Helel and her husband, Marwan Aamer, Eyad Haj, Akiva Leibowitz, Rula and Yousef.

After several consultations with Amin, it was clear that we should establish our school independently from Hand-in-Hand, as we wanted ours to be more rooted in our community, and that we would start with a kindergarten and grow from there. Amin was adamant that the municipality should allocate funds to support the development of the school.

When I suggested the name Hajar, everyone agreed. The only argument was whether it should be the Arabic "Hajar" or the Jewish "Hagar". We ultimately went with the Arabic. Hajar – the wife of the patriarch Abraham – unites us. Her story features in both cultures: a strong woman who was cast out in Beer a-Saba, the place where we were now weaving our histories together.

We started recruiting students and very quickly there was a waiting list for the Arab quota. We only wanted thirty students – fifteen and fifteen – and the Arabs had no good options in Beer a-Saba. The Jews, on the other hand, had a choice of many schools and we needed to recruit more Jewish students. I took Moad and Adan and an armful of bilingual brochures and walked around our local park. I watched as Adan ran over to a woman next to the playground, held out a brochure, and the woman shook her head. "What racism," I thought to myself. "She's only four. Can't you talk to her nicely?" I fumed, rehearsing in my head what I should say to this woman, when Adan ran back over to me and said: "Yuma, Yuma [Mom, Mom] I tried to give that woman a brochure, but she said she has no children that age."

My own prejudice stared me in the face. Adan interpreted the woman's action for what it was. Her mind was purer than mine. That's what I hoped we could create with Hajar.

When our group met with the city mayor Yaakov Turner to talk about the school, he said: "We'll think about it." We spent four months chasing him for a building. Here we were, a group of Arab and Jewish parents who believed that our children could be raised together in an environment that promoted mutual understanding, and the municipality rejected us. At the same time, I raised $375,000 from foreign foundations and private donors to start the school. The mayor thought that we would leave him alone, but when I saw that he wasn't cooperating, I wrote a letter with the heading "Call for Help" and sent it to all the Jewish donors who gave him money, especially the ones in Montreal, since Be'er Sheva is twinned with Montreal.

That got his attention. One morning, after giving a tour of the unrecognized villages to a group from Brandeis University, my cell phone rang. It was Yaakov Turner himself. "Great news. We have a building for you. But you'll need some money to renovate it."

In the opening ceremony, he said: "Peace in the Middle East starts here." It was the first time he'd shown any real commitment to the project and whether he said it as a power-hungry politician or a good-hearted person, I didn't care. He said it and people heard it. After a year, the kindergarten grew into an elementary school that exists to this day. It was a first step towards creating real equality in society: a school where both flags could hang out of the window.

Navigating Minefields

The Yellow Sticker

I WAS INVITED to address universities, non-governmental organizations, European Union human rights committees and conferences and UN committees about a wide range of topics, including Bedouin rights in Israel, Arab–Jewish relations in the country, the role of women in community development, and strategies for organizing communities. If I forgot that I was a second-class citizen or a perceived security threat, I was reminded of that every time I headed to Ben Gurion airport – even if I was crossing an entire continent to talk about my vision for a joint future for Arabs and Jews.

On one of my trips to North America, I was invited to speak at the Jewish Federation in San Francisco to talk about the obstacles to providing early childhood education in the unrecognized villages. I had all my documentation ready – my passport, the address of the federation and the hotel, and my invitation – to avoid any delays at security. When it was my turn at the check-in desk, the officer opened my passport, looked at my face and asked: "Where are you from?"

"Be'er Sheva," I replied in Hebrew.

"Be'er Sheva, Be'er Sheva?"

"Yes. Be'er Sheva, the city."

"Not the villages around it?"

"No. I live in the city."

He didn't like my answer. "I see." He left to speak with another officer who must have been his supervisor and came back.

"What is the purpose of your trip?"

"I am going on a speaking tour."

"*You* are going to speak? Why would they ask you to speak?"

"Why wouldn't they? Don't I look like someone who can give a lecture?" I joked.

"No, but you are a Bedouin. Why would they ask a Bedouin to speak?"

"I think they believe I know a thing or two about community organizing," I said, trying to get him to rethink his question, but he didn't. For him, the situation was entirely absurd: The Bedouin live in deserts, they ride camels, they marry lots of women. Why would anyone invite these primitive people to speak about anything?

"May I see the invitation?" he asked.

After carrying the invitation to his supervisor, he told me to follow him into a small interrogation room where he told me to sit down. I stared at the grey tiled floor, thinking about how I would get through this without losing my mind. I prayed that they wouldn't delve into my luggage and expose my bras and underwear in front of everyone. How could I detach myself and comply?

A female officer came in and asked all the normal questions: "Where are you going? Who packed your luggage? Did anyone give you anything? Do you have any sharp objects?" Despite my answers, she tacked a yellow sticker onto my bag and its garish hue set against my dark blue bag said what no one dared mention. She left and another female officer entered, this one in her early twenties. Even though we were the same height, she still managed to look down her nose at me and order me around like a dog. I removed my boots and shirt. The moment her hands touched my body, my mind ran for cover, my breath shortened and I did my best to endure her handling me like an old bag she'd fished out from the back of her closet. After each corner of me had been patted down, prodded, cupped and grabbed, she stepped aside, still not looking me in the eye, and left me standing there in my bra. Fifteen minutes later, she returned with my passport and compared the face in the photo with the person in front of her. It was only when she was about to leave that she noticed I was crying. She demanded to know why, but I couldn't answer. The anger that stirred inside me didn't have the space to be heard.

She waited for me in the security line with my luggage in front of her. "Open it," she commanded. I obeyed and she pulled out my things while speaking to her colleague about a dress she had bought from Zara. If she had a life outside these four walls, how couldn't she see that I, too, was a person and not just a security threat? She rifled through my bag until she reached my toiletries case and asked me to open it. "You open it," I spat out. "If you want to search it, you open it."

"I can't," she said.

"Well, my body is mine and you had no problem with that."

"We don't have time. Open it."

"I need to see your supervisor," I said to rescue whatever dignity I had left. I wanted to feel like I was fighting instead of taking this humiliation lying down. Jewish travellers staring at me as they passed by were another source of humiliation. They chatted excitedly about their trip and what they planned to buy from the duty-free shop. I could never think about that since I never knew how my journey would end.

She looked around. In that moment, her authority seemed fragile. She was young and clearly didn't know what to do. She left and a large, dark-skinned man stomped over, expressing male authority in his whole body – another type of dominance over me. "We're sorry for the inconvenience," he said without sounding sorry at all. He didn't look me in the eye either, but shouted, "If you want to get to your flight on time, you have to let us do our job," so that the passersby stared at me as though I was a terrorist.

"Is it your job to humiliate people? I have no problem with your job – I have a problem with the way you do it. I wouldn't object if you selected people randomly, but your random doesn't seem so random and I'm not going to cooperate with this."

411

"It's up to you if you want to miss your flight," he snarled.

There was no way I could win this battle. After ten minutes of standing to one side, I opened my toiletries case. The young woman rifled through it and her supervisor went through the files I had on my laptop for my presentation. When they finished, the officer's eyes gloated over his victory. "You can go," he waved me off.

My feet wouldn't budge. I stuffed my things back into my luggage and made sure to stare him in the eye. "People who enjoy humiliating other people must have experienced humiliation themselves. People who abuse power must have been a victim of the same abuse. Ask your parents if you weren't abused as a child."

I walked away, shouting over my shoulder: "Go and get therapy so that your children won't fall into the same cycle of oppression." I didn't look back but I felt as though I had left with my dignity intact.

Another time, at the Jewish General Assembly in Washington DC – an annual meeting of Jewish organizations to discuss Jewish and Israeli issues – while Shimon Peres gave the conference keynote, Vivian held my hand. Every time he spoke about the need to protect the Jews from their enemies, she squeezed it. At the end of his speech, everyone stood for Israel's national anthem, but I remained seated. This song didn't represent me. I am not a Jewish soul.

Vivian shielded me from a hundred reproachful eyes. When we left the hall, the mayor of Ramat Hovav, Shmuel Refman, with whom I'd already had many fights about his views on the Bedouin taking over Jewish land, told me that what I had done wasn't nice. If I didn't feel comfortable, why did I come to these events in the first place, he wanted to know. Vivian swooped in. "You should know by now that Israel is not only about Jewish people – 20 per cent of the population are Arabs."

At the airport on our way back, Vivian and I prepared to be separated and I knew I'd be taken in for security questioning. I saw most of the Israelis who had participated in the General Assembly, including Shimon Peres's staff and the mayors from the Negev and surrounding municipalities waiting in the security area. The security guard held a list with the names of the General Assembly participants. I tugged on Vivian's sleeve to show her that mine was highlighted. "Don't be paranoid," she whispered.

The guard asked me to go with him while the others boarded. Shmuel Refman rushed over to explain that I was with them, but the guard ignored him. He went through the routine questions, and I was happy that all these people who thought that I was inventing such stories were here to witness what I went through each time I travelled.

He asked me who had packed my luggage and who was in my room at the hotel. I looked at the line of government employees and said: "I was with them. With all these people."

"In your room?"

"Yes."

He became very angry and switched to Hebrew: "*Achshav bretzeenuut* [Seriously now]."

"I'm serious. I was with them the whole time."

He let me go. When I passed Shmuel in the line, he apologized for what had happened. "This is nothing," I said. "I don't want you to be sorry for this, I want you to be sorry for annexing Bedouin land to expand your municipality at the expense of unrecognized villages." I didn't wait to hear his answer.

We Made You

WHEN WALKING THROUGH a minefield, one innocent step can trigger a deadly blast. Presenting my story, my solutions-oriented approach to community activism and the human rights issues facing the Bedouin in Israel always triggered anger from every side. I laid out the facts and people hurled abuse back at me. The Inter-Agency Task Force on Israeli Arab issues, an organization committed to raising awareness about minority–majority relations within Israel, invited me as a speaker to several of their conferences.

Once, a day before my presentation at the American University in Washington DC, the organizer called me to say that Palestinian students were going to protest at the conference. He wanted to know if I still felt comfortable giving the presentation. I answered that I would come and share my narrative. Whether I spoke with a Jewish audience or a Palestinian one, my message was the same.

As the white facade appeared in the distance, I saw Palestinian flags waving over a sea of people. Tens of students stood together, shouting slogans and pumping their fists high in the air. The red, white, green and black catching the morning sun gave me goosebumps. I always saw myself standing under that flag. I gathered my courage and walked towards them. I wore my red scarf, the same one which appeared in the poster for the panel, and I greeted the students. "It's important to have you here. Everyone should hear your side of the story. The talk I am going to give inside is about the Bedouin community."

"You are cooperating with them," one of the students yelled. "When you talk here you accept Israel."

"Bedouin are citizens of Israel. Do you know anything about us? To change policies, you need to talk with people who are part of the issue, right?" I spoke loudly and clearly. "Listen. Standing out here is one strategy, but if it's not employed to promote a specific issue, it might serve the Palestinian issue for ten days in the media, but it won't have a lasting impact. You will go home without adding to your knowledge of the real issues that your people face on a daily basis. I suggest you go in and ask your questions. Argue your points. You are welcome to argue mine if you feel that I'm not justly representing the Bedouin case."

Three students stepped out of the crowd and joined me in the conference.

After my presentation, one Jewish woman stood up. She was in her late fifties, and her brow knitted a storm over her face. "How dare you criticize Israel," she said, her hands shaking. "Look around you. Your people have better living conditions than in all the Arab countries. See how Palestinians live in Lebanon. We gave you an education. We made you who you are. Look at you: a strong and educated woman."

The other panellists stepped in to defend me, but I asked to speak for myself. I looked at her and tried to put myself in her place. With people who know what Israel's minorities experience day to day but still decide only to see it through their own lens, I am direct and tough, but for those who speak out of ignorance, I go out of my way to explain. I believe it is on my shoulders to teach people how to treat me.

"Are you a citizen of Israel?" I asked her.

"No, but—"

"I am a citizen. I pay taxes, my people pay taxes, and I am entitled to criticize and demand that the state treats all of its citizens equally. You are right. The Palestinian citizens of Israel have a better standard of life than Palestinians in other Arab countries. This comparison is not a useful one, however. You can't compare tomatoes with apples. You compare apples with apples. Israel is a democratic country. Every morning we wake up hearing that 'Israel claims to be the only democracy in the Middle East'. None of the Arab countries define themselves as a democracy so I have little expectation when it comes to minority rights, but with Israel, one of the main tenets of democracy is minority rights. I suggest you compare my status to yours in the USA or in Canada."

I thanked her for her question and said that I would be happy to discuss this further after my presentation. Before leaving the stage, I folded my notes and said: "And, I would like to use this opportunity to thank my parents for all they did to raise me as a strong and educated woman. My parents are the ones who made me."

Three months later, the Mossawa Center, an organization that promotes the rights of Israel's Arab citizens, invited me to speak at Columbia University about the unrecognized villages. A throng of Jewish student activists entered the room to protest against the talk. The organizers shouted at the students to leave and the whole scene erupted into a shouting match. I walked directly over to one of the Jewish students, introduced myself, and invited him to join the talk and ask his questions.

"Why don't you criticize Arab countries?" he retorted. "They are the ones constantly violating human rights and yet we only hear about Israel."

"Whatever happens in other countries is not the agenda of this talk. I'm here to talk about my people who are citizens of Israel. Why don't you ask your questions and argue your points in a more productive way? I am sure you will learn from it and I promise I will answer all your questions."

I placed my hand on his shoulder and felt the anger and fear pulsing through his body. In his face I saw those same Palestinian students from just three months earlier. If only we spoke with each other and listened with real intention to understand and not defend. Often when I facilitate groups in conflict, I see how each camp is focused solely on how to react, on how to prove that the other side is wrong. If for just one second we cast aside those attitudes – the defence and the attack – then we would be in a different place.

The student followed me when I pulled up a chair for him. One of the Palestinian organizers rushed over.

"What's he doing here?" he asked harshly.

"This is where he's supposed to be. I am here because I want my message to get to him."

"But we can't have him here."

"Just tell me why."

"I don't know. We don't want him here."

"Well, if he is out, then I am out. I can't be part of an event that can't tolerate different opinions. Fundamentalism and not being open to listening are not my way."

The Jewish student stood up to leave but a Palestinian student sitting a few feet from us spoke up. "I think you are in the right place. You can stay."

At the end of the panel, I watched the two students talking to each other. Not screaming, not shouting, but just talking. Talking and listening.

At a conference in London, I was invited to present on the challenges of building a shared space for Arabs and Jews in Israel. I had taken my seat on the panel when one of the conference organizers approached me and quietly asked that I focus on the Bedouin side of my identity rather than the Palestinian so as to garner more sympathy from the audience and not draw attention to the larger issue of Palestinian rights.

When it was my turn to speak, I began my presentation the way I always do – with my life story: the fifth girl who paved the way for boys, a shepherd, a Bedouin, a Palestinian, a feminist and a citizen of Israel. I saw the organizer fidgeting in his seat. Later, one audience member asked me how the Bedouin came to belong to the Palestinian people.

"We didn't migrate to Israel," I said teasingly. "We weren't in your suitcases when you arrived and we didn't fall from the sky. We rose from the sands of the Naqab Negev. The failure to share space arises from the illusion that we can hide the side of our identity that makes others uncomfortable. That will never work. We can't leave any part of our identity behind if we want to build a sustainable shared society. We have to be there exactly as we are. Proud and whole."

Providing international exposure for the Bedouin cause put me on even shakier ground back home. Each of my steps forward provoked a slew of criticism that I could never predict. In this complex reality of competing claims, I was expected to take a clear stance. If my advocacy work addressed issues within my community, I would be accused of being a traitor who was cooperating with the state. When I addressed Bedouin issues within the greater context of minority rights, I would be accused of dissenting from the Palestinian cause by playing into the government's "divide and rule" tactics. And when I stood up against the government for minority rights, the state perceived me as a security threat. Being a woman while navigating all these minefields opened the floodgates to even more criticism.

In 2005, I was asked on a national radio show to respond to the head of the Israeli National Security Council, who had claimed that Bedouin issues were due to the large number of children we had.

"Stop trying to intervene in our bedroom," I said. "The problem is not our wombs, but your policies that leave more than eighty thousand people without high school education, water and basic services. If a woman has a job and an education, she won't have ten children."

The next day, the Bedouin community criticized me for agreeing that having ten children is a problem. One Arab Knesset member stated: "Women in our society should have more children to defeat them [the Jews] demographically."

"Stop politicizing our wombs and using them as your weapons," I shot back.

Womanhood is criticized by both the nationalist apparatus and our patriarchy. In reality, these two forces are similar: both benefit from maintaining a dynamic of the oppressor and the oppressed.

Allah Protect All Muslims

EVERY CHANCE I had to visit Laqiya for work, I stopped off to see my parents. The second I stepped foot in the *hosh,* Ummi's voice raked me over hot coals. "Oh! Poor children! They don't have a real mother! What do you do that we never get to see you?" I longed for tenderness because everywhere I went I was fighting fire, and her harsh tongue sent me running back to my car with fat tears rolling down my cheeks. I would drive around the neighbourhood until I remembered that Ummi didn't really mean what she said and that she loved me. I would come back to find her arms wide open.

Her mother had told her that when I returned from my travels abroad I brought back suitcases full of money. She didn't believe for one second that the house my parents lived in wasn't paid for by this money from overseas. When I heard this, I asked Ummi to set aside two hours just for ourselves. She poured us two cups of coffee from the *bakraj*, settled herself in her chair, and said: "Now, tell me. What exactly do you do and why do people give you money to do what you are doing?"

I explained about AJEEC and its projects, that it was a social change non-profit organization and I was an employee along with forty other people. I explained how we raised money by submitting proposals and grants, and that I met with donors and if they liked what we wanted to do, then they funded it.

"They give you money, you mean?"

"No. They don't give me cash. They send a cheque or deposit money into our account."

"So when you come back from your trips you don't have a suitcase full of cash?"

"No."

"But people say that you get a lot of money."

"Yes. I do. The money is for the programme or project."

I gave her some examples of our programmes and explained that we paid people to run the programmes. I knew what question was coming next.

"If you have all this money, why can't you pay yourself more? You work very hard. You have only one car that you share with Anwar and your living room is very old and I've never seen you buying gold. Women who work as teachers buy gold and I see them all covered in gold, but I see your naked neck and I feel sorry for you."

I told her about salaries and that I was paid according to what people in my position were typically paid. Gold, I said, was a matter of taste, not a measure of wealth – though to this day she hasn't changed her mind about that.

"But *ya bintee*, you travel so much! What do you do? How are the people out there? Are they like us? Why would they give money to support people they don't know?"

"I talk with them."

"So you are only talking? Is this your work?" she asked with wide eyes. "This is not work. Everyone knows how to talk." She leaned in closer. "I hope you're speaking politely to people. I know your big mouth."

"Next time I'll take you and you'll see."

In 2006, I was invited to Istanbul to participate in a three-day conference after being nominated by the Swiss National Council and the Council of Europe as one of the One Thousand Women for the Nobel Peace Prize. I invited Ummi to accompany me.

At the gate at Ben Gurion airport, the security guard, in broken Arabic, asked us what our relationship was. Ummi relinquished her grip on my arm and launched into a meandering explanation about her daughter – me – who travelled the world to speak and who helped people and was the Director of AJEEC.

"Do you know AJEEC?" she asked. "She's also on the TV and the radio. Don't you know her?"

The guard relaxed into a handsome smile. "Of course I know her," he said. "I'm sure that you're very proud of her. I wasn't a good student so my mother was never proud of me."

Ummi clucked her tongue. "She has to thank God for having a boy. School doesn't matter. You are a man and that is enough!"

When Ummi admitted that this was her first time on an airplane, the guard theatrically removed the barrier between us and said: "Well then, it will be my great pleasure to accompany you to the door of the plane. You are my VIP guest."

He accompanied us to the gate, where he wished Ummi a good trip and she told him that if his mother wasn't happy with him, she would adopt him.

As the plane took off, Ummi's calm glow gave way to nail-biting stress. She laid her head in my lap and prayed for Allah's protection while condemning herself for being stupid enough to follow me. By the time her speech was over, the plane was stable and we again chatted excitedly about the sights: the Hagia Sophia, the ferry on the

Bosphorus and the other trips we had planned. As the plane began its descent, that enchanted city appeared through the clouds and I marvelled at Ummi seeing a new world with a bird's eyes for the first time. She offered her wonder to Allah, then turned to me and asked: "Where do they hang their laundry?"

I chuckled and told her I didn't know. It was a question only someone who has lived their whole life close to the ground would ever have thought to ask.

In the evening, after settling in at the hotel, Ummi paced around the room, wringing her hands.

"Should I go with you? I don't know if this is right. You go. I'll stay in the room, but I can't stay here alone. I'm afraid. I've never been alone."

I gave her a gentle "cut it out" tap on the shoulder. "No. You'll be coming with me because the ambassador is waiting to meet you. I've told him about you."

"Oh! I'm not like you, *ya bintee*."

"You said that talking isn't work. Everybody knows how to talk. And you certainly know how to talk."

Out of the nearly one hundred people in the room, we were the only women wearing headscarves. The intricate embroidery on Ummi's long *thobe* stood out among the fitted trouser suits. When I translated for her that the conference organizers had asked each of us to introduce ourselves, Ummi shifted nervously in her seat.

"I don't know what to say. I've never introduced myself to such a large number of strangers. You tell them that I'm your mother."

This assertive, opinionated woman now seemed so vulnerable. My thoughts drifted to her as a young woman: trembling when Abouee and she sat on their marriage bed for the first time, trembling when Jidatee barked orders at her, trembling when she considered what would happen if she didn't produce a son.

"You can do it," I told her softly.

She groaned. "I wish I hadn't come."

I felt the fear in her moist palm. There was still time to escort her out without making a scene. I glanced around the room. Mostly women's faces. Faces that held countless stories that I couldn't even imagine. We were all being celebrated for our commitment to peace and surely these women, like me, must have faced many demons, inner and outer, to be here.

"You are a strong woman," I said. "You know that. No one here has raised thirteen successful children. None of them faced the challenges you did and made it through with pride. Besides, you are the daughter of Aamer a-Sana, a strong man. Imagine him watching you now. How would you introduce yourself?"

My invoking her father's name made her straighten up and her eyes gleam. There were three people to go before it was our turn. Ummi leaned over and whispered: "I'm worried I'll forget my name by the time they reach me!"

"Don't worry, I'll remind you." I winked, then asked: "What's your name again?" We huddled closer in our devious giggles.

"Hello everyone, my name is Amal Elsana Alh'jooj and this is . . ." Ummi stood up. Everyone else had introduced themselves seated, "*Asmi* Hajar a-Sana Aamer a-Sana Um Amal [My name is Hajar Aamer a-Sana mother of Amal]. I wish you all a very fruitful conference and *ya rabb, ahmi kul al-misilmeen* [May Allah protect all Muslims]."

The Arabic speakers in the room cheered. When the organizer translated, the whole room erupted in applause. Under her *shash*, she beamed, perhaps feeling that she had made Aamer a-Sana very proud. Later, at dinner, I explained that there were people here of all backgrounds – Jews, Christians, secular people and other types too.

"Don't worry," she said with a casual wave in my direction, "I prayed for them too."

The next day, I asked one of the participants from Jordan to sit next to Ummi and translate for her during my presentation. As usual, I started with my life story about being the fifth girl whom Ummi didn't want and how they called me Amal, meaning hope, in the hope that I'd bring boys and – hey presto! – five boys were born after me.

When the audience clapped, Ummi stood up and raised her hand.

I invited her onto the stage. As she took her place beside me, my body radiated a pride that stretched beyond the corners of the room.

"I want to tell the story. It's not just Amal's story. It's our story." She pointed at all the women. "No mother on earth can say, 'I don't want my child,' but I needed to pretend that I was sad so they wouldn't blame me." She spoke of how society puts women in such a terrible and difficult place. "Who wouldn't want someone like her?" Her face glowed. "A strong woman, free. Never afraid to speak her mind. I always wanted to say what I thought, but I didn't have the opportunity."

When she finished speaking, everyone stood up to honour her. She bloomed into the Ummi I knew, that woman with a broad back who kept thirteen rowdy children in line. Ummi is one of the millions of women who have never had the opportunity to discover themselves. She lived through us, but despite her humour, I sensed that it wasn't enough. She inspired many conversations about the need for inter-generational dialogue, and after the conference, I submitted a proposal for a programme where Bedouin mothers and their teenage daughters would discuss what it means to be a woman in the hope that we could heal the wounds from the past and usher in an empowered future.

After that trip, Ummi became very curious about my work and where I was travelling to, always asking me questions about the country, the people who lived there and the language they spoke. This didn't mean, however, that she had joined my camp completely.

Once in the waiting room at Soroka Hospital, after her name was announced on the loudspeaker, the woman sitting beside her asked: "Do you know Amal a-Sana?"

"She's from the tribe," Ummi said with a shrug, "you know our tribe is big," and she continued walking down the hall.

The woman called after her: "She opened a day care centre for our children. I wish there were more women like her to help in our community. Please, if you know her, send her my best regards."

Her words tickled my mother's back and she quickly returned to declare with pride that I was in fact her daughter.

"Ummi, why didn't you say that I was your daughter in the first place?" I asked when she told me the story.

"Of course I wouldn't say that you were my daughter! How could I know why that woman was asking about you?"

Ummi will probably always be cautious of me and my work, but we have come a long, long way.

The Influentials

FOR MANY YEARS Jewish and Bedouin organizations and municipalities worked separately until finally we civil society leaders realized that we needed to create one strong address to present the case of the Naqab for both Arabs and Jews in order to win the battle with the state. The Influentials was formed as a result. Comprising civil society leaders and municipal leaders, its main objective was to understand the social, economic and political issues in the Naqab by visiting the anchor institutions in the region.

We were invited to one of the military airbases, formerly an oasis from which the Bedouin were forcibly removed in the 1980s to allow for the base's construction. The surrounding area with its unrecognized villages is scorched with poverty: there are metal shacks, starving sheep and meagre subsistence food plots. But when you enter the gate of the airbase, you might think you were in Silicon Valley. Lush palm trees, luxurious buildings and wide sidewalks. As usual, I was running from another meeting. The rest of the group was already in the auditorium. The cold from the aggressive air conditioning stabbed the nape of my neck where the sweat had pooled. I scurried down the aisle and slid into the empty spot between a colleague from my organization and the mayor of Rahat. The fighter jets neatly parked by the runway flashed again in my mind. My heart clenched. The hairs on the back of my neck stiffened from a learned vigilance. I hated this place.

The commander had just finished his welcoming remarks and told us he would show us a motivational video. The lights dimmed and the screen filled with action footage of those same planes, the F-16s, striking Gaza and zooming back to the base. The rumbling of the engines haunted me. I choked back tears. I raised my hand.

The mayor tugged my sleeve. He begged me: "Please, please don't make trouble, please just be quiet."

"I'm sorry. This is the beginning of the day. If we don't clear this up from the start . . . May I say something?"

Everyone's eyes were on me. The group already knew me and my big mouth. The commander paused the film.

"You called this a 'motivational film'. This might be motivational for people who want to see that Israel has power over Gaza, but power over whom? Power over my own people? I'm sorry, but for me this is not motivational. This is depressing. This is against everything I work for. I don't think you know who we are and what we are trying to promote."

He stared at me for a couple of seconds. He didn't look at the other officers to see what they thought – he was clearly a man who made up his own mind. Putting his hands on the table, he slowly nodded his head, then took a deep breath.

"You are right. Let's start again."

The commander turned off the projector and switched the lights back on. He left his place on the podium and walked towards us. This time, he started the presentation by saying: "Let's hear about the group first. Who are you?"

About a month after that meeting, I received a call from the commander. "Amal," he said, "I've always sat in my office and have only ever seen the Bedouin from my window. I've never seen how they live. I want you to organize a tour for all my pilots. I want them to know their neighbours. I can't allow myself to be here without understanding what's going on in the Bedouin community."

Four months later he came with his officers to my village. Not to have power over us, not to destroy anything, but to learn and to educate themselves.

Volunteering is a Right

SOON AFTER AJEEC was established, my long-term Bedouin colleague and friend Nabhaan Makkaawe and I established another arm of the organization: the Bedouin Volunteer Tent. We recruited young Bedouin from the towns and unrecognized villages by approaching them in Beer a-Saba's air-conditioned malls where they loitered until closing time to escape the dire reality that awaited them back home. In the village or in the city, they were always the first ones blamed for any crimes that took place. In our initial encounters, these boys, some as young as eleven, others as old as nineteen or twenty, used to being on the defensive, would run away or fight us. Slowly we gained their trust, and on the opening day of the Volunteer Tent, they renovated the building and erected a traditional brown, white and black striped tent, large enough to shelter one hundred people beneath it. They brushed elbows with the mothers and grandmothers who had stitched the tent together and with the girls hanging the photographs that showed our history. Ummi sat with these boys and everyone saw that violence subsides when you embrace what has been abandoned.

The Bedouin Volunteer Tent reimagined *al'uuna* – a traditional form of mutual help, such as assisting with the harvest, building a tent, baking bread – to establish volunteering as a structured activity in which youth are empowered through community engagement, and volunteering is a catalyst for social change. Our volunteers worked in schools and early childhood education centres where they developed interventions that supported community growth. By 2005, we had hundreds of volunteers as well as a Gap Year programme for high school students that entailed a full year of volunteering and included skills development workshops which prepared young people for university or for entering the workforce. I tried to pitch our Gap Year programme as a national project for all young Palestinians in Israel, but my proposal fell on deaf ears. I requested a meeting with Knesset members and leaders of other relevant civil society organizations, but only nine of the twenty we had invited showed up, and the ones who did dismissed the project as being applicable to the Bedouin but not to the Arabs in the north. I couldn't understand it at first, but when nothing I said satisfied them, I started to read between the lines: was it really that our model wasn't applicable or was there resistance to the programme because it originated with the Bedouin, who are perceived as less educated and less progressive than the Arabs in the north?

Soon after that meeting, the government released a report stating that 51 per cent of Israel's high school graduates did not serve in the army or in the national service programme – a national volunteer programme that serves as a substitute for army service. The two main groups referred to in the report were the Palestinian minority and Haredi Jews. In response, the government established a department to implement a national service programme among the Palestinian minority. That administration was linked to the Ministry of Defence. The High Follow-up Committee for Arab Citizens of Israel responded with an aggressive campaign called "I Am Not a Servant", attacking the programme for seeking to strip Palestinian youth of their identity and forcing them to demonize their own in order to receive the same rights afforded to those who completed military service.

The High Follow-Up Committee was convinced that our Gap Year programme was affiliated to the National Service programme and they pressured me to publicly denounce the National Service programme to prove my innocence. But I refused. Reactionary moves were no longer my approach. I wanted to respond proactively by putting forward our Gap Year programme as a viable alternative, but the High Follow-Up Committee was only focused on taking down

427

the National Service programme. I met with leaders of NGOs, mayors and Knesset members to promote my approach. I was willing to support a community volunteering programme developed by the community and operating separately from the Ministry of Defence. Volunteering managed by the Ministry of Defence can't be viewed as a civic activity and, further, mandatory volunteering is a contradiction in terms. Behind closed doors, many people agreed with me, but no one dared to support me publicly. At the same time, the department in charge of the National Service programme invited me to a meeting where they offered to fund our Gap Year programme which I refused as long as it operated out of the Ministry of Defence. Even my close friends were pushing me to join the High Follow-Up Committee in denouncing the National Service programme, but I couldn't. A reactionary stance that doesn't offer alternative solutions feeds power, not people. The Committee's campaign rallied people around what they didn't have rather than engage the community in a discussion about what was needed.

Despite all the bad press, the threats from political leaders, and the discord within the community, AJEEC's staff held strong to our position: we were not going to join either camp but would continue creating opportunities for youth empowerment through community engagement. We were doing the work and we took the heat, from every direction. But what kept us going was real: a little boy who now knew how to read, a playground where there used to be a garbage heap, a group of mothers finding support for their children with disabilities. Our work had visible benefits.

Over the next three years, I walked my path alone with nothing but the certainty in my heart and the evidence on the ground telling me that my path was the right one. Among the leaders, no one supported my position, and one morning I saw my name in the Islamic Movement's weekly newspaper linked to the most serious accusation in my entire advocacy career: "Amal el-Sana is bringing the Second Nakba". The journalist condemned the Volunteer Tent as a backdoor to enlisting Palestinian youth in the Israeli army. My heart sank when

I read those words, but my head reassured me. I was the one who pulled the teenagers out of the malls and put them on a path to university, I walked from shack to shack enlisting mothers to take charge of their villages, I inspired young girls to seize a future in which motherhood was only a component and not the end goal. My hands knew people's pain and my feet knew our soil. They accused me of defaming our culture when all of my work had been about raising us to stand as tall above the ground as our roots ran deep beneath it.

My phone erupted in a barrage of death threats that lasted until I finally decided to call one of the leaders of the Islamic Movement, and hold him accountable for this accusation. In the Bedouin tradition, your father would send a *jaaha* to intimidate your accuser, but I refused to play that game. I was trying to bring us into the present, not maintain the customs of the past. I took a deep breath and said to myself: "It's either you or him." I sat in my office on the ninth floor overlooking this city of stone and sand. I straightened in my chair, which now felt like a throne. I dialled the number.

After I'd introduced myself, I tore into him. "As a Muslim, you know that you must first verify anything you hear before you report on it. Did you do any research for this article? Do you have any proof that my programme is operating under the National Service? If that were the case, then you would have all the names and all the IDs of the volunteers because the National Service collects them in order to hand out the benefits afterwards."

He still hadn't said anything, so I continued. I told him that I would not support a passive position when we had more than seventeen thousand young people who weren't in school and weren't able to find jobs. It was our duty to provide an alternative to the government plan and advocate for what was good for us. He didn't even argue. He said he hadn't seen the article. He was going to check and then get back to me. I hung up and looked out of the window with a familiar feeling of betrayal. I wasn't under attack because of my politics – the journalist hadn't even bothered to do his homework. I was under attack for being a woman who stood up to lead.

429

That same year, 2008, I was commemorating Land Day with the Bedouin Tent volunteers by planting olive trees in the unrecognized villages. Later that evening, I walked into the pharmacy to buy detergent. I stood in the aisle, checking the prices, when I felt someone standing behind me. I glanced over my shoulder and saw an agent from the Shabak who always hung around our demonstrations.

"What do you want?" I hissed without turning around.

"Can we talk?" His pleasant tone made me even angrier.

"This is not the place for a conversation. If you want to talk you can invite me to your office. You know how to do that."

"You think radicalizing your volunteers makes them better citizens?"

He wasn't there to discuss minority integration strategies with me. He was there to discredit me. He knew that if someone saw me standing with him in the pharmacy, it would confirm that I worked with the Shabak. I directed all my anger into scrutinizing the detergents. I pulled a light blue one from the shelf and said: "Teaching them about their Palestinian identity builds their self-confidence. Don't speak to me in public again. I know what you're doing."

He let out a hollow laugh. "Amal, why do you do this work? Your own people don't support you. They never will."

I left him standing in the aisle. By the time I got home, it was late. Moad and Adan peeked into my shopping bag and whined that I had forgotten to pick up their favourite snack, Bamba. I pulled my coat back on and ran out to a nearby kiosk, still reeling from my encounter with that snake. Nowhere was safe. Running home, I fell over a few feet from the steps up to my apartment, scraping my knee. I picked myself up, desperate to reach the refuge of my husband and children, and stumbled through the door, holding the Bamba out in front of me like a peace offering, but Anwar had already put the children to bed. My body crumpled on the couch and tears streamed down my cheeks. I was crying everything out.

Later that year, the Volunteer Tent organized a conference called "Volunteering Is a Right". Our aim was to shift the discourse from obligations to rights in order to mobilize our community to advocate for the right to volunteer in the same way that we advocated for the right to clean water and safe housing. Framing the volunteering issue within this discourse finally garnered support from other minority-led civil society organizations and Nabila Espaniolly, Jafar Farah, Nidal Othman and others joined forces with me to establish the Hirakuna Coalition to promote volunteering among the Palestinian minority and pressure the government to remove the National Service programme from the hands of the Ministry of Defence and give it to a different department. We had two strategic aims: to gain the support of The High Follow-Up Committee and of the government. By now, the mayors on the High Follow-Up Committee supported our determination to negotiate with the government because, unlike the Arab Knesset members on the Committee, the mayors were more rooted within their communities. They were aware that if we didn't offer a community volunteering programme that stemmed from our identity needs, their youth might have no choice but to join the National Service programme. At the same time, I met with Avishay Braverman, former president of BGU, who was now the Minister for Minority Affairs, and requested that the National Service programme be moved to a department that dealt with civic issues, such as the Ministry for Welfare or Ministry for Education. Isaac (nicknamed Bougie) Herzog* was the Minister for Welfare and Social Services and I also knew him personally. The best strategy in social change is seizing political opportunity. Braverman agreed with my position and we agreed that he would present the idea to the Mayors' Committee. Everything was falling into place perfectly,

---

* Elected and inaugurated 11th President of Israel in 2021.

but a week before we were supposed to meet, an election was called and the government dissolved.

While that front disintegrated, we finally convinced Ayman Odeh, who was heading the campaign against the National Service programme, of our position and he got us a meeting with the High Follow-Up Committee. This was a big achievement, and Juhayna (the coordinator of the coalition), Nabila and I were excited to be three strong women presenting our vision for Palestinian volunteering to this group of leaders of the Palestinian minority. When we arrived in the room, the dynamic was very different from what I was expecting. I remember thinking: "This is the group responsible for the future of Israel's Palestinian citizens?" I expected them to be more organized, more professional, more dynamic. When one of the members introduced us, his words barely scratched the surface of who we were and the substantial changes we had made to life for Palestinians within Israel. His tone conveyed what he really thought: "Let's hear what these three women have to say and then get back to the real stuff."

Ayman Odeh spoke first to show these men that we had his support. We hadn't even opened our mouths when a representative of the Islamic Movement spat poison at us. "In the name of women's empowerment, these organizations are supported by Jewish money from North America and are serving as an arm of the Zionist movement to weaken and destroy our societies!" It killed me to think that liberty, equality and justice could be considered a foreign agenda when they resided right in the heart of my culture and traditions. My cell phone flashed. It was a text message from my Uncle Talab who was in the room: "Keep calm. They will try to make you angry so you can't be articulate when you present. Just ignore." I glanced over at Ayman whose confident eyes gave me the same message. I squeezed Nabila's hand. She squeezed back.

We started our presentation, but it wasn't long before one of the leaders of the opposition attacked me personally. "How dare you come to speak with us when last week you supported the Goldberg Commission?"*

"I didn't support it. I used its opening to state that the Bedouin are citizens of the state and thus entitled to be treated equally—"

"I don't care!" He slammed his fist on the table. "You are legitimizing this report!"

The meeting couldn't go on. The men sitting beside him tried to calm him down, but his enraged outbursts pursued me out onto the streets of Nazareth.

Those are the men whose validation we need? I thought to myself. I suggested that we proceed with the programme without the High Follow-Up Committee's buy-in, but my colleagues didn't want to proceed on this basis.

On my way back to Beer a-Saba, the desert enrobed in darkness, this dilemma churned in my mind. Were my colleagues right? After that meeting, I doubted it was worth investing my time in trying to convince those leaders. My ringtone pierced the heavy silence. It was one of the High Follow-Up Committee members from the meeting. He was calling to say that I was right and that we shouldn't rely on them to lead change. If we wanted to create real change, we needed to change their working style, train them or replace them.

"Why didn't you say that in there?" I said. "Why did you leave us fighting alone? Three women against twenty-five men."

"I didn't want to bring the fight upon myself. They already know my position and they are not happy with me."

"I appreciate your support. To change them you need to speak your mind – in public. That is what I need from you."

---

*The Goldberg Commission was set up by the Israeli government in 2007 to end the long-running disputes between the state and the Bedouin in the Negev. The report was published in 2011 and recommended that most of the 46 unrecognized villages in a certain location be recognized on condition that they did not interfere with Israel's development plans in the area. It also recommended that most of the illegally built structures in these villages should be legalized and that a committee be set up to hear and settle Bedouin claims relating to traditional land ownership.

Between Bombs and Rockets

EVERY TIME A siren pierced Beer a-Saba's grey skies, Anwar, Adan, Moad and I lay together on the couch. The warmth of Anwar's body next to mine and Moad's head resting on my shoulder provided me with little comfort because I knew that Anwar's family had nowhere to run. The iron dome* isn't made to protect the villages the state refuses to acknowledge. The war on Gaza in December 2008 lasted ten heartbreaking days. The very first time the siren sounded Adan shot upright in her bed. Her face clenched and her lips darkened. I froze in fear, but Anwar swooped down, held her in his protective arms and after a few seconds she started breathing again. He carried her to the couch, where she lay nestled into him until the raid was over. We repeated this routine day after day. Moad barely noticed the blaring. He would sleepwalk over to join us on the couch and then sleepwalk back to bed when it ended, but Adan wouldn't recover for two or three hours.

From our house, we could hear the army planes leaving the military base. After every siren, we knew that in about ten minutes bombs would be dropped on Gaza. Afterwards, I would call my relatives** there to check on them. Anwar's cousin sent her six-year-old daughter to get tomatoes from the neighbour's garden. The little girl had been whining for shakshuka all morning. The blast shook the family's shack and when the mother ran outside, she found her little girl's body lying on the shattered concrete, torn open. "*Maatat ju'aaneh, maatat ju'aaneh* [She died hungry, she died hungry]," her mother wailed in response to this unthinkable crime, surrounded by rubble and despair.

Vivian and I spoke at least twice a day. These check-ins assuaged

* The iron dome is an air-defence system created to intercept short-range rockets and artillery shells.

** In 1948, approximately 90% of Negev Bedouin were expelled – or fled – to Gaza and Jordan. Today the majority of people in the camps in Gaza are Bedouin. Many of Anwar's relatives are there.

my fears for her life – Vivian's kibbutz bordered Gaza – and they prompted an idea that Yehuda considered incredibly dangerous: I wanted to bring all AJEEC's staff together. Yehuda resisted because he had seen how the good work Jews and Palestinians did together was destroyed when they talked politics. He feared that addressing the elephant in the room would see the organization trampled to death. Tensions had never been higher. The news churned out smoke and blood. People feared for their lives and the lives of their children. This, I argued, was the time when we needed each other most. As an organization promoting justice, we needed to demonstrate what was possible; we needed to demonstrate that individual relationships mattered more than political ideology. Vivian was sceptical, but I told her that if, after eight years of working together, the staff couldn't sit together and talk, then we should shut just the organization down.

Two days later, the staff members shuffled in and sat in a large circle. There were thirty of us, some from Jewish cities neighbouring Gaza and Beer a-Saba, some from kibbutzim, and others from Bedouin cities and unrecognized villages. We were truly a mixed group and the gloom that clung to us made us feel like insects caught in an invisible web. We asked people to share their feelings from the previous week. One Jewish staff member shared her fear for her children serving in the army. She couldn't sleep at night. She and her husband lived in the shelter with the rest of their children. A young Bedouin woman of nineteen or twenty, jumped down her throat.

"Oh, it's hard on you in the shelter. What about those in Gaza who have no shelters at all? The hundreds, shredded by your army."

A fellow Bedouin and a mother, joined in this camp. "Why would you send your children there to kill Palestinians?"

Other voices chimed in: "Why would you send your son to the army!" "You call yourself a peace activist!".

The war gave us permission to be cruel because we lived two different versions of it: the Arab staff saw the war from the ground and the Jews saw it from the sky. Our news outlets showed mountains of devastated stone, bodies mangled in the dust, and mothers mourning the dead. Theirs showed aerial footage of smoke: billowy, grey-black clouds which obscured the human loss behind them.

A Jewish staff member, an older man in his sixties, shook his head and shouted above the tumult: "Our army should burn all those people in Gaza."

"Every time a rocket is sent from Gaza I pray that it will hit a Jew and kill him," the young Bedouin woman yelled back.

No one said anything, but their eyes searched each other's for answers. The older Jewish man quickly explained that he meant Hamas, but the young woman didn't say anything. We sat together in the murkiness of all that pain and wondered if we had lost it. How could people who had worked together so closely be so hard on each other? Yehuda looked at Vivian and me with eyes that said: "What did you expect?"

Two others guided the discussion about what we should do as an organization. Should we write a public statement or organize a demonstration against the government?

"You mean against the war?" one corrected.

"No," said another. "It has to be against the government."

"The doing" was much easier to deal with than "the feeling". After the meeting, some of the Jewish staff asked the young Bedouin woman if she had meant what she had said, hoping she would take back her words. She hadn't changed her mind. Later, Vivian and I sat with Yehuda to talk about how to strengthen our organizational resilience in light of what had just happened. "The organization has no place for people who believe in killing other people," Yehuda reasoned. "People who join must believe not only in justice and empowerment but also in peace."

I disagreed. "I am not worried about the young woman. That's exactly what we want. People empowered to share openly, to get all the anger and negative feelings out. She felt safe to do it. It's up to us now to help the staff support each other and not judge."

Vivian and I welcomed the brisk December wind that greeted us as we stepped out of the office. We strolled over to the cafe on the corner and ordered cappuccinos, chatting about other things, but when the waiter brought our coffees, we burst out laughing.

"We came here to escape politics, but here they are," I said pointing to the *magen David* (the star of David) sculpted in the milk foam.

The conflict between the majority and the minority coloured every interaction, right down to a barista's assumption that we wanted a dose of nationalism with our coffee. The waiter took a second look at Vivian and me. Maybe it was my scarf that tipped him off or the colour of my skin, but he took the coffees away and returned with fresh ones, the froth smoothly folded into a heart.

These workshops became essential to building our organizational culture. Everyone continued to work for the organization and we used this first meeting to create a space where the whole person, including challenging thoughts and feelings, could be heard and held. People always want to hear a simple, one-sided story that reinforces what they already believe. At AJEEC, the story we tell doesn't speak about hierarchical pain or who was here first or victimhood without responsibility. The story we tell is about people honouring everything that they are. The story we tell is about building bridges. The story we tell is about a future filled with hope. We will never agree 100 per cent on everything. We just need to find enough common ground to expand that ground together. Even Anwar and I agree on barely 60 percent of what we discuss. What we really need is enough goodwill, enough love, enough respect, enough sympathy and enough recognition.

Love, Hope and Work

BETWEEN THE YEARS 2009 and 2011, my parents harvested what they'd spent more than three decades cultivating. They accompanied us their children from one stage to another as we brought the family six national and international awards. To celebrate our successes, I organized a family retreat – just us, without our spouses and children – at the Dead Sea, which has since become a family tradition. The first time we met in the lobby of the Hod Hamidbar Hotel, my parents milled about awkwardly, their traditional clothes looking out of place against the backdrop of guests lounging in skimpy bathing suits. They also didn't know what to expect. What did I mean, "I wanted to discuss things"? We spoke every day!

We enjoyed refreshments before the "session" started while Nasouh and Ibraheem chased each other around the conference room as though they were little boys. When Abeer announced that she wanted to explain the day's programme, we burst into laughter. It took us fifteen minutes to calm down and then Abeer said: "*Khalas*. Anyone who makes trouble will leave the room," and we were off again. We sat in a circle. Basma, the eldest, in her late forties, sat beside Muntasir, the youngest, then only eighteen years old. Ummi was seated next to Abouee, but moved to be next to Salmaan. "I sat next to you for fifty years! *Khalas!*" We applauded this beautiful gesture of rebellion.

One of the activities was Truth or Dare. The second Abeer finished explaining the game to my parents, Ummi leaped from her seat to be the first to spin the bottle. Abeer whisked the bottle away and punished Ummi's unruly behaviour by handing it to Abouee. Looking straight into Ummi's eyes, he said: "I hope it lands on you so I can ask you the one question I've had for many years."

He spun the bottle and we all watched as it slowed and landed right on Ummi, toasting the lucky spin with a chorus of "*Laaaaaaa* [Nooooooo]."

She pulled her chair closer to challenge him. "Go ahead. Ask whatever. *Yalla!*"

"Remember in our early years, let's say the first twenty-five years, I used to find money missing from my pockets. Have you ever taken money from my pocket without asking me?"

Without taking her eyes off his, she shifted in even closer. "Are you kidding me? Did you think that the twenty or fifty shekels you gave me every morning for the children was enough to take care of the family? Of course I took money from your pocket. I don't regret it for a moment!"

The circle shook with laughter as we saw more and more who was the real sheikh of the family.

That day was the first time Abouee shared with us what helped him raise thirteen successful "human agents" as he called us.

"Neither of you even went to school," Basma said. "How did you do it?"

"I will tell you." Abouee spoke as simply as if he was telling us how to plant a tree. "There are three things that I always made sure I had. Not money. Not connections. But three things."

We all leaned forwards. No one said a word. This was a recipe we were dying to hear.

"What we needed in order to pave our way and overcome all the challenges we faced were love, hope and work."

I felt goosebumps. Every pair of eyes in the circle was shining. We all knew what it felt like to be loved, we all knew Abouee's unshakeable faith, and we all knew his commitment to hard work.

"We gave everything we had to build what we didn't have." He put his hands together to show that there was nothing left to say.

We waited for him to continue, but he remained silent, his eyes challenging us to digest his words on our own.

"Don't take all the credit yourself," Ummi protested. The boys changed seats to sit next to her, and the girls sat with Abouee. Abeer pressed Abouee to continue.

"I am a very optimistic human being," Abouee said. "I have always had a dream. Since I was a child, I have always asked myself what I want to be. When I was working at the moshav, I remember the Jewish father teaching his son how to drive a tractor. I remember saying: "One day I will have a tractor and I will teach my brother Abdallah how to drive. I even saw the tractor in my mind and saw my brother following my instructions.""

As he remembered his younger brother who had died young, his eyes looked soft. "Have a dream." When he lifted his hands, I felt he lifted our souls. "If you don't know where you are going, what does it matter what road you take? It is always about setting a clear goal."

We basked in the hard-earned wisdom he'd given us. The lines etched into his face said it all. He took a deep breath before continuing. "Also, I want you to believe in women," he said looking at my brothers. "Sometimes I feel that I am more open-minded than you when it comes to women. The fact that you grew up with strong sisters doesn't mean that you should take it for granted. You have to make sure that you are always standing up for women's rights." My heart danced at those words and I'm sure my sisters felt the same.

"How does work fit with hope and love?" Nasouh asked.

"To get to your goal, you have to have willpower. A will that can't be broken or compromised under any circumstances. Hard work always bears fruit. *Man jad wajad wa man saar a-tareek wasal.* Seek and you shall find. Plant and you shall harvest. It is clear that hard work always, always pays off. Love . . ." Then he looked at Ummi and we all went: "Oooooooh."

"What glued us together was love. What filled our stomachs when we were hungry and eased our struggles when we were sad was love. Love of my work because I knew that it was bringing me nearer my goals. And love of the people around me. I loved you and everyone around me. This is why I always found good people to support me."

Everyone was enjoying Abouee's lecture except Ummi. She fiddled with her *shash*, clearly irritated, and suddenly declared: "Now I want to talk. Abouee's been going on and on about our journey. It's my turn now."

She put her chair in the middle of the circle, realized her back was to the boys, and quickly returned it to its place and sat down. "Aboukee is always speaking as if he did all this by himself. That's not right."

"I never said that," he protested, but she waved him off. Abeer asked her to continue.

"He is talking about hard work. He always takes the credit for raising you and standing up against the bad traditions. That he was behind my daughters going to college and university. I'm not taking this away from him, but you need to hear the whole story. Yes. He was in front, but he used to be at work. He wasn't in the village to deal with everyone's criticism. He is a man and people didn't dare criticize him. I took all the heat. I didn't fight loudly because I didn't want to trigger the opposition. When Basma went to college, I was the one standing by the door waiting for her to come back. If she was late, I'd be praying that she'd come back before anyone noticed, and if anyone asked where she was, I'd lie and say she was at home."

Salmaan put his arm around Ummi and she patted his cheek.

"God knows how many nights I slept in the *hosh* waiting for my girls to come back from the city. I remember one time when Amal," she pointed to me, "was late. She was young, but she had no fear. She burned my nerves. I walked around the house four times trying to control my thoughts of what might have happened to her. Everyone was sleeping. I hoped if it was something that it would be a car accident. I hoped that she would die, but not bring shame. Can you imagine? Going through your life hoping your daughter will die?" Her voice cracked and she patted her eyes with her *shash*.

Abouee came over and held Ummi's hand. "I never undermined your role in any of this. I trusted you and knew that you would be my partner in achieving this."

She snatched her hand out of his. "I was the one helping you do homework and making sure that the one who knows teaches the one who doesn't. It was me not you." She thrust her chin at Abouee. "We women do the work. We work hard and then the men talk in the *diwaan* as if they did it. It was me who didn't sleep. It was me who stood when my body commanded me to rest. And they say women are weak. Women are weak! Without us you would not only miss the goal but miss the road!"

We cheered her speech and Yousef coyly said: "Ummi, you've become a feminist."

"Yes," she said looking at me, "I am a feminist."

Abouee looked across the circle at Ummi. "Without you this journey won't be complete. You are the love, the hope and *al-waasit* [the central rod of the tent, the foundation] of our hard work."

Whenever Abouee gets emotional, he sings songs by Fareed al-Atrash. Yousef's sweet voice slowly and confidently crooned the opening to one of Abouee's favourites. Ummi squirms at men getting emotional, but Nasouh, Ibraheem and Ousama carried her over to Abouee. She buried her red face in her hands and we all kept singing *al-hayaa helwa* (life is beautiful) until she finally succumbed, for the first time ever, joining Abouee in song.

Later that year, one of the magazines that interviewed me wanted to meet my parents to understand how they had raised thirteen successful children. When the reporter asked my parents about their children, Abouee's face gleamed.

"Let's start with my eldest, Basma. She was the opening of life so I called her Basma – 'smile'. I wanted to start the journey with a big smile. When you smile at life, life smiles back at you. This is what Fareed sings about." He looked at me for approval and I nodded. "Basma was a very assertive, smart child and I knew that she would go far. And she did. She was the first Bedouin woman to become a school principal."

"Then came Na'ama. Do you know what *na'ama* means?" he asked the journalist, but answered the question himself. "It means 'blessing'. And she was a big blessing. When she was born, I got my new job. I was responsible for all the workers in the orange orchard. That was the year of blessing and every time I saw Na'ama, I felt blessed. Na'ama runs the Laqiya Women's Association helping women with employment. Then there was Maryam who is working at a school and was my accountant before she got married. When she was born, I knew that being the father of girls would be a struggle. I wanted strength from her, so I called her Maryam – 'our mother' – a woman who stood strong despite all the rumours about her."

"When my eldest son was born, I named him after my father, a brave, honest person. Salmaan is a pharmacist. I sent him to study in Italy. People told me he wouldn't survive, but I believed in him."

Then Abouee looked at his four fingers and said, "Who is next? I forget . . ." He let out an honest chuckle. Ummi reminded him: "Narjis, the flower."

"Ah yes! Narjis is the flower of the family and you know who came after her," he said, pointing at me. "This girl was born after Narjis when I was praying for a boy and feeling that one was coming. She's the one who came and caused all the trouble."

"She is *mashaakel kibaar bas mish kabeer* [trouble that brought blessings]," Ummi retorted with a loving pat on my arm.

"When she was a child, I knew she would be a leader. I used to watch her play with the other children. She never joined a group. She always sat by herself and invited the other children to join her." The sun danced on his grinning cheeks. "She was even a good leader for the sheep!"

"Then came Yousef who is a lawyer, Abeer who is a social worker, Nasouh, the businessman—"

"Engineer," Ummi corrected.

He looked at her to finish the task.

"Oh! My life was much easier after I had three boys. God gave me Ibraheem and Ousama, two boys, one after the other, *Al-hamdullilah*. Ibraheem studied this thing—"

"He studied computer science at the Technion," I said.

Ummi nodded. "Yes, yes."

"You know the Technion," Abouee said to the journalist. "It's the best."

Ummi continued: "I had a pharmacist to get me medicine, but I needed a doctor to prescribe it, so Ousama studied medicine in Italy." She put her hand on her heart. "Ousama is my eyes. My sons are my eyes. I can't see the world without them."

"And the girls are my eyes. They're my life," Abouee quickly added, noticing the sideways look I'd shot at Ummi.

"The girls belong to their father and I'm the mother of the boys." With this she was just trying to provoke me. I knew by now that a mother never means any harm towards her baby.

"We still have two to go," the journalist said.

"Well, it would have been four if I hadn't taken birth control. I regret it now. After Ousama I wasted three years and then Wafaa was born and she was the queen of the girls. Beautiful like the moon. She is a manager at a health clinic. I waited another three years and then got pregnant with Muntasir. By then I was forty-five years old. I wanted an abortion. All these doctors told me that I was too old for this and that he would be stupid."

"And you listened to them?" Abouee teased.

"No, I listened to you and that is why we ended up having the most brilliant child who studied engineering."

"Can you believe they said that he wouldn't be smart? I was smart to insist on keeping him."

"It was me who brought him into this world."

"Right. He is yours. All the boys are yours."

The Prawer Plan

IN THE ONGOING dispute over Bedouin land, the Prawer Plan was published in June 2011 to execute the recommendations of the Goldberg Commission. Chaired by Ehud Prawer, the plan proposed the relocation of thirty-eight thousand Bedouin from their villages which were not recognized by the state to one of the seven planned Bedouin towns. That September, the High Follow-Up Committee approached several NGOs, including AJEEC, to establish the Supreme Steering Committee for the Negev Arabs in order to protest the numerous injustices this plan presented: the affected communities were given no opportunity to negotiate, the plan rejected any notion of Bedouin land claims, and no Bedouin were consulted in drafting this plan.

In the first Supreme Steering Committee meeting, AJEEC announced its plan to organize a huge demonstration to bring the issue into the public discourse. AJEEC had a wide reach and could mobilize thousands of people, but we needed not only the ones who were already engaged but also the ones who weren't. With the help of the Regional Council for the Unrecognized Villages, we initiated an awareness campaign about the event, but two weeks before the demonstration we realized that it wasn't enough. To add to the challenge, the Supreme Steering Committee announced that they had no budget for the demonstration, implying that they expected us to fund the demonstration. When I heard that, I made it clear that each organization represented in the Supreme Steering Committee should contribute and we agreed that everyone would provide a lump sum to cover the cost of materials, media and transport.

With only a couple of weeks to go till the big event, members of the Supreme Steering Committee and I visited the unrecognized villages to recruit protesters. We'd speak to the people and they'd nod their heads, but at the end of the day, did they really understand why their participation mattered? Would their immediate needs – feeding their children, fetching water, preparing the day's meal – impede them from joining this protest whose outcome might only yield fruit in a future they couldn't see?

One afternoon, driving back to Beer a-Saba, we passed through the city market, ten minutes from where the demonstration would be held, and that's when I had a major "aha" moment. I asked the driver to stop. The last time I'd been there I must have been a student. Things had changed. The sound of Jewish salesmen haggling over scarves and shoes was replaced by the bubbling of rows and rows of Bedouin coffee shops, where thick clouds of sweet-smelling smoke curled around groups of young men circled together. There wasn't a single woman on the street. I ignored my colleagues, who didn't see any hope for these "ignorant young men", and entered the first coffee shop, my arms full of flyers.

Once they caught sight of me, the chatter ceased. A man who clearly felt sorry for me explained that I must be in the wrong place.

"I know where I am," I said, pulling up a stool in the middle of a group of men, one of them looking as young as twelve. "I'm not here for the *nargeela*. I'm here for something much bigger, something that determines your future. Something that determines your life."

I explained about the Prawer plan, the unrecognized villages and their right to be equal citizens. "We must show the government that we cannot be displaced without our consent." The bubbling ceased, the smoke dissipated and only my voice rang out in the dimly lit shop. "What are you waiting for?" Their eyes no longer seemed hazy. They all stood up and cheered. In one coffee shop after another, I handed out my brochures and inspired these men that society had written off as good for nothing to join the cause. After each speech, they would rush over to shake my hand, promising they wouldn't disappoint me. "We'll be the first ones there." I had a feeling they meant it.

One week before the demonstration, we had another meeting with the Supreme Steering Committee. AJEEC's tasks were all accounted for, but when I asked for the money everyone had promised, the room fell silent. For the rest of the meeting, the men argued over who would get to speak on the stage. By that evening, only one committee representative had paid me. The others all had excuses. I called every single one of them, high ranking officials in the Arab-Israeli political landscape, and told them blankly that only those who sponsored the demonstration would speak at the rally. Before the next meeting, they had all paid.

On October 6th, the day of the demonstration, I drove my car, overflowing with banners, to the location and saw waves of Bedouin men walking from the market in the same direction. I had been working around the clock to ensure the day's success and seeing the men marching for their rights was everything I could have asked for. When time came for the speeches, I made sure I was up there. Of course, I had hoped that someone would nominate me, but by now I realized I needed to nominate myself.

This demonstration was the biggest in the history of Bedouin participation, with more than ten thousand attendees, including women and young adults from the unrecognized villages. And the government noticed. In response, MK Benny Begin was asked to conduct an inquiry to understand our complaints against the Prawer plan. I saw this as a landmark achievement for an advocacy campaign, but the Supreme Steering Committee wanted to boycott the process. What was the point of campaigning if we weren't going to negotiate with the government? The voices in the room were demanding that the government drop the plan entirely before we sat down to talk, but that was a zero-sum game. I believed that if we presented a compelling case, Benny Begin would support it. The Chair of the Supreme Steering Committee phoned me later that day to tell me that any dealings I had with Begin would not be supported by the committee. He criticized me for not supporting the Bedouin. Since when did he care about the Bedouin, I fired back.

I ignored him and together with a female Bedouin lawyer, we analysed the Prawer plan and wrote our proposal for our meeting with Begin. We sent our paper to the media before the meeting so that no one could accuse us of being co-opted by the state. We were nine women in the meeting. The lawyer spoke about the plan's legal consequences and I presented the social ones. We stated it clearly: this is a bad plan and it won't settle the Bedouin land issue. Expelling thirty thousand people from their homes was not the solution of a problem but the creation of one. The core of the issue is that Bedouin land claims must be acknowledged first. Then we can negotiate land development. I watched Begin as the other women spoke about housing demolition and lack of basic services. He asked thoughtful questions and responded sincerely, even when we condemned this plan as an example of systemic discrimination. At the end of the meeting he shook our hands and said: "The men are making a big mistake by not letting you lead. I have never received a document that is as clear, compelling and professional as yours."

The next day, Abouee called me to ask if he should meet with Begin to present his own land claim.

"Of course!" I told him. "Why not?"

The day after Abouee met with Begin, I visited him in the village. He sat under the olive tree fixing his horse saddle and gave me a telling smile.

"Wallah, Aboukee was strong. You should be proud of me." I clasped my arms around him and planted a kiss on his forehead. "Benny Begin asked me: 'What if we give you a percentage of the land?'"

Abouee held his head high and pulled his shoulders back as if Begin was standing right there in the *hosh*. "'Your Honour,' I told him, 'your question needs to be rephrased. It's the wrong question.' He looked puzzled. I said firmly – you know Aboukee: 'The question should be: "What if I give you back your land?" Your honour, this is my land not yours. Let's first resolve this. Believe me. If you recognize my ownership and acknowledge that this land is mine and not yours, I will donate all my land towards the development of the Bedouin community.'"

The following week, the Supreme Steering Committee held a meeting which I wasn't invited to, but I attended anyway. Their eyes expressed what their silence didn't: that I was a traitor. They acted as if I wasn't there and I was prepared to swallow that, but I wouldn't leave the battleground for them to do whatever they pleased. The discussion turned to strategies to prevent people from meeting with Begin. Their short-sightedness made my blood boil. Why put all this energy into making people feel even more helpless?

"Our people are suffering and they need solutions," I declared. "We can't fight for the sake of fighting. You think the government is stupid? They don't need your blessing to implement this plan. They'll speak with the sheikhs individually. I say we prepare people to meet with Begin. We explain to them exactly what they shouldn't compromise on and show the government that we know our rights, that we're here to negotiate as equals."

We had always held demonstrations to air our anger, but the state did what it wanted anyway. For the first time, we had someone with whom to hold a constructive negotiation and I believed we had to put our demands on the table as one strong, unified people. Of course my community didn't believe in Begin. A disadvantaged minority can't trust a government that holds them down with one hand and beckons them forward with another. We needed these leaders to change their mindset from resistance to reconciliation, but that vision could cost them their power and weak leaders won't ever risk losing power.

One of the leaders of the Islamic Movement interrupted me. "We're talking about a serious matter. This is a land issue."

"Yes," said another man across the table. "This is a land issue. It's not for a woman to decide."

I didn't back down. "Because it is a serious issue we women have to be here. And besides, I guarantee that 50 percent of you haven't even read the plan."

A member of the Islamic Movement cut me off again. "Could you stop your niece?" he snapped at my uncle Talab.

"With all due respect," I said before my uncle had the chance to speak, "here, in this room, you are a member of the committee." Looking each one of them in the eye, I continued: "If you think I will put the future of my children," my heart clenched, "in your hands knowing that you didn't even read the entire plan, you are wrong."

I walked out. I didn't want them to enjoy my tears. Their warring voices followed me down the stairs: "She is right! She knows what she is doing," and "No. We can't let women lead us." I finally made it to the street, but the evening bustle couldn't drown out the echo of their words in my head.

Ultimately, Benny Begin made efforts to listen, but his plan was rejected by the right-wing government in power at that time.

The Shepherd's Cave

T HE EVENING I drove back from the meeting with the Supreme
Steering Committee about the Prawer Plan, my tears competed
with the droplets falling hard against my windshield. All those years
of challenging exclusionary practices and showing a new model in
which women could make change – change driven by love and
compassion, work based on respecting my people and believing in
them – disappeared in the cavernous dark beside the desert road. My
love had turned to rage. My twenty years of proven success at
elevating the status of the Bedouin community didn't grant me the
same political power as the other people sitting around that table.
And why? There was only one answer: the political struggle was
entrenched in the patriarchal system and, according to that system,
my opinions, a woman's opinions, didn't matter.

I arrived at our apartment and took a deep breath. I didn't want
Anwar and the children to see my red eyes. When Anwar asked me
if everything was all right, I lied. Moad ran over to show me that his
face was healing from when he fell off the back of the donkey he was
riding with his cousins in Awaajaan. I touched the scars next to his
left eye and kissed him.

"We're waiting for you to tell us a story," he said.

"Your dad will read you one," I answered, doing my best to hide
the crack I felt widening down the centre of my chest.

Adan heard my voice and came running to show me the story
that she was writing. "No, we want a story from your head. Tell us
about when you lost your little lamb!"

My children loved my stories and I loved sharing them, but that
day, if I started talking about my childhood, my tears would flow
forever. I missed the days when I felt like I owned the world and that
nothing could stop me. Anwar sensed something was wrong and he
made a deal with them that tonight he'd tell them the story about the
dog he had when he was a little boy. They scurried to their room to
build the tent they always built for story time.

I went to the kitchen and tucked into Anwar's famous ravioli. I didn't feel like eating, but I was on autopilot. I sat down at the table and checked my email. There was an email from Jim Torczyner, with whom I had done my master's, and who had become like a second father to me, asking if we could Skype. I pulled my laptop out of my bag and logged on. This had to be from the Almighty. Although we were close, we hadn't spoken in over four years and this was the moment I needed someone to hear me out. Someone with an objective voice. Someone to shepherd me out of the rain. Jim's face appeared on the screen and he howled my name gleefully, but before he'd had the chance to say why he wanted to speak, I began sobbing. I had never cried in front of Jim before, but his presence drew out all the poison from my soul. Between the tears I expressed to him my devastation: firstly, at the misogyny I experienced continually within my own community despite my proven track record of positive change and secondly, that even after all these years of actively building partnerships with the state, the Prawer Plan had been developed without consulting a single Bedouin and the rejection of the findings from Benny Begin's hearings proved that my community was still invisible. He listened intently, nodding and groaning in all the right places, and gave my anger, grief and rage a cave in which to rest.

"Maybe it's time to take a break," he said after a short silence. "It's been fifteen years since you finished your master's and since then you've been working intensively, organizing people. That is not an easy job, especially when you're dealing with your own people. It doubles your anger and frustration. This is not a good place to continue from. You're angry and you might hurt yourself or your people. You need to take a break."

"What kind of break? I've never even taken a vacation! I don't know what it means not to work. I was climbing the walls those four months of maternity leave."

"What about coming back to McGill to do your PhD?"

"What? Jim, you know I've always criticized academia for being so passive when it comes to caring about impact. My academic friends spend all their time thinking and rethinking theories and concepts. They can't help people in their head."

"Not all academics are like that. You can combine both. I did. I teach what I do and I do what I teach."

A few days later it rained even harder. Slimaan, the Director of the Volunteer Tent, woke me in the early hours of the morning to tell me that someone had set fire to the building. This was the third attempt within a week, and this time they had succeeded. The tent we had erected inside the building was completely destroyed, along with the offices and all the photos we had collected over the years showing the Arab history of Beer a-Saba. We could always find another tent and the building could be fixed, but those photos were rare glimpses of a contested history. We didn't know who had done it: Jewish extremists trying to stop us from exercising our rights as equal citizens or members of our own community trying to stop us from exercising our rights as women? Whatever message they were trying to send, our message needed to be louder. We blocked off the main road and built a solidarity tent where within a few hours a crowd had gathered in support. I spoke about community empowerment, Arab–Jewish partnership, and Bedouin rights as fundamental to a healthy society. I reminded everyone of the role of civil society in promoting those values. I saw there imams and rabbis, representatives from Arab and Jewish organizations, and the Jewish people who lived next to the centre but had never walked in, and I knew that all the fires I'd faced had been worth it, that my work here had gone some way to shaping a society in which everyone shared the same rights.

I hadn't yet told anyone about Jim's suggestion – it was an escape route I wasn't sure I wanted to take. Was it time to reflect on my practice, to condense fifteen years of community organizing into lessons learned? Every shepherd knows that when the rain starts really coming down, you find a cave for your sheep and yourself to shelter in until the rain lets up because, no matter how stubborn you are, you won't survive the flood that could follow.

Anwar loved the idea right away. He believes that a homeland is the place where you feel comfortable, the place where you feel you belong. Returning to Montreal brought with it the promise of feeling like a human being, like an equal citizen who didn't have to fight for everything.

For AJEEC, the news landed like a thunderstorm in the middle of a sunny day.

"It's the wrong decision. You were born to create new realities. You can't do that by doing your PhD. If you are tired, take a break. Don't leave," Yehuda pleaded.

He was almost crying. He so believed in my ability to change the situation for the Palestinian minority and to bring about the peace that we all had been longing for since the very beginning.

"Amal," he said, the crease in his forehead deepening, "you are making history and you're leaving in the middle of it!"

Yehuda had been my professional mentor since we started the organization. He was always there to remind me of our grand vision.

"It's only three years," I said. "And I'll be back."

"If you leave, I don't know if you'll come back."

"I'll never leave my community," I promised.

That year, I travelled to Holland to present a five-year plan for the advancement of early childhood education in the Bedouin community and we signed a one-million-euro contract with the Van Leer Foundation. When I informed the grant director of my plan to leave, he told me he was worried.

"Do you think the organization can manage without you?"

The grant was for AJEEC, not for me, I told him, and the success of the organization was due to the hard work of the team. I knew that AJEEC didn't need me to be successful at upscaling its programmes at national level.

Before I left, there was talk of my going into politics, but I didn't feel that was the right place for me. Not only was the impact of the Arab Knesset members minimal, but I truly believed that the impact

I was able to make in civil society far outweighed what I could do in politics.

"Finally, you'll have time for another pregnancy!" Ummi declared when I told her the plan. She had been pressuring me to give Moad another brother and Adan another sister. How evil I was not to think about them and how lonely they would be compared to me with my twelve siblings!

Abouee, on the other hand, held me in his loving gaze and said simply: "There is never an end to education. There is always something new to learn in life." It was a lesson I'd heard before, but this time it had a ring of longing.

We sat drinking tea in the *hosh*, under the olive tree that had shaded my sisters and brothers and me from when we were toddlers. Ummi set down her cup. "We thought we were done with our worries and now you are taking your children overseas! God knows if we'll see you again. Who knows who will live and who will die. I won't sleep, worrying about you and your children!"

I removed the pillow between us and nestled my body into hers. "Don't worry. We'll be OK. I'm not a child anymore."

"I will worry until you return," she said, as if she was reminding herself. "We are worried for the young until they grow up, for the sick until they recover, for the absent until they return."

After lunch at my parents' house, Moad, Adan and I walked across Abouee's land and admired his orchard. We walked up to the mountains and I showed them where I used to herd my sheep. They skipped around chasing a butterfly. I sat on a rock, the kiss of the spring sun and the playful breeze caressing me. I wanted to fill my lungs with the village air before I left. I was basking in the moment, seeing, hearing, smelling and feeling only what God creates, when my cell phone rang. It was the president of the Hebrew University in Jerusalem.

"I'm calling you because I made a promise to myself when I first met you in 2003. At that time, I was the Knesset member on the education committee, and you invited us for a tour of the unrecognized villages. That was the first time I had seen the conditions people lived in but what I remember most was the hope you gave me. I promised myself that if I was in a position to give someone an award one day, I would give it to you. And here I am, the President of the Hebrew University, and I want to give you the award for—"

His words disappeared into the elation that arose within me, not because he was handing me some fancy award with a ceremony, but because he said I had given him hope and that eight years later he still carried that hope within him.

Because of my travel plans, my parents decided to organize Wafaa's and Ousama's respective weddings in July before I left. Weddings are my paradise: I dance from one dawn to the next. Even as a child, whenever I saw a tent with a red and white flag, I would take my *dorbaka* (drum) there and join the women in dance. I remember one day Abouee asked my seventh grade teacher how I was doing. "She has an A in all subjects, but a C in discipline," he said. "If you drum on a metal container, she'll dance." Those dances that summer were my dances for all the successes, all the failures, all the pain. A dance for all the women who had changed their stars and all the women who couldn't be there to dance with us. Bare feet, worn and alive, shimmering in the glory of the women's tent where Jidatee smiled at us from her seat in heaven.

For the rest of the summer, I moved back in with my parents to spend time with them and my siblings before we left. These were the best of times. I would sleep in Ummi's bed and we would talk through the night. I no longer saw her as a dictator or a servant. We had finally stopped throwing stones at each other and were now gathering them together, two strong women supporting one another, side by side, epitomizing the matriarchy: power with, not power over.

As the plane took off from Tel Aviv, I felt my roots being ripped from the warm familiar soil that in the name of history and God is ravaged by war and conflict, to be replanted in a cold foreign land that in contrast is peaceful and welcoming. But no matter where I am, I will always hear my mother's voice calling me back.